Macroeconomic Analysis

Macroeconomic Analysis

Dirk Niepelt

The MIT Press
Cambridge, Massachusetts
London, England

This book was set in Times Roman by the author.

Printed and bound in the United States of America.

Library of Congress Cataloging-in-Publication Data

Names: Niepelt, Dirk, 1969– author.
Title: Macroeconomic analysis / Dirk Niepelt.
Description: Cambridge, MA : MIT Press, [2019] | Includes bibliographical
   references and index.
Identifiers: LCCN 2019015697 | ISBN 9780262043472 (hardcover : alk. paper)
Subjects: LCSH: Macroeconomics—Study and teaching (Higher)
Classification: LCC HB172.5 .N54 2019 | DDC 339—dc23 LC record available at
   https://lccn.loc.gov/2019015697

10 9 8 7 6 5 4 3 2 1

Meinen Lieben

Contents

List of Figures

List of Tables

Preface

This book offers an introduction into modern, mainstream macroeconomic theory. It is designed to be concise, accessible, and broad.

Audience The target audience are master students or beginning doctoral students in economics who are familiar with microeconomics and calculus at the undergraduate level. The text may also serve as a reference for more advanced readers.

Structure Models help organize one's thinking. The book attempts to organize models and to show how they build on and relate to each other. The design is decidedly bottom-up: Models of individual decision making are covered prior to models of general equilibrium, which in turn are covered prior to positive and normative theories of government and economic policy. Simpler—and often, the simplest possible—environments are analyzed before more complex settings. And models without frictions precede models with frictions.

Contents Chapter 1 reviews the microeconomic foundations of macroeconomics and discusses the primitives of an economic model. Chapter 2 analyzes the dynamic optimization problem of a household with a finite or infinite horizon and consistent or inconsistent preferences, which consumes a single or multiple goods. Chapter 3 embeds the household problem in the two workhorse models of dynamic general equilibrium theory—the representative-household model and the overlapping generations model—and analyzes the efficiency properties of equilibrium.

Chapter 4 introduces risk and studies the implications for household choices and macroeconomic outcomes when markets are complete or incomplete. Chapter 5 analyzes equilibrium asset returns and prices as well as bubbles. Chapter 6 introduces labor supply choice along the intensive and extensive margin and studies wage and consumption inequality; the chapter also covers growth and business cycles, both technology- and sunspot-driven. Chapter 7 introduces open economy issues including the current account, the real exchange rate, and gains from trade.

Chapter 8 introduces frictions and analyzes their macroeconomic consequences: The chapter covers convex and nonconvex capital adjustment costs; matching frictions in the labor market; and frictions in financial markets, which give important roles to net worth, collateral, and pecuniary externalities. Chapter 9 focuses on models of money as a unit of account, store of value, and medium of exchange. Chapter 10 analyzes price setting by monopolistically competitive firms and the macroeconomic consequences of price rigidity.

The last three chapters focus on the government and economic policy. Chapter 11 covers the macroeconomic effects of tax, debt, social security, and monetary policy; equivalence relations between policies; fiscal-monetary policy interaction; and the determinacy of inflation and output. Chapter 12 characterizes optimal (Ramsey) fiscal and monetary policies. Chapter 13 analyzes sequential policy choice in (politico-economic) equilibrium with applications to capital income taxation, sovereign debt and default, politically motivated redistribution, and monetary policy biases.

Mathematical Tools and Technical Discussions Appendix A collects mathematical tools for optimization and the analysis of dynamic systems. Appendix B contains discussions about transversality conditions; the representative household construct; nonexpected utility; linear rational expectations models; Ramsey taxation; and probabilistic voting.

Literature and Related Topics Bibliographic notes at the end of each chapter point to classic articles and other related papers. They also touch upon topics that are connected with the material but not discussed in the chapter and they indicate when other textbooks cover the material in more detail. The hope is that this helps the reader to gain an overview of the field.

Style Conciseness was a key objective. Nevertheless, the text is self-contained and generally includes derivations of the results. When these derivations are missing, then they are most likely the subject of an exercise (see below).

Exercises and Additional Material A companion text with exercises for all chapters is available on the author's website, www.niepelt.ch/book; the solutions manual may be obtained from the publisher. The website also points to computer code and other useful (teaching) material as well as to a list of typos and corrections. Links and content will be updated over time in response to helpful critique and suggestions.

Theory and Measurement The book focuses on theoretical models—formal, abstract parables that are internally consistent and convey general insights. It has nothing to say about "the" data. (What passes as a stylized fact may change over time and be country specific.)

To meaningfully confront abstract parables with real-world macroeconomic data requires a sound understanding not only of theory, which the text is about, but also of data sources, aggregation, and econometric methods, which it is not.

Teaching   The book grew out of lecture notes for MA and PhD courses taught at European universities. It focuses on theory (see above) and lecturers using the text in class will likely opt to supplement the theory with real-world examples.

A one-semester, two-hour-per-week introduction to macroeconomics may be based on material in chapters 1–3 as well as selected topics covered in chapters 4–7.

One-semester advanced courses may be based on the remaining topics from chapters 4–7 or on material covered in chapters 8–10.

A one-semester advanced course on government and economic policy may follow selected sections in chapters 11–13.

Alternatively, it is easy to blend the analysis of models with and without government and economic policy by taking turns between chapters 3, 4, and 10 on the one hand and chapters 11–13 on the other; the uniform notation and cross-references help in this respect.

Conventions   Throughout the text, additions like "for all i" or "$t = 0, 1, 2, \ldots$" generally are omitted. When a statement needs qualification, however (e.g., "for all i except $i = 5$" or "$t \geq 1$"), then the qualification is included.

Technical or key terms are *italicized* when they are introduced or more thoroughly explained for the first time. Only italicized terms are included in the subject index.

Acknowledgments   This text has benefited from the inputs of many colleagues, students, and other contributors.

For insightful discussions, I thank Fabrice Collard, Jordi Galí, Piero Gottardi, Robert King, Per Krusell, Cyril Monnet, Sergio Rebelo, Emmanuel Saez, Robert Shimer, Alexander Wolman, and in particular, Fernando Alvarez, George-Marios Angeletos, as well as my coauthors in recent years—Markus Brunnermeier, Harris Dellas, and Martín Gonzalez-Eiras.

For comments on earlier drafts, I am grateful to Daria Finocchiaro, Martín Gonzalez-Eiras, Nils Herger, Philip Letsch, Thomas Mertens, Cyril Monnet, Christian Myohl, Klaus Neusser, Pascal Paul, and Lukas Voellmy. Fabio Canetg, Michel Habib, Philipp Harms, Leo Kaas, Ricardo Reis, and Heinz Zimmermann provided particularly detailed feedback on draft chapters, for which I am very thankful. Lorenz Driussi read a complete draft and assisted with the figures; his help is much appreciated.

At MIT Press, I thank Jane McDonald for bringing me on board, as well as Emily Taber, Laura Keeler, and team members for managing the book project. I also thank anonymous referees who offered helpful comments.

At Westchester Publishing Services, I thank JodieAnne Sclafani and collaborators for the efficient cooperation. I am also grateful to the LaTeX community for developing and maintaining such a remarkable program.

My interest in macroeconomics was inspired by great instructors. I am indebted to Daron Acemoglu, Olivier Blanchard, Ricardo Caballero, and Peter Diamond at MIT, as well as to lecturers at the Study Center Gerzensee and elsewhere who introduced me to general equilibrium theory and macroeconomics.

Last but not least, I am grateful to those close to me: for love, laughter, and learning; challenges, meaning, and backing. πάντα ῥεῖ.

D. Niepelt
August 2019

1 Microeconomic Foundations

Modern macroeconomic models are micro-founded and dynamic. They are derived from assumptions about microeconomic primitives, specifically preferences and technology; explicitly model intertemporal links and expectation formation; and describe economic outcomes as the result of optimizing choices by households and firms, subject to affordability and feasibility constraints. This contrasts with frameworks such as the IS-LM model, which posit relations between macroeconomic aggregates (e.g., aggregate consumption and income) and often are static.

To prepare for the subsequent micro-founded macroeconomic analysis, we review key microeconomic concepts from *general equilibrium* theory; unlike *partial equilibrium* analysis of a single market, general equilibrium analysis accounts for feedback effects across markets. We also introduce standard assumptions about the primitives.

1.1 Microeconomics

1.1.1 Allocation, Feasibility, Optimality

An *allocation* consists of a *consumption* vector for each household and a net *production* vector for each firm. For example, an allocation in an economy with one household, one firm, and three goods could be {(1, 2, 1), (−1, 1, −1)}: The household consumes one unit each of the first and third good and two units of the second good, while the firm uses one unit each of the first and third good as inputs and supplies one unit of the second good. In a model with government, the allocation also includes a consumption and production vector for the government. In an open economy model, the allocation also includes a consumption and production vector for the rest of the world.

An allocation is *feasible* if for each good, total consumption does not exceed the endowment plus net production. For example, the allocation given above is feasible if the endowment vector equals (2, 1, 2) but it is not feasible if the endowment vector equals (2, 2, 1).

A feasible allocation Pareto dominates another feasible allocation if at least one household strictly prefers the former and no household strictly prefers the latter. A feasible allocation is *Pareto optimal* or Pareto efficient if it is not Pareto dominated by any other feasible allocation. The set of Pareto optimal allocations traces the Pareto frontier.

1.1.2   Competitive Equilibrium

The *consumption set* of a household contains all consumption vectors that the household conceivably could consume in the absence of budgetary restrictions. For example, the consumption set might exclude negative quantities of apples.

The *budget set* of a household contains all consumption vectors in the household's consumption set that the household can afford to consume. The budget set is determined by household endowments, the prices of all goods, and firm profits which are distributed to households according to prespecified ownership rights.

The *production set* of a firm contains all production vectors that are feasible given the firm's technology.

A *competitive equilibrium* or *Walrasian equilibrium* is an allocation and a set of prices satisfying three conditions, conditional on endowments, firm production sets, and household preferences:

i.   The allocation is feasible.

ii. Taking prices as given, each firm's production choice is profit-maximizing in the firm's production set.

iii. Taking prices and firm profits as given, each household's consumption choice is utility-maximizing in the household's budget set.

The equilibrium is competitive because firms and households take prices as given. Alternative, noncompetitive equilibria might exist as well, where agents perceive their choices to affect prices or firm profits and they exploit this feature. For example, a firm might want to reduce output in order to raise the equilibrium price of its product. We mostly abstract from noncompetitive behavior and focus on competitive equilibria.

A competitive equilibrium with lump-sum transfers between households that sum to zero is a *price equilibrium with transfers*.

1.1.3   Walras's Law

Let p denote the vector of prices across goods. Let $z_g^h(p)$ denote household h's *net demand function* for good g—the household's desired consumption net of its endowment and share of firm profits as a function of p. Let $z^h(p)$ denote the vector of household h's net demand functions across goods. Let $z_g(p) \equiv \sum_h z_g^h(p)$ denote the aggregate excess demand function for good g. Finally, let $z(p) \equiv \sum_h z^h(p)$ denote the vector of excess demand functions across goods. If all households satisfy their budget constraints, then $p \cdot z^h(p) = 0$ for all h. By implication, *Walras's law* holds: The values of excess demands sum to zero, $p \cdot z(p) = 0$.

Walras's law has two important consequences. First, in an equilibrium with strictly positive prices, all markets clear. To see this, note that the equilibrium requirements optimization and feasibility (subject to free disposal) imply $z(p) \leq 0$. If a good has strictly positive price, excess demand for that good thus must be zero (otherwise, $p \cdot z(p) \neq 0$). Second, with strictly positive prices, market clearing in all markets but one implies market clearing in the remaining market. To see this, suppose all markets except market j clear, $z_g(p) = 0$ for all $g \neq j$, such that $\sum_{g \neq j} p_g z_g(p) = 0$. Since $p_j > 0$, $z_j(p)$ also must equal zero (otherwise, $p \cdot z(p) \neq 0$).

1.1.4 Fundamental Theorems of Welfare Economics

The fundamental theorems of welfare economics relate equilibrium allocations to Pareto optimal allocations.

The *first fundamental theorem of welfare economics* formalizes the notion of an *invisible hand*. It states that, if an allocation and price system constitute a price equilibrium with transfers (in particular, a competitive equilibrium) and certain conditions (spelled out below) are satisfied, then the allocation is Pareto optimal. Decentralized choices by price-taking individuals thus are consistent with Pareto optimality, and this holds true even if lump-sum transfers occur before market transactions take place.

Let x^h, e^h, and y^f denote household h's consumption and endowment vectors as well as firm f's net production vector, respectively. An allocation $(\{x^h\}_h, \{y^f\}_f)$ is feasible if $\sum_h (x^h - e^h) \leq \sum_f y^f$. Let $(\{x^{h\star}\}_h, \{y^{f\star}\}_f, p^\star)$ be a competitive equilibrium with equilibrium price vector $p^\star$ and assume that preferences are locally nonsatiated; markets are complete (all goods are traded); and the market value of endowments is finite (e.g., because the number of households is finite). The theorem claims that under these conditions, no feasible allocation Pareto dominates $(\{x^{h\star}\}_h, \{y^{f\star}\}_f)$.

The proof by contradiction proceeds in three steps:

i. Suppose that a feasible Pareto dominating allocation, $(\{x^{h\bullet}\}_h, \{y^{f\bullet}\}_f)$, exists such that all households weakly prefer consumption in the $\bullet$ allocation and some strictly prefer it. Local nonsatiation, price taking, market completeness, and optimality imply that for all households, consumption in the $\bullet$ allocation is at least as expensive under $p^\star$ as in the $\star$ allocation, and for some households it is unaffordable.

ii. Since the market value of endowments is finite, we can sum over all households to find

$$\sum_h p^\star \cdot (x^{h\bullet} - e^h) > \sum_f p^\star \cdot y^{f\star}.$$

iii. Firm optimization implies $\sum_f p^\star \cdot y^{f\star} \geq \sum_f p^\star \cdot y^{f\bullet}$ and thus,

$$\sum_h p^\star \cdot (x^{h\bullet} - e^h) > \sum_f p^\star \cdot y^{f\bullet}.$$

But feasibility of $(\{x^{h\bullet}\}_h, \{y^{f\bullet}\}_f)$ implies the reverse inequality. We have established a contradiction and this proves the theorem.

The *second fundamental theorem of welfare economics* formalizes the notion that Pareto optimal allocations can be decentralized through markets and lump-sum transfers. It states that for every Pareto optimal allocation, there exists a set of prices such that the allocation and the prices constitute a price equilibrium with transfers. Necessary conditions include convex production sets as well as convex and locally nonsatiated preferences.

1.2   Primitives

The *primitives* of a modern macroeconomic model—the objects we take as given—include those of a microeconomic model, most importantly households with preferences and endowments, and firms with technologies. An event tree serves to describe the dynamic and stochastic formation of the economy.

1.2.1   Event Tree

Time is denoted by t. It runs from zero, the initial date, to some final date T or to infinity. To represent exogenous risk we let ϵ^t denote the *history* of realizations of the *state of nature* up to and including date t. From the perspective of date $t = 0$, history ϵ^0 is known but history $\epsilon^t, t \geq 1$, is a random variable unless there is no risk.

The *event tree* in figure 1.1 illustrates a three-period example. At date $t = 1$, one of two possible realizations occurs—"up" (for example promotion) or "down" (demotion). The same happens at date $t = 2$. History ϵ^1 thus takes two values, up or down, and history ϵ^2 four: (up, up), (up, down), (down, up), or (down, down).

Except for deterministic settings, variables need to be indexed by history to avoid ambiguity. Consider for instance a variable c—say, consumption of fruit. Indexing c by ϵ^t accounts for the fact that fruit in different histories at the same date constitutes different commodities, and that the quantities of fruit consumed in different histories may differ. In the environment of figure 1.1, fruit consumption at date $t = 2$ can take four values— $c_2(\text{up, up})$, $c_2(\text{up, down})$, $c_2(\text{down, up})$, or $c_2(\text{down, down})$.

A variable may be indexed by date t and history ϵ^s, $s < t$. This indicates that the variable takes the same value across all histories at date t that are continuation histories of history ϵ^s. For example, in the environment of figure 1.1, $c_2(\text{up})$ would indicate that fruit consumption at date $t = 2$ in histories (up, up) and (up, down) is the same.

1.2.2   Preferences

In the simplest dynamic model, *households* consume a single good (which might represent a composite), c, in each history. They trade off consumption across time and histories, in parallel to the static tradeoff between apples and oranges, say, in a microeconomic model. As we will see in chapters 2 and 4, the optimality conditions in dynamic and static settings are isomorphic under specific assumptions about the market structure.

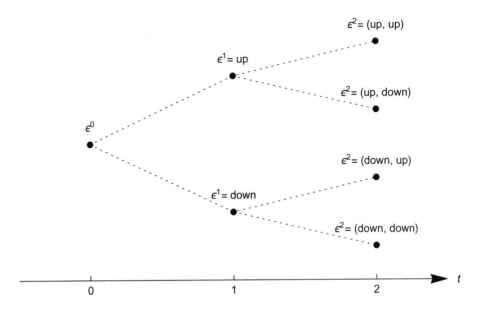

Figure 1.1
Event tree: An economy with three periods and two states of nature each at dates $t = 1, 2$.

Preferences map a sequence of history-contingent consumption into utility,

$$U\left(c_0, \{c_1(\epsilon^1)\}_{\epsilon^1}, \ldots, \{c_T(\epsilon^T)\}_{\epsilon^T}\right).$$

The *lifetime utility function* U increases in all its arguments. The notation $\{c_t(\epsilon^t)\}_{\epsilon^t}$ indicates that consumption at date t takes multiple values, depending on history. For example, in the environment of figure 1.1, we have $\{c_1(\epsilon^1)\}_{\epsilon^1} = (c_1(\text{up}), c_1(\text{down}))$.

Let $c \equiv (c_0, \{c_1(\epsilon^1)\}_{\epsilon^1}, \ldots, \{c_T(\epsilon^T)\}_{\epsilon^T})$ denote a stochastic consumption path and let U be differentiable, strictly increasing, and concave. The *marginal rate of substitution* between $c_t(\epsilon^t)$ and $c_s(\epsilon^s)$ equals

$$\frac{\partial U(c)/\partial c_t(\epsilon^t)}{\partial U(c)/\partial c_s(\epsilon^s)}.$$

Function U is *homothetic* if marginal rates of substitution do not change when c is scaled up or down. With homothetic preferences, relative demands are invariant to shifts of the budget line—that is, homothetic preferences generate linear Engel curves. Suppose that $U(c) = g(h(c))$ where g is strictly increasing and h is homogeneous of degree $n \geq 1$. By Euler's homogeneous function theorem the partial derivatives $\partial h(c)/\partial c_t(\epsilon^t)$ and $\partial h(c)/\partial c_s(\epsilon^s)$ then are homogeneous of degree $n - 1$. This implies that U is homothetic.

We often assume that preferences are *additively separable* across time and histories—that is, U is a weighted sum. The weight attached to date t equals β^t where $\beta \in [0, 1)$

denotes the psychological *discount factor* which measures the degree of patience. The weight attached to a particular history equals the probability that this history occurs. A consumption sequence thus is evaluated according to the discounted *expected utility* that it generates,

$$U = \mathbb{E}_0 \left[\sum_{t=0}^{T} \beta^t u(c_t(\epsilon^t)) \right],$$

where $\mathbb{E}_s$ denotes the mathematical expectation conditional on information available at date s, history ϵ^s, and u denotes the *period utility function* or *felicity function*. Separability across time and histories implies that the marginal utility of consumption at a date and history is independent of consumption at other dates and histories.

Function u exhibits strictly positive, decreasing marginal utility. Unless otherwise noted, we assume that it is continuously differentiable; marginal utility is strictly decreasing; and consumption at each date is essential, $\lim_{c \downarrow 0} u'(c) = \infty$.

We sometimes restrict u to be of the *constant intertemporal elasticity of substitution* (CIES) or equivalently, *constant relative risk aversion* form. Function u then is given by

$$u(c) = \frac{c^{1-\sigma} - 1}{1 - \sigma} \text{ for } \sigma > 0, \ \sigma \neq 1.$$

This functional form is not defined for $\sigma = 1$, but applying L'Hôpital's rule implies $\lim_{\sigma \to 1} u(c) = \ln(c)$; the logarithmic function thus constitutes a limiting case.

As the name suggests, CIES preferences exhibit constant relative risk aversion and a constant intertemporal elasticity of substitution.[1] To see the former, recall that the *coefficient of relative risk aversion* is defined as $-u''(c)c/u'(c)$; with CIES preferences this reduces to σ. To see the latter, recall that the *elasticity of substitution* measures how strongly a change in relative price, which equals the marginal rate of substitution in equilibrium, affects relative demand. With CIES preferences, the elasticity of the ratio c_{t+1}/c_t with respect to the relative price of c_{t+1} and c_t reduces to $1/\sigma$. As we will see in chapter 2, CIES preferences simplify the equilibrium conditions in dynamic models.

Figure 1.2 illustrates the role of σ in the CIES case. The top row of the figure plots $u(c)$ and the bottom row plots indifference curves of $U = u(c_0) + \beta u(c_1)$. As σ increases the indifference curves gain curvature; variations in c_1/c_0 therefore are associated with larger changes in the marginal rate of substitution.

1.2.3   Technology

Firms employ a *production function*, f, that maps inputs of physical capital, K, and labor, L, into output. Unless otherwise noted, we assume that the production function is *neo-*

---

[1] Risk aversion and the intertemporal elasticity of substitution are conceptually distinct even if they are functionally related when preferences take the CIES form. Appendix B.4 discusses a preference specification in which risk aversion and the intertemporal elasticity of substitution are decoupled.

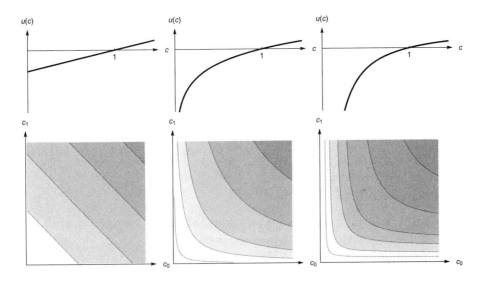

Figure 1.2
CIES preferences: Period utility function and indifference curves for very small, intermediate, and large σ (from left to right).

classical. That is, f exhibits strictly positive and diminishing marginal products as well as *constant returns to scale,*

$$f_K(K,L), f_L(K,L) > 0; \quad f_{KK}(K,L), f_{LL}(K,L) < 0; \quad \phi f(K,L) = f(\phi K, \phi L), \quad \phi > 0.$$

Here, subscripts denote partial derivatives, $f_K(K,L) = \partial f(K,L)/\partial K$ and $f_{KK}(K,L) \equiv \partial^2 f(K,L)/(\partial K)^2$; we use this notation throughout the book.

With constant returns to scale, output coincides with total factor payments to the suppliers of K and L if the rental rates of K and L equal the respective marginal products. In competitive factor markets, this is the case. Moreover, with constant returns to scale, output per worker as well as marginal products only depend on the capital–labor ratio, $k \equiv K/L$, not on K and L individually. This follow from Euler's homogeneous function theorem.

The production function satisfies the *Inada conditions* when

$$\lim_{K \downarrow 0} f_K(K,L) = \lim_{L \downarrow 0} f_L(K,L) = \infty, \quad \lim_{K \to \infty} f_K(K,L) = \lim_{L \to \infty} f_L(K,L) = 0.$$

The Inada conditions help guarantee interior equilibria—that is, equilibria with strictly positive, finite factor inputs.

The *constant elasticity of substitution* (CES) production function,

$$f(K,L) = \left(\alpha K^{1-\frac{1}{\theta}} + (1-\alpha)L^{1-\frac{1}{\theta}} \right)^{\frac{\theta}{\theta-1}}, \quad \theta > 0, \ \alpha \in (0,1),$$

constitutes a tractable example of a neoclassical production function. The elasticity of substitution of the CES function between K and L is constant and equals θ. For $\theta \to \infty$, the CES production function approaches a linear production function; for $\theta \to 0$ the Leontief production function; and for $\theta \to 1$ it converges to the *Cobb-Douglas production function*,

$$f(K, L) = K^{\alpha} L^{1-\alpha}.$$

When production factors are paid their marginal products, the Cobb-Douglas production function implies constant factor shares, $K f_K(K, L)/f(K, L) = \alpha$ and $L f_L(K, L)/f(K, L) = 1 - \alpha$.

1.3   Bibliographic Notes

The Walrasian equilibrium notion is due to Walras (1874) and other representatives of the (pre)marginalist school (von Thünen, Cournot, Dupuis, Gossen, Jevons, Menger). Arrow and Debreu (1954) and McKenzie (1954) use fixed-point arguments to prove the existence of general equilibrium and Debreu (1959) proves the welfare theorems. Bewley (1972) proves that in economies with a finite number of *infinitely* lived, impatient households, an equilibrium exists and is Pareto optimal.

   Arrow (1953; 1964) and Debreu (1959, chapter 7) define commodities with reference to the event tree. Cobb and Douglas (1928) discuss the production function named after them.

Related Topics and Additional References   The notion of macroeconomic *equilibrium* has evolved since Walras (1874). Hicks (1939) envisions interdependent markets that operate sequentially and he distinguishes between *temporary equilibrium* in spot markets (conditional on expectations about the future), and *equilibrium over time* where expected and actual prices coincide. Stigum (1969) relaxes the restriction on expectations and Grandmont (1977) discusses the notion of a *sequence of temporary equilibria*, possibly including learning.[2] Common price expectations across agents and consistent plans based on these expectations form an *equilibrium of plans, prices, and price expectations* (Hahn, 1971; Radner, 1972). When agents have heterogeneous information sets, market prices may reveal some of the unobserved fundamentals and agents may use a model of the relationship between equilibrium prices and fundamentals to infer the latter; in a *rational expectations equilibrium* the prediction model used by the agents in the model is the correct model (Lucas, 1972). Barro and Grossman (1971) study a general *disequilibrium* model where excess supplies and demands in different markets affect each other.

   More broadly, the methodological approach to studying *macroeconomics* has changed profoundly over the last 60 years. In the late 1950s, microeconomic reasoning coexisted

---

[2] For macroeconomic models with learning dynamics, see Evans and Honkapohja (1999; 2001).

with Keynesian arguments (Keynes, 1936; Hicks, 1939), which often rest on weaker choice theoretic foundations. During the 1960s, empirical macroeconomics suffered setbacks, not least because the *Phillips curve* relationship between observed unemployment and (wage) inflation proved less stable than expected. Friedman (1968, p. 8) argues that the Phillips curve presumes "a world in which everyone anticipated that nominal prices would be stable . . . whatever happened," stimulating the search for models that better reconcile micro- and macroeconomics, as in Phelps (1970). Building on Muth (1961), Sargent (1971) and Lucas (1972) promote the rational expectations consistency requirement.

By the late 1970s, the profession lost faith in the *neoclassical synthesis* (Samuelson, 1955) of Keynesian and neoclassical economics and in particular, in policy analysis based on large-scale macroeconometric models. It became clear that optimizing behavior also concerns expectation formation; reduced-form relationships in models without micro-foundations are not policy-invariant (Lucas, 1976); and "claims for identification in [large-scale statistical macroeconomic] models" are unfounded (Sims, 1980, p. 1). Early micro-founded dynamic general equilibrium models in the 1980s and their empirical counterparts improved on these weaknesses but lacked plausible frictions and abstracted from heterogeneity, which limits their relevance for applied purposes. Modern macroeconomic models for applied purposes—models of dynamic stochastic general equilibrium—feature heterogeneity, time, risk, and diverse frictions.

Mas-Colell et al. (1995) cover microeconomic theory and Eatwell et al. (1989) provide an overview of topics in general equilibrium theory. Niehans (1994) covers the history of economic thought until 1980.

2 Consumption and Saving

Saving generates opportunities for future consumption. A household's savings choice thus reflects the costs and benefits of consuming at different points in time. In turn, these costs and benefits depend on household preferences and relative prices, among other factors.

We specify the household's dynamic utility maximization problem in finite and infinite horizon environments and introduce techniques to solve it. We analyze the consumption–saving tradeoff, which forms the backbone of macroeconomic models, and we derive the household's demand functions for current and future consumption. For now, we abstract from risk and assume that utility in a period depends on a single consumption good.

2.1 Consumption Smoothing

Consider a household that owns a (possibly negative) stock of assets, a_t. The household receives (or pays) interest income on the assets, $a_t(R_t - 1)$, where R_t denotes the exogenous gross interest rate. It also receives exogenous wage income, w_t. The stock of assets and the two incomes fund consumption, c_t, as well as asset holdings carried into the next period, a_{t+1}. The *dynamic budget constraint*

$$a_{t+1} = a_t R_t + w_t - c_t$$

represents the resulting asset dynamics. Rearranging terms, the dynamic budget constraint states that the change in the asset position, $a_{t+1} - a_t$, equals *saving* or income minus consumption.

2.1.1 Two Periods

Suppose the household lives for two periods and has no assets to start with ($a_0 = 0$). Its objective is given by

$$u(c_0) + \beta u(c_1)$$

and the dynamic budget constraints at the two dates read

$$a_1 = w_0 - c_0,$$
$$a_2 = a_1 R_1 + w_1 - c_1.$$

Since the household dies at the end of date $t = 1$, nobody will lend it resources at that date; terminal household assets therefore must be nonnegative, $a_2 \geq 0$. Moreover, carrying strictly positive assets into date $t = 2$ would be wasteful because the household cannot consume after its death. The optimal saving choice at date $t = 1$ thus equals $a_2 = 0$.

Using this result and combining the two dynamic budget constraints, we arrive at the *intertemporal budget constraint*

$$c_0 + \frac{c_1}{R_1} = w_0 + \frac{w_1}{R_1}.$$

The terms on the left-hand side represent total spending on the two goods, consumption in the first and second period—c_0 and c_1, respectively. Consumption in the first period is the *numeraire*; its price is normalized to unity. The relative price of consumption in the second period is given by the inverse of the gross interest rate, $1/R_1$. Intuitively, reducing consumption in the first period by one unit raises saving and increases consumption in the second period by R_1 units. One unit of first-period consumption therefore buys R_1 units of second-period consumption, or one unit of second-period consumption costs $1/R_1$ units of first-period consumption.

The terms on the right-hand side of the intertemporal budget constraint represent the household's wealth; that is, the date $t = 0$ market value of first- and second-period wage income. Note that the intertemporal budget constraint is isomorphic to the budget constraint in a static model of consumer choice. In the static model, apples and oranges, say, replace first- and second-period consumption; the market value of the endowments constitutes wealth; and the price of oranges in terms of apples replaces the inverse gross interest rate.

To find the household's optimal level of saving in the first period, we may solve the dynamic budget constraints for consumption and substitute the resulting expressions into the objective function. The household's program then reads

$$\max_{a_1} u(w_0 - a_1) + \beta u(a_1 R_1 + w_1).$$

An interior solution to this program satisfies the first-order condition

$$u'(c_0) = \beta R_1 u'(c_1) \quad \text{or} \quad \frac{u'(c_0)}{\beta u'(c_1)} = R_1,$$

where we reintroduce the variables c_0 and c_1 for ease of notation. This first-order condition is referred to as the *Euler equation*. The second-order condition for a maximum, $u''(c_0) +$

$\beta R_1^2 u''(c_1) < 0$, is satisfied as long as u is strictly concave. Strict concavity also implies that the maximum is a unique global maximum (see appendix A.1).

The second representation of the Euler equation states that the marginal rate of substitution between current and future consumption is equated with the relative price of the two goods. This is the same condition as in a static model. Represented graphically, the condition states that the price line is tangent to an indifference curve.

The Euler equation characterizes optimal second-period consumption relative to first-period consumption and thus, the slope of the optimal consumption path but not its level. Three factors determine whether and how strongly consumption increases or decreases over time. First, β. More patience increases the weight given to future utility and thus, the slope of the optimal consumption path. Formally, a higher β implies a higher ratio $u'(c_0)/u'(c_1)$ and thus (if u is strictly concave), a higher c_1/c_0. Second, R_1. A higher interest rate renders second-period consumption cheaper, also implying a higher c_1/c_0. Third, the curvature of the marginal utility function (recall figure 1.2). It determines how strongly a change of β or R_1 translates into a steeper or flatter consumption profile. More curvature implies a stronger *consumption-smoothing* motive; that is, less willingness to intertemporally substitute.

To solve for the equilibrium consumption levels we combine the Euler equation and the intertemporal budget constraint (or the two dynamic budget constraints). If the period utility function is of the CIES type (such that the Euler equation reads $c_0^{-\sigma} = \beta R_1 c_1^{-\sigma}$) this yields

$$c_0 = \left(w_0 + \frac{w_1}{R_1}\right) \Big/ \left(1 + \frac{(\beta R_1)^{1/\sigma}}{R_1}\right).$$

From the budget constraint, we may also solve for a_1 and c_1.

We have completely characterized optimal consumption conditional on β, u, R_1, w_0, and w_1. Two important results emerge. First, optimal consumption depends on wealth, $w_0 + w_1/R_1$, or *permanent income*, not only on contemporaneous income as with a Keynesian consumption function. This is a consequence of the household's desire to smooth consumption over the life cycle if marginal utility is decreasing ($u'' < 0$), and its ability to do so by means of saving or borrowing.

Second, a change of interest rate affects optimal consumption threefold, through wealth, income, and substitution effects. (The terms "wealth effect" and "income effect" often are used interchangeably.) First, if $w_1 > 0$, an increase in the interest rate reduces wealth because it lowers the date $t = 0$ market value of future labor income, w_1/R_1. This leads the household to consume less in both periods—a negative *wealth effect*. Second, for given quantities c_0 and $c_1 > 0$, an increase in the interest rate lowers the cost of the bundle (c_0, c_1) expressed in terms of the numeraire because it lowers the cost of c_1. The higher purchasing power leads the household to consume more of both goods—a positive *income effect*. Finally, from the Euler equation, it is optimal to substitute toward the cheaper good.

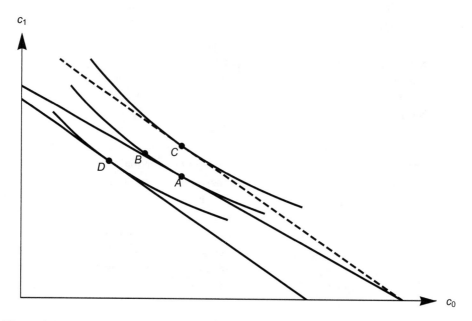

Figure 2.1
Effects of an interest rate change: Wealth, income, and substitution effects.

An increase in the interest rate thus leads the household to increase c_1 relative to c_0. The strength of this *substitution effect* depends on the intertemporal elasticity of substitution, $1/\sigma$. Note that the income and substitution effects on c_0 cancel if $\sigma = 1$ as $(\beta R_1)^{1/\sigma}/R_1$ is independent of R_1 in this case.

Figure 2.1 illustrates the three effects. Point A depicts the equilibrium at a low interest rate; it is the tangency point of the budget line and the highest indifference curve that the household may attain. Point D depicts the equilibrium at a higher interest rate, represented by a steeper budget line. The substitution effect corresponds to the distance between points A and B; the income effect to the distance between points B and C; and the wealth effect to the distance between points C and D. The figure is plotted for the logarithmic utility case, $\sigma = 1$. The income and substitution effects on c_0 exactly cancel in this case.

2.1.2   More Periods

More generally, the household's program comprises a multiperiod objective function and multiple dynamic budget constraints in addition to the initial and terminal conditions:

$$\max_{c_0,\dots,c_T,a_1,\dots,a_{T+1}} \sum_{t=0}^{T} \beta^t u(c_t) \ \text{ s.t. } \ a_{t+1} = a_t R_t + w_t - c_t, \ a_0 R_0 \text{ given, } a_{T+1} \geq 0.$$

In parallel with the strategy adopted in the two-period case, we may confront this problem by solving the dynamic budget constraints for consumption and substituting the resulting expressions into the objective function. Conjecturing again that a_{T+1} optimally equals zero, this yields

$$\max_{a_1,\dots,a_T} \sum_{t=0}^{T} \beta^t u(a_t R_t + w_t - a_{t+1}) \text{ s.t. } a_0 R_0 \text{ given, } a_{T+1} = 0.$$

Differentiating with respect to the choice variables, we find an Euler equation for each date t.

2.1.2.1   Lagrangian   An alternative strategy uses the intertemporal budget constraint. The latter can be derived, as before, by combining the dynamic budget constraints:

$$
\begin{aligned}
a_{T+1} &= a_T R_T + w_T - c_T \\
&= (a_{T-1} R_{T-1} + w_{T-1} - c_{T-1}) R_T + w_T - c_T \\
&= \cdots \\
&= a_0 R_0 R_1 \cdots R_T + (w_0 - c_0) R_1 R_2 \cdots R_T + (w_1 - c_1) R_2 \cdots R_T \\
&\quad + \dots + (w_{T-1} - c_{T-1}) R_T + (w_T - c_T).
\end{aligned}
$$

Let $q_t \equiv (R_1 R_2 \cdots R_t)^{-1}$ denote the price of date-t consumption at the initial date and define $q_0 \equiv 1$. Multiplying the intertemporal budget constraint by q_T and using the optimality condition $a_{T+1} = 0$ yields

$$q_T a_{T+1} = 0 = a_0 R_0 + \sum_{t=0}^{T} q_t(w_t - c_t) \text{ or } \sum_{t=0}^{T} q_t c_t = a_0 R_0 + \sum_{t=0}^{T} q_t w_t.$$

In parallel to the two-period case, the intertemporal budget constraint equates lifetime consumption spending and wealth.

Replacing the $T + 1$ dynamic budget constraints with the single intertemporal budget constraint, the household's program can be expressed as

$$\max_{c_0,\dots,c_T} \sum_{t=0}^{T} \beta^t u(c_t) \text{ s.t. } a_0 R_0 + \sum_{t=0}^{T} q_t(w_t - c_t) = 0.$$

Forming the *Lagrangian* (see appendix A.1),

$$\mathcal{L} = \sum_{t=0}^{T} \beta^t u(c_t) + \lambda \left[a_0 R_0 + \sum_{t=0}^{T} q_t(w_t - c_t) \right],$$

and differentiating yields T first-order conditions,

$$\beta^t u'(c_t) = \lambda q_t.$$

They state that marginal utility from consumption at date t equals the price of consumption in that period, q_t, times the *multiplier* attached to the intertemporal budget constraint, λ. Since the multiplier measures the effect of a marginal relaxation of the constraint on the maximized objective function or equivalently, the *shadow cost* of the constraint, λ represents the *shadow value of wealth*.

Combining the first-order conditions at date t and $t+1$ yields the Euler equation, $u'(c_t) = \beta R_{t+1} u'(c_{t+1})$. To solve for the optimal consumption levels, we combine the Euler equations and the intertemporal budget constraint.

Yet another approach to solving the household's program relies on forming a Lagrangian that incorporates the dynamic budget constraints and the terminal condition $a_{T+1} \geq 0$. This approach allows us to derive the optimality condition $a_{T+1} = 0$ rather than imposing it. The Lagrangian now reads (see appendix A.1)

$$\mathcal{L} = \sum_{t=0}^{T} \{\beta^t u(c_t) - \lambda_t [a_{t+1} - (a_t R_t + w_t - c_t)]\} + \mu a_{T+1}.$$

The first-order conditions with respect to c_t and a_{t+1} are given by

$$\beta^t u'(c_t) = \lambda_t,$$
$$\lambda_t = \lambda_{t+1} R_{t+1}, \ t = 0, \ldots, T-1,$$

respectively. The first-order condition with respect to a_{T+1} is $\lambda_T = \mu$ and the complementary slackness condition is given by $\mu a_{T+1} = 0$.

Combining the first-order conditions with respect to consumption again yields the Euler equation, $u'(c_t) = \beta R_{t+1} u'(c_{t+1})$. Moreover, nonsatiation ($u' > 0$) implies $\lambda_T > 0$ and thus $\mu > 0$, which in turn implies $a_{T+1} = 0$, the *transversality condition* we had informally argued before.

2.1.2.2 Dynamic Programming We may also solve the consumption–saving program by means of *dynamic programming* techniques. Consider the household's program at date t. Its value—the maximized objective—is a function of household assets at date t, a_t, as well as of the program's other parameters. We denote the value by $V_t(a_t)$ where V_t is the *value function* at date t, and we refer to the parameters of the program as the *state* or the *state variables*. Note that the value function is an *indirect utility function*; it gives the maximum utility over the remaining lifetime as a function of the parameters of the optimization problem.

The state contains exogenous and endogenous elements. Wages and interest rates over the planning horizon are exogenous state variables, as is the remaining time horizon of the program and the structure of preferences. In contrast, the initial asset level, a_t, is an endogenous state variable: At date t, it constitutes a parameter, which summarizes the effect of past (savings) decisions, but in the program at date $t-1$ it constitutes a choice variable.

To simplify the notation, we do not include the exogenous state variables as arguments of the value function; instead, we implicitly represent them by the time subscript.

Let DBC_t denote the dynamic budget constraint at date t and let C denote the set of dynamic budget constraints at date $t+1$ and later as well as the terminal condition, $a_{T+1} \geq 0$. The value function at date t then satisfies

$$V_t(a_t) = \max_{\{c_s, a_{s+1}\}_{s=t}^{T}} \sum_{s=t}^{T} \beta^{s-t} u(c_s) \text{ s.t. } DBC_t, C, a_t \text{ given.}$$

Exploiting the additive separability of preferences, we can alternatively represent this condition recursively:

$$
\begin{aligned}
V_t(a_t) &= \max_{\{c_s, a_{s+1}\}_{s=t}^{T}} \sum_{s=t}^{T} \beta^{s-t} u(c_s) \text{ s.t. } DBC_t, C, a_t \text{ given} \\
&= \max_{c_t, a_{t+1}} u(c_t) + \left(\max_{\{c_s, a_{s+1}\}_{s=t+1}^{T}} \sum_{s=t+1}^{T} \beta^{s-t} u(c_s) \text{ s.t. } C, a_{t+1} \text{ given} \right) \text{ s.t. } DBC_t, a_t \text{ given} \\
&= \max_{c_t, a_{t+1}} u(c_t) + \beta \left(\max_{\{c_s, a_{s+1}\}_{s=t+1}^{T}} \sum_{s=t+1}^{T} \beta^{s-(t+1)} u(c_s) \text{ s.t. } C, a_{t+1} \text{ given} \right) \text{ s.t. } DBC_t, a_t \text{ given} \\
&= \max_{c_t, a_{t+1}} u(c_t) + \beta V_{t+1}(a_{t+1}) \text{ s.t. } DBC_t, a_t \text{ given.}
\end{aligned}
$$

We are confronted with a *functional equation* referred to as the *Bellman equation*. It stipulates that the function of a_t on the left-hand side of the equality is identical to the function on the right-hand side. Substituting the dynamic budget constraint, we arrive at a more compact representation of the Bellman equation at date t,

$$V_t(a_t) = \max_{a_{t+1}} u(a_t R_t + w_t - a_{t+1}) + \beta V_{t+1}(a_{t+1}).$$

Since T is finite we face a finite system of Bellman equations which we can solve by backward induction. To start the induction, note that $V_{T+1}(a_{T+1}) = 0$ for any a_{T+1} because the household is no longer alive at date $t = T + 1$. At date $t = T$, this implies the optimal choice $a_{T+1} = 0$ and thus, the value function $V_T(a_T) = u(a_T R_T + w_T)$. Using this result and the Bellman equation at date $t = T - 1$, we can characterize the optimal choice and the value function at date $t = T - 1$. Proceeding backward, we solve for all value functions V_t and *policy functions* g_t, say; the latter give the optimal value of the choice variable as a function of the state, $a_{t+1} = g_t(a_t)$. To automate this iterative process we can approximate the functions V_t and g_t (e.g., by vectors over a finite grid that approximates the continuous state space) and use a computer program with loops to find V_t and g_t conditional on V_{t+1} for $t = T, T - 1, \ldots$.

From the Bellman equation, we may also derive the Euler equation—even if we do not know the value functions. According to the right-hand side of the Bellman equation, the optimal value of the choice variable maximizes $u(a_t R_t + w_t - a_{t+1}) + \beta V_{t+1}(a_{t+1})$; that is, it solves the first-order condition

$$u'(c_t) = \beta V'_{t+1}(a_{t+1}).$$

Intuitively, the optimal savings choice balances the marginal utility loss from lower contemporaneous consumption with the marginal gain due to a higher discounted *continuation value*.

To derive an expression for the marginal continuation value, we differentiate the Bellman equation with respect to the state variable to find the *envelope condition*,

$$
\begin{aligned}
V'_t(a_t) &= u'(c_t)(R_t - g'_t(a_t)) + \beta V'_{t+1}(a_{t+1}) g'_t(a_t) \\
&= u'(c_t) R_t,
\end{aligned}
$$

where c_t represents consumption at the optimum. The second equality in the envelope condition follows from substituting the first-order condition—this is the envelope theorem at work (see below). Combining the first-order condition and the envelope condition (at date $t + 1$) yields the Euler equation, $u'(c_t) = \beta R_{t+1} u'(c_{t+1})$. Using the policy function, we can also express the Euler equation as a functional equation,

$$u'(a_t R_t + w_t - g_t(a_t)) = \beta R_{t+1} u'(g_t(a_t) R_{t+1} + w_{t+1} - g_{t+1}(g_t(a_t))),$$

which holds for all feasible values of a_t.

Figure 2.2 illustrates the envelope condition. The figure plots the level curves of the right-hand side of the Bellman equation at date $t = T - 1$, $\mathrm{RHS}(a_T; a_{T-1}) \equiv u(a_{T-1} R_{T-1} + w_{T-1} - a_T) + \beta u(a_T R_T + w_T)$, against a_{T-1} (the state variable) and a_T (the choice variable). Darker areas indicate higher values of RHS. For a given value of the state, for instance the horizontal coordinate of point A, the maximand is a concave function of the choice variable. This function reaches a maximum at the optimal choice, in this case the vertical coordinate of point A; the level curve through point A thus is vertical at point A.

Consider now a small increase in the state, indicated by the solid arrow. This has two effects on RHS: A direct, positive one because higher assets increase consumption at date $t = T - 1$; and an indirect one, because the household optimally adjusts saving, which reduces consumption at date $t = T - 1$ but increases it at date $t = T$. The increase in saving is indicated by the dashed arrow to point B. The level curve through point B is exactly vertical at B while the level curve through the tip of the solid arrow (not plotted) is negatively sloped at the tip. If the increase in the state is infinitesimally small, however, then the level curve through the tip of the solid arrow is "nearly" vertical because the tip of the arrow is close to point A. The increase of RHS due to the adjustment in saving—that is, due to the movement along the dashed arrow—thus is of second order. Accordingly, the only first-order effect of the infinitesimal change in the state variable on the value function is the direct one.

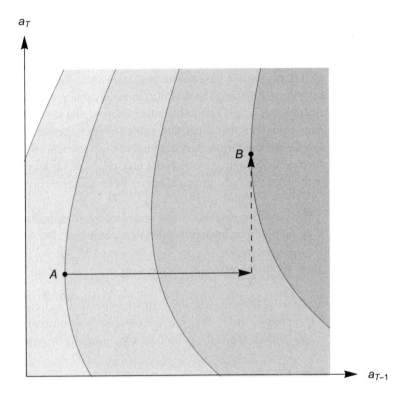

Figure 2.2
Envelope condition: Level curves of the right-hand side of the Bellman equation.

2.1.3   Infinite Horizon

There are several reasons to consider optimization over an *infinite horizon*, $T \to \infty$. First, because this can be interpreted as reflecting intergenerational altruism: Parents care about the utility of their children, who in turn care about the utility of their children, and so on. Second, because an infinite horizon can be interpreted as reflecting a time-invariant survival probability. And third, because eliminating time as a state variable renders the program simpler in some dimensions, as we will see below.

To derive the household's intertemporal budget constraint in the infinite horizon case, we need to specify an appropriate terminal condition. This is given by the *no-Ponzi-game condition*,

$$\lim_{T \to \infty} q_T a_{T+1} \geq 0.$$

Note that the no-Ponzi-game condition generalizes the constraint $q_T a_{T+1} \geq 0$ from the finite horizon case, not its reduced form, $a_{T+1} \geq 0$. In fact, a generalization of the latter, to $\lim_{T \to \infty} a_{T+1} \geq 0$, would constitute an unnecessarily tight constraint that prevents the household from holding any debt in the long run.

In contrast, the no-Ponzi-game condition only rules out paths along which debt in the long run grows at a weakly higher rate than the interest rate—that is, along which a_{T+1} grows faster than q_T shrinks as $T \to \infty$. The no-Ponzi-game condition thus prevents the household from permanently rolling over debt, including interest, and never servicing it. While the no-Ponzi-game condition guarantees that going forward, the present value of debt service fully covers the outstanding debt, it does not impose restrictions on the time profile of the debt service. For example, the household may once and for all pay back all outstanding debt, or it may never repay the principal but instead pay interest on the liability forever after.

Using the no-Ponzi-game condition and following the same steps as in the finite horizon case, we can derive the infinite-horizon intertemporal budget constraint

$$a_0 R_0 + \lim_{T \to \infty} \sum_{t=0}^{T} q_t(w_t - c_t) = \lim_{T \to \infty} q_T a_{T+1} \geq 0.$$

By the same logic as in the finite horizon case, optimality requires setting $\lim_{T \to \infty} q_T a_{T+1}$ as small as possible (see appendix B.1). The intertemporal budget constraint therefore reduces to $a_0 R_0 + \sum_{t=0}^{\infty} q_t(w_t - c_t) = 0$ and the household's program can be represented as

$$\max_{\{c_t\}_{t \geq 0}} \sum_{t=0}^{\infty} \beta^t u(c_t) \ \text{ s.t. } \ a_0 R_0 + \sum_{t=0}^{\infty} q_t(w_t - c_t) = 0.$$

Forming the Lagrangian,

$$\mathcal{L} = \sum_{t=0}^{\infty} \beta^t u(c_t) + \lambda [a_0 R_0 + \sum_{t=0}^{\infty} q_t(w_t - c_t)],$$

and differentiating yields the same first-order conditions as before,

$$\beta^t u'(c_t) = \lambda q_t,$$

and thus, the Euler equation.

Turn next to dynamic programming. With an infinite horizon, the household's planning horizon is independent of how many periods have gone by. The structure of the optimization problem therefore is independent of time—the problem is *time autonomous*—unless wages, interest rates, or preferences are time dependent. In the time-autonomous case, the Bellman equation can be expressed as

$$V(a_\circ) = \max_{a_+} u(a_\circ R + w - a_+) + \beta V(a_+).$$

Note that the value functions on the left- and right-hand side are identical (the functions do not have time subscripts), in contrast with the finite horizon case. The state variable $a_\circ$ and the choice variable a_+ are written without time subscripts to indicate the time-autonomous nature of the program.

Although there exists no final period in the infinite horizon case, we can nevertheless find the value function V of the infinite horizon problem by means of an iterative procedure that parallels the solution strategy in the finite horizon case. This follows from mathematical results which establish that under certain conditions, (i) the value function V solving the time-autonomous Bellman equation is unique, and (ii) starting from any value function guess (for example, the function that started the recursion in the finite horizon case, $V_{T+1}(a_{T+1}) = 0$), the iterative procedure applied in the finite horizon case yields a sequence of value functions that converges to V (see appendix A.2). When working with a computer, an approximation of the infinite horizon value function thus can be found by running exactly the same code as in the finite horizon case, except that the iteration only stops when the sequence of value function approximations has converged.

2.2 Extensions

2.2.1 Borrowing Constraint

We have assumed that households may freely borrow as long as they satisfy the intertemporal budget constraint—that is, as long as they are *solvent*. But borrowing against future wage income may be difficult; for example, because a potential lender does not have sufficient information about the future income stream or cannot enforce repayment. This renders future wage income *illiquid* and gives rise to a new constraint—a *liquidity* or *borrowing constraint*—in addition to the intertemporal budget constraint.

The simplest borrowing constraint excludes all borrowing against future wage income, such that the household's financial assets must be positive at all times, $a_{t+1} \geq 0$. If the constraint binds, then this is costly because it prevents consumption smoothing. To see this, consider a two-period model with strictly concave preferences and suppose that absent a borrowing constraint, optimal consumption in the first period exceeds *liquid wealth*, $w_0 + a_0 R_0$. Implementing the optimal consumption plan thus would require borrowing, $a_1 < 0$, but the borrowing constraint renders this infeasible. The constrained optimal consumption path then equals $(c_0, c_1) = (w_0 + a_0 R_0, w_1)$—that is, consumption follows income, as with a Keynesian consumption function. Note that we have identified a new saving motive: reduced borrowing (that is, increased saving) due to a binding borrowing constraint.

More formally, the Lagrangian associated with the constrained saving problem reads

$$\mathcal{L} = u(c_0) + \beta u(c_1) - \lambda \left(c_0 + \frac{c_1}{R_1} - w_0 - \frac{w_1}{R_1} - a_0 R_0 \right) + \mu(w_0 + a_0 R_0 - c_0),$$

where the nonnegative multiplier μ represents the shadow cost of the borrowing constraint, $w_0 + a_0 R_0 - c_0 \geq 0$. Differentiating with respect to c_0 and c_1 and combining the two conditions yields the modified Euler equation

$$u'(c_0) = \beta R_1 u'(c_1) + \mu.$$

A binding borrowing constraint, $\mu > 0$, increases the slope of the equilibrium consumption path. Moreover, $\mu > 0$ and the complementary slackness condition, $\mu(w_0 + a_0 R_0 - c_0) = 0$, imply $c_0 = w_0 + a_0 R_0$, in line with the heuristic argument above.

2.2.2   Nongeometric Discounting and Time Consistency

We have posited so far that the sequence of psychological discount factors is geometrically declining, $1, \beta, \beta^2, \beta^3, \ldots$. Under this assumption, a household that reoptimizes period by period opts to continue with the consumption plan chosen earlier in time. That is, if the household optimally chose the consumption plan $(c_t, \overrightarrow{c_{t+1}})$ with $\overrightarrow{c_{t+1}} \equiv \{c_{t+1}, c_{t+2}, \ldots\}$ at date t, then pursuing the plan $\overrightarrow{c_{t+1}}$ once time has progressed to date $t + 1$ remains optimal. As a consequence, it does not matter whether we assume that the household chooses the consumption plan at date $t = 0$ once and for all, under *commitment*, or whether it reoptimizes period by period. In this sense, the initial consumption plan is *time consistent*.

Under more general assumptions about the psychological discount factor sequence, the consumption plan at date $t = 0$ need not be time consistent. Two households, one reoptimizing period by period and the other acting under commitment, may end up with different consumption paths although their preferences at date $t = 0$ and their budget sets are identical.

Consider an extreme example in a setting with three periods, where the household discounts all future utility at factor $\beta < 1$. At date $t = 0$, the household has preferences $u(c_0) + \beta(u(c_1) + u(c_2))$ while at date $t = 1$, preferences are given by $u(c_1) + \beta u(c_2)$. For simplicity, let $R_t = 1, w_t = w$. The optimal consumption path as of date $t = 0$ then solves the problem

$$\max_{c_0, c_1, c_2} u(c_0) + \beta(u(c_1) + u(c_2)) \text{ s.t. } c_0 + c_1 + c_2 = 3w + a_0,$$

which yields $c_1 = c_2$ (assuming $u'' < 0$). A committed household implements this solution. Absent commitment, in contrast, a household reoptimizing at date $t = 1$ solves

$$\max_{c_1, c_2} u(c_1) + \beta u(c_2) \text{ s.t. } c_1 + c_2 = 2w + a_1,$$

which yields $c_1 > c_2$. That is, the household does not implement the path that is optimal from the perspective of date $t = 0$.

Without commitment, the ex-ante optimal consumption plan cannot be implemented because it is *time inconsistent*. In equilibrium, the two selves of the household play a game against each other. The first self chooses c_0 and a_1. The second self chooses c_1, a_2 and c_2 conditional on a_1. Since the second self chooses $c_1 > c_2$, the first self cannot implement the ex-ante optimal plan. Anticipating the second self's choice, the first self solves

$$\max_{c_0, c_1, c_2} u(c_0) + \beta(u(c_1) + u(c_2)) \text{ s.t. } c_0 + c_1 + c_2 = 3w + a_0, u'(c_1) = \beta u'(c_2)$$

where the second constraint, the Euler equation of the second self, reflects the consumption choice from date $t = 1$ onward. By choosing a_1, the first self affects the state variable at date $t = 1$ and may thus influence the action taken by the second self.

Instruments that serve as state variables at date $t = 1$ can be helpful for the first self, even if these instruments would be irrelevant under commitment. Ulysses, for example, manages to bypass the island of the Sirens by having his crew put wax into their ears (so that they cannot hear the Sirens sing) and himself tied to the mast (so that he cannot change the course of the vessel).

2.2.3 Multiple Goods

Consider a two-period lived household that consumes two goods in each period. Their quantities, d_t and e_t, are aggregated into a CES consumption index,

$$c_t(d_t, e_t) = \left(\delta^{\frac{1}{\theta}} d_t^{1-\frac{1}{\theta}} + \varepsilon^{\frac{1}{\theta}} e_t^{1-\frac{1}{\theta}} \right)^{\frac{\theta}{\theta-1}}, \ \delta + \varepsilon = 1, \ \theta > 0, \ \theta \neq 1,$$

with elasticity of substitution equal to θ. The price of d_t is normalized to unity and the relative price of e_t is denoted p_t. Intertemporal preferences are described by the utility function $u(c_0) + \beta u(c_1)$.

The household's consumption choice has an *intratemporal* dimension (the tradeoff between d_t and e_t) and an *intertemporal* one (the tradeoff between c_0 and c_1). Focusing first on the intratemporal tradeoff, consider the problem of maximizing c_t subject to a given amount of spending, $z_t = d_t + p_t e_t$. The solution to this problem is given by

$$d_t = \delta \frac{z_t}{\delta + \varepsilon p_t^{1-\theta}}, \ e_t = \varepsilon p_t^{-\theta} \frac{z_t}{\delta + \varepsilon p_t^{1-\theta}}, \ c_t = \left(\delta + \varepsilon p_t^{1-\theta} \right)^{\frac{1}{\theta-1}} z_t.$$

Solving the third equation for z_t we derive a price index, $\mathcal{P}_t$: One unit of the consumption index c_t costs

$$\mathcal{P}_t = \left(\delta + \varepsilon p_t^{1-\theta} \right)^{\frac{1}{1-\theta}}.$$

For $p_t = 1$, the price index equals unity. For $p_t \to \infty$, it increases with p_t if $\theta < 1$ but converges to a constant if $\theta > 1$. Intuitively, how strongly the relative price increase translates into a higher price index depends on the household's willingness to substitute across goods. Using the price index, we also have $d_t = \delta c_t \mathcal{P}_t^{\theta}$ and $e_t = \varepsilon c_t (\mathcal{P}_t / p_t)^{\theta}$.

Equipped with these results, we turn to the intertemporal program. The dynamic budget constraints are given by $w_0 = \mathcal{P}_0 c_0 + a_1$ and $a_1 R_1 + w_1 = \mathcal{P}_1 c_1$, where wage income and assets are expressed in terms of the numeraire, d_t. The household's program therefore reads

$$\max_{c_0, c_1} u(c_0) + \beta u(c_1) \text{ s.t. } \mathcal{P}_0 c_0 + \frac{\mathcal{P}_1 c_1}{R_1} = w_0 + \frac{w_1}{R_1}$$

and the Euler equation characterizing the optimal intertemporal consumption allocation is given by

$$u'(c_0) = \beta R_1 \frac{\mathcal{P}_0}{\mathcal{P}_1} u'(c_1).$$

As usual, the marginal rate of substitution, $u'(c_0)/(\beta u'(c_1))$, is equated with the marginal rate of transformation. With a consumption index, the marginal rate of transformation is given by the *own rate of interest*, $R_1 \mathcal{P}_0/\mathcal{P}_1$. The latter differs from the marginal rate of transformation for the numeraire good, R_1, whenever $\mathcal{P}_t$ (and thus, p_t) changes over time.

2.3   Bibliographic Notes

Modigliani and Brumberg (1954) and Friedman (1957) derive consumption functions from microeconomic principles. Friedman (1957) emphasizes the role of permanent as opposed to current income and Modigliani and Brumberg (1954), among others, stress life cycle considerations.

Strotz (1956), Pollak (1968), and Phelps and Pollak (1968) analyze time inconsistency and Laibson (1997) explores consequences of hyperbolic discounting. Krusell and Smith (2003) and Cao and Werning (2018) analyze determinacy of the saving function of an infinitely lived household with time inconsistent preferences. Homer (800 B.C.E., book 12) describes Ulysses and the Sirens. Dixit and Stiglitz (1977) analyze a model with a CES consumption index.

Related Topics and Additional References   Deaton (1992) covers consumption.

3 Dynamic Competitive Equilibrium

We have studied how households trade off current and future consumption conditional on wages and interest rates. The same wages and interest rates affect firms' demand for factors of production and their supply of goods. For markets to clear in general equilibrium, the demands and supplies must be compatible with each other. The market clearing requirement thus pins down equilibrium wages and interest rates.

We analyze general equilibrium and its efficiency properties in two models of capital accumulation. In the first model, we assume that all households are alike and live over the same period; each household thus is representative of the others and the household sector behaves like a single, representative agent. The representative household assumption is convenient but restrictive, as we discuss in appendix B.2; only under specific conditions may heterogeneous households be represented by a single surrogate. In the second model, we study the interaction between overlapping cohorts of households. Each cohort constitutes a representative household but members of different cohorts differ by age and wealth. In subsequent chapters, we generalize these models, for instance by introducing risk or a labor–leisure choice.

3.1 Representative Agent and Capital Accumulation

Our first general equilibrium model is the *representative agent* or *Ramsey model*.

3.1.1 Economy

The economy is inhabited by a continuum of identical households of mass one, as well as a continuum of identical firms of mass one. Both households and firms take prices as given; households also take firm profits as given. Since households and firms are homogeneous we can represent them as a *representative household* and a *representative firm*, respectively.

3.1.2   Firms

Firms solve static profit maximization problems. In each period, they rent capital, K_t, at *rental rate r_t* and labor, L_t, at *wage w_t* from households to produce *output* (the numeraire) with a neoclassical production function, f. Profits are distributed to households.

Taking rental rates and wages as given, the representative firm maximizes

$$\max_{K_t, L_t} f(K_t, L_t) - K_t r_t - L_t w_t.$$

The first-order conditions,

$$f_K(K_t, L_t) = r_t, \tag{3.1}$$

$$f_L(K_t, L_t) = w_t, \tag{3.2}$$

define demand correspondences for capital and labor: For any (r_t, w_t), the conditions imply a set of factor demands with typical element (K_t, L_t); due to constant returns to scale, each element in the set has the same capital–labor ratio, K_t/L_t.

The budget constraint of the representative firm reads

$$f(K_t, L_t) = K_t r_t + L_t w_t + z_t \tag{3.3}$$

where z_t denotes profits. In equilibrium, profits equal zero, due to constant returns to scale and price taking.

3.1.3   Households

The representative household maximizes $\sum_{t=0}^{\infty} \beta^t u(c_t)$. The dynamic budget constraint and Euler equation, respectively, are given by

$$a_{t+1} = a_t R_t + w_t - c_t + z_t,$$

$$u'(c_t) = \beta R_{t+1} u'(c_{t+1}).$$

Since all households are alike (and the economy is closed and there is no government sector) they do not hold claims vis-à-vis each other or third parties. Accordingly, household assets correspond to the physical capital stock in the economy: The capital stock per worker, k_t, equals a_t. Capital *depreciates* at rate δ per period. The gross *interest rate* thus equals the rental rate of capital paid by firms, r_t, plus the unit of capital net of depreciation: $R_t = 1 + r_t - \delta$.

Combining these conditions yields

$$k_{t+1} = k_t(1 + r_t - \delta) + w_t - c_t + z_t, \tag{3.4}$$

$$u'(c_t) = \beta(1 + r_{t+1} - \delta)u'(c_{t+1}). \tag{3.5}$$

Households also satisfy the transversality condition $\lim_{T \to \infty} q_T k_{T+1} = 0$ or equivalently, using the Euler equation, $\lim_{T \to \infty} \beta^T u'(c_T) k_{T+1} = 0$.[3] The initial capital stock, k_0, is given.

3.1.4 Market Clearing

There are three goods in each period: Labor, capital (inherited from the last period), and output, which can be used for consumption and *investment* (accumulation of new capital). Since there is one representative household whose time endowment per period equals unity, labor and capital market clearing requires firms to demand one unit of labor and k_t units of capital:

$$K_t = k_t, \tag{3.6}$$
$$L_t = 1. \tag{3.7}$$

By Walras's law, market clearing in all but one market implies that the remaining market clears as well if all agents satisfy their budget constraints. In the economy considered here, this can be seen by combining (3.3), (3.4), (3.6), and (3.7) to find

$$k_{t+1} = k_t(1 + r_t - \delta) + w_t - c_t + f(k_t, 1) - k_t r_t - 1 w_t$$

which simplifies to the *resource constraint*

$$k_{t+1} = k_t(1 - \delta) + f(k_t, 1) - c_t.$$

The resource constraint states that the market for the output good clears. Equivalently, *gross investment* plus consumption equals output, or saving equals *net investment*. The condition represents the GDP identity in a closed economy without a government sector.

3.1.5 General Equilibrium

In general equilibrium, the transversality condition as well as conditions (3.1)–(3.7), and thus the resource constraint, hold at all dates. These equilibrium conditions can be represented as (i) the transversality condition; (ii) two core equations in capital and consumption; and (iii) five remaining conditions that determine r_t, w_t, z_t, K_t, and L_t. The two core equations are given by the resource constraint and the Euler equation with the rental rate of capital expressed in terms of the marginal product of capital:

$$k_{t+1} = k_t(1 - \delta) + f(k_t, 1) - c_t, \tag{3.8}$$
$$u'(c_t) = \beta(1 + f_K(k_{t+1}, 1) - \delta)u'(c_{t+1}). \tag{3.9}$$

Note that, conditional on k_t and c_t, these two equations pin down k_{t+1} and c_{t+1}.

---

[3] With a finite horizon, the transversality condition reduces to $k_{T+1} = 0$.

For a given initial capital stock, k_0, conditions (3.8) and (3.9) completely pin down the equilibrium sequences of capital and consumption once a starting value for consumption, c_0, is specified. The choice of this starting value is constrained by the requirement that the sequences also must satisfy the transversality condition,

$$\lim_{T \to \infty} \beta^T u'(c_T) k_{T+1} = 0.$$

As we will see below, there is a unique c_0 such that the paths implied by (k_0, c_0) as well as (3.8) and (3.9) satisfy the transversality condition.

3.1.6   Social Planner Allocation and Pareto Optimality

We have derived the equilibrium conditions in the *decentralized economy* with firms and households. Alternatively, we can characterize the *social planner allocation* in a *Robinson Crusoe economy*. This economy is inhabited by a single consumer-producer that operates the production function f and saves in the form of capital. Robinson Crusoe solves

$$\max_{\{c_t, k_{t+1}\}_{t \geq 0}} \sum_{t=0}^{\infty} \beta^t u(c_t) \text{ s.t. } k_{t+1} = k_t(1 - \delta) + f(k_t, 1) - c_t, \ k_0 \text{ given, } k_{t+1} \geq 0.$$

The nonnegativity constraint on capital is not binding if f satisfies the Inada conditions. Solving this program yields exactly the same conditions as those characterizing the decentralized equilibrium: conditions (3.8) and (3.9) and the transversality condition (see appendix B.3).

Since the social planner allocation is the feasible allocation preferred by the representative household, it necessarily is Pareto optimal. The decentralized equilibrium allocation therefore is Pareto optimal as well. This is not surprising because the economy satisfies the conditions of the first welfare theorem. In fact, given that these conditions are satisfied, we could have directly characterized the equilibrium allocation (and also prices) by solving the *social planner problem*.

This alternative strategy is available much more generally. As long as the conditions of the welfare theorems are satisfied, the set of Pareto optimal allocations corresponds to the set of competitive equilibria, possibly subject to transfers between different groups of households. Rather than solving the conditions characterizing the decentralized equilibrium, we may then find the equilibrium allocation directly by solving a corresponding social planner problem (see subsection 8.3.3 for an application in a model with heterogeneous households).

3.1.7   Analysis

3.1.7.1   Phase Diagram   Since (3.8) and (3.9) constitute nonlinear first-order difference equations, the model cannot generally be solved in closed form. However, we may qualitatively characterize equilibrium by means of a *phase diagram* which illustrates the system dynamics. The phase diagram is constructed based on the relations

$$c_t = f(k_t, 1) - \delta k_t, \tag{3.10}$$

$$1 = \beta(1 + f_K(k_{t+1}, 1) - \delta). \tag{3.11}$$

Condition (3.10) follows from (3.8) when the capital stock is constant over time, $k_t = k_{t+1}$. In this case, consumption plus *replacement investment* equals output. Condition (3.11) follows from (3.9) when $c_t = c_{t+1}$. For consumption to be constant over time, βR_{t+1} must equal unity.

In figure 3.1, relations (3.10) and (3.11) are represented by the solid concave schedule and vertical line, respectively. Their intersection indicates the *steady state* of the system, (k, c), where all equilibrium conditions are satisfied and all variables do not change over time.

From (3.10), consumption is maximized subject to a time-invariant capital stock when the latter equals the *golden-rule* capital stock, k^{gr}, which satisfies

$$f_K(k^{\mathrm{gr}}, 1) = \delta.$$

The steady-state or *modified-golden-rule* capital stock is lower than the golden-rule capital stock, $k < k^{\mathrm{gr}}$, because from (3.11)

$$f_K(k, 1) = \delta + \beta^{-1} - 1 > \delta.$$

Capital stock dynamics off steady state are determined by the resource constraint (3.8). Suppose that $c_t > f(k_t, 1) - \delta k_t$—that is, c_t lies above the concave schedule. Gross investment then falls short of the replacement investment necessary to maintain the capital stock, and as a consequence $k_{t+1} < k_t$. Conversely, a choice of c_t below the concave schedule implies $k_{t+1} > k_t$.

Consumption dynamics off steady state are determined by the Euler equation (3.9). If the capital stock is smaller than k, then the marginal product of capital, and thus the gross interest rate, are higher than in steady state and consumption rises, $c_{t+1} > c_t$. Conversely, a capital stock larger than k implies $c_{t+1} < c_t$.

The system dynamics therefore differ across the four regions separated by (3.10) and (3.11): If $k_t < k$ and $c_t < f(k_t, 1) - \delta k_t$, then both the capital stock and consumption rise over time. If $k_t > k$ and $c_t < f(k_t, 1) - \delta k_t$, then the capital stock rises and consumption falls. If $k_t < k$ and $c_t > f(k_t, 1) - \delta k_t$, then the capital stock falls and consumption rises. Finally, if $k_t > k$ and $c_t > f(k_t, 1) - \delta k_t$, then both the capital stock and consumption fall.

The paths indicated by dots and arrows in figure 3.1 illustrate the system dynamics. Consider a low initial capital stock, say $k_0 = k/2$. The figure illustrates three candidate adjustment paths that start at different initial consumption levels, c_0. All these candidate paths satisfy (3.8) and (3.9) but only one—the path toward the steady state indicated by dots—also meets the transversality condition. Too low an initial consumption level implies

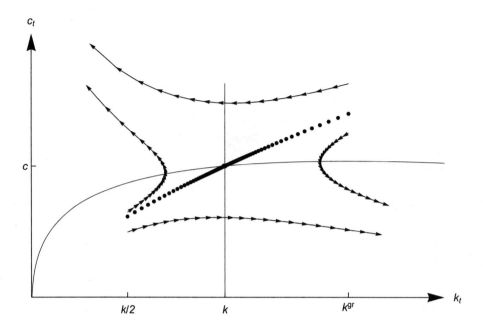

Figure 3.1
Dynamics in the representative household model: Steady state, saddle path, and off-equilibrium dynamics.

nonconvergent dynamics to the bottom right (indicated by arrows), where the interest rate is negative, and thus the transversality condition violated. Too high an initial consumption level implies nonconvergent dynamics to the top left (also indicated by arrows), where the Euler equation prescribes consumption growth but household assets tend to zero.

Similarly, for a high initial capital stock, say $k_0 = k^{gr}$, too low or too high an initial consumption value implies nonconvergent dynamics, indicated by the paths marked with arrows that start above k^{gr}, while an appropriate intermediate starting value implies convergent dynamics, indicated by the dotted path toward the steady state.

For any initial capital stock, k_0, there exists a consumption level guaranteeing convergent equilibrium dynamics, $c_0(k_0)$. The function $c_0(k_0)$ traces out the *saddle path*. The saddle path gives the equilibrium initial consumption level for an initial capital stock, and it indicates the path along which convergent equilibrium dynamics occur. The dotted path in figure 3.1 illustrates the segment of the saddle path between $0.5k$ and k^{gr}.

Based on the phase diagram, we may not only analyze equilibrium dynamics in environments with constant technology and preferences but also the response to changing fundamentals. Suppose, for example, that the production function is known to change from f to g, say at some future date $t = T$. From that future date onward, system dynamics are governed by the Euler equation and resource constraint associated with g rather than f. Before date $t = T$, in contrast, the Euler equation and resource constraint associated with f determine the dynamic behavior.

To characterize the economy's equilibrium dynamics in this scenario we consider both the "old" (associated with f) and "new" (associated with g) saddle path. After date $t = T$, (k_t, c_t) moves along the new saddle path toward the long-run steady state. But before date $t = T$, when dynamics are still governed by the old system, (k_t, c_t) does *not* advance along the old saddle path because this would require it to traverse from the old to the new saddle path at some point—in violation of the Euler equation or the resource constraint. Before date $t = T$, (k_t, c_t) rather moves *off* the old saddle path toward the new saddle path, which it meets exactly at date $t = T$.

3.1.7.2 Solution Methods Beyond the phase diagram, we may use several strategies to solve the model. One, described below, is based on a *linear approximation* of the difference equation system (3.8) and (3.9); it involves eigenvalue and eigenvector operations. Another strategy is based on simply trying different starting values c_0 conditional on k_0 and checking whether the induced system dynamics are convergent. Finally, one may solve the social planner's program numerically, using dynamic programming methods.

The approximation strategy rests on linearizing (3.8) and (3.9) around the steady state. For example, totally differentiating (3.8) and evaluating at the steady state yields

$$dk_{t+1} + dc_t = (f_K(k, 1) + 1 - \delta)dk_t,$$
$$\Rightarrow \quad \hat{k}_{t+1} + \hat{c}_t \frac{c}{k} = \beta^{-1}\hat{k}_t,$$

where a circumflex denotes infinitesimal relative deviations from the corresponding steady state value, for example, $\hat{c}_t \equiv (c_t - c)/c$. Similarly, taking logarithms in (3.9), totally differentiating and evaluating at the steady state yields (letting $\sigma \equiv -u''(c)c/u'(c)$)

$$\ln(u'(c_t)) = \ln(\beta) + \ln(1 + f_K(k_{t+1}, 1) - \delta) + \ln(u'(c_{t+1})),$$
$$\Rightarrow \quad -\sigma\frac{dc_t}{c} = \frac{f_{KK}(k, 1)dk_{t+1}}{1 + f_K(k, 1) - \delta} - \sigma\frac{dc_{t+1}}{c},$$
$$\Rightarrow \quad \hat{c}_t = -\frac{\beta}{\sigma}f_{KK}(k, 1)\, k\, \hat{k}_{t+1} + \hat{c}_{t+1}.$$

Approximating the original system to the first order means that we apply the linearized system to deviations from steady state even if they are larger than infinitesimal.

Next, we represent the linearized equations in vector and matrix form as

$$M_1\begin{bmatrix} \hat{c}_{t+1} \\ \hat{k}_{t+1} \end{bmatrix} = M_0\begin{bmatrix} \hat{c}_t \\ \hat{k}_t \end{bmatrix}, \quad M_1 \equiv \begin{bmatrix} 1 & -\frac{\beta}{\sigma}f_{KK}(k, 1)k \\ 0 & 1 \end{bmatrix}, \quad M_0 \equiv \begin{bmatrix} 1 & 0 \\ -\frac{c}{k} & \beta^{-1} \end{bmatrix}.$$

Multiplying by the inverse of M_1 yields

$$\begin{bmatrix} \hat{c}_{t+1} \\ \hat{k}_{t+1} \end{bmatrix} = M \begin{bmatrix} \hat{c}_t \\ \hat{k}_t \end{bmatrix}, \quad M \equiv M_1^{-1} M_0 = \begin{bmatrix} 1 - \frac{c}{\sigma} \beta f_{KK} & \frac{f_{KK} k}{\sigma} \\ -\frac{c}{k} & \beta^{-1} \end{bmatrix}.$$

Finally, we express the linearized system in terms of the eigenvalues ρ_1 and ρ_2, as well as the corresponding eigenvectors v_1 and v_2 of the matrix M. An eigenvalue of M satisfies $\det(M - \rho I) = 0$; that is, it solves the characteristic equation $C(\rho) = 0$ with $C(\rho) \equiv \rho^2 - \rho(1 + \beta^{-1} - c\beta f_{KK}(k, 1)/\sigma) + \beta^{-1}$. The latter is a continuous quadratic function satisfying $C(0) > 0$, $C(1) < 0$, and $\lim_{\rho \to \infty} C(\rho) = \infty$. It follows that $0 < \rho_1 < 1 < \rho_2$. In fact, $\rho_2 = 1/(\beta\rho_1)$. Using standard results (see appendix A.3), we have

$$\begin{bmatrix} \hat{c}_t \\ \hat{k}_t \end{bmatrix} = \varphi_1 \rho_1^t v_1 + \varphi_2 \rho_2^t v_2,$$

where φ_1, φ_2 are arbitrary constants that remain to be determined. The requirement that system dynamics be stable (reflecting the transversality condition) implies that φ_2 must equal zero because ρ_2^t grows without bound as $t \to \infty$. The second constant, φ_1, is pinned down by the initial condition for the capital stock, $\hat{k}_0 = \varphi_1 v_{1[2]}$, where $v_{1[2]}$ denotes the second element of the eigenvector v_1. In conclusion,

$$\begin{bmatrix} \hat{c}_t \\ \hat{k}_t \end{bmatrix} = \rho_1^t v_1 \frac{\hat{k}_0}{v_{1[2]}}.$$

The saddle path of the linearized system (expressed in terms of deviations from steady state) is given by the function

$$\hat{c}_0(\hat{k}_0) = \frac{\hat{k}_0}{v_{1[2]}} v_{1[1]}.$$

The slope of the saddle path in (k, c) space satisfies

$$\frac{dc_0}{dk_0} = \frac{c}{k} \frac{v_{1[1]}}{v_{1[2]}}.$$

For $\sigma \to \infty$ or $f_{KK} k / f_K \to 0$, the slope approaches $(1 - \beta)/\beta$. Lower values of σ (a higher intertemporal elasticity of substitution) or more negative elasticities of the marginal product with respect to k increase dc_0/dk_0.

The *speed of convergence* to the steady state is determined by the stable eigenvalue, ρ_1. The higher this eigenvalue, the slower the convergence.

3.1.8   Population Growth

Suppose the number of household members grows at gross rate v per period and the household's objective thus equals $\sum_{t=0}^{\infty} \beta^t v^t u(c_t)$, where c_t denotes per-capita consumption as before. Normalizing the population size at date $t = 0$ to unity, the resource constraint now

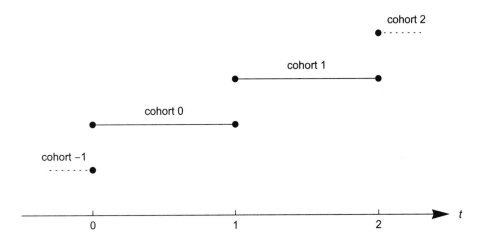

Figure 3.2
Overlapping generations.

is given by

$$v^{t+1}k_{t+1} = v^t k_t (1 - \delta) + f(v^t k_t, v^t) - v^t c_t,$$

where k_t continues to denote the capital stock per capita. Equivalently,

$$vk_{t+1} = k_t(1 - \delta) + f(k_t, 1) - c_t.$$

Intuitively, positive population growth implies that the capital–labor ratio at date $t + 1$ is smaller (by the factor v) than the per-capita resources not consumed at date t. Except for this difference, the conditions characterizing the centralized or decentralized equilibrium are not affected by population growth.

3.2 Overlapping Generations and Capital Accumulation

Our second general equilibrium model is the *overlapping generations model.*

3.2.1 Economy

There is an infinite number of two-period lived cohorts. Subsequent generations overlap (see figure 3.2): In each period, a continuum of young and old households of mass one each inhabit the economy. Young households are born without assets; they work, consume, and save for retirement. Old households retire, consume the return on their saving (i.e., households leave no bequests), and die. The assets held by the retirees correspond to the economy's capital stock. (With two-period lived overlapping generations, there is no scope for intergenerational borrowing or lending.) At date $t = 0$ the old cohort is endowed with the initial capital stock, k_0.

3.2.2   Firms

The firm sector is identical to the one in the representative agent model and conditions (3.1)–(3.3) apply. Profits are distributed to old households.

3.2.3   Households

The dynamic budget constraints of a worker and a retiree at date t, as well as the Euler equation of a young household, are given by

$$k_{t+1} = w_t - c_{1,t}, \tag{3.12}$$

$$c_{2,t} = k_t(1 + r_t - \delta) + z_t, \tag{3.13}$$

$$u'(c_{1,t}) = \beta(1 + r_{t+1} - \delta)u'(c_{2,t+1}), \tag{3.14}$$

respectively. Here, $c_{1,t}$ and $c_{2,t}$ denote consumption at date t of a young and old household, respectively.

3.2.4   Market Clearing

Labor and capital market clearing requires that firms demand one unit of labor and k_t units of capital, implying the equilibrium conditions (3.6) and (3.7). By Walras's law, market clearing in all but one market implies that the remaining market clears as well if all agents satisfy their budget constraints. Combining (3.3), (3.6), (3.7), (3.12), and (3.13) and letting $c_t \equiv c_{1,t} + c_{2,t}$ yields

$$\begin{aligned} k_{t+1} &= w_t - c_{1,t} + k_t(1 + r_t - \delta) - c_{2,t} + z_t \\ &= k_t(1 + r_t - \delta) + w_t - c_t + f(k_t, 1) - k_t r_t - 1 w_t. \end{aligned}$$

This simplifies to the same resource constraint as in the representative agent model,

$$k_{t+1} = k_t(1 - \delta) + f(k_t, 1) - c_t.$$

3.2.5   General Equilibrium

In general equilibrium, conditions (3.1)–(3.3), (3.6)–(3.7), and (3.12)–(3.14), and thus the resource constraint, hold simultaneously. These equilibrium conditions can be represented as three core equations,

$$\begin{aligned} k_{t+1} &= k_t(1 - \delta) + f(k_t, 1) - c_{1,t} - c_{2,t}, \\ c_{2,t} &= k_t(1 + f_K(k_t, 1) - \delta), \\ u'(c_{1,t}) &= \beta(1 + f_K(k_{t+1}, 1) - \delta)u'(c_{2,t+1}), \end{aligned}$$

as well as five remaining conditions that determine r_t, w_t, z_t, K_t, and L_t. Compared with the representative agent model, an additional budget constraint is present; it determines how consumption is split between workers and retirees. The Euler equation characterizes the slope of the consumption profile over the household's life cycle.

Conditional on k_t, the second core equation pins down $c_{2,t}$. Moreover, since $c_{2,t+1} = k_{t+1}(1 + f_K(k_{t+1}, 1) - \delta)$, the first and third conditions pin down $c_{1,t}$ and k_{t+1}. For an initial capital stock, k_0, the core equations therefore completely determine the equilibrium paths of capital and consumption over the infinite horizon.

An alternative representation of equilibrium uses the *saving function*. Let $a_{t+1} = a(w_t, R_{t+1})$ denote equilibrium saving of a worker. The saving function a combines the Euler equation and the intertemporal budget constraint, which extends over two periods; it depends on wealth (given by the wage) and the interest rate. Combined with the equilibrium relations between factor prices and the capital–labor ratio, the saving function defines a *law of motion* for capital,

$$k_{t+1} = a(w_t, R_{t+1}) \quad \text{where} \quad w_t = f_L(k_t, 1), \ R_{t+1} = 1 - \delta + f_K(k_{t+1}, 1), \tag{3.15}$$

which maps k_t into k_{t+1}. Under specific functional form assumptions, this law of motion can be solved in closed form.

Depending on preferences and technology, the function $k_{t+1}(k_t)$ defined by (3.15) may intersect the 45-degree line in (k_t, k_{t+1}) space never, once, or multiple times; accordingly, no steady state with a strictly positive capital stock, a unique such steady state, or multiple steady states may exist. A steady state is stable and nonoscillating if in a neighborhood around it, k_{t+1} increases in k_t, but by less than one-to-one. Writing (3.15) as $k_{t+1} = \tilde{a}(k_t, k_{t+1})$ and totally differentiating implies

$$\frac{dk_{t+1}}{dk_t} = \frac{\partial \tilde{a}(k_t, k_{t+1})/\partial k_t}{1 - \partial \tilde{a}(k_t, k_{t+1})/\partial k_{t+1}}.$$

A steady state thus is stable and nonoscillating if the value of the expression on the right-hand side, evaluated at steady state, lies between zero and one.

3.2.6 Analysis

In contrast to the representative agent model, households in the overlapping generations model are heterogeneous. As a consequence, average saving in the economy differs from the saving of young or old households, and the slope of the consumption profile of a young household need not match the slope of the aggregate consumption profile.

This has important implications for the steady state. While the first steady-state condition of the representative agent model, condition (3.10), also applies in the overlapping generations model, the second one, condition (3.11), does not. In the representative agent model, this second condition follows from the requirement that aggregate, and thus individual consumption, is constant over time. In the overlapping generations model, in contrast, constancy of aggregate consumption (or of young-age consumption or old-age consumption) does not imply that the consumption profile of an individual household is flat over the life cycle. The steady-state capital stock—the fixed point of (3.15)—therefore need not satisfy the condition $\beta(1 - \delta + f_K(k, 1)) = 1$. In fact, depending on preferences and the production function, it can be smaller or larger than the golden-rule capital stock.

3.2.7   Pareto Optimality

Since the steady-state capital stock in the overlapping generations model may exceed the golden-rule capital stock, the steady-state interest rate may be negative, $R < 1$. This contrasts sharply with the steady state in the representative agent model. As we will see below, a negative steady-state interest rate indicates an inefficient allocation. The equilibrium allocation in the overlapping generations model thus may be *Pareto inefficient*, unlike in the representative agent model.

To establish inefficiency of an equilibrium with negative steady-state interest rates, we first consider an endowment economy. Suppose that young and old agents receive endowments $\bar{w}$ and $\underline{w}$, respectively, where $\bar{w} > \underline{w}$. Each household consumes its endowment because trade between two-period lived overlapping cohorts is not possible. Welfare of a young household thus equals $u(\bar{w}) + \beta u(\underline{w})$. We can reinterpret this autarky outcome as the competitive equilibrium in a slightly modified economy, where households are infinitely rather than two-period lived, but nevertheless are economically active only at two successive dates; that is, households in cohort t receive endowments at dates t and $t + 1$ and value consumption only in these two periods, but since they live forever, they can trade endowments and consumption on a competitive market at date $t = 0$. In this modified economy, there exists an equilibrium with the autarky allocation and an interest rate, R, that satisfies the Euler equation $u'(\bar{w}) = \beta R u'(\underline{w})$.

Suppose that $R < 1$. A transfer scheme that takes a marginal unit of the good from each young household and gives it to each old household then makes everybody better off: The old in the first period gain because they receive a transfer without ever having to contribute; and young households in all periods are strictly better off as well since

$$-u'(\bar{w}) + \beta u'(\underline{w}) > -u'(\bar{w}) + \beta R u'(\underline{w}) = 0,$$

where we use the Euler equation and the fact that $R < 1$. We conclude that a steady state with $R < 1$ entails an *inefficient allocation of consumption* across cohorts. Note that the inefficiency is present both in the original and the modified economy. This implies that it is not the absence of trade in the overlapping generations economy that causes the inefficiency. Rather, it is the fact that the equilibrium conditions do not rule out a negative interest rate.

The possibility of Pareto improving transfers (or similar measures, see subsection 5.3.2 and section 9.2) in an inefficient overlapping generations economy hinges on the assumption of an infinite horizon. If there existed a last period, then transferring resources from the young to the old would hurt the young in that last period and the transfer scheme would not lead to a Pareto improvement. Related, with a negative interest rate the market value of all endowments is infinite if the horizon is infinite (reflecting the *double infinity* of households and commodities) but finite if the horizon is finite. The proof of the first welfare theorem, which relies on a finite market value of endowments, therefore does not go through in an infinite horizon overlapping generations economy when interest rates are negative.

With capital, inefficiency in the overlapping generations economy also manifests itself in the form of *capital overaccumulation* or *dynamic inefficiency*. When $R = 1 - \delta + f_K(k, 1) < 1$, the marginal unit of capital reduces steady-state consumption since its marginal contribution to output, $f_K(k, 1)$, falls short of the marginal replacement investment, δ. When $R < 1$, a reduction of the capital stock therefore frees resources both for immediate consumption and for consumption in all future periods. Accordingly, a steady-state allocation with $R < 1$ is wasteful.

To take a stark example, suppose that capital does not contribute to production at all ($f_K(K_t, L_t) = 0$, capital accumulation amounts to storage) and depreciates at a strictly positive rate (a fraction of the stored goods spoils). The condition for dynamic inefficiency, $R < 1$, then is met and capital accumulation is wasteful. Nevertheless, households do accumulate capital in equilibrium because they must satisfy their budget constraints and need to finance old-age consumption.

Intergenerational transfers reduce overaccumulation because they *crowd out* private savings. Intuitively, as the transfer scheme takes resources from households in young age and provides them in old age, the incentive to save becomes smaller. In the example introduced above, the efficient level of capital equals zero and the optimal level of transfers from a dynamic inefficiency perspective thus equals the level that eliminates storage. The same level of transfers cures the inefficient allocation of consumption. To see this, let k denote storage, which pays a rate of return $1 - \delta < 1$, and let Δ denote transfers. Young- and old-age consumption then equals $\bar{w} - k - \Delta$ and $\underline{w} + k(1 - \delta) + \Delta$, respectively. A marginal increase of transfers helps the old in the initial period and it also improves welfare of all other cohorts if $-u'(\bar{w} - k - \Delta) + \beta u'(\underline{w} + k(1 - \delta) + \Delta) \geq 0$ (using the envelope condition). But from the Euler equation, $-u'(\bar{w} - k - \Delta) + \beta(1 - \delta)u'(\underline{w} + k(1 - \delta) + \Delta) = 0$ as long as households store. An expansion of the transfer scheme thus improves welfare of all generations as long as the Euler equation holds with equality, that is, as long as households store.

3.2.8 Population Growth

Suppose the number of young households grows at gross rate v per period and normalize the cohort size at date $t = 0$ to unity. Maintaining the definition of k_t as capital stock per worker as well as $c_{1,t}$ and $c_{2,t}$ as per-capita consumption, the budget constraints in equilibrium now read

$$
\begin{aligned}
c_{1,t} &= w_t - k_{t+1}v, \\
c_{2,t} &= k_t(1 + r_t - \delta)v
\end{aligned}
$$

and the resource constraint is given by

$$v^{t+1}k_{t+1} = v^t k_t(1 - \delta) + f(v^t k_t, v^t) - v^t c_{1,t} - v^{t-1}c_{2,t}$$

or

$$vk_{t+1} = k_t(1 - \delta) + f(k_t, 1) - c_{1,t} - c_{2,t}/v.$$

The condition for inefficiency generalizes to

$$f_K(k, 1) < \delta + v - 1 \quad \text{or} \quad R < v,$$

relating the net marginal product of capital or the interest rate to the net growth rate of the economy.

3.3   Bibliographic Notes

The representative agent, Ramsey, or neoclassical growth model is due to Ramsey (1928), Cass (1965), and Koopmans (1965). According to the Fisher (1930) *separation theorem* a firm's objective is to maximize the present value of profits, independently of the owners' preferences and of financing decisions. Negishi (1960) characterizes competitive equilibrium by solving a social planner problem.

The overlapping generations model builds on Allais (1947) and is due to Samuelson (1958); Diamond (1965) introduces capital in the model. Modigliani and Brumberg (1954) discuss life cycle saving as well as the aggregation of heterogeneous consumption profiles. Shell (1971) and Balasko and Shell (1980) analyze inefficiency in overlapping generations endowment economies. Malinvaud (1953), Phelps (1965), and Cass (1972) analyze capital overaccumulation.

Related Topics and Additional References   Gale (1973) analyzes overlapping generations endowment economies and studies determinacy of the equilibrium allocation; see also Kehoe and Levine (1985) on indeterminacy and Grandmont (1985) on endogenous cycles in overlapping generations economies.

Chattopadhyay and Gottardi (1999) analyze inefficiency in overlapping generations economies with endowment risk. Zilcha (1990) analyzes capital overaccumulation in environments with stochastic production; see also Barbie et al. (2007).

Yaari (1965) and Blanchard (1985) analyze models of *perpetual youth* in which households face a constant probability of death while new cohorts enter the economy.

See chapter 6 for models of sunspot-driven business cycles and chapter 9 for money in the overlapping generations model.

4 Risk

We have assumed so far that households optimize in a deterministic environment. Now we introduce *risk*. Random wages or returns on saving introduce insurance considerations into the household's problem because the consumption-smoothing motive applies both across time and histories.

We study wage and return risk and its effect on the consumption–saving tradeoff when markets are complete or incomplete. Thereafter, we analyze risk sharing among heterogeneous households and study how uninsurable income risk affects capital accumulation in general equilibrium. Throughout, we assume that households evaluate random consumption sequences according to the expected utility criterion; in appendix B.4 we discuss a model that relaxes this assumption.

4.1 Consumption, Saving, and Insurance

4.1.1 Incomplete Markets

Suppose that there are two periods. In the second period, one of two histories is realized, $\epsilon^1 = h$ or $\epsilon^1 = l$, with probability $\eta(h)$ and $\eta(l)$ respectively. The wage in the second period, $w_1(\epsilon^1)$, varies by history; it equals $w_1(h)$ or $w_1(l)$. The household saves in one asset, a_1, and maximizes expected discounted utility from consumption, $u(c_0) + \beta\mathbb{E}_0[u(c_1(\epsilon^1))]$. The program reads

$$\max_{a_1,c_0,c_1(h),c_1(l)} \quad u(c_0) + \beta(\eta(h)u(c_1(h)) + \eta(l)u(c_1(l)))$$

$$\text{s.t.} \quad a_1 = w_0 - c_0, \quad c_1(\epsilon^1) = a_1 R_1 + w_1(\epsilon^1).$$

Note that the return on savings is not history-contingent, in contrast to the wage. This assumption is not critical. What is crucial—and renders *markets incomplete*—is that fewer assets than states of nature are available. Note also that consumption in the second period is history-contingent.

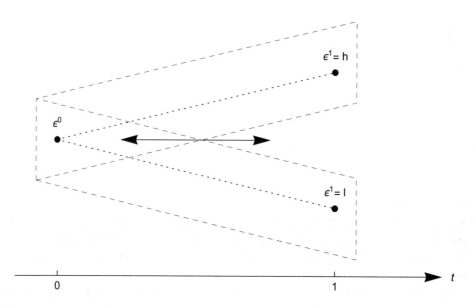

Figure 4.1
Incomplete markets: Two intertemporal budget constraints and one adjustment margin.

Substituting the second- into the first-period dynamic budget constraint, we find one intertemporal budget constraint for each history,

$$c_0 + \frac{c_1(h)}{R_1} = w_0 + \frac{w_1(h)}{R_1} \quad \text{and} \quad c_0 + \frac{c_1(l)}{R_1} = w_0 + \frac{w_1(l)}{R_1}.$$

If the second-period wage assumes the high value, then lifetime consumption expenditures discounted at the interest rate R_1 must equal $w_0 + w_1(h)/R_1$. If it assumes the low value, then they must equal $w_0 + w_1(l)/R_1$.

The household faces incomplete markets because it cannot exchange consumption in history h against consumption in history l. Figure 4.1 illustrates this. The dashed parallelograms indicate the range of the two intertemporal budget constraints: One connects the initial period and the high state in the second period, the other the initial period and the low state. The arrows indicate the household's single margin of adjustment, corresponding to the choice of a_1: Purchasing power can be shifted over time—saving reduces c_0 and increases *both* $c_1(h)$ and $c_1(l)$—but it cannot be shifted across nodes at date $t = 1$.

To characterize the solution to the household's problem we can substitute the dynamic budget constraints into the objective function and differentiate with respect to a_1. This yields the *stochastic Euler equation*

$$u'(c_0) = \beta R_1 \mathbb{E}_0 \left[u'(c_1(\epsilon^1)) \right].$$

Intuitively, the cost of saving represented on the left-hand side is balanced with the average benefit across histories represented on the right-hand side.

4.1.1.1 Precautionary Saving Assume that $\beta R_1 = 1$ such that the Euler equation reduces to $u'(c_0) = \mathbb{E}_0\left[u'(c_1(\epsilon^1))\right]$. Without risk, the equilibrium consumption profile would be flat in this case. With risk, in contrast, it cannot be flat in all histories ϵ^1 because $w_1(\epsilon^1)$ is stochastic. In fact, the consumption profile generally is not even flat on average. To see this, assume that preferences are not only strictly concave, $u' > 0, u'' < 0$, as usual, but marginal utility also is convex, $u''' > 0$. Most commonly used period utility functions satisfy this condition. By Jensen's inequality we then have $\mathbb{E}_0\left[u'(c_1(\epsilon^1))\right] > u'(\mathbb{E}_0\left[c_1(\epsilon^1)\right])$ and the Euler equation therefore stipulates $u'(c_0) > u'(\mathbb{E}_0\left[c_1(\epsilon^1)\right])$ or $c_0 < \mathbb{E}_0\left[c_1(\epsilon^1)\right]$. We conclude that convex marginal utility implies strictly positive average consumption growth, in spite of $\beta R_1 = 1$; saving is higher than in the absence of risk, reflecting a *precautionary saving* motive or *prudence*. In contrast, linear marginal utility would imply $c_0 = \mathbb{E}_0\left[c_1(\epsilon^1)\right]$ and concave marginal utility $c_0 > \mathbb{E}_0\left[c_1(\epsilon^1)\right]$.

Figure 4.2 illustrates the precautionary saving motive. The solid line indicates the marginal utility function. Suppose first that the wage is deterministic and equal to w_0 in both periods. Since $\beta R_1 = 1$, optimal consumption then equals w_0 in both periods and saving equals zero. Consider next the case with a risky wage in the second period, $w_1(l)$ or $w_1(h)$. If the household does not save, then first-period consumption equals w_0 and history-contingent second-period consumption equals $w_1(l)$ or $w_1(h)$. Due to the convexity of the marginal utility function, expected marginal utility of second-period consumption, indicated by the circle on the dashed line, exceeds marginal utility of first-period consumption, indicated by the circle on the marginal utility function, and the Euler equation is violated. Intuitively, the downside risk affects average marginal utility more strongly than the upside. To satisfy the Euler equation, saving must rise, first-period consumption must fall to c_0, and history-contingent second-period consumption must rise to $c_1(l)$ and $c_1(h)$. In equilibrium, marginal utility in the first period and expected marginal utility in the second period, indicated by the black dots, coincide.

4.1.1.2 Certainty Equivalence Strict convexity of the marginal utility function in combination with risky consumption renders it more difficult to solve the model. A linear marginal utility specification (quadratic utility) circumvents this problem—at the cost of doing away with the precautionary saving motive—because it implies $\mathbb{E}_0[u'(c_1(\epsilon^1))] = u'(\mathbb{E}_0[c_1(\epsilon^1)])$, and thus the Euler equation $u'(c_0) = \beta R_1 u'(\mathbb{E}_0[c_1(\epsilon^1)])$. Note that the latter equation corresponds to the condition in the deterministic case, except that risk-free second-period consumption is replaced by the conditional expectation of risky second-period consumption. The fact that the equilibrium condition only contains the conditional mean (rather than also higher-order moments) of the random variable is referred to as *certainty equivalence*.

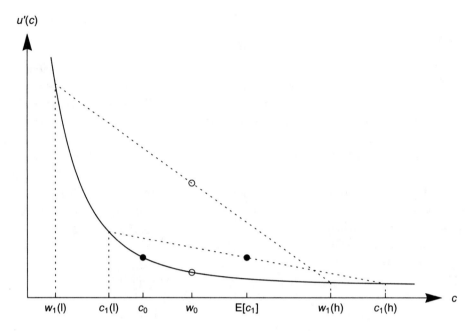

Figure 4.2
Precautionary saving: Convex marginal utility and income risk.

To appreciate the gain in tractability due to certainty equivalence, consider a three-period model with quadratic utility and $\beta R_t = 1$ at all times. The intertemporal budget constraint along each history reads

$$c_0 + \beta c_1(\epsilon^1) + \beta^2 c_2(\epsilon^2) = w_0 + \beta w_1(\epsilon^1) + \beta^2 w_2(\epsilon^2)$$

and the Euler equations imply that consumption follows a *Martingale*—the conditional expectation of the change in consumption equals zero: $c_0 = \mathbb{E}_0[c_1(\epsilon^1)]$ and $c_1(\epsilon^1) = \mathbb{E}_1[c_2(\epsilon^2)]$. Using the law of iterated expectations, we can combine these results to find

$$c_0(1 + \beta + \beta^2) = w_0 + \beta \mathbb{E}_0[w_1(\epsilon^1)] + \beta^2 \mathbb{E}_0[w_2(\epsilon^2)].$$

At date $t = 1$, history ϵ^1, the intertemporal budget constraint conditional on saving in the initial period ($a_1 = w_0 - c_0$) reads

$$c_1(\epsilon^1) + \beta c_2(\epsilon^2) = (w_0 - c_0)\beta^{-1} + w_1(\epsilon^1) + \beta w_2(\epsilon^2),$$

and the Euler equation is given by $c_1(\epsilon^1) = \mathbb{E}_1[c_2(\epsilon^2)]$. Taking expectations and combining the two conditions yields

$$c_1(\epsilon^1)(1 + \beta) = (w_0 - c_0)\beta^{-1} + w_1(\epsilon^1) + \beta \mathbb{E}_1[w_2(\epsilon^2)].$$

Comparing the results for c_0 conditional on information at date $t = 0$ and for $c_1(\epsilon^1)$ conditional on information at date $t = 1$, we note that

$$(c_1(\epsilon^1) - c_0)(1 + \beta) = (\mathbb{E}_1 - \mathbb{E}_0)[w_1(\epsilon^1) + \beta w_2(\epsilon^2)].$$

We conclude that the sign and magnitude of the innovation $c_1(\epsilon^1) - \mathbb{E}_0[c_1(\epsilon^1)]$ reflects how the expected present value of income in and after date $t = 1$ changes as the information set changes from date $t = 0$ to date $t = 1$.

4.1.1.3 Risk of Binding Borrowing Constraint A binding borrowing constraint reduces consumption relative to the situation without a constraint. It also affects consumption earlier in time, before the constraint binds. In a stochastic environment, this effect is present whenever a borrowing constraint may bind later in time with strictly positive probability. We illustrate this in a three-period model with stochastic income $w_1(\epsilon^1)$ in the second period and nonstochastic income w_0 and w_2 otherwise. For simplicity, we let $\beta = 1$ and assume that the gross interest rate also equals unity. Only borrowing at date $t = 1$ is prohibited, $a_2(\epsilon^1) \geq 0$.[4]

We start by deriving the value function at date $t = 1$ when uncertainty is resolved. In histories where $a_1 + w_1(\epsilon^1) \geq w_2$, the preferred level of a_2 is positive and the borrowing constraint does not bind. Consumption in the second and third period is equal in these histories and given by $(a_1 + w_1(\epsilon^1) + w_2)/2$. In histories where $a_1 + w_1(\epsilon^1) < w_2$, in contrast, the borrowing constraint does bind and consumption in the second and third period equals $a_1 + w_1(\epsilon^1)$ and w_2, respectively. The value function thus satisfies

$$V_1(a_1 + w_1(\epsilon^1)) = \begin{cases} u(a_1 + w_1(\epsilon^1)) + u(w_2) & \text{if } w_1(\epsilon^1) < w_2 - a_1 \\ 2 \cdot u\left(\frac{a_1 + w_1(\epsilon^1) + w_2}{2}\right) & \text{if } w_1(\epsilon^1) \geq w_2 - a_1 \end{cases}.$$

Note that the derivative of the value function has a kink at the critical value $a_1 + w_1(\epsilon^1) = w_2$, below which consumption cannot be smoothed: $\lim_{\delta \downarrow 0} V_1''(w_2 - \delta) = u''(w_2)$ whereas $V_1''(w_2) = u''(w_2)/2$. That is, the derivative is convex around the critical level, independently of whether marginal utility is convex or not; all that is required for the convexity of V' is that preferences are strictly concave.

Consider now the effect of the potentially binding borrowing constraint at date $t = 1$ on saving in the initial period, a_1. While the household's program

$$\max_{a_1} u(w_0 - a_1) + \mathbb{E}_0[V_1(a_1 + w_1(\epsilon^1))]$$

[4] Recall why a_2, the level of assets carried into date $t = 2$, is indexed by ϵ^1 rather than ϵ^2: This level is chosen at date $t = 1$ and as a consequence, it is the same in each history ϵ^2 subsequent to history ϵ^1. Formally, a_2 is measurable with respect to ϵ^1.

yields the usual Euler equation, $u'(c_0) = \mathbb{E}_0[V_1'(a_1 + w_1(\epsilon^1))]$, the convexity of V' leads the household to save more at date $t = 0$ than if no risk of a binding borrowing constraint were present. The intuition mirrors the one for precautionary saving, although it is the risk of a binding borrowing constraint in combination with strictly concave preferences—not convexity of marginal utility—which drives the result.

4.1.1.4   Buffer Stock Saving   Consider an impatient household in an environment with constant interest rates, $\beta R < 1$. Absent risk, this household would choose a declining consumption path. With risk, in contrast, the precautionary saving motive or the risk of a future binding borrowing constraint work in the opposite direction and encourage saving.

The net effect on saving depends on household wealth. When consumption is a concave function of liquid wealth—the sum of financial wealth and the current wage income—then the motives that encourage saving weaken as the household becomes wealthier. Intuitively, when consumption is a concave function, then the marginal propensity to consume declines in liquid wealth; for a wealthier household, a given wage risk therefore translates into lower consumption risk, and thus a weaker precautionary saving motive. The wealth-dependent saving motive on the one hand, and impatience on the other, give rise to a target ratio of financial assets relative to the average wage. The household builds up a *buffer stock* of financial assets when its asset-to-income ratio is low and vice versa.

4.1.2   Complete Markets

Turning to *complete markets*, consider again the environment with two periods and two histories. In contrast to the incomplete market setting, the household now has access to two assets with linearly independent returns. For simplicity, we assume that these two assets are *Arrow securities*; that is, securities that only pay off in one history each (we relax this assumption later). We denote by a_1^1 the savings in the first Arrow security, which pays off if and only if $\epsilon^1 = h$, and we denote the history-dependent gross rate of return on this security by $R_1^1(\epsilon^1)$ with $R_1^1(l) = 0$. Similarly, a_1^2 denotes savings in the second Arrow security, which pays off if and only if $\epsilon^1 = l$, and its return is denoted $R_1^2(\epsilon^1)$ with $R_1^2(h) = 0$. The household's program reads

$$\max_{a_1^1, a_1^2, c_0, c_1(h), c_1(l)} \quad u(c_0) + \beta(\eta(h)u(c_1(h)) + \eta(l)u(c_1(l)))$$

$$\text{s.t.} \quad a_1^1 + a_1^2 = w_0 - c_0, \quad c_1(\epsilon^1) = a_1^1 R_1^1(\epsilon^1) + a_1^2 R_1^2(\epsilon^1) + w_1(\epsilon^1).$$

As in the incomplete market setting, three dynamic budget constraints bind. In contrast to the incomplete market setting, however, these three constraints can be combined into a single intertemporal budget constraint rather than separate ones for each history:

$$c_0 + \frac{c_1(h)}{R_1^1(h)} + \frac{c_1(l)}{R_1^2(l)} = w_0 + \frac{w_1(h)}{R_1^1(h)} + \frac{w_1(l)}{R_1^2(l)}.$$

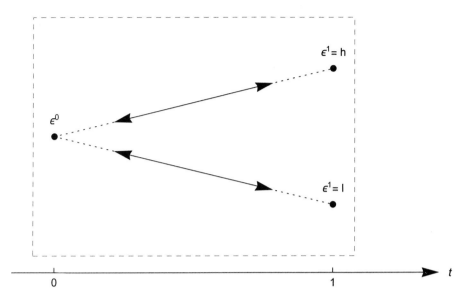

Figure 4.3
Complete markets: One intertemporal budget constraint and two adjustment margins.

The situation is akin to a static or deterministic environment where the household can exchange all goods ($c_0, c_1(h)$, and $c_1(l)$) against each other—the household faces complete markets. In particular, and in contrast to the incomplete market setting, the two assets do not only allow the household to shift purchasing power across time (that is, exchange c_0 against a *bundle* of $c_1(h)$ and $c_1(l)$) but also to specific nodes in the event tree. Equivalently, they allow the shift of purchasing power across histories at date $t = 1$, by buying less of one Arrow security and more of the other. Since consumption in the two histories can be chosen independently of each other, the household may achieve full insurance ($c_1(h) = c_1(l)$) even if $w_1(h) \neq w_1(l)$, unlike in the incomplete markets case.

Figure 4.3 illustrates the complete market setting. The dashed rectangle indicates the range of the single intertemporal budget constraint that connects the initial period and both histories in the second period. The arrows indicate the two margins of adjustment, corresponding to the choices of a_1^1 and a_1^2. Note that a simultaneous reduction of a_1^1 and increase of a_1^2 (or vice versa) allows the reallocation of purchasing power across the two histories.

The first-order conditions of the program with Arrow securities are given by the Euler equations

$$u'(c_0) = \beta R_1^1(h)\eta(h)u'(c_1(h)) \text{ and } u'(c_0) = \beta R_1^2(l)\eta(l)u'(c_1(l)).$$

These conditions do not contain an expectation operator because the choice of a_1^1 or a_1^2 affects second-period consumption only in one history each. If returns are actuarially fair— that is, return differentials compensate for risk such that $R_1^1(h)/R_1^2(l) = \eta(l)/\eta(h)$—then the household perfectly smoothes consumption across histories, $c_1(h) = c_1(l)$. If, moreover, $\beta R_1^1(h)\eta(h) = 1$, then it also smoothes consumption perfectly over time.

4.1.2.1   Generalizations   A complete set of Arrow securities is sufficient but not necessary for market completeness; completeness only requires as many assets with linearly independent returns as there are branches of the event tree. To understand the independence requirement, consider an example with two histories and two assets with general return structure, $R_1^i(\epsilon^1) \geq 0, i = 1, 2; \epsilon^1 = h, l$. (With Arrow securities, $R_1^1(l) = R_1^2(h) = 0$.) The dynamic budget constraints in the second period can be expressed as

$$\begin{bmatrix} c_1(h) - w_1(h) \\ c_1(l) - w_1(l) \end{bmatrix} = \begin{bmatrix} R_1^1(h) & R_1^2(h) \\ R_1^1(l) & R_1^2(l) \end{bmatrix} \begin{bmatrix} a_1^1 \\ a_1^2 \end{bmatrix}.$$

If the return vectors $R_1^1(\epsilon^1)$ and $R_1^2(\epsilon^1)$ are linearly independent, then the matrix on the right-hand side has full rank and its determinant, $D = R_1^1(h)R_1^2(l) - R_1^1(l)R_1^2(h)$, differs from zero. The matrix then can be inverted, and thus the equation solved for a_1^1 and a_1^2. Substituting the resulting expressions into the first-period dynamic budget constraint yields the single intertemporal budget constraint

$$w_0 - c_0 + (w_1(h) - c_1(h))\frac{R_1^2(l) - R_1^1(l)}{D} + (w_1(l) - c_1(l))\frac{R_1^1(h) - R_1^2(h)}{D} = 0.$$

(When $R_1^1(l) = R_1^2(h) = 0$, this reduces to the constraint in the case with Arrow securities derived earlier.)

The term $(R_1^2(l) - R_1^1(l))/D$ in the intertemporal budget constraint represents the price of second-period consumption in history h, expressed in terms of first-period consumption. To see this, note that purchasing ϕ units of the first asset and $-\phi R_1^1(l)/R_1^2(l)$ units of the second yields an absolute return of $\phi(R_1^1(h) - R_1^2(h)R_1^1(l)/R_1^2(l))$ in history h and zero in history l. To secure one additional unit of consumption in history h, the household thus must acquire $\phi = (R_1^1(h) - R_1^2(h)R_1^1(l)/R_1^2(l))^{-1} = R_1^2(l)/D$ units of the first asset and $-R_1^1(l)/D$ units of the second, at a cost of $(R_1^2(l) - R_1^1(l))/D.$[5] Similarly, $(R_1^1(h) - R_1^2(h))/D$ represents the price of consumption in history l.

---

[5] When $R_1^1(l) = R_1^2(l)$ but $D \neq 0$, then the return on one asset strictly dominates the return on the other: In history l both assets generate the same return, but in history h one generates a strictly higher return than the other (if $D > 0$ the first asset returns more, if $D < 0$ the second does). Buying the asset with the strictly higher return and selling the one with the lower return increases consumption in history h without lowering consumption in the initial period or in history l; the price of consumption in state h therefore equals zero. See also section 5.3.

In an interior equilibrium, the Euler equations now read

$$u'(c_0) = \beta(R_1^1(h)\eta(h)u'(c_1(h)) + R_1^1(l)\eta(l)u'(c_1(l))),$$
$$u'(c_0) = \beta(R_1^2(h)\eta(h)u'(c_1(h)) + R_1^2(l)\eta(l)u'(c_1(l))).$$

Linear combinations of these equations recover the Euler equations for the Arrow securities. For example, multiplying the first equation by $R_1^2(l)$ and the second by $-R_1^1(l)$ and summing yields

$$u'(c_0) = \beta \frac{D}{R_1^2(l) - R_1^1(l)} \eta(h)u'(c_1(h)).$$

Market completeness does not require all date- and history-contingent goods to be traded in the initial period (either by means of Arrow securities or combinations of assets with linearly independent returns). It suffices when at each node of the event tree, there are securities that enable the household to shift purchasing power across adjacent branches of the event tree, and if all goods can be traded on spot markets.

To see this, consider an economy with three periods, $t = 0, 1, 2$; S states of nature in both the second and the third period and thus, S^2 histories at date $t = 2$; G goods at each node of the event tree in the second and third period; and one good at date $t = 0$. At each node, the first good serves as numeraire. A complete set of time-, history-, and good-specific Arrow securities includes $(S + S^2)G$ securities, namely SG for the delivery of history-contingent goods at date $t = 1$ and S^2G for delivery at date $t = 2$. Note that the returns on the Arrow securities define relative prices between the goods in each node, and between the numeraire goods in different nodes.

Consider next an alternative market structure, where only S assets with linearly independent rcturns (e.g., S Arrow securities) are traded at date $t = 0$. Once uncertainty is resolved at date $t = 1$, the numeraire good is traded against the other goods on spot markets and again, S assets with linearly independent returns are traded. When uncertainty is resolved at date $t = 2$, spot markets reopen. This alternative market structure only uses $S + (G - 1) + S + (G - 1)$ markets but it provides the same trading opportunities as the complete set of Arrow securities. It also generates the same budget set when the spot market prices and asset returns correspond to the relative prices in the environment with Arrow securities.

4.1.3   General Case

We have seen that the household faces a single intertemporal budget constraint when markets are complete and multiple constraints when they are incomplete. To clarify this point under more general conditions, consider a two-period setup with a finite number of histories and a finite number of assets indexed by i. Markets may be complete or incomplete.

The household's program reads

$$\max_{c_0, \{a_1^i\}_i, \{c_1(\epsilon^1)\}_{\epsilon^1}} \quad u(c_0) + \beta \mathbb{E}_0 \left[u(c_1(\epsilon^1)) \right]$$

$$\text{s.t.} \quad \sum_i a_1^i = w_0 - c_0, \ c_1(\epsilon^1) = \sum_i a_1^i R_1^i(\epsilon^1) + w_1(\epsilon^1).$$

For each asset i that the household purchases or sells, the corresponding Euler equation $u'(c_0) = \beta \mathbb{E}_0[u'(c_1(\epsilon^1)) R_1^i(\epsilon^1)]$ holds. Expressed differently, $1 = \mathbb{E}_0[m_1(\epsilon^1) R_1^i(\epsilon^1)]$ where $m_1(\epsilon^1) \equiv \beta u'(c_1(\epsilon^1))/u'(c_0)$ denotes the household's *stochastic discount factor*, namely the marginal rate of substitution normalized by the conditional probability of history ϵ^1. Note that

$$\sum_i a_1^i = \mathbb{E}_0 \left[m_1(\epsilon^1) \sum_i a_1^i R_1^i(\epsilon^1) \right]$$

because the household either is invested in asset i, in which case $a_1^i = \mathbb{E}_0[m_1(\epsilon^1) a_1^i R_1^i(\epsilon^1)]$, or it is not invested, in which case $a_1^i = 0$.

Multiplying the dynamic budget constraints at date $t = 1$ by $m_1(\epsilon^1)$ and taking expectations yields

$$\mathbb{E}_0[m_1(\epsilon^1) c_1(\epsilon^1)] = \mathbb{E}_0 \left[m_1(\epsilon^1) \sum_i a_1^i R_1^i(\epsilon^1) \right] + \mathbb{E}_0[m_1(\epsilon^1) w_1(\epsilon^1)].$$

Adding the dynamic budget constraint at date $t = 0$, we arrive at the equilibrium condition

$$c_0 + \mathbb{E}_0[m_1(\epsilon^1) c_1(\epsilon^1)] = w_0 + \mathbb{E}_0[m_1(\epsilon^1) w_1(\epsilon^1)]. \tag{4.1}$$

Condition (4.1) holds independently of whether markets are complete or incomplete. It integrates all dynamic budget constraints and uses the household's Euler equations to express prices in terms of stochastic discount factors. When markets are complete, the single intertemporal condition (4.1) fully represents the household's budgetary restrictions conditional on the equality of marginal rates of substitution and prices. When markets are incomplete, in contrast, condition (4.1) represents the budgetary restrictions only partially because it does not account for the market incompleteness that prevents purchasing power from being shifted across time and histories in arbitrary ways. That is, market incompleteness imposes constraints in addition to condition (4.1).

As an example, recall the saving problem with incomplete markets and a risk-free return considered earlier. The history-contingent intertemporal budget constraint and the Euler equation are given by

$$w_0 - c_0 + \frac{w_1(\epsilon^1) - c_1(\epsilon^1)}{R_1} = 0, \ \frac{1}{R_1} = \mathbb{E}_0 \left[m_1(\epsilon^1) \right].$$

Summing the intertemporal budget constraints for the two histories, weighted by the respective probabilities and stochastic discount factors, yields condition (4.1) once the Euler equation is imposed. But condition (4.1) does not imply the two intertemporal budget constraints.

4.2 Risk Sharing

4.2.1 Borch's Rule

Consider an economy with groups of households who buy or sell assets with contingent returns. Households are homogeneous within but heterogeneous across groups. In equilibrium at date t,

$$1 = \mathbb{E}_t[m_{t+1}^h(\epsilon^{t+1})R_{t+1}^i(\epsilon^{t+1})]$$

for all assets i where m_{t+1}^h denotes the stochastic discount factor of the representative household in group h. Similarly, the stochastic discount factors of the representative households from two different groups, say l and n, satisfy

$$\mathbb{E}_t[(m_{t+1}^l(\epsilon^{t+1}) - m_{t+1}^n(\epsilon^{t+1}))R_{t+1}^i(\epsilon^{t+1})] = 0.$$

Each asset with a linearly independent return vector imposes an additional constraint of this type. When markets are complete, the combined restrictions imply that $m_{t+1}^l(\epsilon^{t+1}) = m_{t+1}^n(\epsilon^{t+1})$ in each history. This is most easily seen in the case where the assets include a complete set of Arrow securities.

When markets are complete such that $m_{t+1}^l(\epsilon^{t+1}) = m_{t+1}^n(\epsilon^{t+1})$ and if both households have the same utility function, then

$$\frac{u'(c_t^n(\epsilon^t))}{u'(c_t^l(\epsilon^t))} = \frac{u'(c_{t+1}^n(\epsilon^{t+1}))}{u'(c_{t+1}^l(\epsilon^{t+1}))}. \tag{4.2}$$

Condition (4.2) is referred to as *Borch's rule*. It states that households *share risk*—whenever marginal utility of one household is high or low, the same holds true for the other. The ratio of marginal utilities reflects differences in wealth. When household preferences are homothetic then condition (4.2) simplifies to

$$\frac{c_t^n(\epsilon^t)}{c_t^l(\epsilon^t)} = \frac{c_{t+1}^n(\epsilon^{t+1})}{c_{t+1}^l(\epsilon^{t+1})}.$$

Risk sharing is Pareto optimal. To see this, consider the problem of maximizing the welfare of group l subject to the other groups attaining given levels of welfare, $\{\bar{U}^h\}_{h\neq l}$. The Lagrangian associated with this program reads

$$\mathcal{L} = \mathbb{E}_0\left[\sum_{t=0}^{\infty}\beta^t u(c_t^l(\epsilon^t))\right] + \sum_{h\neq l}\lambda^h\mathbb{E}_0\left[\sum_{t=0}^{\infty}\beta^t u(c_t^h(\epsilon^t)) - \bar{U}^h\right]$$
$$+ \sum_{t,\epsilon^t}\mu_t(\epsilon^t)\left\{\ldots - c_t^l(\epsilon^t) - \sum_{h\neq l}c_t^h(\epsilon^t) + \ldots\right\},$$

where we assume that the number of households is the same in each group; λ^h denotes the multiplier associated with the reservation utility requirement for group h; and $\mu_t(\epsilon^t)$ denotes the multiplier associated with the resource constraint. We do not need to be specific about the production side of the economy, thus the dots. Differentiating with respect to consumption yields

$$u'(c_t^l(\epsilon^t)) = \lambda^h u'(c_t^h(\epsilon^t))$$

at all dates, which implies the risk-sharing condition (4.2).

4.2.2   Aggregate and Idiosyncratic Risk

Suppose that the endowment of households in group h, $w_t^h(\epsilon^t)$, has an *aggregate* and an *idiosyncratic* (group-specific) component. The former, $w_t(\epsilon^t)$, is the same across all groups, while the latter, $\iota_t^h(\epsilon^t)$, differs across groups; the sum of the idiosyncratic components across groups equals zero in all histories. Markets are complete, and in equilibrium households thus share risk.

Let φ^h denote wealth of group h relative to average wealth. With identical and homothetic preferences, condition (4.2) then implies $c_t^h(\epsilon^t) = \varphi^h c_t(\epsilon^t)$ where $c_t(\epsilon^t)$ denotes average consumption. Using the resource constraint, $w_t(\epsilon^t) = c_t(\epsilon^t)$, this yields

$$c_t^h(\epsilon^t) = \varphi^h w_t(\epsilon^t).$$

Note that consumption of all households is proportional to the average endowment in the economy. In other words, with complete markets, consumption of households only reflects aggregate shocks and idiosyncratic risk is fully insured.

4.3   Uninsurable Labor Income Risk and Capital Accumulation

Suppose now that—in stark contrast to the environment with risk sharing—insurance is ruled out. Household consumption thus reflects aggregate and idiosyncratic shocks. We abstract from the former and study the consequences of *uninsurable idiosyncratic labor income risk* for capital accumulation.

4.3.1   Economy

The structure of the economy is the same as in the representative agent model of section 3.1, except for one difference: The effective, productivity-weighted time endowment of each household is random. Formally, there is a continuum of measure one of infinitely lived households, indexed by $h \in [0, 1]$. The time endowment of household h at date t is given by $1 + \iota_t^h$; it is strictly positive, bounded, and i.i.d. across households with minimum value $1 + \underline{\iota}$ and mean 1. Aggregate labor supply thus equals unity at all times. We assume that the time endowment follows a *Markov process*; that is, the probability that the endowment takes a specific value at date t only depends on the realized value at date $t - 1$.

Households have access to a risk-free asset with gross interest rate R_t. Aggregate net financial assets of the household sector correspond to the economy's capital stock, k_t. Firms rent labor at the competitive wage w_t per unit of time, and capital at the competitive rate r_t. Capital depreciates at rate δ, and thus $R_t = 1 + r_t - \delta$.

We consider a *stationary equilibrium*: While the time endowment and asset of each household changes from period to period, the joint distribution of time endowments and assets across the population is time-invariant. Accordingly, the aggregate capital stock, and thus the interest rate and wage, are time-invariant as well.

4.3.2   Households

Household h maximizes $\mathbb{E}_0[\sum_{t=0}^{\infty} \beta^t u(c_t^h(\epsilon^t))]$. Its dynamic budget constraint is given by

$$a_{t+1}^h(\epsilon^t) = a_t^h(\epsilon^{t-1})R + w(1 + \iota_t^h(\epsilon^t)) - c_t^h(\epsilon^t).$$

Consumption cannot be negative. Because debt must be serviced under all circumstances this implies a *natural borrowing limit*. Specifically, a household's debt must not rise above a critical value, $-\underline{a}$, which equals the market value of future labor income in the worst possible history, namely the history with recurring realizations of the lowest possible time endowment:

$$a_{t+1}^i(\epsilon^t) \geq \underline{a} \equiv -w(1 + \underline{\iota})\frac{1}{R-1}.$$

A tighter borrowing constraint may bind, for example, if households are excluded from borrowing at all; in this case, the natural borrowing limit is replaced by the restriction $a_{t+1}^h(\epsilon^t) \geq 0$.

At date t the state variables (other than the constant wage and interest rate) in the household's program are $a_t^h(\epsilon^{t-1})$ and $\iota_t^h(\epsilon^t)$, and the choice variables are $a_{t+1}^h(\epsilon^t)$ and consumption. Adopting recursive notation, let $(a_\circ^h, \iota_\circ^h)$ and (a_+^h, ι_+^h) denote the state in the current and subsequent period, respectively. Since the program is time autonomous, the Bellman equation for household h reads

$$V(a_\circ^h, \iota_\circ^h; w, R) = \max_{a_+^h} u(a_\circ^h R + w(1 + \iota_\circ^h) - a_+^h) + \beta \mathbb{E}\left[V(a_+^h, \iota_+^h; w, R)|\iota_\circ^h\right]$$

subject to the borrowing constraint; the expectation is conditioned on $\iota_\circ^h$ because the current time endowment may contain information about the probability distribution of the next period's endowment (the Markov assumption implies that $\iota_\circ^h$ contains all such information).

If ι risk were absent (or equivalently, if markets were complete and households insured each other), the household would face a risk-free, constant labor income stream. With $\beta R = 1$, its optimal consumption would be time-invariant and equal to $a_\circ^h(R - 1) + w$. With risk and incomplete markets, in contrast, optimal consumption cannot be constant and finite because constant and finite consumption cannot be consistent with the worst-case scenario of minimum time endowments forever after and at the same time optimally respond to more favorable time endowment realizations.

Uninsurable income risk implies that households accumulate infinite assets if $\beta R \geq 1$. To see this, suppose that the condition holds. The first-order and envelope conditions then yield

$$V_a(a_o^h, \iota_o^h; w, R) = Ru'(c_o^h) \geq \mathbb{E}\left[V_a(a_+^h, \iota_+^h; w, R)|\iota_o^h\right] = R\mathbb{E}\left[u'(c_+^h)|\iota_o^h\right],$$

where the inequality reflects the possibly binding borrowing constraint as well as $\beta R \geq 1$. With $u' > 0, u'' < 0$, this condition implies that optimal consumption stochastically converges to infinity as the household accumulates more and more assets to *self-insure* against low future realizations of the time endowment.

Formally, the Euler equation $u'(c_o^h) \geq \mathbb{E}\left[u'(c_+^h)|\iota_o^h\right]$ implies that marginal utility follows a submartingale, which converges. Strict concavity of the utility function implies that marginal utility only converges if consumption converges. Since an income shock translates into a change in consumption unless asset holdings are infinite, convergence of marginal utility requires that asset holdings converge to infinity. We conclude that for households to accumulate a finite level of assets, the interest rate must satisfy $\beta R < 1$.

4.3.3   General Equilibrium

The stationary equilibrium in the hypothetical economy without risk (or with insurance) would satisfy $R = \beta^{-1} = 1 + r - \delta$, $f_K(k, 1) = r$, and $f_L(k, 1) = w$. Aggregate consumption would equal $k(R - 1) + w$.

In the stationary equilibrium in the economy with risk and incomplete markets, in contrast, R is strictly smaller than β^{-1}. If R equaled or exceeded β^{-1}, the market for capital would not clear because supply by households would grow without bound, while firms' demand would be bounded. In equilibrium, households accumulate assets when their time endowment is high and run them down when it is low. The capital stock in the economy is constant and because $R < \beta^{-1}$, it is strictly larger than in the economy without risk, and so are wages. Although the risk is purely idiosyncratic and washes out in the aggregate, self-insurance gives rise to a higher capital stock.

Suppose for simplicity that the time endowment can assume m possible values and asset holdings of a household n values; both m and n are finite. The $m \times m$ transition matrix Π^ι, whose rows sum to unity, contains the exogenous transition probabilities of the time endowment; the (i, j) element of Π^ι gives the probability that ι_+^h takes the j-th of the m possible values conditional on ι_o^h taking the i-th such value.

The time-varying elements of household h's state, (a_o^h, ι_o^h), then can take mn values. The transition matrix for this state, say Π, which is of size $mn \times mn$, follows from the transition matrix Π^ι and the household's optimal decision rule. The (i, j) element of Π gives the probability that (a_+^h, ι_+^h) takes the j-th of the mn possible values conditional on (a_o^h, ι_o^h) taking the i-th such value.

Let $\Pi^\top$ denote the transpose of Π, and let d of size $mn \times 1$ denote the probability distribution of households over the possible states; the elements of d sum to one. Note that conditional on $d_\circ$, the probability distribution in the subsequent period is given by $d_+ = \Pi^\top d_\circ$. A *stationary distribution* therefore satisfies $d = \Pi^\top d$; it is the normalized eigenvector associated with the unit eigenvalue of $\Pi^\top$. The stationary distribution d, which reflects the optimal household choices given the wage and interest rate, implies a stationary distribution over the n asset values. In equilibrium, the latter stationary distribution is consistent with the aggregate capital stock associated with the wage and interest rate.

4.4 Bibliographic Notes

von Neumann and Morgenstern (1944) introduce expected utility. Modigliani and Brumberg (1954) discuss the precautionary savings motive and Friedman (1957, p. 16) discusses saving as a "reserve for emergencies." Phelps (1962) and Levhari and Srinivasan (1969) study dynamic optimization problems with risky returns on saving. Leland (1968) relates the precautionary saving motive to the convexity of marginal utility, and Sandmo (1970) analyzes the differences between return and labor income risk. The analysis of the saving problem with quadratic utility is due to Hall (1978). Kimball (1990) defines prudence as the sensitivity of an optimal choice (here saving) to risk. Zeldes (1989a; 1989b) analyzes how the risk of a binding borrowing constraint and precautionary motives affect the consumption function. Deaton (1991) analyzes buffer stock saving in a model with borrowing constraints, precautionary motive, and impatience, and Carroll (1997) shows that impatient households with a precautionary motive target a wealth-to-permanent-income ratio. Arrow (1953; 1964) and Radner (1972) analyze equilibrium with sequential trading.

Borch (1962) derives the risk-sharing condition.

Aiyagari (1994) analyzes idiosyncratic risk and capital accumulation in stationary equilibrium. Chamberlain and Wilson (2000) prove that consumption grows without bound in such an environment when $\beta R \geq 1$.

Related Topics and Additional References Cass and Shell (1983) analyze the efficiency implications of risk and *limited participation* in an overlapping generations economy. They show that even with complete markets and a finite horizon, extrinsic risk (sunspots) can cause a Pareto inefficient allocation because the yet unborn do not participate in markets.

The Aiyagari (1994) model introduces capital into frameworks developed by Bewley (1977; 1980; 1986) and Huggett (1993) (see sections 5.6, 9.4, and 9.5). Angeletos (2007) analyzes the implications of *uninsurable idiosyncratic capital income risk*. As in Aiyagari (1994), the interest rate is lower than with complete markets but unlike in that model, the capital stock need not exceed the complete markets level; this is due to a risk premium, which drives a wedge between the interest rate and the marginal product of capital.

Werning (2015) studies the effect of market incompleteness on aggregate consumption.

Deaton (1992) covers consumption. Laffont (1989) and Gollier (2001) cover models of risk, time, and information.

See section 8.3 for models with financial frictions.

5 Asset Returns and Asset Prices

We have previously characterized the consumption and saving choices of households conditional on asset returns. Now, we change the perspective: We analyze asset returns and prices conditional on equilibrium consumption.

We start from the observation that a household that invests in multiple assets is indifferent between them at the margin. We derive the implications of this indifference for the return characteristics of assets and we relate asset returns to asset prices and their components, fundamental values and bubbles. Thereafter, we study the implications of equilibrium asset prices for the term structure of interest rates and we analyze a simple general equilibrium model of asset prices. Throughout, we assume that households maximize expected utility; the model in appendix B.4 relaxes this assumption.

5.1 Euler Equation

Consider the equilibrium in an economy with two periods and risk. Markets may be complete or incomplete. We saw in subsection 4.1.3 that for each asset i and each household h that holds or shorts the asset, an Euler equation of the form

$$u'(c_0^h) = \beta \mathbb{E}_0[u'(c_1^h(\epsilon^1))R_1^i(\epsilon^1)] \;\; \text{or} \;\; 1 = \mathbb{E}_0[m_1^h(\epsilon^1)R_1^i(\epsilon^1)]$$

holds, where $m_1^h(\epsilon^1) \equiv \beta u'(c_1^h(\epsilon^1))/u'(c_0^h)$ denotes household h's stochastic discount factor.

This has two important implications. First, when asset i is held by different households, l and n say, then the stochastic discount factors of these households satisfy $\mathbb{E}_0[m_1^l(\epsilon^1)R_1^i(\epsilon^1)] = \mathbb{E}_0[m_1^n(\epsilon^1)R_1^i(\epsilon^1)]$; that is, the return-weighted average stochastic discount factors coincide. When l and n hold multiple assets this imposes multiple restrictions. When markets are complete, these restrictions imply that $m_1^l(\epsilon^1) = m_1^n(\epsilon^1)$ for each history (see subsection 4.2.1).

The second implication concerns return differentials across assets, to which we turn next.

5.2   Excess Returns

5.2.1   C-CAPM

When a household with stochastic discount factor $\{m_1(\epsilon^1)\}_{\epsilon^1}$ purchases or sells multiple assets, say j and k, then the rates of return on these assets satisfy $\mathbb{E}_0[m_1(\epsilon^1)R_1^j(\epsilon^1)] = \mathbb{E}_0[m_1(\epsilon^1)R_1^k(\epsilon^1)]$; that is, the stochastic-discount-factor-weighted average returns on the assets coincide. Expressing the equality as $\mathbb{E}_0[m_1(\epsilon^1)(R_1^j(\epsilon^1) - R_1^k(\epsilon^1))] = 0$ and using the definition of covariance yields

$$\mathbb{E}_0[m_1(\epsilon^1)]\mathbb{E}_0[R_1^j(\epsilon^1) - R_1^k(\epsilon^1)] + \mathbb{C}\mathrm{ov}_0[m_1(\epsilon^1), R_1^j(\epsilon^1) - R_1^k(\epsilon^1)] = 0.$$

Equilibrium therefore imposes restrictions on *expected returns* and *return covariances* of assets. The latter reflect how strongly asset returns covary with the stochastic discount factor.

Let f index an asset with risk-free return, $R_1^f(\epsilon^1) = R_1^f$, and suppose that the household holds this asset such that $1 = \mathbb{E}_0[m_1(\epsilon^1)]R_1^f$ and

$$\mathbb{E}_0[m_1(\epsilon^1)](\mathbb{E}_0[R_1^j(\epsilon^1)] - R_1^f) + \mathbb{C}\mathrm{ov}_0[m_1(\epsilon^1), R_1^j(\epsilon^1)] = 0.$$

The *excess return* on asset i—that is, the expected rate of return net of the risk-free return— then satisfies

$$\mathbb{E}_0[R_1^i(\epsilon^1)] - R_1^f = -\frac{\mathbb{C}\mathrm{ov}_0[m_1(\epsilon^1), R_1^i(\epsilon^1)]}{\mathbb{E}_0[m_1(\epsilon^1)]} = -\mathbb{C}\mathrm{ov}_0[m_1(\epsilon^1), R_1^i(\epsilon^1)]R_1^f.$$

According to this *consumption capital asset pricing model* (C-CAPM) result, the excess return is proportional to the covariance between the asset's return and the stochastic discount factor. Note that the excess return compensates for covariation of the asset return with marginal utility, not for return volatility per se.

Since β and $u'(c_0)$ in $m_1(\epsilon^1)$ are constants, the sign of the excess return depends on the sign of the covariance between $R_1^i(\epsilon^1)$ and $u'(c_1(\epsilon^1))$. The asset pays zero excess return if this covariance is zero; for example, because utility is linear (risk neutrality) or consumption is deterministic (full insurance). If the asset return covaries negatively with the stochastic discount factor and thus (if utility is strictly concave) positively with $c_1(\epsilon^1)$, then the excess return is positive. Intuitively, the asset is a bad *hedge* in this case; it tends to pay more when the marginal benefit from additional resources is small. To induce the household to nevertheless hold the asset, its return must be high. If the asset return covaries negatively with $c_1(\epsilon^1)$, in contrast, then the excess return is negative; when the asset is a good hedge it need not pay a high average return.

The C-CAPM implies a *mean-variance frontier* that bounds the absolute value of an asset's excess return given the standard deviation of its return:

$$\mathbb{E}_0[R_1^i(\epsilon^1)] - R_1^f = -\frac{\mathbb{C}ov_0[m_1(\epsilon^1), R_1^i(\epsilon^1)]}{\mathbb{E}_0[m_1(\epsilon^1)]}$$

$$\Rightarrow \quad |\mathbb{E}_0[R_1^i(\epsilon^1)] - R_1^f| \leq \frac{\mathbb{S}td_0[m_1(\epsilon^1)]\mathbb{S}td_0[R_1^i(\epsilon^1)]}{\mathbb{E}_0[m_1(\epsilon^1)]}.$$

Here, we use the fact that the covariance equals the product of the standard deviations and the correlation coefficient, which lies between minus and plus one.

5.2.2   CAPM

The C-CAPM establishes a linear relation between the equilibrium excess return on an asset and the covariance between the asset return and the stochastic discount factor. The *capital asset pricing model* (CAPM) similarly establishes such a linear relation; but in the case of the CAPM it is the covariance between the asset return and the return on the *market portfolio* encompassing all risky assets which enters the relation.

The CAPM follows from the C-CAPM under the assumption that consumption is a linear function of the rate of return on the market portfolio—the *market return* $R_1^m(\epsilon^1)$—and the marginal utility function is accurately approximated to the first order. The stochastic discount factor, $m_1(\epsilon^1)$, then is a linear function of $R_1^m(\epsilon^1)$,

$$\mathbb{E}_0[R_1^i(\epsilon^1)] - R_1^f = \mathbb{C}ov_0\left[R_1^m(\epsilon^1), R_1^i(\epsilon^1)\right]\phi R_1^f,$$

where ϕ denotes a factor of proportionality. In particular, the excess return on the market portfolio satisfies

$$\mathbb{E}_0[R_1^m(\epsilon^1)] - R_1^f = \mathbb{C}ov_0[R_1^m(\epsilon^1), R_1^m(\epsilon^1)]\phi R_1^f.$$

Substituting into the previous equation yields

$$\mathbb{E}_0[R_1^i(\epsilon^1)] - R_1^f = \frac{\mathbb{C}ov_0[R_1^m(\epsilon^1), R_1^i(\epsilon^1)]}{\mathbb{V}ar_0[R_1^m(\epsilon^1)]}(\mathbb{E}_0[R_1^m(\epsilon^1)] - R_1^f).$$

The ratio on the right-hand side of the last equality represents asset i's *beta*, the normalized covariance between the asset return and the market return. (Formally, beta represents the projection of $R_1^i(\epsilon^1)$ on $R_1^m(\epsilon^1)$.) According to the CAPM, the excess return equals the product of the asset's beta and the market's excess return.

The CAPM also follows under the assumption that a representative household values the mean return on its portfolio and dislikes return variance. The optimal *portfolio choice* then implies a linear relation between an asset's excess return and the covariance between the asset and portfolio returns. Moreover, market clearing requires that the household's portfolio choice corresponds to the market portfolio, and thus the portfolio return to the market return.

Formally, let e denote the $n \times 1$ vector of expected returns on n risky assets; and V the $n \times n$ variance-covariance matrix of the returns. The household chooses the portfolio shares invested in the risky assets, represented by the $n \times 1$ vector x, and maximizes the expected portfolio return minus γ times the portfolio variance, where γ reflects risk aversion. Letting a T superscript denote transposition and $\bar{x}$ the portfolio share $1 - \sum_{i=1}^{n} x_i$ invested in the risk-free asset, the household's problem reads

$$\max_{x} \quad x^T e + (1 - \bar{x})R^f - \gamma x^T V x$$

and yields the first-order condition

$$e^T - R^f = 2\gamma\, x^T V.$$

Post multiplying the last condition by x and combining the result with the first-order condition yields

$$e^T - R^f = \frac{x^T V}{x^T V x}[(e^T - R^f)x].$$

Market clearing implies that the shares chosen by the household, x, correspond to the shares of the risky assets in the market portfolio (the former are $1 - \bar{x}$ times the latter). The ratio on the right-hand side of the equation thus corresponds to the vector of betas; and the expression in brackets corresponds to the excess return on the market portfolio. The difference on the left-hand side represents the vector of excess returns.

5.3   Asset Prices

To derive the implications of the C-CAPM for *asset prices*, we use the definition of a return: The gross rate of return between date t and $t + 1$, $R_{t+1}^i(\epsilon^{t+1})$, equals the payoff at date $t + 1$ relative to the asset price at date t, $p_t^i(\epsilon^t)$; and the payoff consists of the asset price, $p_{t+1}^i(\epsilon^{t+1})$, and the dividend, $d_{t+1}^i(\epsilon^{t+1})$:

$$R_{t+1}^i(\epsilon^{t+1}) \equiv \frac{p_{t+1}^i(\epsilon^{t+1}) + d_{t+1}^i(\epsilon^{t+1})}{p_t^i(\epsilon^t)}. \tag{5.1}$$

We can therefore rewrite the equilibrium condition $1 = \mathbb{E}_t[m_{t+1}(\epsilon^{t+1})R_{t+1}^i(\epsilon^{t+1})]$ as

$$p_t^i(\epsilon^t) = \mathbb{E}_t[m_{t+1}(\epsilon^{t+1})(p_{t+1}^i(\epsilon^{t+1}) + d_{t+1}^i(\epsilon^{t+1}))].$$

Conditional on $\{m_{t+1}(\epsilon^{t+1})\}_{\epsilon^{t+1}}$ and a probability distribution over histories, any asset with specified payoffs can be priced by computing the expectation of the stochastic discount factor times the payoff.

Financial economists also refer to the stochastic discount factor as the *asset pricing kernel*. Rather than relating the pricing kernel to the marginal rate of substitution, and thus consumption, they often take it as given. The *law of one price* in financial economics states that portfolios with identical payoffs have the same price; the law holds when the price of every portfolio with a zero payoff in each history equals zero. When markets are complete, the law of one price implies a unique asset pricing kernel and unique prices for all Arrow securities, referred to as *state prices*. An *arbitrage* is a portfolio with a strictly negative price that pays off a nonnegative amount in every history, or a portfolio with a zero price that pays off a nonnegative amount in every history and a strictly positive amount in some histories. Absence of arbitrage is equivalent to strictly positive state prices. If utility functions are strictly increasing, equilibrium therefore requires the absence of arbitrage. In the presence of portfolio restrictions (e.g., short-sale constraints) the law of one price may not hold and equilibrium does not require the absence of arbitrage.

5.3.1   Fundamental Value

With multiple periods, iterating the pricing equation forward T times yields

$$
\begin{aligned}
p_0^i &= \mathbb{E}_0\left[m_1(\epsilon^1)\left(d_1^i(\epsilon^1) + \mathbb{E}_1\left[m_2(\epsilon^2)\left(d_2^i(\epsilon^2) + \ldots + \mathbb{E}_{T-1}\left[m_T(\epsilon^T)d_T^i(\epsilon^T)\right]\right)\right]\right)\right] \\
&\quad + \mathbb{E}_0\left[m_1(\epsilon^1)\mathbb{E}_1\left[m_2(\epsilon^2)\cdots\mathbb{E}_{T-1}\left[m_T(\epsilon^T)p_T^i(\epsilon^T)\right]\right]\right] \\
&= \mathbb{E}_0\left[\sum_{s=1}^{T}(m_1(\epsilon^1)\cdots m_s(\epsilon^s))d_s^i(\epsilon^s)\right] + \mathbb{E}_0\left[(m_1(\epsilon^1)\cdots m_T(\epsilon^T))p_T^i(\epsilon^T)\right] \\
&= \mathbb{E}_0\left[\sum_{s=1}^{T}\beta^s\frac{u'(c_s(\epsilon^s))}{u'(c_0)}d_s^i(\epsilon^s)\right] + \mathbb{E}_0\left[\beta^T\frac{u'(c_T(\epsilon^T))}{u'(c_0)}p_T^i(\epsilon^T)\right],
\end{aligned}
$$

where we use the law of iterated expectations and the fact that

$$
m_1(\epsilon^1)\cdots m_s(\epsilon^s) = \beta\frac{u'(c_1(\epsilon^1))}{u'(c_0)}\cdots\beta\frac{u'(c_s(\epsilon^s))}{u'(c_{s-1}(\epsilon^{s-1}))} = \beta^s\frac{u'(c_s(\epsilon^s))}{u'(c_0)}.
$$

The asset price has two components: The expected present value of the dividend stream until date $t = T$; and the expected present value of the price at this date.

When T is the final period, then the second component of the asset price equals zero because $p_T^i(\epsilon^T) = 0$; the first component is referred to as the *fundamental value*. When the asset has infinite maturity, in contrast, then its price satisfies

$$
p_0^i = \lim_{T\to\infty}\mathbb{E}_0\left[\sum_{s=1}^{T}\beta^s\frac{u'(c_s(\epsilon^s))}{u'(c_0)}d_s^i(\epsilon^s)\right] + \lim_{T\to\infty}\mathbb{E}_0\left[\beta^T\frac{u'(c_T(\epsilon^T))}{u'(c_0)}p_T^i(\epsilon^T)\right].
$$

The first component of the price represents the fundamental value and the second component represents a *bubble*. Whether the bubble is strictly positive, and thus p_0^i exceeds the fundamental value, depends on whether $p_T^i(\epsilon^T)$ grows more quickly than $\beta^T u'(c_T(\epsilon^T))/u'(c_0)$ shrinks as $T \to \infty$. We turn next to the question of whether this is possible.

5.3.2 Bubble

For simplicity, suppose that the utility function is linear and dividends are constant, such that $m_t(\epsilon^t) = \beta$, $d_t^i(\epsilon^t) = d^i$, and

$$p_0^i = \lim_{T\to\infty} \sum_{s=1}^{T} \beta^s d^i + \lim_{T\to\infty} \beta^T \mathbb{E}_0[p_T^i(\epsilon^T)].$$

One solution to this equation is a constant price that equals the fundamental value, $p_t^i = d^i\beta/(1-\beta)$; the bubble component equals zero in this case. Another candidate solution is $p_t^i = d^i\beta/(1-\beta) + \text{bubble}_t^i$ where $\{\text{bubble}_t^i\}_{t\geq 0}$ is a strictly positive sequence that satisfies $\text{bubble}_t^i = \beta\,\text{bubble}_{t+1}^i$; that is, the bubble grows at the rate of interest.[6] This candidate solution satisfies the asset pricing equation because

$$p_t^i = d^i\frac{\beta}{1-\beta} + \text{bubble}_t^i = \beta d^i + \beta d^i\frac{\beta}{1-\beta} + \beta\,\text{bubble}_{t+1}^i = \beta(d^i + p_{t+1}^i).$$

To check whether the candidate solution with a bubble component is consistent with rational expectations, suppose first that the number of potential investors is finite. In this case it is impossible that all households purchasing the asset at a bubbly price expect somebody else to purchase it at an even higher bubbly price in the future. A bubbly price therefore is inconsistent with common knowledge, rational expectations, and a finite number of investors.

Suppose next that new potential investors enter the economy as time progresses. A household may then purchase the asset at a bubbly price expecting to resell it to subsequent investors with similar expectations. When the interest rate strictly exceeds the economy's growth rate, then such expectation formation cannot be rational; a bubble growing at the rate of interest would eventually outgrow the economy and newcomers would not be able to purchase the bubble any longer. But when the interest rate falls short of the growth rate, then a bubble may be sustained in rational expectations equilibrium.

Recall that the growth rate in an inefficient overlapping generations economy exceeds the interest rate (see subsection 3.2.8). Such an environment therefore admits bubbles. In fact, a bubble can play exactly the same role as a Pareto improving intergenerational transfer scheme (see subsection 3.2.7): When an initial old cohort creates a bubble and old households in each period sell the bubble to young ones, the latter transfer resources to the former; this absorbs savings of the young and reduces or eliminates capital overaccumulation. A bubble of this type can be interpreted as money (see sections 9.2 and 9.4). While equilibrium imposes restrictions on the growth rate of the bubble, it is consistent with different bubble sizes. That is, the equilibrium allocation with a bubble is *indeterminate*.

---

[6] Other candidate solutions involve stochastic bubbles that grow at a faster rate but collapse stochastically.

5.4   Term Structure of Interest Rates

The price of a risk-free one-period bond that pays off unity equals

$$p_t^{f1}(\epsilon^t) = \mathbb{E}_t \left[m_{t+1}(\epsilon^{t+1}) \, 1 \right],$$

and the risk-free one-period gross interest rate, $R_{t+1}^{f1}(\epsilon^t)$, equals the inverse of the bond price (from condition (5.1)). (Note that the risk-free interest rate is indexed by ϵ^t because the return is the same across all histories ϵ^{t+1} subsequent to ϵ^t.) More generally, a risk-free s-period bond that pays off unity is priced at

$$p_t^{fs}(\epsilon^t) = \mathbb{E}_t \left[m_{t+1}(\epsilon^{t+1}) \cdots m_{t+s}(\epsilon^{t+s}) \, 1 \right]$$

and the risk-free s-period gross interest rate, $R_{t+s}^{fs}(\epsilon^t)$, equals the inverse of $p_t^{fs}(\epsilon^t)$.

Because $\{ m_{t+1}(\epsilon^{t+1}) \}_{\epsilon^{t+1}}$ affects both short- and longer-term interest rates, these rates satisfy cross-restrictions. Consider $R_{t+1}^{f1}(\epsilon^t)$ and $R_{t+2}^{f2}(\epsilon^t)$. By the law of iterated expectations,

$$
\begin{aligned}
\left(R_{t+2}^{f2}(\epsilon^t) \right)^{-1} &= \mathbb{E}_t \left[m_{t+1}(\epsilon^{t+1}) m_{t+2}(\epsilon^{t+2}) \right] = \mathbb{E}_t \left[m_{t+1}(\epsilon^{t+1}) \mathbb{E}_{t+1} \left[m_{t+2}(\epsilon^{t+2}) \right] \right] \\
&= \mathbb{E}_t \left[m_{t+1}(\epsilon^{t+1}) \left(R_{t+2}^{f1}(\epsilon^{t+1}) \right)^{-1} \right] \\
&= \left(R_{t+1}^{f1}(\epsilon^t) \right)^{-1} \mathbb{E}_t \left[\left(R_{t+2}^{f1}(\epsilon^{t+1}) \right)^{-1} \right] + \mathbb{C}\text{ov}_t \left[m_{t+1}(\epsilon^{t+1}), \left(R_{t+2}^{f1}(\epsilon^{t+1}) \right)^{-1} \right].
\end{aligned}
$$

Accordingly, there are two drivers of (the inverse of) the long-term interest rate, $R_{t+2}^{f2}(\epsilon^t)$. First, current and expected future (inverse) short-term rates. Second, a *term premium* which reflects the covariance between the inverse short-term interest rate and the stochastic discount factor in the subsequent period. Suppose that this covariance is positive—that is, consumption tends to be high when the short-term interest rate is high, and vice versa. The inverse long-term interest rate then exceeds the product of the inverse (expected) short-term rates; that is, the long-term interest rate is lower than the product of the (expected) short-term interest rates. Intuitively, a higher than expected short-term interest rate in the future is associated with a capital loss on the long-term bond. When such capital losses tend to occur in histories with high consumption, and capital gains in histories with low consumption, then the long-term bond is a good hedge and this lowers its average equilibrium return.

The *expectations hypothesis* stipulates that the term premium is negligible. Inverse long-term interest rates then equal the product of inverse (expected) short-term rates.

To compare the returns on bonds of different maturities, it is useful to express them in normalized form, over time intervals of the same length (e.g., on an annual basis). The *term structure* of interest rates,

$$\left\{ R_{t+1}^{f1}(\epsilon^t), \; \sqrt[2]{R_{t+2}^{f2}(\epsilon^t)}, \; \sqrt[3]{R_{t+3}^{f3}(\epsilon^t)}, \dots \right\},$$

collects the normalized returns, and the *yield curve* illustrates the term structure by plotting the normalized returns against maturity. The yield curve is upward sloping when the normalized return increases in maturity; for example, because investors expect short-term interest rates to rise in the future.

5.5   Equilibrium Asset Prices in an Endowment Economy

In general equilibrium, both consumption and asset prices are endogenous. Characterizing the latter requires solving for the former. A particularly tractable equilibrium asset pricing framework results in a model where equilibrium saving effectively is exogenous. We now turn to such a framework.

5.5.1   Economy

Consider an economy with a continuum of mass one of infinitely lived homogeneous households who own a fixed capital stock that consists of a continuum of mass one of *trees*. Dividends—the *fruit* of the trees—are exogenous, stochastic, and cannot be stored. They are the only source of income for the households. The budget constraint of household h reads

$$c_t^h(\epsilon^t) + p_t^{tr}(\epsilon^t)\left(tr_{t+1}^h(\epsilon^t) - tr_t^h(\epsilon^{t-1})\right) = tr_t^h(\epsilon^{t-1})d_t^{tr}(\epsilon^t),$$

where $p_t^{tr}(\epsilon^t)$ denotes the tree price; $tr_{t+1}^h(\epsilon^t)$ the household's stock of trees between t and $t+1$; and $d_t^{tr}(\epsilon^t)$ the dividend.

5.5.2   General Equilibrium

While an individual household perceives its tree holdings and consumption to be endogenous, market clearing requires that each household owns one tree, $tr_{t+1}^h(\epsilon^t) = 1$, and consumes the dividend in full. The market price of trees supports this choice. Absent bubbles, it therefore satisfies

$$p_t^{tr}(\epsilon^t) = \mathbb{E}_t\left[\sum_{s=1}^{\infty} \beta^s \frac{u'(d_{t+s}^{tr}(\epsilon^{t+s}))}{u'(d_t^{tr}(\epsilon^t))} d_{t+s}^{tr}(\epsilon^{t+s})\right].$$

Using the equilibrium stochastic discount factor we can also determine the price of arbitrary other assets, including those that are in zero net supply and not actually traded. For example, the price of a risk-free one-period bond that pays off unity is given by

$$p_t^{f1}(\epsilon^t) = \mathbb{E}_t\left[\beta \frac{u'(d_{t+1}^{tr}(\epsilon^{t+1}))}{u'(d_t^{tr}(\epsilon^t))}\right],$$

and the price of an *option* that gives the right to sell a tree in the subsequent period at price $\bar{p}$ equals

$$p_t^{option}(\epsilon^t) = \mathbb{E}_t\left[\beta \frac{u'(d_{t+1}^{tr}(\epsilon^{t+1}))}{u'(d_t^{tr}(\epsilon^t))} \max\left[0, \bar{p} - p_{t+1}^{tr}(\epsilon^{t+1})\right]\right].$$

The capital stock in an economy may be viewed as a fruit-yielding tree and we may thus associate the tree price with the price of a diversified portfolio of assets, for example a stock market index. According to that interpretation, the excess return on the tree equals the *equity premium*—the excess return on stocks.

5.6   Bibliographic Notes

The CAPM is due to Sharpe (1964), Lintner (1965), and Mossin (1966); see also Ross (1976). The C-CAPM is due to Lucas (1978) and Breeden (1979).

Tirole (1982) rules out speculative price bubbles in economies with a finite number of investors with common knowledge of rational expectations and common priors (but possibly different information sets). Tirole (1985) analyzes bubbles in overlapping generations economies with or without assets that generate rents.

Campbell (1986) characterizes stock prices and the term structure of interest rates when consumption is autoregressive log-normal. Cox et al. (1985) analyze a general equilibrium model of the term structure.

The model of asset prices in an endowment economy is due to Lucas (1978).

Related Topics and Additional References   Bewley (1980) studies bubbly money in a stochastic incomplete markets environment (see sections 4.4, 9.4, and 9.5). On bubbly government debt, see subsection 11.2.2 and section 11.7. Weil (1987) studies stochastic bubbles and Santos and Woodford (1997) analyze rational asset price bubbles in environments with symmetric information, incomplete markets, and incomplete participation. Martin and Ventura (2012) analyze wealth effects of bubbles that reallocate resources between unproductive and productive agents.

Cochrane (2001), Cvitanić and Zapatero (2004), Duffie (2001), LeRoy and Werner (2014), and Campbell (2018) cover financial economics and asset pricing. Magill and Quinzii (1996) cover equilibrium in economies with incomplete financial markets and heterogeneous agents; see also section 8.3. Brunnermeier and Oehmke (2013) and Martin and Ventura (2018) cover asset price bubbles.

See appendix B.4 for asset pricing implications of nonexpected utility.

6 Labor Supply, Growth, and Business Cycles

We have assumed so far that supplying labor is costless for households, and thus that hours worked are exogenous. We now introduce an opportunity cost of working: The utility from forgone leisure. This gives rise to a tradeoff between earning income and consuming goods on the one hand and enjoying leisure on the other, thereby rendering labor supply endogenous.

We first analyze whether and how much a household optimally works, and how wage inequality affects consumption inequality. Subsequently, we embed household choices in extensions of the representative agent model analyzed in section 3.1. These extensions focus on economic growth and business cycles. We analyze the determinants of economic growth under different assumptions about technology and study how the economy responds to productivity and sunspot shocks. We also illustrate how to represent equilibrium recursively. Throughout, we normalize the time endowment of each household to one unit per period.

6.1 Goods versus Leisure Consumption

6.1.1 One Period

Consider first a static model. Utility u is strictly increasing and concave in the consumption of goods, c, and *leisure*, x. The time spent working equals $\ell \equiv 1 - x$.

A household may adjust *labor supply* along the intensive or the extensive margin. Marginally increasing or decreasing hours worked constitutes *intensive margin* adjustment while entering or leaving the labor market represents adjustment along the *extensive margin*. We consider the two margins in turn.

6.1.1.1 Intensive Margin When labor supply is a continuous choice, the household's program reads

$$\max_{c,x} u(c, x) \text{ s.t. } c = w(1 - x),$$

where w denotes the wage. Note that the wage represents the price of leisure relative to goods consumption. This is also evident when we express the budget constraint as

$$c + wx = w,$$

equating expenditures for goods and leisure consumption (on the left-hand side) with wealth, all expressed in terms of the good.

An interior optimal choice satisfies the first-order condition

$$u_x(c, x) = u_c(c, x)w;$$

that is, the household equates the relative price of leisure and goods consumption with the marginal rate of substitution, $u_x(c, x)/u_c(c, x)$. Combining the budget constraint and the first-order condition yields the solution to the program.

A wage change alters both the household's wealth and the price of leisure relative to goods consumption. Accordingly, it induces income and substitution effects. The *compensated* or *Hicksian labor supply elasticity* is defined as the elasticity of ℓ with respect to w when utility is held constant. In contrast, the *Frisch labor supply elasticity* is defined as the elasticity of ℓ with respect to w for a fixed marginal utility of wealth.

Assume for example that

$$u(c, x) = \bar{u}(c) - \gamma \frac{\ell^{1+\varphi}}{1 + \varphi}$$

for some strictly increasing and concave function $\bar{u}$ with $\varphi > 0$. Letting λ denote the multiplier associated with the budget constraint—the marginal utility of wealth—the household's labor supply satisfies

$$\gamma \ell^\varphi = \lambda w$$

and the Frisch elasticity of labor supply equals $d \ln(\ell)/d \ln(w)|_\lambda = \varphi^{-1}$.

6.1.1.2   Extensive Margin   When workers may either work $\ell > 0$ units of time or not at all—that is, when the labor supply choice occurs along the extensive margin—then the aggregate labor supply elasticity can substantially exceed φ^{-1}.

To see this, consider a household with a continuum of identical members. Fraction η of members works ℓ units of time and fraction $1 - \eta$ does not work. Aggregate labor supply thus equals $\eta\ell$. All members are equally likely to work. The household maximizes the expected utility of its members; it solves

$$\max_{\eta, c^0, c^1} \eta\bar{u}(c^1) + (1 - \eta)\bar{u}(c^0) - \gamma \frac{\eta\ell^{1+\varphi} + (1 - \eta)0}{1 + \varphi} \text{ s.t. } \eta c^1 + (1 - \eta)c^0 = \eta\ell w,$$

where c^1 and c^0 denote consumption of working and nonworking household members, respectively. Risk sharing implies $c^1 = c^0 = c$ (see section 4.2). Letting

$$\bar{\gamma} \equiv \gamma \frac{\ell^{1+\varphi}}{1+\varphi} > 0, \; \bar{w} \equiv \ell w,$$

the program can be expressed as

$$\max_{\eta, c} \; \bar{u}(c) - \bar{\gamma}\eta \; \text{ s.t. } \; c = \eta\bar{w},$$

which corresponds to the intensive margin program of a household with preference parameter $\varphi = 0$ that faces wage $\bar{w}$. We conclude that the household labor supply elasticity at the extensive margin equals infinity.

6.1.2   More Periods

With two (and similarly, with more) periods, the household's choice at the intensive margin solves

$$\max_{c_0, c_1, x_0, x_1} \; u(c_0, x_0) + \beta u(c_1, x_1) \; \text{ s.t. } \; c_0 + \frac{c_1}{R_1} = w_0\ell_0 + \frac{w_1\ell_1}{R_1},$$

where β and R_1 denote the discount factor and the gross interest rate, respectively. The first-order conditions yield the standard Euler equation as well as the intratemporal first-order condition that we found in the static model,

$$u_c(c_0, x_0) \;\; = \;\; \beta R_1 u_c(c_1, x_1),$$
$$u_x(c_t, x_t) \;\; = \;\; u_c(c_t, x_t)w_t.$$

The intertemporal first-order condition can also be expressed as

$$u_x(c_0, x_0) = \beta R_1 \frac{w_0}{w_1} u_x(c_1, x_1),$$

which equates the relative price of leisure in the first and second period, $R_1 w_0/w_1$, with the corresponding marginal rate of substitution. If u is additively separable, leisure consumption rises and labor supply falls over time if and only if $\beta R_1 w_0/w_1 > 1$.

Assume that

$$u(c, x) = \ln(c) - \gamma \frac{\ell^{1+\varphi}}{1+\varphi}$$

with $\varphi > 0$. The first-order conditions then imply $c_1 = \beta R_1 c_0$, as well as

$$\gamma\ell_t^{\varphi} \;\; = \;\; w_t \frac{1}{c_t},$$
$$\ell_0 \;\; = \;\; \left(\frac{w_0}{w_1}\beta R_1\right)^{\frac{1}{\varphi}} \ell_1.$$

According to the first condition, the Frisch elasticity equals

$$d \ln(\ell_t)/d \ln(w_t)|_{c_0} = \varphi^{-1}.$$

According to the second condition, the Frisch elasticity determines the *intertemporal elasticity of substitution* of labor supply,

$$d \ln\left(\frac{\ell_0}{\ell_1}\right) / d \ln\left(\frac{w_0 R_1}{w_1}\right) = \varphi^{-1}.$$

As φ increases, relative labor supply responds less to wage differentials. In the limit of $\varphi \to \infty$, labor supply is constant over time.

Substituting the intertemporal first-order conditions into the intertemporal budget constraint yields

$$\ell_0 \left(w_0 + \left(\frac{w_0}{w_1}\beta R_1\right)^{-\frac{1}{\varphi}} \frac{w_1}{R_1} \right) = c_0(1 + \beta).$$

When we additionally use the intratemporal first-order condition we find

$$\gamma \ell_0^{1+\varphi} \left(1 + \left(\frac{w_0}{w_1}\beta R_1\right)^{-\frac{1}{\varphi}} \frac{w_1}{w_0 R_1} \right) = 1 + \beta.$$

The conditions make clear that φ shapes both intra- and intertemporal tradeoffs.

6.1.3   Wage Inequality and Risk Sharing

Random shocks to wages (or labor productivity) expose households to consumption risk (see subsection 4.1.1) but this risk can partly be hedged by making labor supply contingent on the wage. Households can also insure consumption risk directly, by sharing risk on insurance markets (see section 4.2). The consequences of *wage inequality* for *consumption inequality* therefore depend both on preferences and the market structure.

Consider a three-period economy with stochastic, household-specific wages and no capital or storage. There is a continuum of groups, indexed by g, and in each group there is a continuum of households, indexed by i. Each group has the same size and the period utility function of households is given by

$$u(c, x) = \frac{c^{1-\sigma}}{1 - \sigma} - \frac{\ell^{1+\varphi}}{1 + \varphi},$$

where $\sigma > 0, \sigma \neq 1, \varphi > 0$.

The log wage of household i in group g at date $t = 1, 2$, history ϵ^t, $\ln(w_{git}(\epsilon^t))$, consists of three components: a permanent, group-specific component, $\zeta_{gt}(\epsilon^t)$, which follows a random walk; a permanent, household-specific component, $\theta_{git}(\epsilon^t)$, which also follows a random walk; and a temporary, household-specific component, $\iota_{git}(\epsilon^t)$:

$$
\begin{aligned}
\ln(w_{git}(\epsilon^t)) &= \zeta_{gt}(\epsilon^t) + \theta_{git}(\epsilon^t) + \iota_{git}(\epsilon^t), \\
\zeta_{gt}(\epsilon^t) &= \zeta_{g,t-1}(\epsilon^{t-1}) + \iota^{\zeta}_{gt}(\epsilon^t), \\
\theta_{git}(\epsilon^t) &= \theta_{gi,t-1}(\epsilon^{t-1}) + \iota^{\theta}_{git}(\epsilon^t).
\end{aligned}
$$

The lagged values at date $t = 1$ are normalized to zero, $\zeta_{g0}(\epsilon^0) = \theta_{gi0}(\epsilon^0) = 0$. All innovations $\iota^{\zeta}_{gt}(\epsilon^t)$, $\iota^{\theta}_{git}(\epsilon^t)$, and $\iota_{git}(\epsilon^t)$ are independent draws from component-specific but time-invariant distributions that are the same for all groups and households.

The timing of events is as follows. At date $t = 0$, households are assigned to groups. At date $t = 1$, the group-specific permanent component, $\zeta_{g1}(\epsilon^1) = \iota^{\zeta}_{g1}(\epsilon^1)$, of each group is realized. Subsequently, households enter an insurance market where claims can only be conditioned on household-specific risks. That is, households may issue or buy a risk-free bond (to self-insure, see section 4.3), which is in zero net supply, or they can write insurance contracts that stipulate payment conditional on the realization of $\theta_{gi1}(\epsilon^1)$ and $\iota_{gi1}(\epsilon^1)$ at date $t = 1$ and $\theta_{gi2}(\epsilon^2)$ and $\iota_{gi2}(\epsilon^2)$ at date $t = 2$. Finally, the household-specific risks are realized, households supply labor, and they consume. At date $t = 2$, risks are realized, households supply labor, and they consume. The objective of household i in group g is to maximize $\mathbb{E}[u(c_{gi1}(\epsilon^1), x_{gi1}(\epsilon^1)) + \beta u(c_{gi2}(\epsilon^2), x_{gi2}(\epsilon^2))|\zeta_{g1}(\epsilon^1)]$.

Because of CIES preferences and because the innovations are identically distributed across households, the bond is not traded in equilibrium; moreover, there is complete insurance within groups and no insurance across groups. To establish this result, we conjecture that it is correct and check consistency. Consider group g at date $t = 1$. Since insurance markets are complete within the group, the date-$t = 1$ equilibrium allocation conditional on $\zeta_{g1}(\epsilon^1)$ solves a planner problem with the choice variables $\{c_{gi1}(\epsilon^1), x_{gi1}(\epsilon^1)\}_{i,\epsilon^1}$ that can be divided into subprograms for each history. Fix a history ϵ^1 and let λ denote the multiplier attached to the group's resource constraint in that history, which requires group consumption to equal group labor income. The Lagrangian associated with the subprogram reads

$$
\mathcal{L} = \int_i \frac{\left(c_{gi1}(\epsilon^1)\right)^{1-\sigma}}{1-\sigma} - \frac{\left(\ell_{gi1}(\epsilon^1)\right)^{1+\varphi}}{1+\varphi} di - \lambda \int_i \left(c_{gi1}(\epsilon^1) - \ell_{gi1}(\epsilon^1)w_{gi1}(\epsilon^1)\right) di.
$$

The first-order conditions for consumption imply that consumption is equalized across group members, $c_{gi1}(\epsilon^1) = c_{g1}(\epsilon^1)$, reflecting perfect insurance of idiosyncratic risks (see section 4.2). Moreover, from the first-order conditions for labor supply,

$$
\left(\ell_{gi1}(\epsilon^1)\right)^{\varphi} = \left(c_{g1}(\epsilon^1)\right)^{-\sigma} w_{gi1}(\epsilon^1).
$$

Substituting these results into the resource constraint for history ϵ^1 yields

$$\ln\left(\ell_{gi1}(\epsilon^1)\right) = \frac{1-\sigma}{\sigma+\varphi}\zeta_{g1}(\epsilon^1) - \frac{\sigma}{\sigma+\varphi}\ln\left(\Theta_{g1}(\epsilon^1)\right) + \frac{\theta_{gi1}(\epsilon^1) + \iota_{gi1}(\epsilon^1)}{\varphi}, \qquad (6.1)$$

$$\ln\left(c_{g1}(\epsilon^1)\right) = \frac{1+\varphi}{\sigma+\varphi}\zeta_{g1}(\epsilon^1) + \frac{\varphi}{\sigma+\varphi}\ln\left(\Theta_{g1}(\epsilon^1)\right), \qquad (6.2)$$

where we define

$$\Theta_{g1}(\epsilon^1) \equiv \int_i \exp\left\{(\theta_{gi1}(\epsilon^1) + \iota_{gi1}(\epsilon^1))(1 + \varphi^{-1})\right\} di.$$

Parallel conditions hold in all other histories and at date $t = 2$.

Consider now the stochastic Euler equation of household i in group g for a risk-free bond with gross interest rate R_2. If the conjecture is correct, then the Euler equation is satisfied at the allocation where no household is exposed to the bond; that is, for the consumption expressions derived above. Using these expressions the Euler equation reduces to

$$1 = \beta R_2 \mathbb{E}\left[\left(\exp\left\{\frac{1+\varphi}{\sigma+\varphi}(\zeta_{g2}(\epsilon^1) - \zeta_{g1}(\epsilon^1))\right\}\left(\frac{\Theta_{g2}(\epsilon^2)}{\Theta_{g1}(\epsilon^1)}\right)^{\frac{\varphi}{\sigma+\varphi}}\right)^{-\sigma}\Big|\zeta_{g1}(\epsilon^1)\right].$$

Since the innovations are independent, the expression inside the expectation is the same for all households. This establishes that all households share the same expected stochastic discount factor, and thus that they all choose zero bond holdings. The allocation characterized above thus indeed constitutes an equilibrium allocation.

According to condition (6.1), more productive households in a group work more than unproductive ones. Since *insurable wage shocks* have no income effect, and thus no effect on the marginal utility of wealth, the elasticity of labor supply with respect to these shocks is given by the Frisch elasticity. *Uninsurable shocks*, in contrast, do have an income effect. When $\sigma < 1$, the substitution effect dominates the income effect and a positive uninsurable wage shock increases labor supply; when $\sigma > 1$, the income effect dominates and labor supply decreases.

According to condition (6.2), consumption only responds to uninsurable, group-specific shocks. This reflects the fact that the wage component $\theta_{gi1}(\epsilon^1) + \iota_{gi1}(\epsilon^1)$ is fully diversified and preferences are separable. The elasticity of consumption with respect to the uninsurable wage component, $(1 + \varphi)/(\sigma + \varphi)$, declines with σ because a higher value for σ strengthens the income effect on leisure. When $\sigma = 1$, the income and substitution effects of an uninsurable wage shock on labor supply cancel and the elasticity of consumption equals unity.

Wage inequality as measured by the variance of (the logarithm of) wages across groups and households is given by

$$\mathbb{V}\text{ar}\left[\ln(w_{gi1}(\epsilon^1))\right] = \mathbb{V}\text{ar}[\zeta_{g1}(\epsilon^1)] + \mathbb{V}\text{ar}[\theta_{gi1}(\epsilon^1) + \iota_{gi1}(\epsilon^1)].$$

Consumption inequality equals

$$\mathbb{V}\mathrm{ar}\left[\ln(c_{g1}(\epsilon^1))\right] = \left(\frac{1+\varphi}{\sigma+\varphi}\right)^2 \mathbb{V}\mathrm{ar}[\zeta_{g1}(\epsilon^1)].$$

Even if all wage risk is uninsurable—that is, $\theta_{gi1}(\epsilon^1) = \iota_{gi1}(\epsilon^1) = 0$—consumption inequality is smaller than wage inequality when the income effect on labor supply dominates the substitution effect ($\sigma > 1$) such that labor supply changes dampen the impact of uninsurable wage shocks on income. In this case, a higher Frisch elasticity (smaller value for φ) also reduces consumption inequality.

The covariances between (log) consumption and wages and between consumption and labor supply, respectively, equal

$$\mathbb{C}\mathrm{ov}\left[\ln(c_{g1}(\epsilon^1)), \ln(w_{gi1}(\epsilon^1))\right] = \frac{1+\varphi}{\sigma+\varphi}\mathbb{V}\mathrm{ar}[\zeta_{g1}(\epsilon^1)],$$

$$\mathbb{C}\mathrm{ov}\left[\ln(c_{g1}(\epsilon^1)), \ln(\ell_{gi1}(\epsilon^1))\right] = \frac{1+\varphi}{\sigma+\varphi}\frac{1-\sigma}{\sigma+\varphi}\mathbb{V}\mathrm{ar}[\zeta_{g1}(\epsilon^1)].$$

When $\sigma = 1$, the covariance between consumption and wages equals the variance of the uninsurable shock while consumption and labor supply are uncorrelated.

6.2   Growth

We now introduce the labor–leisure tradeoff into the general equilibrium model analyzed in section 3.1. Our aim is to identify the sources of *economic growth* and the restrictions that growth imposes on preferences and technology.

6.2.1   Exogenous Growth

We first consider *exogenous growth* driven by exogenous increases in productivity. While we maintain the assumption of constant returns to scale in capital and labor, we adopt a general specification of productivity growth: We assume that per-capita output, y_t, depends on calendar time, in addition to the per-capita capital stock, k_t, and per-capita labor input, $1 - x_t$,

$$y_t = \tilde{f}(k_t, 1 - x_t, t).$$

For given t, the production function $\tilde{f}$ satisfies the Inada conditions and exhibits decreasing marginal products. We also allow for exogenous gross population growth at rate v.

In this environment, the welfare theorems apply. The decentralized equilibrium therefore solves the social planner problem

$$\max_{\{c_t, x_t, k_{t+1}\}_{t\geq 0}} \sum_{t=0}^{\infty} \beta^t v^t u(c_t, x_t) \tag{6.3}$$

$$\text{s.t.} \quad v k_{t+1} = k_t(1 - \delta) + \tilde{f}(k_t, 1 - x_t, t) - c_t, \quad k_0 \text{ given, } k_{t+1} \geq 0.$$

Before deriving the equilibrium conditions, we analyze the conditions for a *balanced growth path* along which all variables are strictly positive and grow at constant (but possibly different) rates.

6.2.1.1   Balanced Growth Path Restrictions

Suppose that the economy starts to grow along a balanced growth path at date $t = T$ and let γ_z denote the gross growth rate of a generic variable z along the balanced growth path. Note that we must have $\gamma_x = 1$ since the time endowment is bounded. Dividing the resource constraint in program (6.3) at date $t > T$ by γ_k^{t-T} and rearranging yields

$$k_T(v\gamma_k - 1 + \delta) = y_T(\gamma_y/\gamma_k)^{t-T} - c_T(\gamma_c/\gamma_k)^{t-T}.$$

Since the left-hand side of this equality is independent of t, the right-hand side must be time independent as well. Moreover, since $y_T, k_T, c_T > 0$, this implies $\gamma_y = \gamma_k = \gamma_c$.

Denoting the common gross growth rate of per-capita output, capital, and consumption by γ we thus have established

$$k_T(v\gamma - 1 + \delta) = y_T - c_T \text{ and } y_T\gamma^{t-T} = \tilde{f}(k_T\gamma^{t-T}, 1 - x_T, t).$$

The latter equality and constant returns to scale imply

$$\tilde{f}(k_T, 1 - x_T, T) = y_T = \frac{1}{\gamma^{t-T}}\tilde{f}(k_T\gamma^{t-T}, 1 - x_T, t) = \tilde{f}\left(k_T, \frac{1 - x_T}{\gamma^{t-T}}, t\right).$$

Comparing the left- and rightmost expressions, we conclude that the only form of technological progress consistent with a balanced growth path is *labor augmenting technological progress* at the gross growth rate γ.

Up to some normalization of the initial level of productivity, output per capita thus depends on the per-capita capital stock and per-capita labor supply in *efficiency units*, $(1 - x_t)\gamma^t$: For any t (on or off the balanced growth path)

$$y_t = f(k_t, (1 - x_t)\gamma^t),$$

where f denotes the neoclassical production function considered in section 3.1. In the special case of a Cobb-Douglas production function, labor augmenting (or *Harrod-neutral*) technological progress is isomorphic to progress that is capital augmenting (*Solow-neutral*) or multiplying $f(k, 1 - x)$ (*Hicks-neutral*).

Balanced growth path dynamics also impose restrictions on preferences. To see this, consider the Euler equation and intratemporal first-order condition implied by program (6.3). These conditions read

$$\frac{u_c(c_t, x_t)}{\beta u_c(c_{t+1}, x_{t+1})} = 1 - \delta + f_K(k_{t+1}, (1 - x_{t+1})\gamma^{t+1}),$$

$$\frac{u_x(c_t, x_t)}{u_c(c_t, x_t)\gamma^t} = f_L(k_t, (1 - x_t)\gamma^t).$$

Due to constant returns to scale, the terms on the right-hand side—which in equilibrium correspond to the gross interest rate, R_{t+1}, and the wage per efficiency unit, w_t/γ^t—are constant along a balanced growth path. Consistency therefore requires that the elasticity of u_c with respect to consumption is constant (so that the ratio of marginal utilities of consumption does not change along a balanced growth path) and that u_x/u_c grows at the same rate as consumption. These two requirements imply

$$u(c, x) = \begin{cases} \frac{c^{1-\sigma}v(x)}{1-\sigma}, & \sigma > 0, \sigma \neq 1 \\ \ln(c) + v(x), & \sigma = 1 \end{cases},$$

where the function v needs to satisfy additional conditions to guarantee that u is increasing and concave.

To gain intuition for the preference restrictions, note that along a balanced growth path consumption and wages grow at the same rate such that the intratemporal first-order condition takes the form

$$u_c(w_T\gamma^{t-T}\xi, x_T)w_T\gamma^{t-T} = u_x(w_T\gamma^{t-T}\xi, x_T)$$

for all $t > T$ where $\xi > 0$ denotes some constant. To satisfy this condition, preferences must give rise to income and substitution effects on leisure that offset each other in a static environment (see subsection 6.1.1). Along the balanced growth path, the model then generates a constant capital–output ratio, constant wage growth and interest rates, and constant factor shares in national income.

A final condition that we need to impose on the primitives concerns the growth rate of technological progress, γ: it must not be too high because otherwise, the objective is unbounded. To see this, note that

$$\sum_{t=T}^{\infty} \beta^{t-T}\gamma^{t-T}\frac{(c_T\gamma^{t-T})^{1-\sigma}v(x_T)}{1-\sigma} = \sum_{t=T}^{\infty}(\beta v\gamma^{1-\sigma})^{t-T}\chi_1,$$

where χ_1 denotes a constant. Boundedness requires $\beta v\gamma^{1-\sigma} < 1$.

6.2.1.2 Representation in Detrended Form It is useful to express program (6.3) in terms of detrended variables. To this end, we divide all variables except leisure by the cumulative balanced growth path growth rate, γ^t. Letting a bar denote detrended variables, this yields

$$\max_{\{\bar{c}_t, x_t, \bar{k}_{t+1}\}_{t \geq 0}} \sum_{t=0}^{\infty} \beta^t v^t \gamma^{t(1-\sigma)} u(\bar{c}_t, x_t) \tag{6.4}$$

$$\text{s.t.} \quad v\gamma\bar{k}_{t+1} = \bar{k}_t(1-\delta) + f(\bar{k}_t, 1-x_t) - \bar{c}_t, \quad \bar{k}_0 \text{ given, } \bar{k}_{t+1} \geq 0,$$

where u satisfies the restrictions discussed above. Defining $\beta^\star \equiv \beta\nu\gamma^{1-\sigma}$, the first-order conditions simplify to

$$u_x(\bar{c}_t, x_t) = f_L(\bar{k}_t, 1 - x_t)u_c(\bar{c}_t, x_t), \tag{6.5}$$

$$\nu\gamma u_c(\bar{c}_t, x_t) = \beta^\star(1 - \delta + f_K(\bar{k}_{t+1}, 1 - x_{t+1}))u_c(\bar{c}_{t+1}, x_{t+1}). \tag{6.6}$$

Condition (6.5) is equivalent to the intratemporal first-order condition in the decentralized equilibrium,

$$u_x(c_t, x_t) = f_L(k_t, (1 - x_t)\gamma^t)\gamma^t u_c(c_t, x_t) = w_t u_c(c_t, x_t),$$

and condition (6.6) is equivalent to the standard Euler equation

$$u_c(c_t, x_t) = \beta(1 - \delta + f_K(\bar{k}_{t+1}, 1 - x_{t+1}))u_c(c_{t+1}, x_{t+1}) = \beta R_{t+1} u_c(c_{t+1}, x_{t+1}).$$

Since along the balanced growth path, per-capita consumption grows at the gross rate γ, and thus marginal utility at rate $\gamma^{-\sigma}$, the Euler equation implies that the gross *interest rate* satisfies

$$R = \gamma^\sigma / \beta.$$

When $\gamma \neq 1$, the interest rate does not only reflect the psychological discount factor (as in the model without growth) but also the curvature of preferences and the growth rate. Intuitively, in a growing (or shrinking) economy, per-capita consumption grows (or shrinks) as well. Since the curvature of preferences determines the intertemporal elasticity of substitution, it also affects by how much the interest rate changes in order to induce the equilibrium growth rate of consumption. A lower willingness to intertemporally substitute (higher σ) implies that the gross interest rate differs more from β^{-1}.

6.2.2   Endogenous Growth

Long-run per-capita growth in the model of the previous subsection reflects exogenous productivity growth. The model explains why per-capita output, investment, and consumption grow at the same rate as productivity, but it does not explain why productivity—and thus, the economy—grows.

At the root of the model's inability to endogenously generate sustained per-capita growth lies an Inada condition: As the capital intensity rises, the marginal product of capital declines and the incentive to further accumulate falls. We now relax this condition and show that models with a suitably modified production function *endogenously* generate sustained per-capita *growth*. Throughout the subsection, we abstract from productivity and population growth, $\gamma = \nu = 1$, as well as from leisure, $x_t = 0$.

6.2.2.1   *Ak* Technology   Consider first an extreme production function,

$$f(K, L) = AK, \ A > 0.$$

Function f exhibits constant returns to scale but does not feature decreasing marginal products; in fact, the marginal product of capital is constant. With this *Ak technology* the resource constraint reads

$$k_{t+1} = k_t(1 - \delta) + Ak_t - c_t,$$

wages equal zero, and the interest rate is constant at value $R_t = 1-\delta+A$. The Euler equation therefore implies that marginal utility grows at a constant rate. With CIES preferences,

$$\left(\frac{c_{t+1}}{c_t}\right)^\sigma = \beta(1 - \delta + A),$$

and from the resource constraint (and the transversality condition), the capital stock grows at this rate as well. Dividing the resource constraint by k_t and substituting the expression for the growth rate yields the equilibrium initial consumption level, c_0, for a given initial capital stock, k_0:

$$[\beta(1 - \delta + A)]^{\frac{1}{\sigma}} = 1 - \delta + A - \frac{c_0}{k_0}.$$

The economy exhibits sustained positive per-capita growth if $\beta R > 1$ but household utility only is well defined if $\sum_{t=0}^{\infty} \beta^t c_t^{1-\sigma} < \infty$; that is, if $\beta(c_{t+1}/c_t)^{1-\sigma} < 1$. Both conditions are satisfied if

$$\beta(1 - \delta + A) > 1 > \beta(1 - \delta + A)^{1-\sigma}.$$

Note that both technology (A and δ) and preferences (β and σ) affect the equilibrium growth rate, unlike with a neoclassical production function. If policy affected the interest rate paid to investors (e.g., by taxing or subsidizing capital income), it would also affect the growth rate.

Since the initial consumption–capital ratio, c_0/k_0, is maintained forever and the growth rate is constant, the economy immediately reaches the balanced growth path. Unlike with a neoclassical production function, there are no transition dynamics and the initial capital stock has a permanent effect on consumption.

6.2.2.2 Two Sectors An unappealing feature of the *Ak* model is the assumption that labor is not productive (unless it is treated as a form of human capital). A *two-sector model*, where the first sector operates a neoclassical technology to produce the consumption good while the second produces investment goods with an *Ak* technology, remedies this problem. More importantly, the two-sector model makes clear that endogenous growth does not require a linear technology in all sectors; it suffices for the marginal product in the sector where the accumulated factor of production (capital) is produced, to be bounded from below.

Let k_t^c denote the capital stock employed in the production of consumption goods; the remaining capital stock, $k_t - k_t^c$, is used to produce investment goods. We assume a Cobb-Douglas production function with capital share $\alpha \in (0, 1)$ in the consumption goods sector and normalize labor to one. Market clearing thus requires $c_t = (k_t^c)^\alpha$ and the equilibrium wage equals the marginal product of labor. The welfare theorems apply so that we can solve the social planner problem to characterize equilibrium:

$$\max_{\{k_t^c, k_{t+1}\}_{t \geq 0}} \quad \sum_{t=0}^{\infty} \beta^t u((k_t^c)^\alpha)$$

$$\text{s.t.} \quad k_{t+1} = k_t(1 - \delta) + A(k_t - k_t^c), \quad k_0 \text{ given}, \quad k_{t+1} \geq 0, \quad k_t \geq k_t^c \geq 0.$$

The first-order conditions with respect to k_t^c and k_{t+1} yield

$$u'(c_t)\alpha(k_t^c)^{\alpha-1} = u'(c_{t+1})\alpha(k_{t+1}^c)^{\alpha-1}\beta(1 - \delta + A).$$

Along a balanced growth path, k_t^c and k_t grow at the same rate. Using this fact as well as the production function in the consumption goods sector and imposing CIES preferences, we find the following relation between the balanced growth path gross growth rates of consumption and capital, γ_c and γ_k respectively:

$$\gamma_c = \gamma_k^\alpha = [\beta(1 - \delta + A)]^{\frac{\alpha}{1-\alpha+\alpha\sigma}}.$$

Consumption grows more slowly than the capital stock because the marginal product of capital in the consumption goods sector decreases. In the decentralized equilibrium, the growth differential is reflected in a trend increase of the *price of consumption relative to investment goods*; this price differential renders investors indifferent between the two sectors, although the marginal product of capital in the consumption goods sector faces a secular decline.

6.2.2.3 Externalities
Endogenous growth does not require the marginal product to be bounded from below at the level of an individual firm; it suffices to have an aggregate production function with this property, and technological spillovers may cause the marginal products of capital at the aggregate and the firm level to differ.

To see this, consider a one-sector model where the representative firm operates the technology

$$y_t = A_t f(k_t, 1) = A_t k_t^\alpha.$$

Labor is normalized to unity, the capital share $\alpha \in (0, 1)$, and A_t denotes productivity which households and firms take as given.

Suppose that productivity depends positively on the average capital stock in the economy, which in equilibrium equals the capital stock owned by the representative household. Specifically, we assume that

$$A_t = A k_t^{1-\alpha}.$$

In equilibrium, per-capita output then is a linear function of the capital–labor ratio, $y_t = A k_t$, while at the level of an individual firm, the production function is neoclassical.

Since investment by an individual firm increases the productivity of all firms—it generates a positive *externality*—the conditions of the first welfare theorem are violated. To characterize the competitive equilibrium, we therefore need to derive the household and firm optimality conditions rather than those of a social planner. The program of the representative household that takes productivity as given reads

$$\max_{\{c_t, k_{t+1}\}_{t \geq 0}} \quad \sum_{t=0}^{\infty} \beta^t u(c_t)$$
$$\text{s.t.} \quad k_{t+1} = k_t(1 - \delta) + A_t k_t^\alpha - c_t, \quad k_0 \text{ given}, \quad k_{t+1} \geq 0.$$

Assuming CIES preferences, the first-order conditions of this program combined with the relation between productivity and the average capital stock reduce to

$$\left(\frac{c_{t+1}}{c_t} \right)^\sigma = \beta(1 - \delta + \alpha A).$$

Wages and interest rates are determined by firms' marginal products, taking productivity as given.

Under parameter conditions similar to those discussed earlier, equilibrium growth is strictly positive and the objective function is bounded. In contrast to the growth models considered so far, however, equilibrium growth is inefficiently low. Unlike individual households, a social planner would take into account that $A_t = A k_t^{1-\alpha}$ when solving the program. As a consequence, the social planner would implement an allocation with a higher growth rate than in competitive equilibrium.

6.3   Business Cycles

Next, we extend the general equilibrium model analyzed in section 3.1 to a *dynamic stochastic general equilibrium model*. We consider the economy's response to productivity shocks and sunspot shocks.

6.3.1   Real Business Cycles

To study productivity-driven or *real business cycles*, we modify the neoclassical growth model analyzed in subsection 6.2.1 in one respect: We assume that productivity does not only grow deterministically, at gross rate γ, but may also fluctuate stochastically. Specifically, we assume that per-capita capital stock, k_t, and per-capita labor supply, $1 - x_t$, generate per-capita output

$$y_t = f(k_t, (1 - x_t)\gamma^t) \cdot A_t,$$

where A_t—the new model element—stochastically fluctuates around a mean value of one. We assume that in period t and history ϵ^t, the relative deviation of $A_t(\epsilon^t)$ from its mean, $\hat{A}_t(\epsilon^t) \equiv A_t(\epsilon^t) - 1$, is governed by the first-order stochastic difference equation

$$\hat{A}_t(\epsilon^t) = \rho_A \hat{A}_{t-1}(\epsilon^{t-1}) + \iota_t(\epsilon^t), \quad 0 \leq \rho_A < 1,$$

where $\iota_t(\epsilon^t)$ is i.i.d. with mean zero.

The fundamental theorems of welfare economics apply. Accordingly, we can characterize the equilibrium in the real business cycle model by solving the planner's problem, corresponding to program (6.4) augmented by the stochastic productivity term. To simplify the notation, we adopt a recursive formulation and let $(\bar{k}_\circ, A_\circ)$ denote the state, $(\bar{c}_\circ, x_\circ, \bar{k}_+)$ the choice variables, and ι_+ the productivity innovation in the subsequent period. The Bellman equation reads

$$V(\bar{k}_\circ, A_\circ) = \max_{\bar{c}_\circ, x_\circ, \bar{k}_+} \left\{ u(\bar{c}_\circ, x_\circ) + \beta^\star \mathbb{E}\left[V(\bar{k}_+, A_+) | \bar{k}_\circ, A_\circ \right] \right\} \qquad (6.7)$$

$$\text{s.t.} \quad v\gamma \bar{k}_+ = \bar{k}_\circ(1 - \delta) + f(\bar{k}_\circ, 1 - x_\circ)A_\circ - \bar{c}_\circ,$$

$$A_+ = 1 + \rho_A(A_\circ - 1) + \iota_+,$$

where $\beta^\star \equiv \beta v\gamma^{1-\sigma}$, and the controls are bounded. The first-order conditions and envelope condition reduce to

$$u_x(\bar{c}_\circ, x_\circ) = f_L(\bar{k}_\circ, 1 - x_\circ)A_\circ u_c(\bar{c}_\circ, x_\circ), \qquad (6.8)$$

$$v\gamma u_c(\bar{c}_\circ, x_\circ) = \beta^\star \mathbb{E}[\{1 - \delta + f_K(\bar{k}_+, 1 - x_+)A_+\} u_c(\bar{c}_+, x_+) | \bar{k}_\circ, A_\circ], \qquad (6.9)$$

where $(\bar{c}_+, x_+)$ denote optimal choices in the subsequent period. These equilibrium conditions differ from (6.5) and (6.6) only insofar as marginal products are augmented by the corresponding A terms and future outcomes are weighted by their respective conditional probabilities.

In the special case with a Cobb-Douglas production function, full depreciation, and a utility function that is logarithmic in consumption and additively separable, analytical solutions for $(\bar{c}_\circ, x_\circ, \bar{k}_+)$ are available. To derive the equilibrium allocation under more general assumptions, we may resort to an approximate solution based on the linearized equilibrium conditions.

For the latter strategy, consider first the deterministic balanced growth path that results when A_t always equals one. The steady-state values of the detrended variables, $(\bar{k}, \bar{c}, x)$, satisfy

$$v\gamma \bar{k} = \bar{k}(1 - \delta) + f(\bar{k}, 1 - x) - \bar{c},$$

$$u_x(\bar{c}, x) = f_L(\bar{k}, 1 - x)u_c(\bar{c}, x),$$

$$v\gamma u_c(\bar{c}, x) = \beta^\star(1 - \delta + f_K(\bar{k}, 1 - x))u_c(\bar{c}, x).$$

Linearizing the resource constraint in program (6.7), as well as the optimality conditions (6.8) and (6.9) around the steady state values $(\bar{k}, \bar{c}, x)$, yields a system of linear difference equations. In forming this system, we exploit the certainty equivalence property: Approximating a nonlinear function h of the variable z_+ to the first order around z yields $\mathbb{E}_\circ[h(z_+)] \approx \mathbb{E}_\circ[h(z) + h'(z) \cdot (z_+ - z)] = h(z) + h'(z) \cdot (\mathbb{E}_\circ[z_+] - z)$; that is, the linearized system only includes the conditional mean (and no higher moments) of the random variable. Using this property and substituting the linearized intratemporal first-order condition into the other two linearized equilibrium conditions, we arrive at (switching to sequence notation)

$$
\begin{bmatrix} \hat{k}_{t+1}(\epsilon^t) \\ \mathbb{E}_t[\hat{c}_{t+1}(\epsilon^{t+1})] \end{bmatrix} = M \begin{bmatrix} \hat{k}_t(\epsilon^{t-1}) \\ \hat{c}_t(\epsilon^t) \end{bmatrix} + N_1 \mathbb{E}_t[\hat{A}_{t+1}(\epsilon^{t+1})] + N_0 \hat{A}_t(\epsilon^t)
$$

$$
= M \begin{bmatrix} \hat{k}_t(\epsilon^{t-1}) \\ \hat{c}_t(\epsilon^t) \end{bmatrix} + N \hat{A}_t(\epsilon^t).
$$

Here, a circumflex denotes relative deviations from the steady-state value (e.g., $\hat{c}_t \equiv (\bar{c}_t - \bar{c})/\bar{c}$); the elements of the 2×2 matrices M, N_0, and N_1 contain parameters and functions evaluated at the steady-state values; and $N \equiv \rho_A N_1 + N_0$.

This system with one predetermined (capital) and one nonpredetermined endogenous variable (consumption) differs twofold from the system analyzed previously, in the context of the deterministic representative agent model (see subsection 3.1.7). First, matrices M and N do not only reflect the linearized resource constraint and Euler equation in general equilibrium but they also incorporate the intratemporal first-order condition that relates leisure to consumption, the capital stock, and productivity. Second, the presence of temporary productivity variation introduces an exogenous shock process. As noted before, stochasticity of the productivity shock does not introduce any additional complication because of certainty equivalence.

We solve the system using essentially the same approach as in the deterministic environment (see subsection 3.1.7). When the matrix M has one stable and one unstable eigenvalue, the equilibrium value $\hat{c}_t(\epsilon^t)$ is uniquely determined by the requirement that conditional on the state, the difference equation system generates paths for expected consumption and capital that converge to their steady-state values, $(\bar{c}, \bar{k})$. Moreover, given $\hat{k}_t(\epsilon^{t-1})$, $\hat{A}_t(\epsilon^t)$, and $\hat{c}_t(\epsilon^t)$, the intratemporal first-order condition uniquely determines $x_t(\epsilon^t)$. Appendix B.5 contains further discussion.

Figures 6.1–6.3 illustrate the response of the model economy to a *productivity shock*. We let

$$
u(c, x) = \ln(c) - \omega \frac{\ell^{1+\varphi}}{1 + \varphi}, \ \varphi > 0,
$$

where $\ell \equiv 1 - x$ and $\omega > 0$.[7] We compare three scenarios, distinguished by the autocorrelation coefficient, ρ_A, and the willingness of households to intertemporally substitute labor supply, $1/\varphi$.

Figure 6.1 illustrates the response to a temporary productivity shock, $\rho_A = 0$, when the elasticity of substitution equals unity, $\varphi = 1$. Productivity increases by one percent at date

---

[7] We also assume a Cobb-Douglas production function with capital share 0.3, a depreciation rate of 5 percent, and a discount factor $\beta = 0.98$. We choose ω such that steady-state labor supply equals 0.5.

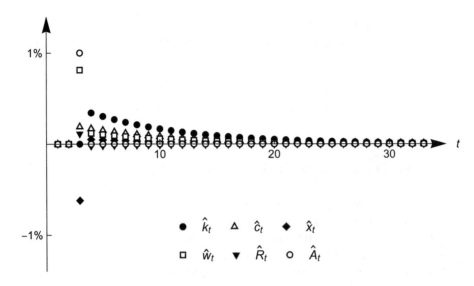

Figure 6.1
Effects of a productivity shock: $\rho_A = 0$ and $\varphi = 1$.

$t = 3$, $\iota_3 > 0$, and reverts to its steady-state value, A, at date $t = 4$. The endogenous variables, except for the predetermined capital stock, contemporaneously respond to the productivity shock. Wages and consumption rise relative to their steady-state values and eventually revert to the latter. Leisure falls on impact before rising in the subsequent period and similarly embarking on a path back to its steady-state value. The interest rate responds inversely, and the capital stock increases at date $t = 4$ before converging back to steady state.

To interpret these paths, consider a household in the decentralized equilibrium. Following the productivity shock, the household faces an increased wage and anticipates higher wages and lower interest rates in the future. The positive wealth effect induces higher consumption, while the lower interest rates induce a substitution effect toward present consumption (see the Euler equation (6.9)). In the labor market, the productivity increase shifts the labor supply schedule inward (due to an income effect) and the demand schedule outward. The high wage at date $t = 3$ induces a substitution effect from leisure to goods consumption (see condition (6.8)) and hours increase. In subsequent periods, the wealth effect on leisure consumption dominates the substitution effect, leading to an increase in leisure consumption relative to steady state.

The higher output due to increased productivity and stronger labor supply at date $t = 3$ is not fully consumed. Part of it is saved and invested, generating a higher capital stock in subsequent periods. It is this higher capital stock from date $t = 4$ onward that keeps wages persistently elevated and interest rates subdued. From date $t = 4$ onward, negative

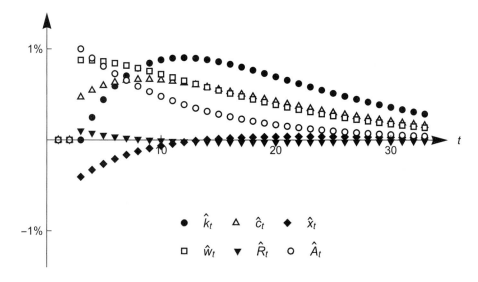

Figure 6.2
Effects of a productivity shock: $\rho_A = 0.9$ and $\varphi = 1$.

net investment generates resources for consumption. Capital accumulation at date $t = 3$ and the reversal starting at date $t = 4$ thus supports consumption smoothing.

By construction, the equilibrium dynamics satisfy the resource constraint and the optimality conditions (6.8) and (6.9) at all times. Note, however, that the Euler equation only prescribes equality of the marginal rate of substitution and the marginal rate of transformation in expectation. At the time of the shock, $t = 3$, the marginal rates of substitution and transformation differ. Accordingly, the realized interest and consumption growth rates do not satisfy the deterministic version of the Euler equation. Equilibrium goods and leisure consumption in the shock period are determined in a forward-looking way, by the requirement that their choice places the economy on the saddle path subject to the expected productivity shock sequence.

Figure 6.2 illustrates the response under the assumption that the shock is persistent, $\rho_A = 0.9$. We keep the elasticity of substitution unchanged. The persistent technological improvement gives rise to a similarly persistent rise in wages. Capital is accumulated over a longer period. The persistent rise of the interest rate coupled with the strong wealth effect due to higher wages induces households to choose a hump-shaped consumption path. Because of the persistent rise of wages, leisure consumption remains subdued—and labor supply is stimulated—over an extended period.

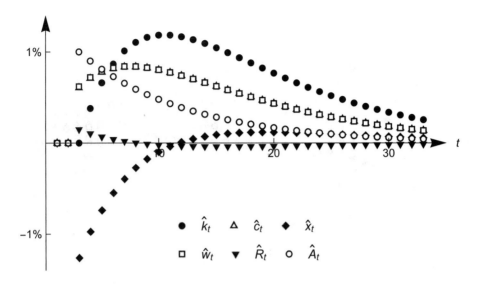

Figure 6.3
Effects of a productivity shock: $\rho_A = 0.9$ and $\varphi = 0.01$.

Finally, figure 6.3 illustrates the response under the assumption that the shock is persistent, $\rho_A = 0.9$, and the elasticity of substitution very high, $\varphi = 0.01$.[8] The higher elasticity implies a more pronounced labor supply response. The logarithmic utility of consumption and the inelastic disutility of labor supply imply (from the intratemporal first-order condition) that consumption and wages exceed their respective steady-state values by the same proportion.

6.3.1.1   Recursive Competitive Equilibrium   We have characterized equilibrium dynamics by solving the system of linear difference equations that approximates the nonlinear equilibrium conditions. Alternatively, we may use recursive methods. This is straightforward in the baseline real business cycle model, where the decentralized equilibrium allocation corresponds to the allocation chosen by a social planner. It suffices to (numerically) solve the planner's program (6.7); equilibrium dynamics then are fully described by the planner's policy functions.

We can also represent the decentralized equilibrium recursively, as a *recursive competitive equilibrium*, and solve for it numerically based on that representation. This solution strategy is available independently of whether the decentralized equilibrium allocation solves a social planner problem or not. It requires, however, that we carefully distinguish

---

[8] We adjust the value for ω to keep steady-state labor supply at the same level as in the first two scenarios.

between the state variables of individual agents (e.g., the capital stock of an individual household) and aggregate state variables that individuals take as given (e.g., the economy-wide capital stock that determines equilibrium wages and interest rates). Without this distinction, we would characterize the equilibrium in an economy where individuals choose aggregate variables.

The objects in a recursive competitive equilibrium are functions of the state. They include value functions as well as policy functions of the optimizing agents; price functions; and laws of motion for the aggregate state variables, which describe how decision makers perceive these variables to evolve over time.

In the case of the real business cycle model, the aggregate state variables are productivity, $A_\circ$, and the economy-wide capital stock, $\bar{K}_\circ$; the state of the representative household additionally includes the household's capital stock, $\bar{k}_\circ$. In equilibrium, $\bar{k}_\circ = \bar{K}_\circ$. The recursive competitive equilibrium is given by a value function and policy functions, $V, \bar{k}', c, x$, respectively, which are functions of the household's state; as well as price functions and a law of motion for capital, $w, R, \bar{K}'$, respectively, which are functions of the aggregate state, such that the following conditions are satisfied: First, the value function satisfies the household's Bellman equation subject to the budget constraint, law of motion for productivity, law of motion for aggregate capital, and price taking,

$$
\begin{aligned}
V(\bar{k}_\circ, A_\circ, \bar{K}_\circ) &= \max_{c_\circ, x_\circ, \bar{k}_+} \left\{ u(c_\circ, x_\circ) + \beta^\star \mathbb{E}\left[V(\bar{k}_+, A_+, \bar{K}_+) | \bar{k}_\circ, A_\circ, \bar{K}_\circ \right] \right\} \\
c_\circ &= R(A_\circ, \bar{K}_\circ)\bar{k}_\circ + w(A_\circ, \bar{K}_\circ)(1 - x_\circ) - \nu\gamma\bar{k}_+, \\
A_+ &= 1 + \rho_A(A_\circ - 1) + \iota_+, \\
\bar{K}_+ &= \bar{K}'(A_\circ, \bar{K}_\circ);
\end{aligned}
$$

and the policy functions are associated with the optimal household choices. Second, the price functions reflect constant returns to scale and competitive firm behavior, and both the price functions and the law of motion for capital are consistent with the policy functions and market clearing,

$$
\begin{aligned}
w(A_\circ, \bar{K}_\circ) &= f_L(\bar{K}_\circ, 1 - x(\bar{K}_\circ, A_\circ, \bar{K}_\circ))A_\circ, \\
R(A_\circ, \bar{K}_\circ) &= 1 - \delta + f_K(\bar{K}_\circ, 1 - x(\bar{K}_\circ, A_\circ, \bar{K}_\circ))A_\circ, \\
\bar{K}'(A_\circ, \bar{K}_\circ) &= \bar{k}'(\bar{K}_\circ, A_\circ, \bar{K}_\circ).
\end{aligned}
$$

In a more general environment with heterogeneous agents, the equilibrium is given by several value functions and associated policy functions, and the consistency and market clearing requirements account for the heterogeneous groups.

To find an approximate solution to the above system, we may discretize the aggregate state space as well as the state space of the representative household on grids and represent the functions by vectors whose sizes correspond to the sizes of the respective grids. (For notational simplicity, in what follows we do not distinguish between the original functions and the vectors.) Next, we guess $w, R, \bar{K}'$, and given that guess, we solve the household's problem by standard dynamic programming techniques. We check whether the consistency requirements are satisfied at each grid point. If they are not satisfied we update the guess and solve the household's problem again. This procedure is repeated until the consistency requirements are (approximately) satisfied.

6.3.2   Sunspot-Driven Business Cycles

In the real business cycle model, fluctuations are driven by exogenous shocks to productivity. A level of productivity and its expected future path is associated with a unique equilibrium sequence for each endogenous variable. The uniqueness reflects the saddle-path property of the dynamic system: Conditional on the predetermined capital stock, only specific values for consumption and leisure are consistent with the equilibrium conditions, including the requirement that system dynamics be stable. In turn, the saddle-path property reflects the fact that the number of unstable eigenvalues in the dynamic system equals the number of nonpredetermined variables.

Consider now a different dynamic system where the number of stable eigenvalues is strictly larger than the number of predetermined variables. Conditional on the predetermined capital stock, consumption and leisure then are *indeterminate*—multiple initial values are consistent with the equilibrium conditions; see appendix B.5. As a consequence, the endogenous variables may not only respond to fundamental shocks (e.g., productivity shocks) but also to nonfundamental *sunspot shocks*. The latter do not affect technology, preferences, or other fundamentals in the economy; their only role is to coordinate rational expectations that are not pinned down by fundamentals. We now analyze this possibility.

We assume that there are no fundamental shocks at all, and that due to a modification of the production function, the number of stable eigenvalues exceeds the number of predetermined variables by one, such that the system does not exhibit the saddle-path property. Conditional on the capital stock, the equilibrium conditions including the stability requirement then leave one degree of freedom for the initial level of consumption or leisure, and this opens up the possibility for a nonfundamental sunspot shock to select an equilibrium.

Specifically, we assume that the production function exhibits *increasing returns to scale*, similar to the production function in the growth model with externalities (see subsection 6.2.2); output per capita is given by

$$y_t = f(k_t, (1 - x_t)\gamma^t) \cdot A_t,$$

where A_t does not exogenously fluctuate as in the real business cycle model, but instead is determined by aggregate factor inputs that each individual firm and household takes as given:

$$A_t = f(k_t, (1 - x_t)\gamma^t)^\chi, \ \chi \geq 0.$$

For $\chi = 0$, the model reduces to the real business cycle model with constant productivity.

Due to increasing returns to scale, the economy does not satisfy the conditions of the welfare theorems. To characterize the decentralized equilibrium, we therefore rely on the resource constraint as well as the private sector first-order conditions. These equilibrium conditions differ from the conditions in the real business cycle model (equations (6.7)–(6.9)) because A_t is replaced by $f(k_t, (1 - x_t)\gamma^t)^\chi$. We conjecture a balanced growth path along which per-capita consumption, capital, and output grow at the common gross rate, μ. The equilibrium conditions in terms of detrended variables then read (suppressing histories and writing ℓ_t for $1 - x_t$)

$$
\begin{aligned}
\nu\mu\bar{k}_{t+1} &= \bar{k}_t(1 - \delta) + \mu^{-t}f(\bar{k}_t\mu^t, \ell_t\gamma^t)^{1+\chi} - \bar{c}_t, \\
u_x(\bar{c}_t, x_t)\mu^t &= f_L(\bar{k}_t\mu^t, \ell_t\gamma^t)\gamma^t f(\bar{k}_t\mu^t, \ell_t\gamma^t)^\chi u_c(\bar{c}_t, x_t), \\
\nu\mu u_c(\bar{c}_t, x_t) &= \beta^\star \mathbb{E}_t[\{1 - \delta + f_K(\bar{k}_{t+1}\mu^{t+1}, \ell_{t+1}\gamma^{t+1})f(\bar{k}_{t+1}\mu^{t+1}, \ell_{t+1}\gamma^{t+1})^\chi\}u_c(\bar{c}_{t+1}, x_{t+1})],
\end{aligned}
$$

where $\beta^\star \equiv \beta\nu\mu^{1-\sigma}$. With Cobb-Douglas technology a balanced growth path indeed exists. The growth rate along this path is given by

$$
\mu \equiv \gamma^{\frac{(1-\alpha)(1+\chi)}{1-\alpha(1+\chi)}},
$$

where α denotes the capital share in production; note that μ reduces to γ if $\chi = 0$. The steady state of the detrended variables, $(\bar{k}, \bar{c}, x)$, is unique.

Linearizing the system of equilibrium conditions around the steady state and reducing it to a system of two difference equations in capital and consumption yields the system

$$
\begin{bmatrix} \hat{k}_{t+1}(\epsilon^t) \\ \mathbb{E}_t[\hat{c}_{t+1}(\epsilon^{t+1})] \end{bmatrix} = M \begin{bmatrix} \hat{k}_t(\epsilon^{t-1}) \\ \hat{c}_t(\epsilon^t) \end{bmatrix}.
$$

A circumflex denotes relative deviations from the steady state and the elements of the 2×2 matrix M contain parameters and functions evaluated at steady-state values.

If φ is sufficiently small (marginal utility of leisure is inelastic) and χ sufficiently large (output has large positive externalities), the matrix M has two stable eigenvalues. Intuitively, when households are willing to work more at nearly the same wage and the marginal product of labor *increases* with labor input, then different combinations of consumption and leisure satisfy the intratemporal first-order condition.

Figure 6.4 illustrates the economy's response to a sunspot shock at date $t = 3$, which coordinates expectations to anticipate a contemporaneous rise in productivity. No additional sunspot shocks occur later in time; that is, all variables assume their expected values from date $t = 4$ onward. As before, we assume logarithmic utility of consumption as well as inelastic disutility of labor ($\varphi = 0.01$); the intratemporal first-order condition therefore implies $\hat{c}_t(\epsilon^t) \approx \hat{w}_t(\epsilon^t)$.

In response to the anticipated productivity increase, labor supply and output rise and actual productivity therefore rises as well, confirming the beliefs. This is reflected in a higher wage, a higher interest rate, higher consumption, and capital accumulation. In the

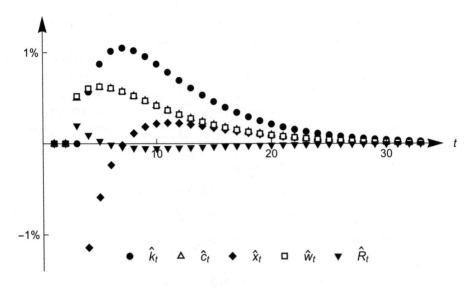

Figure 6.4
Effects of a sunspot shock: $\varphi = 0.01$.

subsequent period, labor supply starts to revert while the capital stock continues to grow; the interest rate falls but remains elevated and consumption and wages increase further. During the transition, labor supply and the interest rate fall below their initial levels before eventually, all variables monotonically converge to their steady-state values.

6.4   Bibliographic Notes

Becker (1965) studies the allocation of time in a static model. Lucas and Rapping (1969) and Heckman (1974) analyze intertemporal labor supply. Hansen (1985) and Rogerson (1988) study economies with indivisible labor. Subsection 6.1.3 follows Constantinides and Duffie (1996) and Heathcote et al. (2014).

The restrictions on technology in the model of subsection 6.2.1 are due to Uzawa (1961); the proof follows Schlicht (2006). King et al. (1988) derive the restrictions on preferences; see also King et al. (2002, p. 94). The balanced growth path restrictions imply that the model replicates the Kaldor (1961) *stylized facts* including a constant capital–output ratio, constant wage growth and interest rates, and constant factor shares in national income. The two-sector model in subsection 6.2.2 is due to Rebelo (1991) and the model with externalities follows Romer (1986); see also Jones and Manuelli (1990).

Mirrlees (1965) and Brock and Mirman (1972) analyze the stochastic growth model without a labor–leisure choice. The real business cycle model is due to Kydland and Prescott (1982), Long and Plosser (1983), and King et al. (1988); see also Cooley (1995). King et al.

(2002) describe the solution strategy followed in the text. Lucas and Prescott (1971) analyze a recursive competitive equilibrium; see also Prescott and Mehra (1980) and Stokey and Lucas (1989). The model with sunspots follows Benhabib and Farmer (1994).

Related Topics and Additional References Krusell and Smith (1998) introduce aggregate risk in the Aiyagari (1994) model. They represent the wealth distribution, which is an element of the state, based on a few moments; computed approximate equilibrium dynamics suggest that the wealth distribution has a minor effect on aggregate investment and consumption because poor households save and consume little and the rich self-insure well.

Lucas (1987, chapter 3) assesses the cost of business cycles based on a comparison of the utility of two consumption sequences, one following a deterministic growth path and the other fluctuating around such a path. Alvarez and Jermann (2004) relate the marginal cost of consumption fluctuations to asset prices.

Azariadis (1981) analyzes sunspot-driven business cycles in overlapping generations models.

First-order approximations of equilibrium conditions are inappropriate when nonlinearities are key for the object of interest. For instance, a linear approximation of the Euler equation cannot capture the precautionary savings motive, which hinges on the convexity of the marginal utility function. Schmitt-Grohé and Uribe (2004) discuss higher-order approximations based on *perturbation methods*.

Acemoglu (2009) covers economic growth and Benhabib and Farmer (1999) cover indeterminacy and sunspots.

7 The Open Economy

We have so far studied closed economies. In an open economy, agents import and export goods and services and they save, borrow, and insure internationally. The real exchange rate and its variation over time affects these choices, and the current account and net foreign asset position of a country reflects them.

We introduce these variables and study the determinants of international trade, investment, and insurance. We also analyze the welfare implications of economic integration.

7.1 Current Account and Net Foreign Assets

A country's *trade balance* is defined as domestic production net of absorption. The *current account* equals the trade balance plus income from net foreign assets and net transfers from abroad; absent capital gains or losses, it also equals the change in *net foreign assets*. Ceteris paribus, a trade surplus implies an equal-sized current account surplus and net foreign asset accumulation, as foreigners finance their acquisition of resources by selling assets to domestic agents.

Consider the economy with homogeneous households, firms, and capital accumulation analyzed in section 3.1, where we now allow for a nonzero trade balance, tb_t, current account, ca_t, and net foreign asset position, nfa_t. Abstracting from net transfers and capital gains, and letting a_t denote total household assets (at home and abroad) and k_t the domestic capital stock, the trade balance, current account, and net foreign assets satisfy

$$
\begin{aligned}
tb_t &= f(k_t, 1) - c_t - (k_{t+1} - k_t(1 - \delta)), \\
ca_t &= f(k_t, 1) - c_t - (k_{t+1} - k_t(1 - \delta)) + (R_t - 1)nfa_t, \\
nfa_t &= a_t - k_t,
\end{aligned}
$$

where f and c_t denote the neoclassical production function and consumption, respectively.

We assume that the economy is not only *open* but also *small*; that is, domestic saving does not affect world interest rates and net foreign assets can freely adjust. We also assume that physical capital can costlessly be moved across borders (see section 8.1 for models with capital adjustment costs), such that the domestic and international rental rates on capital,

r_t, coincide. Firms take this rate as given and optimally choose labor and capital inputs. The firms' optimality conditions combined with the labor market clearing condition imply

$$f_K(k_t, 1) = r_t,$$
$$f_L(k_t, 1) = w_t.$$

The first condition pins down the capital stock and the second determines the wage, w_t. Note that with constant world rental rates and time-invariant technology, domestic capital stock and wages are constant at all times.

The remaining equilibrium conditions include the dynamic budget constraint of households and the Euler equation,

$$a_{t+1} = a_t R_t + w_t - c_t,$$
$$u'(c_t) = \beta R_{t+1} u'(c_{t+1}),$$

where the gross interest rate reflects the rental rate and depreciation, $R_t = 1 + r_t - \delta$. Households also satisfy a transversality condition. From the definition of net foreign assets as well as the budget constraints of households and firms,

$$nfa_{t+1} = nfa_t R_t + k_t R_t - k_{t+1} + w_t - c_t = nfa_t R_t - k_{t+1} + f(k_t, 1) + k_t(1 - \delta) - c_t.$$

The current account identity therefore implies $ca_t = nfa_{t+1} - nfa_t$.

To solve for equilibrium consumption, we iterate the dynamic budget constraint forward (see subsections 2.1.2–2.1.3). Assuming for simplicity that $R_t = R = \beta^{-1}$ (such that consumption is constant over time), we find

$$c_t \sum_{s=0}^{\infty} R^{-s} = a_t R + \sum_{s=0}^{\infty} R^{-s} w_{t+s} \text{ or } c_t = \rho \left(a_t R + \sum_{s=0}^{\infty} R^{-s} w_{t+s} \right), \qquad (7.1)$$

where we define the annuity factor $\rho \equiv 1/\left(\sum_{s=0}^{\infty} R^{-s} \right) = (R - 1)/R$. As usual, equilibrium consumption reflects wealth. Unlike in closed-economy general equilibrium models, however, the interest rate is exogenous and net foreign assets allow for a decoupling of domestic saving and investment, and thus consumption and capital accumulation.

Now abstract from production and capital (such that $a_t = nfa_t$) and let $\{w_{t+s}\}_{s\geq0}$ in equation (7.1) denote a possibly time-varying endowment sequence. The trade balance then equals $tb_t = w_t - c_t$. Let $\tilde{w}_t$ denote the *permanent income* corresponding to the endowment sequence,

$$\tilde{w}_t \equiv \rho \sum_{s=0}^{\infty} R^{-s} w_{t+s}.$$

From the household's dynamic budget constraint, consumption equals $nfa_t R + w_t - nfa_{t+1}$, and from optimality condition (7.1), it equals $\rho \, nfa_t R + \tilde{w}_t$. Equalizing the two expressions implies $nfa_t R(\rho - 1) + nfa_{t+1} = w_t - \tilde{w}_t$ or

$$ca_t = nfa_{t+1} - nfa_t = w_t - \tilde{w}_t. \tag{7.2}$$

Condition (7.2) states that net foreign assets increase (decrease) when the endowment exceeds (falls short of) permanent income, reflecting the usual consumption-smoothing motive (see chapter 2).

Introducing endowment risk does not affect these findings (except that w_{t+s} in condition (7.1) is replaced by $\mathbb{E}_t[w_{t+s}(\epsilon^{t+s})]$) as long as certainty equivalence holds (see subsection 4.1.1).

7.2   Real Exchange Rate

Suppose next that the endowment has two components, a *nontradable* component, w_t^N, and a *tradable* component, w_t^T. Nontradables only can be consumed domestically, while tradables can both be consumed domestically and shipped abroad at no cost. The tradable good serves as numeraire and the price of nontradables is denoted p_t.

Household consumption is a CES aggregate of the tradable and the nontradable goods,

$$c_t = c(c_t^T, c_t^N). \tag{7.3}$$

The price of c_t, which increases in p_t, is denoted $\mathcal{P}_t$ (see subsection 2.2.3 for the formula of $\mathcal{P}_t$). We define the *real exchange rate* as the price of one unit of domestic consumption relative to the price of a consumption unit abroad that we normalize to unity. The real exchange rate thus equals $\mathcal{P}_t$ and it increases in p_t—a higher price of nontradables implies a real exchange rate appreciation.

The household takes world interest rates as given and maximizes $\sum_{t=0}^{\infty} \beta^t u(c_t)$ subject to (7.3), the dynamic budget constraint,

$$
\begin{aligned}
a_{t+1} &= a_t R_t + w_t^T + w_t^N p_t - c_t \mathcal{P}_t \\
&= a_t R_t + w_t^T + w_t^N p_t - c_t^T - c_t^N p_t
\end{aligned}
$$

(assets are denominated in terms of the numeraire), and a no-Ponzi-game condition. The first-order conditions are given by (see subsection 2.2.3)

$$u'(c_t)/\mathcal{P}_t = \beta R_{t+1} u'(c_{t+1})/\mathcal{P}_{t+1}, \tag{7.4}$$

$$u'(c_t) c_T(c_t^T, c_t^N) = \beta R_{t+1} u'(c_{t+1}) c_T(c_{t+1}^T, c_{t+1}^N), \tag{7.5}$$

$$p_t = \frac{c_N(c_t^T, c_t^N)}{c_T(c_t^T, c_t^N)}, \tag{7.6}$$

where c_N and c_T denote partial derivative functions. Condition (7.4) represents the Euler equation for c_t; note that the own rate of interest for the consumption index equals $R_{t+1}\mathcal{P}_t/\mathcal{P}_{t+1}$. Condition (7.5) gives the Euler equation for tradable consumption whose own rate of interest equals R_{t+1}. Finally, condition (7.6) equalizes the relative price of nontradables and tradables and the corresponding marginal rate of substitution.

Assume that $\beta R_t = 1$ and $w_t^N = w^N$ in all periods. Imposing market clearing, $c_t^N = w^N$, conditions (7.5) and (7.6) then reduce to

$$u'(c_t)c_T(c_t^T, w^N) = u'(c_{t+1})c_T(c_{t+1}^T, w^N),$$

$$p_t = \frac{c_N(c_t^T, w^N)}{c_T(c_t^T, w^N)}.$$

From the first condition, the consumption index and both its components are constant over time. Domestic market clearing ($c_t^N = w^N$) and the household's intertemporal budget constraint then imply that c_t^T equals the net interest on net foreign assets plus permanent income from the tradable endowment sequence (condition (7.1) with c_t replaced by c_t^T and w_{t+s} replaced by w_{t+s}^T). Tradable consumption thus increases in the initial net asset position and the permanent income from tradable goods. In a slightly extended model with differentiated export and import goods, it also increases in the *terms of trade*—the price of exports relative to imports—since improved terms of trade increase the market value of the tradable endowment.

The second condition pins down the real exchange rate. Recall that nontradable consumption is fixed, while tradable consumption reflects the net asset position and the tradable endowment sequence (possibly accounting for the terms of trade). Higher net foreign assets or permanent income from tradables therefore increase the marginal rate of substitution on the right-hand side of the condition, and thus the price of nontradables and the real exchange rate. Intuitively, higher household wealth raises the demand for tradables and nontradables but with the latter in fixed supply, their equilibrium price must rise for markets to clear. We conclude that a wealthier economy (measured in terms of tradables) or one with a stronger preference for nontradables has a more appreciated real exchange rate.

Over longer horizons, the supply of nontraded goods is not given by an exogenous endowment sequence but determined by optimizing firms that shift production between the tradable and the nontradable sector, depending on where the marginal return is highest. This undermines the link between household wealth and the real exchange rate; in fact, the latter may be completely determined on the supply side.

To see this, suppose that competitive domestic firms employ capital and labor. Output of tradables and nontradables, respectively, is given by $A_t^T f^T(K_t^T, L_t^T)$ and $A_t^N f^N(K_t^N, L_t^N)$, where A_t^T and A_t^N denote productivity levels and the arguments of the constant-returns-to-scale functions f^T and f^N denote capital and labor inputs in the two sectors. Capital is internationally mobile and earns the exogenous rental rate r_t, while labor is mobile across sectors and earns the wage w_t.

For competitive firms to produce both goods, the marginal value products of all inputs must equal their respective rental rates, implying

$$A_t^T f_K^T(K_t^T, L_t^T) = r_t,$$
$$p_t A_t^N f_K^N(K_t^N, L_t^N) = r_t,$$
$$A_t^T f_L^T(K_t^T, L_t^T) = w_t,$$
$$p_t A_t^N f_L^N(K_t^N, L_t^N) = w_t.$$

Due to constant returns to scale, the marginal products are functions of the respective capital–labor ratios, k_t^T or k_t^N. Conditional on A_t^T, A_t^N, r_t (and independently of household preferences), the four conditions thus pin down $k_t^T, k_t^N, w_t,$ and p_t.

Higher tradable-sector productivity raises the price of nontradables. This follows from the fact that a higher A_t^T raises k_t^T (from the first condition), and thus w_t (from the third condition); that a higher w_t raises either p_t or k_t^N (from the fourth condition); and that p_t and k_t^N adjust in the same direction (from the second condition, because A_t^N and r_t are fixed). Intuitively, higher productivity in the tradable sector at given rental rates increases equilibrium wages. To attract workers, nontradable sector firms must pay higher wages even if their productivity is unchanged. For the marginal value products of capital and labor in the nontradable sector to remain unchanged and rise, respectively, both p_t and k_t^N must rise. Similar reasoning establishes that an increase in non-tradable-sector productivity lowers p_t.

For an alternative perspective, consider the zero-profit conditions of firms,

$$A_t^T f^T(k_t^T, 1) = w_t + k_t^T r_t,$$
$$p_t A_t^N f^N(k_t^N, 1) = w_t + k_t^N r_t,$$

which are implied by constant returns to scale and competition. Totally differentiating the zero-profit condition in the tradable sector (holding the rental rate fixed) and using the first-order condition with respect to K_t^T to cancel terms yields $dA_t^T f^T(k_t^T, 1) = dw_t$. This can be expressed as $\hat{A}_t^T = \hat{w}_t \sigma_t^T$ where a circumflex denotes an infinitesimal relative deviation and $\sigma_t^T \equiv w_t/(A_t^T f^T(k_t^T, 1))$ denotes the labor share in the tradable sector. Similarly, totally differentiating the zero-profit condition in the nontradable sector, using the first-order condition with respect to K_t^N to cancel terms and letting $\sigma_t^N \equiv w_t/(p_t A_t^N f^N(k_t^N, 1))$, yields $\hat{p}_t + \hat{A}_t^N = \hat{w}_t \sigma_t^N$.

Combining the two expressions, we find

$$\hat{p}_t = \hat{A}_t^T \frac{\sigma_t^N}{\sigma_t^T} - \hat{A}_t^N,$$

which confirms that an increase in tradable-sector productivity raises p_t while an increase in non-tradable-sector productivity decreases it. Intuitively, an increase in tradable-sector productivity lowers the unit cost of the tradable good. As a consequence, competition pushes up wages and the nontradable sector breaks even only if its output price rises. If productivity in both sectors rises, p_t still increases as long as tradable-sector productivity grows more quickly and the labor share in the nontradable sector is larger than in the tradable sector. When these two conditions are satisfied, the model predicts the *Baumol-Bowen effect*—the secular increase of the relative price of nontradables—as well as the *Harrod-Balassa-Samuelson effect*, namely real appreciations in countries with faster productivity growth, and thus higher incomes.

A change in the world interest rate also affects the real exchange rate. Calculations similar to the previous ones establish that, for constant productivity levels,

$$\hat{p}_t = \frac{dr_t}{p_t f^N}(k_t^N - k_t^T) = \frac{\hat{r}_t}{\sigma_t^T}(\sigma_t^T - \sigma_t^N).$$

A higher rental rate thus causes a decline in the price of nontradables (and a real depreciation) when the labor share in the tradable sector is smaller than in the nontradable sector. This result mirrors the *Stolper-Samuelson theorem*, according to which a price change benefits the production factor that is employed more intensively in the expanding sector.

7.3   Gains From Trade

Trade allows countries to mutually exploit *comparative advantage* that results from relative productivity or endowment differences. In addition to static gains, opening economies up generates *gains from trade* across time (saving and borrowing) and histories (risk sharing). Here, we analyze the intertemporal gains from trade.

Consider a model with one sector of production. The domestic economy is endowed with one unit of labor per period and a constant-returns-to-scale production function, f, that is the same as in the rest of the world (as is the depreciation rate, δ). Domestic assets equal the domestic capital stock plus net foreign assets, $a_t = k_t + nfa_t$. The budget constraint of the economy is given by

$$c_t = f(a_t - nfa_t, 1) + nfa_t r_t + a_t(1 - \delta) - a_{t+1}.$$

When the economy is closed, $nfa_t = 0$.

Suppose first that households are homogeneous. When the economy is closed, the household's saving choice satisfies the Euler equation

$$u'(c_t^c) = \beta(1 - \delta + f_K(a_{t+1}^c, 1))u'(c_{t+1}^c),$$

where the superscript "c" denotes closed economy outcomes. In the open economy, both the stock of domestic assets and its components—capital and net foreign assets—adjust as physical capital is reallocated across borders. The endogenous variables now satisfy

$$\begin{aligned} u'(c_t) &= \beta(1 - \delta + r_{t+1})u'(c_{t+1}), \\ r_t &= f_K(a_t - nfa_t, 1). \end{aligned}$$

From the budget constraint, a marginal change in net foreign assets affects consumption by $dc_t/d\,nfa_t = r_t - f_K(a_t - nfa_t, 1)$. Starting from the allocation in the closed economy, the welfare effect from marginally increasing nfa_t thus equals

$$u'(c_t)(r_t - f_K(a_t, 1)).$$

Note that the product $(r_t - f_K(a_t, 1))d\,nfa_t$ is positive, implying that disposable income rises and the welfare effect is positive. Intuitively, when capital flows into the economy, $d\,nfa_t < 0$, the marginal product of capital falls from $f_K(a_t, 1)$ to r_t and output benefits from productive capital that is financed by cheap foreign loans. Conversely, when capital flows out, $d\,nfa_t > 0$, the marginal product rises and domestic production falls but the inframarginal units of freed capital earn a rental rate abroad that exceeds the marginal product in autarky.

While capital in- or outflows unambiguously raise disposable income, they affect the returns on capital and labor unequally. When the international capital–labor ratio exceeds the domestic ratio in autarky, then opening up the economy lowers the rental rate but raises domestic wages. With homogeneous households this affects all households symmetrically. With heterogeneous households, in contrast, the opposing factor price effects have *distributive implications*; they imply that capital flows may benefit some groups while hurting others.

Consider, for example, the overlapping generations model with two-period lived households (see section 3.2), where the capital stock is owned by the old. Opening up the economy then affects the old differently from the young. In particular, capital inflows harm the old by lowering interest rates and benefit the young by increasing wages. Aggregate disposable income rises; with sufficiently high transfers from the young to the old, all cohorts benefit.

7.4 International Risk Sharing

The (aggregate) gains from intertemporal trade reflect efficiency gains due to the international equalization of marginal rates of transformation and substitution. Similar gains arise from the equalization of the marginal rate of substitution across histories; that is, from *international risk sharing*.

Consider the framework with tradable and nontradable endowments analyzed in section 7.2 and suppose that endowments are risky and households can trade a complete set of Arrow securities denominated in the tradable good (the numeraire). The equilibrium stochastic discount factor expressed in terms of the tradable good at date t, history ϵ^t, for date $t + s$, history ϵ^{t+s},

$$\beta^s \frac{u'(c_{t+s}(\epsilon^{t+s}))}{u'(c_t(\epsilon^t))} \frac{c_T(c_{t+s}^T(\epsilon^{t+s}), w_{t+s}^N(\epsilon^{t+s}))}{c_T(c_t^T(\epsilon^t), w_t^N(\epsilon^t))},$$

then is the same for all households in all countries. Equivalently, the stochastic discount factor expressed in terms of the consumption index, corrected for variation in the real exchange rate,

$$\beta^s \frac{u'(c_{t+s}(\epsilon^{t+s}))/\mathcal{P}_{t+s}(\epsilon^{t+s})}{u'(c_t(\epsilon^t))/\mathcal{P}_t(\epsilon^t)},$$

also is the same across countries. This follows from the risk-sharing result in section 4.2 (see condition (4.2)) and the equilibrium conditions (7.4) and (7.5) once we allow for risk.

If all goods are tradable, the real exchange rate is constant and marginal utility of the consumption index is perfectly correlated across countries. Country-specific shocks are perfectly diversified away in this case and consumption only reflects aggregate (global) shocks. If there are nontradable goods, in contrast, the real exchange rate is not necessarily constant, and marginal utilities of the consumption index are not perfectly correlated. In fact, marginal utility grows faster in countries whose consumer price index grows more quickly.

With incomplete financial markets, the correlation is even weaker. For example, when only a risk-free bond (denominated in tradables) is traded, then the expected stochastic discount factor corrected for the price index,

$$\beta^s \frac{\mathbb{E}_t[u'(c_{t+s}(\epsilon^{t+s}))/\mathcal{P}_{t+s}(\epsilon^{t+s})]}{u'(c_t(\epsilon^t))/\mathcal{P}_t(\epsilon^t)},$$

is equalized across countries. This follows from the stochastic Euler equation variant of condition (7.4).

7.5   Bibliographic Notes

Buiter (1981), Obstfeld (1982), Sachs (1981), and Svensson and Razin (1983) propose models of the current account with intertemporally optimizing agents. Kraay and Ventura (2000) study the current account implications of portfolio choice.

Baumol and Bowen (1966) describe the Baumol-Bowen effect. The Harrod-Balassa-Samuelson effect is named after Harrod (1933), Balassa (1964), and Samuelson (1964). Stolper and Samuelson (1941) analyze the effects of trade on factor prices.

Samuelson (1939) discusses the (static) gains from trade; Fried (1980) and Buiter (1981) analyze intergenerational welfare effects of dismantling barriers to international capital flows.

Backus and Smith (1993) analyze international risk sharing with nontradable goods.

Related Topics and Additional References   Dornbusch et al. (1977) study a tractable model of the terms of trade.

Obstfeld and Rogoff (1996), Harms (2016), and Uribe and Schmitt-Grohé (2017) cover international macroeconomics.

8 Frictions

We have so far mostly abstracted from frictions that delay adjustment or undermine trade. Important exceptions were borrowing constraints and other forms of market incompleteness that prevent an equalization of marginal rates of substitution and transformation. We now introduce (more of) such frictions.

We first focus on investment and analyze how costs of adjusting the capital stock and irreversibility impact investment behavior. Thereafter, we focus on the labor market and study how frictions in the process of matching workers and firms, as well as wage bargaining between the two parties, affect employment and the economy's response to technological change. Finally, we focus on financial contracts and markets. We analyze how asymmetric information and misaligned incentives shape financial contracts and render investment dependent on the investor's net worth, collateral, or asset prices. We also study the welfare implications of pecuniary externalities.

8.1 Capital Adjustment Frictions

In the models considered so far, physical investment contributes one-for-one to the buildup of capital. Departing from this assumption, we now posit investment frictions that take the form of *capital adjustment costs*. In the presence of such costs, firms solve dynamic optimization problems. Rather than renting capital on spot markets, they install and own capital with a view on current and future adjustment costs.

8.1.1 Convex Adjustment Costs and Tobin's q

Suppose that an increase of the capital stock, K_t, by the quantity I_t requires resources $I_t + \Xi(I_t, K_t)$, where Ξ denotes an adjustment cost function. We abstract from depreciation ($\delta = 0$) and assume the following properties of Ξ: Adjustment costs are weakly positive; equal to zero when there is no adjustment; as well as smooth and strictly *convex* in I_t. Moreover, a larger preexisting capital stock reduces the adjustment cost per unit of capital buildup. Formally, $\Xi(I, K) \geq 0$; $\Xi(0, K) = 0$; $\Xi_I(0, K) = 0$; $\Xi_{II}(I, K) > 0$; and $\Xi_K(I, K) < 0$.

Consider a firm operating a neoclassical production function, f, that faces wages, w_t, and a constant (for simplicity) gross interest rate, R, and chooses investment, I_t, and labor demand, L_t, to maximize the present value of profits. The Lagrangian associated with the firm's program reads

$$\mathcal{L} = \sum_{t=0}^{\infty} R^{-t} \left(f(K_t, L_t) - I_t - w_t L_t - \Xi(I_t, K_t) - q_t(K_{t+1} - K_t - I_t) \right),$$

where we attach the multiplier q_t to the law of motion for the capital stock. This multiplier—*Tobin's q*—represents the shadow value of *installed capital* relative to the price of investment goods or *outside capital*, which is normalized to unity. To see this, note that a marginal relaxation of the law of motion for capital increases the value of the firm's program by q_t. The first-order conditions with respect to L_t, K_{t+1}, and I_t, respectively, are given by

$$f_L(K_t, L_t) = w_t,$$
$$f_K(K_{t+1}, L_{t+1}) = \Xi_K(I_{t+1}, K_{t+1}) - q_{t+1} + Rq_t,$$
$$q_t = 1 + \Xi_I(I_t, K_t).$$

The first condition represents the usual labor demand relation: Conditional on installed capital, the firm equalizes the marginal product of labor and the wage. The second condition can be written as an asset pricing relation,

$$q_t = \frac{f_K(K_{t+1}, L_{t+1}) - \Xi_K(I_{t+1}, K_{t+1}) + q_{t+1}}{R}.$$

It states that the shadow price of installed capital equals the discounted shadow price in the subsequent period, plus the discounted dividend from installed capital; the dividend in turn equals the marginal product of capital (as usual) plus the reduction in future adjustment costs due to the higher capital stock (recall that $\Xi_K < 0$). Iterating the equation forward yields (absent bubbles)

$$q_0 = \sum_{t=1}^{\infty} \frac{f_K(K_t, L_t) - \Xi_K(I_t, K_t)}{R^t}.$$

Note that in the absence of adjustment costs, $q_t = 1$ and $f_K(K_t, L_t) = R - 1$, corresponding to our findings in the baseline model. Absent adjustment costs, it is therefore irrelevant whether firms own or rent the capital stock.

According to the condition $q_t = 1 + \Xi_I(I_t, K_t)$, the shadow price of installed capital equals the replacement cost of capital plus the marginal adjustment cost. Due to the convexity of Ξ, this condition yields a unique mapping from q_t to I_t (conditional on K_t)—for a given stock of installed capital, q is a sufficient statistic for investment.

The end-of-period value of the firm at date $t = 0$, V_0, is given by

$$V_0 = \sum_{t=1}^{\infty} \frac{f(K_t, L_t) - w_t L_t - \Xi(I_t, K_t) - I_t}{R^t},$$

evaluated at the optimal investment and labor demand. If both f and Ξ exhibit constant returns to scale, then the value of a marginal unit of installed capital, q_t, and the average value of installed capital, V_t / K_{t+1}, coincide (*marginal* and *average q* coincide). This follows from

$$
\begin{aligned}
K_{t+1} q_t &= \frac{f_K(K_{t+1}, L_{t+1}) K_{t+1} - \Xi_K(I_{t+1}, K_{t+1}) K_{t+1} + q_{t+1} K_{t+1}}{R} \\
&= \frac{f(K_{t+1}, L_{t+1}) - w_{t+1} L_{t+1} - \Xi_K(I_{t+1}, K_{t+1}) K_{t+1} + (1 + \Xi_I(I_{t+1}, K_{t+1}))(K_{t+2} - I_{t+1})}{R} \\
&= \frac{f(K_{t+1}, L_{t+1}) - w_{t+1} L_{t+1} - \Xi(I_{t+1}, K_{t+1}) - I_{t+1} + q_{t+1} K_{t+2}}{R} \\
&= \sum_{s=t+1}^{\infty} \frac{f(K_s, L_s) - w_s L_s - \Xi(I_s, K_s) - I_s}{R^{s-t}} = V_t.
\end{aligned}
$$

The fact that marginal and average q coincide implies that the gross rate of return on shares of the firm equals R.

Suppose that Ξ is a quadratic function, $\Xi(I, K) = \xi I^2/(2K)$ where $\xi > 0$. Assuming for simplicity that labor demand is fixed at L, the optimality conditions derived earlier then reduce to

$$I_t \xi = (q_t - 1) K_t,$$

$$R q_t - q_{t+1} =$$

$$f_K(K_{t+1}, L) + \frac{\xi}{2}\left(\frac{I_{t+1}}{K_{t+1}}\right)^2 = f_K\left(K_t\left(1 + \frac{q_t - 1}{\xi}\right), L\right) + \frac{1}{2\xi}(q_{t+1} - 1)^2.$$

In steady state, the capital stock K satisfies $R = 1 + f_K(K, L)$ and investment and the shadow price are given by $I = 0$ and $q = 1$.

A first-order Taylor expansion around the steady state yields the following linear dynamic system in the variables $dK_t \equiv K_t - K$ and $dq_t \equiv q_t - 1$:

$$
\begin{aligned}
dK_{t+1} &= dK_t + \frac{K}{\xi} dq_t, \\
dq_{t+1} &= \left(R - \frac{K f_{KK}(K, L)}{\xi}\right) dq_t - f_{KK}(K, L) dK_t.
\end{aligned}
$$

The matrix governing the system dynamics,

$$M \equiv \begin{bmatrix} 1 & K/\xi \\ -f_{KK}(K, L) & R - K f_{KK}(K, L)/\xi \end{bmatrix},$$

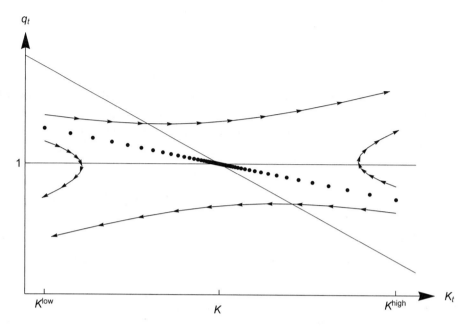

Figure 8.1
Dynamics of installed capital and its shadow price: Steady state, saddle path, and off-equilibrium
dynamics.

has one stable and one unstable eigenvalue. Since capital is predetermined while the
shadow price can instantaneously adjust, the linear system is saddle-path stable: For any
initial level of installed capital, K_0, there exists a unique shadow price, q_0, such that starting
from (K_0, q_0), the dynamic system prescribes a path that converges to the steady state.

Figure 8.1 illustrates the dynamics by means of a phase diagram in (K, q) space. The
horizontal line depicts points at which the capital stock is constant, $K_{t+1} = K_t$. Below
(above) that locus, $q_t < (>)1$ and the capital stock falls (grows). The decreasing line
depicts points with time-invariant shadow prices, $q_{t+1} = q_t$. To the left (right) of that
locus, the marginal product of capital is high (low) and the shadow price falls (rises). The
paths indicated by dots and arrows represent adjustment paths starting from two initial
capital stocks, K^{low} and K^{high}. All these paths satisfy the two conditions governing system
dynamics, but only the dotted paths follow the saddle path and converge to the steady state,
$(K, 1)$.

Using the phase diagram, we can analyze the effect of productivity and interest rates
on investment. Both higher productivity and lower interest rates increase the discounted
marginal products of capital; this is reflected in an outward shift of the steady-state shadow
price relation (the decreasing line in figure 8.1). The saddle path therefore shifts out as well,

and for a given initial level of capital the shadow price and thus firm value rise. Intuitively, the value of installed capital increases because the discounted marginal products are higher, and the marginal products are higher because the capital stock does not immediately adjust. Over time, the firm builds up capital until the shadow price reaches its steady-state value of one.

In general equilibrium, the capital stock and q_t interact with household consumption and saving. As usual, the household Euler equation relates the growth rate of consumption to the gross interest rate which now equals

$$R_{t+1} = \frac{f_K(K_{t+1}, L_{t+1}) - \Xi_K(I_{t+1}, K_{t+1}) + q_{t+1}}{q_t}.$$

8.1.2 Nonconvex Adjustment Costs

If the adjustment cost function is not convex, then q_t ceases to be a sufficient statistic for investment. We analyze this case in a two-period model. Throughout, we assume that the firm has an initial stock of installed capital, K_0; chooses investment or disinvestment, I_0; and maximizes firm value, $(f(K_1, L) + K_1)/R - \Xi(I_0, K_0) - I_0$, subject to the law of motion for capital, $K_1 = K_0 + I_0$.[9]

Consider first the case without adjustment costs, $\Xi(I_0, K_0) \equiv 0$. Let $K_1^\star$ denote the optimal capital stock at date $t = 1$ in this case, that is $f_K(K_1^\star, L) = R - 1$. Clearly, in equilibrium, $I_0 = K_1^\star - K_0$ and $q_0 = 1$.

Second, with convex adjustment costs of the type discussed in subsection 8.1.1, equilibrium is characterized by the conditions

$$q_0 = \frac{f_K(K_1, L) + 1}{R},$$
$$q_0 = 1 + \Xi_I(I_0, K_0).$$

Investment or disinvestment is weakly smaller than in the frictionless case. Moreover, $q_0 \neq 1$ unless $K_1^\star = K_0$. The solid lines in figure 8.2 illustrate the relation between K_0, q_0, and I_0 in the case with convex adjustment costs.

Turning next to *nonconvex adjustment costs*, consider a *fixed cost*, that is $\Xi(I_0, K_0) = \Xi > 0$ if $I \neq 0$ and zero otherwise. The optimal policy then consists of either not adjusting the capital stock at all, or fully adjusting it to the frictionless level. In the former case, q_0 differs from unity while in the latter, it does not. Either way, q_0 is not a sufficient statistic for investment. The dashed lines in figure 8.2 illustrate the case with a fixed adjustment cost.

Finally, as another example of nonconvex adjustment costs, consider *proportional costs* of adjustment, $\Xi(I_0, K_0) = \xi|I_0|, \xi > 0$. Now, the firm faces a constant marginal cost of

---

[9] We also assume that there are no adjustment costs in the second period, such that $q_1 = 1$ and $\Xi_K(I_1, K_1) = 0$. Second-period capital, K_1, therefore contributes one-to-one to second-period profits.

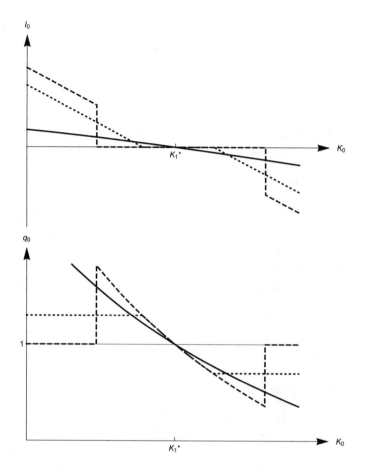

Figure 8.2
Convex and nonconvex adjustment costs: Optimal investment (top) and Tobin's q (bottom) when adjustment costs are strictly convex, fixed, or proportional.

adjusting. If $K_1^\star - K_0$ is small in absolute value, then the marginal gain of adjusting is smaller than ξ; consequently, $I_0 = 0$ and q_0 differs from unity. If the absolute value of $K_1^\star - K_0$ is large, in contrast, then the firm adjusts to the point where the marginal gain of further adjustment equals the marginal cost. That is, $I_0 \neq 0$ but the adjustment is incomplete and q_0 does not reach unity. The dotted lines in figure 8.2 illustrate this case.

8.1.3   Irreversibility and the Option Value of Waiting

Consider a risk neutral firm that chooses whether to invest a fixed amount I at date $t = 0$ or possibly later. The investment is *irreversible* and once undertaken, pays a return ρ per period forever. The return can either be high or low, ρ^h or ρ^l respectively. Conditional on information available at date $t = 0$, the former occurs with probability η^h and the latter with probability $\eta^l = 1 - \eta^h$. At date $t = 1$, uncertainty is resolved and the firm learns ρ with certainty. The gross discount factor is given by $R = 1 + r > 1$.

Consider first the strategy of investing at date $t = 0$. The payoff of this strategy, V, equals

$$V = -I + (\eta^h \rho^h + \eta^l \rho^l)\left(\frac{1}{R} + \frac{1}{R^2} + \ldots\right) = -I + \frac{\eta^h \rho^h + \eta^l \rho^l}{r}.$$

We assume that $V > 0$ (the project is profitable on average) but $-I + \rho^l/r < 0$ (the project is not profitable when the low return is realized).

Consider next the strategy of waiting and only investing at date $t = 1$ if this is profitable. The payoff of this second strategy, W, is given by

$$W = \frac{\eta^h \max[0, -I + \rho^h/r] + \eta^l \max[0, -I + \rho^l/r]}{R} = \frac{\eta^h(-I + \rho^h/r)}{R},$$

where we use the fact that the project is profitable in the high but unprofitable in the low state.

If η^h is sufficiently close to one, then $V > W$ because the second strategy delays a project that is profitable with very high probability and delay is costly ($R > 1$). Investing at date $t = 0$ then is optimal. For smaller values of η^h, in contrast, $V < W$ because the benefit of avoiding an unprofitable investment with probability η^l outweighs the cost of delaying a profitable investment with probability η^h. Investing at date $t = 0$ therefore is suboptimal in this case, although $V > 0$.

Intuitively, irreversibility and the risky investment return imply that the firm forgoes an option when it starts the investment project, namely the option to invest now *or later* if and when uncertainty has been resolved in a favorable way. This option has the value $\max[V, W]$. When $0 < V < \max[V, W]$, investing early is profitable but not sufficiently profitable to warrant forgoing the more valuable option and sacrificing flexibility; the option is *in the money* at date $t = 0$ but it is not yet optimal to exercise it.

Note that a mean-preserving spread of ρ does not change V while it increases W. In a more risky environment, the firm invests more cautiously because the downside risk of ending up with an unprofitable project gains in importance.

If the investment were reversible the firm could fully recover its investment at date $t = 1$. It would make use of this possibility in the low state and the payoff of investing early would equal

$$-I + \eta^h \frac{\rho^h}{r} + \eta^l I = \eta^h\left(-I + \frac{\rho^h}{r}\right) = RW,$$

which exceeds W when delay is costly. Early investment therefore would be optimal.

8.2   Labor Market Frictions

In the baseline model of labor supply and demand discussed in chapter 6, workers and firms meet in a centralized market and the competitive wage is determined by the market clearing requirement. We now modify this assumption and introduce *matching frictions*.

8.2.1   Economy

The economy is inhabited by a representative firm and a representative household with a continuum of members that insure each other, as in the extensive margin model considered in subsection 6.1.1. At date t, a fraction x_t of household members consumes leisure; a fraction y_t supplies labor; and a fraction $z_t = 1 - x_t - y_t$ searches for a job. Workers employed by the firm perform two types of tasks: A share $1 - v_t$ contributes to production and the remaining share, v_t, searches for new employees; that is, the number of the firm's *vacancies* equals $y_t v_t$. The firm accumulates capital, k_t, which it uses jointly with productive labor, $y_t(1 - v_t)$, to produce output subject to the constant-returns-to-scale production function f. This function also depends on productivity, A_t, which is exogenous and labor augmenting.

Vacancies are filled, and job seekers are employed, according to a constant-returns-to-scale *matching function*, g. When the household has z_t job seekers and the firm v_t vacancies, then $g(z_t, v_t)$ vacancies and job seekers are matched, where

$$g(z_t, v_t) = z_t \, g\left(1, \frac{v_t}{z_t}\right) \equiv z_t \, g(1, \theta_t).$$

Variable $\theta_t \equiv v_t / z_t$ denotes *labor market tightness*, the ratio of vacancies to job seekers. At date t, the share $\eta(\theta_t) \equiv g(1, \theta_t)/\theta_t = g(z_t, v_t)/v_t$ of vacancies is filled; the function η is decreasing. Correspondingly, the share $\theta_t \eta(\theta_t) = g(z_t, v_t)/z_t$ of job seekers (which increases in θ_t) gets employed. Both households and firms take labor market tightness as given. Employment is a state variable and employment relationships end with an exogenous probability, s.

For notational simplicity, we abstract from aggregate (productivity) risk and formulate the equilibrium conditions recursively. Let a_t denote household financial assets at date t, and q_{t+1} the price at date t of an asset that pays off one unit at the subsequent date.

8.2.2   Firms

The firm's value function, W, depends on the firm's capital stock and employment as well as on time. It solves

$$
\begin{aligned}
W(k_t, y_t, t) \quad = \quad & \max_{k_{t+1}, v_t} \; cf_t + q_{t+1} W(k_{t+1}, y_{t+1}, t+1) \\
\text{s.t.} \quad & cf_t = f(A_t, k_t, y_t(1 - v_t)) + k_t(1 - \delta) - k_{t+1} - y_t w_t, \\
& y_{t+1} = y_t(1 - s) + \eta(\theta_t) y_t v_t, \\
& 0 \le v_t \le 1,
\end{aligned}
$$

where cf_t denotes cash flow; $\delta \geq 0$ is the depreciation rate; and w_t denotes the wage. The first constraint defines cash flow as output net of gross investment and the wage bill; the second represents the law of motion for employment from the firm's perspective; and the third reflects the fact that the number of recruiters cannot exceed the number of employees.

The first-order conditions with respect to capital and recruiting, respectively, are

$$1 = q_{t+1} W_k(k_{t+1}, y_{t+1}, t+1),$$

$$f_y(A_t, k_t, y_t(1 - v_t)) = \eta(\theta_t) q_{t+1} W_y(k_{t+1}, y_{t+1}, t+1).$$

The firm equates the resource cost of investment to the discounted marginal increase in firm value due to a higher capital stock; and the output loss due to more intense recruiting to the discounted marginal increase in firm value from higher employment, weighted by the probability of filling a vacancy.

Using the envelope conditions for capital and employment,

$$W_k(k_t, y_t, t) = f_k(A_t, k_t, y_t(1 - v_t)) + 1 - \delta,$$

$$W_y(k_t, y_t, t) = f_y(A_t, k_t, y_t(1 - v_t)) - w_t + (1 - s)q_{t+1} W_y(k_{t+1}, y_{t+1}, t+1),$$

we find

$$1 = q_{t+1} \left(f_k(A_{t+1}, k_{t+1}, y_{t+1}(1 - v_{t+1})) + 1 - \delta \right), \tag{8.1}$$

$$f_y(A_t, k_t, y_t(1 - v_t)) = \eta(\theta_t) q_{t+1}$$
$$\times \left(f_y(A_{t+1}, k_{t+1}, y_{t+1}(1 - v_{t+1})) \left(1 + \frac{1 - s}{\eta(\theta_{t+1})} \right) - w_{t+1} \right), \tag{8.2}$$

$$W_y(k_t, y_t, t) = f_y(A_t, k_t, y_t(1 - v_t)) \left(1 + \frac{1 - s}{\eta(\theta_t)} \right) - w_t. \tag{8.3}$$

The first equation is standard. The second equates the cost and benefit of recruiting. The last condition states that the marginal value of employment equals the marginal product of labor, net of the wage, plus the recruitment cost that the firm saves when employment is higher: One employee at date t generates $1 - s$ units of employment at date $t + 1$; $1/\eta(\theta_t)$ recruiters at date t increase employment at date $t + 1$ by one unit; an additional employee at date t thus saves $(1 - s)/\eta(\theta_t)$ recruiters who can instead be employed in production.

8.2.3   Households

The date t period utility of the representative household is given by $u(c_t) - \gamma(y_t + z_t)$, where c_t denotes consumption and $\gamma > 0$ measures the disutility of work or job search. We assume logarithmic preferences. The household's value function, V, solves

$$V(a_t, y_t, t) = \max_{a_{t+1}, z_t} \ln(c_t) - \gamma(y_t + z_t) + \beta V(a_{t+1}, y_{t+1}, t+1)$$

$$\text{s.t.} \quad c_t = a_t + w_t y_t - q_{t+1} a_{t+1},$$

$$y_{t+1} = y_t(1 - s) + \theta_t \eta(\theta_t) z_t,$$

$$0 \le z_t \le 1 - y_t.$$

The household also satisfies the natural borrowing limit. The first constraint is the budget constraint. The second constraint represents the law of motion for employment from the household's perspective, and the third constraint is the time use constraint.

The first-order condition with respect to assets,

$$\frac{1}{c_t} q_{t+1} = \beta V_a(a_{t+1}, y_{t+1}, t+1),$$

relates the intertemporal marginal rate of substitution to the price. The optimality condition with respect to labor market search,

$$\gamma = \beta \theta_t \eta(\theta_t) V_y(a_{t+1}, y_{t+1}, t+1),$$

equates the cost of job search (forgone utility from leisure) and the marginal benefit; the latter equals the discounted continuation value of employment, multiplied by the probability of a match.

Using the envelope conditions

$$V_a(a_t, y_t, t) = \frac{1}{c_t},$$

$$V_y(a_t, y_t, t) = \frac{w_t}{c_t} - \gamma + \beta(1 - s)V_y(a_{t+1}, y_{t+1}, t+1),$$

we arrive at the equilibrium conditions

$$q_{t+1} = \beta \frac{c_t}{c_{t+1}}, \tag{8.4}$$

$$\gamma = \beta \theta_t \eta(\theta_t) \left(\frac{w_{t+1}}{c_{t+1}} - \gamma + \gamma \frac{1 - s}{\theta_{t+1} \eta(\theta_{t+1})} \right), \tag{8.5}$$

$$V_y(a_t, y_t, t) = \frac{w_t}{c_t} - \gamma + \gamma \frac{1 - s}{\theta_t \eta(\theta_t)}. \tag{8.6}$$

The first condition is the standard Euler equation. The second equates the cost and benefit of job search. The third condition states that higher employment generates two benefits: Marginal utility due to higher labor income, net of the disutility from work; and marginal utility from leisure because of reduced job search. An additional unit of employment at date t generates $1 - s$ units at date $t + 1$, thus saving the household $(1 - s)/(\theta_t \eta(\theta_t))$ job seekers at date t.

8.2.4 Market Clearing and Wage Determination

Goods market clearing implies

$$c_t = f(A_t, k_t, y_t(1 - v_t)) + k_t(1 - \delta) - k_{t+1}. \tag{8.7}$$

Employment, y_t, is a state variable that changes in response to exogenous separations and endogenous hires. When a job seeker and a firm with a vacancy meet they form a *bilateral monopoly* since neither the former nor the latter has the possibility to be matched with another party in the same period. Accordingly, the job seeker is willing to accept any wage above its opportunity cost, and similarly for the firm. The two parties negotiate and if they can agree on a wage then they form a new employment relationship.

We assume that the wage is determined by Nash bargaining. Let $\tilde{V}_y(a_t, y_t, t, \Delta w_t)$ and $\tilde{W}_y(k_t, y_t, t, \Delta w_t)$ denote the value to the household and the firm, respectively, of a marginal hire whose wage exceeds the market wage at date t by Δw_t, but in the future equals the market wage. From the two envelope conditions derived earlier,

$$\tilde{V}_y(a_t, y_t, t, \Delta w_t) = \frac{\Delta w_t}{c_t} + V_y(a_t, y_t, t),$$
$$\tilde{W}_y(k_t, y_t, t, \Delta w_t) = -\Delta w_t + W_y(k_t, y_t, t).$$

The generalized *Nash bargaining solution* to the wage determination problem maximizes the weighted average of the surpluses of the negotiating parties,

$$\mathcal{J}(\Delta w_t) \equiv \left(\tilde{V}_y(a_t, y_t, t, \Delta w_t) \right)^\phi \left(\tilde{W}_y(k_t, y_t, t, \Delta w_t) \right)^{1-\phi},$$

where ϕ and $1 - \phi$ denote the bargaining weights of the job seeker and the firm, respectively.[10] That is, the equilibrium wage satisfies $\mathcal{J}'(0) = 0$ or equivalently,

$$\phi \frac{1}{c_t} \frac{1}{V_y(a_t, y_t, t)} = (1 - \phi) \frac{1}{W_y(k_t, y_t, t)}.$$

Using conditions (8.3) and (8.6) and solving for the *wage*, we find

$$w_t = \gamma c_t \left(1 - \frac{1-s}{\theta_t \eta(\theta_t)} \right)$$
$$+ \phi \left\{ f_y(A_t, k_t, y_t(1 - v_t)) \left(1 + \frac{1-s}{\eta(\theta_t)} \right) - \gamma c_t \left(1 - \frac{1-s}{\theta_t \eta(\theta_t)} \right) \right\}. \tag{8.8}$$

The equilibrium wage has two components, represented by the two terms on the right-hand side of equation (8.8): First, the household's opportunity cost or *outside value*, namely the forgone utility from leisure net of the saved search cost (both in consumption terms);

---

[10] We have assumed that agents take the wage as given when choosing a or k, although these state variables may affect the bargaining outcome. To reconcile these assumptions one could assume that counter parties do not observe individual assets or that the firm negotiates a uniform wage for all workers.

and second, the share ϕ of the *joint surplus* expressed in terms of consumption units, $W_y(k_t, y_t, t) + c_t V_y(a_t, y_t, t)$. The joint surplus equals the sum of the household's and the firm's marginal values from a hire, net of the outside values of the two parties; the firm's outside value equals zero.

8.2.5   Equilibrium

In equilibrium, household assets represent the value of the representative firm; labor market tightness reflects optimal firm and household choices, $\theta_t = y_t v_t / z_t$; and the laws of motion for employment as perceived by the firm and the household reduce to

$$y_{t+1} = y_t(1 - s) + \eta\left(\frac{y_t v_t}{z_t}\right) y_t v_t. \tag{8.9}$$

Conditional on the state variables in the initial period, an equilibrium is characterized by (8.1), (8.2), (8.4), (8.5), (8.7)–(8.9) as well as the definition of θ_t; the household budget constraint; and the borrowing limit.

Using (8.4) and (8.8), we can reexpress conditions (8.2) and (8.5) as

$$\frac{f_y(A_t, k_t, y_t(1 - v_t))}{c_t} = \beta\eta(\theta_t)(1 - \phi)\Omega_{t+1}, \tag{8.10}$$

$$\gamma = \beta\theta_t\eta(\theta_t)\phi\Omega_{t+1}, \tag{8.11}$$

respectively, where we define (dropping arguments of the marginal product function for legibility)

$$\Omega_{t+1} \equiv \frac{f_y(t+1)}{c_{t+1}} - \gamma + \frac{1 - s}{\eta(\theta_{t+1})}\left(\frac{f_y(t+1)}{c_{t+1}} + \frac{\gamma}{\theta_{t+1}}\right). \tag{8.12}$$

We will use these conditions below.

8.2.6   Constrained Pareto Optimality

Job seekers and firms with vacancies are *rationed*: They are willing to form employment relationships at the going wage but are unable to do so until being matched. When labor market tightness is high, then firms are typically rationed for an extended period while job seekers quickly find a job; when tightness is low the situation is reversed. In either case, job seekers and firms exert negative *congestion externalities* and positive *thick market externalities*: Their search renders it harder for agents of the same type, but easier for agents of the other type to be matched.

A social planner cannot avoid the matching friction. But the planner internalizes the externalities, in contrast to firms and job seekers in the decentralized equilibrium. As a consequence, the (constrained optimal) social planner allocation typically differs from the equilibrium allocation. It is only when the bargaining weight of job seekers and firms assumes a particular value that the equilibrium allocation is constrained efficient.

To see this, consider the social planner's program. Letting P denote the value function of the social planner, we have

$$P(k_t, y_t, t) \;=\; \max_{v_t, z_t} \ln(c_t) - \gamma(y_t + z_t) + \beta P(k_{t+1}, y_{t+1}, t+1)$$

$$\text{s.t.} \quad (8.7), (8.9),$$

$$0 \le z_t \le 1 - y_t,$$

$$0 \le v_t \le 1.$$

The first-order and envelope conditions reduce to a first-order condition for capital accumulation, which corresponds to (8.1) and (8.4), as well as to

$$\frac{f_y(A_t, k_t, y_t(1 - v_t))}{c_t} \;=\; -\gamma \frac{\eta'(\theta_t)\theta_t + \eta(\theta_t)}{\eta'(\theta_t)\theta_t^2}, \tag{8.13}$$

$$\gamma \;=\; -\beta \eta'(\theta_t)\theta_t^2 \Phi_{t+1}, \tag{8.14}$$

where we define (dropping again arguments)

$$\Phi_{t+1} \equiv \frac{f_y(t+1)}{c_{t+1}} - \gamma + \gamma \frac{1 - s}{-\eta'(\theta_{t+1})\theta_{t+1}^2}.$$

Note the $\eta'(\theta_t)$ terms in the planner's optimality conditions; they reflect that the planner internalizes the search externalities. Note also that $-\eta'(\theta_t)\theta_t^2 = g_z(z_t, v_t)$ and $\eta'(\theta_t)\theta_t + \eta(\theta_t) = g_v(z_t, v_t)$.

Condition (8.13) states that the planner equalizes the relative costs and benefits of recruiting and job search: Recruiting generates $g_v(z_t, v_t)$ matches and has opportunity cost $f_y(A_t, k_t, y_t(1 - v_t))$, while job search generates $g_z(z_t, v_t)$ matches and has opportunity cost γc_t in consumption units. Condition (8.14) characterizes the efficient intensity of job search. It equalizes the utility cost of job search and the discounted, probability-weighted benefit from a marginal match. This benefit reflects utility from consumption, net of the utility loss from working, plus the cost saving from reduced job search.

Let $\varphi(\theta_t)$ denote the elasticity of the matching function with respect to job search,

$$\varphi(\theta_t) \equiv \frac{g_z(z_t, v_t)}{g(z_t, v_t)} z_t = \frac{g_z(z_t, v_t)}{\eta(\theta_t)\theta_t}.$$

If the bargaining weight of the job seeker, ϕ, coincides with this elasticity—that is, if the *Hosios condition* is satisfied—then the decentralized equilibrium allocation and the social planner allocation coincide and in particular, conditions (8.10)–(8.11) and (8.13)–(8.14) are identical.

This can be shown as follows: Using (8.11), the right-hand side of (8.10) can be expressed as $\gamma(1 - \phi)/(\phi\theta_t)$ and thus (using the Hosios condition and the constant-returns-to-scale property of the matching function), $\gamma g_v(z_t, v_t)/g_z(z_t, v_t)$. Moreover, using the modified condition (8.10), the last term of Ω_{t+1} in (8.12) can be expressed as $(1 - s)\gamma/(\phi\eta(\theta_{t+1})\theta_{t+1})$.

The Hosios condition and the above definition of the elasticity then implies $\Omega_{t+1} = \Phi_{t+1}$ and the result follows.

Intuitively, the Hosios condition guarantees that the private gains from job seeking or posting vacancies (which households or firms internalize) equal the social contributions of these activities. When the elasticity $\varphi(\theta_t)$ is high, then job search strongly increases the odds that a vacancy is filled but it only has a minor negative effect on the probability that a job seeker is matched. In contrast, recruiting strongly reduces the odds that a vacancy is filled in this case, while it only has a minor positive effect on the job-finding probability of a job seeker. When $\varphi(\theta_t)$ is high, it is therefore efficient to give strong incentives for job seeking; that is, pay high wages.

8.2.7   The Case without Capital

Returning to the decentralized equilibrium, consider a variant of the model without capital; that is, let $f(A_t, k_t, y_t(1 - v_t)) = A_t y_t(1 - v_t)$. The first-order conditions for v_t and z_t, the wage condition, the resource constraint, and the budget constraint then reduce to

$$\frac{A_t}{c_t} = \beta\eta(\theta_t)\left(\frac{A_{t+1}}{c_{t+1}}\left(1 + \frac{1-s}{\eta(\theta_{t+1})}\right) - \frac{w_{t+1}}{c_{t+1}}\right),$$

$$\gamma = \beta\theta_t\eta(\theta_t)\left(\frac{w_{t+1}}{c_{t+1}} - \gamma + \gamma\frac{1-s}{\theta_{t+1}\eta(\theta_{t+1})}\right),$$

$$\frac{w_t}{c_t} = \gamma\left(1 - \frac{1-s}{\theta_t\eta(\theta_t)}\right) + \phi\left\{\frac{A_t}{c_t}\left(1 + \frac{1-s}{\eta(\theta_t)}\right) - \gamma\left(1 - \frac{1-s}{\theta_t\eta(\theta_t)}\right)\right\},$$

$$\frac{c_t}{A_t} = y_t(1 - v_t),$$

respectively.

Note that productivity, consumption, and the wage only appear in pairs as ratios. Productivity thus is fully reflected in consumption and the wage, and different productivity sequences are associated with the same equilibrium sequences for employment, recruiting, job search, and labor market tightness.

Intuitively, holding wages and consumption (and thus, interest rates) constant, a contemporaneous productivity increase renders recruiting more expensive relative to production, thereby inducing firms to recruit less and produce more (see the first condition). But higher production raises consumption, and less recruiting lowers future production and consumption. In equilibrium, this requires a fall in the interest rate (from the Euler equation), raising the incentive to invest in vacancies. With logarithmic preferences, the direct, negative effect on the incentive to recruit and the indirect, positive effect cancel. With capital, this result only would hold in steady state since capital cannot instantaneously adjust in line with productivity.

Exogenously imposed *wage stickiness* renders labor market outcomes more responsive to productivity. When firms anticipate elevated productivity but unchanged wages, then recruiting becomes more profitable (see the optimality condition for v_t above). Employment therefore rises more strongly than in an environment with Nash bargaining, where wages increase with productivity. Note that wage stickiness is individually rational in the sense that it does not give rise to inefficiencies from the joint perspective of a job seeker and a firm as long as the wage remains within the bargaining set delimited by the pair's reservation wages.

8.2.8   A Model without Capital and Leisure

To further simplify the analysis, we abstract from leisure; that is, we assume that households are either employed or unemployed (searching for a job), $z_t = 1 - y_t$. We also assume that workers are risk neutral and that each firm has one job. To fill a vacancy, a firm must post it, which costs b, and must be matched with an unemployed worker. A filled job generates output A. A worker consumes the wage income when employed and the return on home production, γ, when unemployed.

Let V, V^0, W, and W^0 denote the steady-state values of an employed and unemployed worker and a firm with a worker and a vacancy, respectively. For a given wage, w, and labor market tightness, $\theta \equiv v/z$, these values solve the Bellman equations

$$
\begin{aligned}
W &= A - w + \beta\big((1-s)W + sW^0\big), \\
W^0 &= -b + \beta\big(\eta(\theta)W + (1-\eta(\theta))W^0\big), \\
V &= w + \beta\big((1-s)V + sV^0\big), \\
V^0 &= \gamma + \beta\big(\theta\eta(\theta)V + (1-\theta\eta(\theta))V^0\big).
\end{aligned}
$$

Due to *free entry*, a firm entering the labor market and posting a vacancy just breaks even,

$$
W^0 = 0,
$$

implying

$$
\begin{aligned}
V - V^0 + W &= \frac{A - \gamma + b\theta}{1 - \beta(1-s) + \beta\theta\eta(\theta)}, \\
w &= A - b\frac{1 - \beta(1-s)}{\beta\eta(\theta)}, \\
W &= \frac{b}{\beta\eta(\theta)}.
\end{aligned}
$$

Intuitively, the joint surplus $V - V^0 + W$ reflects output net of home production as well as saved posting costs (we assume that the joint surplus is positive). Moreover, a higher cost of posting a vacancy or a lower probability of filling it (due to higher labor market tightness) must be compensated by a lower wage and a higher value W. Finally, the wage increases in output.

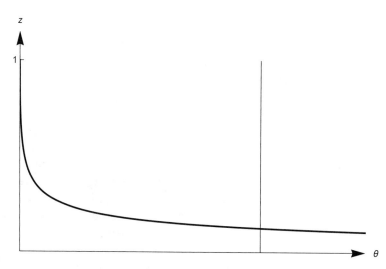

Figure 8.3
Steady-state labor market equilibrium: Labor market tightness and the Beveridge curve.

To close the model we assume the Nash bargaining solution for the wage. Maximizing $(V - V^0)^\phi (W - W^0)^{1-\phi}$ with respect to w (taking continuation values in the Bellman equations as given) implies that the surplus appropriated by the firm equals the joint surplus times the firm's bargaining weight,

$$W = (1 - \phi)(V - V^0 + W).$$

An equilibrium is a collection $(W, W^0, V, V^0, w, \theta)$ that solves the above equations.

The vertical line in figure 8.3 indicates the equilibrium level of labor market tightness. When the bargaining power of workers, ϕ, rises or their outside options, γ, improve, or when the cost of posting a vacancy, b, increases, then the incentive for firms to post vacancies can only be maintained by a corresponding increase in the probability of filling vacancies. This requires lower labor market tightness; that is, a leftward shift of the line.

The decreasing schedule in figure 8.3 depicts the *Beveridge curve* relationship between steady-state unemployment and labor market tightness. To derive the curve we use the fact that with constant employment (and abstracting from leisure), the law of motion (8.9) implies $g(z, v) = s(1 - z)$ or

$$z = \frac{s}{s + \theta \eta(\theta)}.$$

The Beveridge curve is decreasing because both unemployment (job search) and vacancies increase the number of matches. In steady state, net inflows into employment equal zero. Additional vacancies thus must be accompanied by fewer job seekers, both to reduce the number of matches and to increase the number of outflows from employment, $s(1 - z)$.

Since $\theta\eta(\theta)$ is concave, the Beveridge curve is convex. (The same holds true when the curve is plotted in (v, z) space.)

Steady-state unemployment and vacancies are determined by the intersection of the Beveridge curve and the vertical line representing the equilibrium conditions. Note that *structural unemployment* is strictly positive in equilibrium; if it equaled zero firms would not recruit. When the matching technology improves or the separation rate, s, falls then the Beveridge curve shifts down and the vertical line shifts outward; structural unemployment falls.

8.3 Financial Frictions

Financial frictions limit the ability of agents to engage in trade across time or histories. One source of such frictions are conflicts of interest in combination with contracting or information problems. Consider a borrower and a lender. Ex ante, when the two parties agree on the loan, their interests are aligned—both sides benefit from the intertemporal trade. Ex post, when the loan is due for repayment, however, their interests are no longer aligned since the repayment constitutes a transfer from the borrower to the lender. When it is difficult to enforce or incentivize repayment, then the misalignment ex post may undermine the viability of the loan in the first place (see also section 13.4).

Incentive problems are mitigated when investors have high *net worth* or *equity* such that they do not need to raise external financing. To generate a role for incentive problems and thus financial frictions, we impose conditions under which investors have limited net worth and rely on external financing.

8.3.1 Net Worth and External Finance Premium

8.3.1.1 Costly State Verification Consider an investor with net worth nw who borrows $z - nw$ from a lender and invests z into a project with risky payoff; the payoff equals R^h with probability η^h and $R^l < R^h$ with probability $\eta^l = 1 - \eta^h$. Both the lender and the investor are risk neutral. The lender's required gross rate of return is given by R.

The *information* about the project return is *asymmetric*: While the investor observes the payoff at zero cost the lender only observes it after paying a *verification cost*, γ. One possible financial arrangement between the lender and the investor could stipulate a non-contingent loan repayment to avoid the need for costly verification by the lender; but this would limit the maximum debt repayment to R^l (because the investor would pretend that the payoff was low even if it was not) and thus severely delimit the loan size. Another possible arrangement could foresee that the lender always observes the actual return; but this would be suboptimal as well, since verification is costly and not always needed.

To find the constrained optimal financial arrangement, we compare *mechanisms* that map the investor's announcement about the project payoff into a contingent observation choice by the lender and contingent payments to the investor and the lender. A mechanism must satisfy the lender's *participation constraint* and the investor's *incentive compatibility constraint*. The former requires the lender to break even in equilibrium and the latter requires the investor's optimal contingent announcement under the mechanism to conform with the intended announcement. By the *revelation principle*, we may without loss of generality restrict attention to direct mechanisms that induce truth telling. Accordingly, we search for the arrangement that is optimal for the investor, subject to inducing truth telling and letting the lender break even.

Let ρ^h (ρ^l) denote the payment to the investor after announcing a high (low) project return and when the lender does not observe the payoff; let ψ^h (ψ^l) denote the payment after announcing a high (low) project return and when the lender does observe the payoff and verifies the announcement; and let θ^h (θ^l) denote the probability that the lender observes the payoff after an announcement of a high (low) return. A truth-telling investor then receives ρ^h or ψ^h in the high state (with probability $1 - \theta^h$ and θ^h, respectively) and ρ^l or ψ^l in the low state (with probability $1 - \theta^l$ and θ^l, respectively); and the lender receives $R^h - \rho^h$, $R^h - \psi^h - \gamma$, $R^l - \rho^l$, and $R^l - \psi^l - \gamma$ in the four cases. The mechanism design program reads

$$\max_{\rho^h, \rho^l, \psi^h, \psi^l, \theta^h, \theta^l} \quad \sum_{s=h,l} \eta^s \left(\theta^s \psi^s + (1 - \theta^s) \rho^s \right)$$

$$\text{s.t.} \quad \sum_{s=h,l} \eta^s \left(R^s - \theta^s (\psi^s + \gamma) - (1 - \theta^s) \rho^s \right) \geq R(z - nw),$$

$$\rho^h, \rho^l, \psi^h, \psi^l \geq 0,$$

$$\theta^h \psi^h + (1 - \theta^h) \rho^h \geq \theta^l 0 + (1 - \theta^l) \left(\rho^l + R^h - R^l \right),$$

$$0 \leq \theta^h, \theta^l \leq 1.$$

The first constraint is the lender's participation constraint. It states that the expected project return net of payments to the investor and verification costs must let the lender break even. The second constraint reflects *limited liability*: Since the investor cannot be forced to contribute additional funds ex post, the payments to the investor must be nonnegative. The third constraint imposes incentive compatibility when the project return is high:[11] The investor must find it advantageous to truthfully report R^h and receive either ψ^h or ρ^h rather than incorrectly reporting R^l and receiving zero in case of detection or ρ^l plus the return differential, $R^h - R^l$, when there is no detection. Note that detection of an incorrect report triggers a payment of zero to the investor; limited liability prevents a harsher punishment. Without the limited liability restriction, the incentive compatibility constraint could be rendered nonbinding. The last constraint states that probabilities lie between zero and one.

Inspection reveals that we can simplify the constraint set. First, the participation constraint holds with equality; otherwise the objective function could be increased without vi-

---

[11] We rule out the possibility that the investor announces a high payoff although it is low. Accordingly, we only impose an incentive constraint for the high state.

olating a constraint, by raising ψ^h or ψ^l. Second, the participation constraint (with equality) implies that the objective can be reexpressed as the minimization of the expected verification costs, $\gamma \sum_s \eta^s \theta^s$. Third, it is weakly beneficial to lower ρ^l and ψ^l to zero (the benefit is strictly positive when θ^l is strictly smaller than unity and strictly larger than zero, respectively); we therefore set $\rho^l = \psi^l = 0$. Finally, holding $\theta^h \psi^h + (1 - \theta^h)\rho^h$ constant, a reduction of θ^h to zero relaxes the participation constraint and lowers expected verification costs; this implies $\theta^h = 0$. In conclusion, the program can be rewritten as

$$\min_{\rho^h, \theta^l} \quad \gamma \eta^l \theta^l$$

$$\text{s.t.} \quad \eta^h(R^h - \rho^h) + \eta^l(R^l - \theta^l \gamma) = R(z - nw),$$

$$\rho^h \geq (1 - \theta^l)(R^h - R^l),$$

$$0 \leq \theta^l \leq 1.$$

There are two possibilities: Either there exists a (first-best) solution to the program with $\theta^l = 0$; from the participation and incentive compatibility constraints (which are slack in this case), this requires $R^l \geq R(z - nw)$; that is, the lender's required return is smaller than the lowest project return. The loan is risk-free in this case. Or, the latter inequality is violated; the optimal arrangement involves stochastic verification; and the lender's return on the loan is risky. The verification costs constitute deadweight losses or *agency costs*. They drive a wedge—the expected verification costs, $\gamma \eta^l \theta^l$—between the expected project return and the expected returns received by the investor, $\eta^h \rho^h$, and the lender, $R(z - nw)$. Since the lender receives the required return the verification costs effectively are born by the investor. This implies a positive *external finance premium*: Raising funds externally is more expensive than contributing internal funds because the return paid to lenders must cover both their opportunity costs and the verification costs.

When $nw = z$, the investor does not need external financing and thus does not bear agency costs. When external financing is needed and $R(z - nw)$ exceeds R^l, in contrast, then both the participation and incentive compatibility constraints bind, implying

$$\theta^l = \frac{R(z - nw) - R^l}{\eta^h(R^h - R^l) - \gamma \eta^l}.$$

Note that higher investor net worth reduces agency costs; the agency costs per unit of the loan, $\gamma \eta^l \theta^l / (z - nw)$, increase with the loan size.

8.3.1.2   Persistent Effects of Net Worth Shocks   To analyze the dynamic implications of net worth shocks, we consider an overlapping generations economy with investors and lenders. Output is a function of capital, which cannot be consumed; labor; and an i.i.d. productivity shock.

Young investors and lenders inelastically supply labor and earn a competitive wage, w_t, which constitutes their net worth. Investors only consume when old; they invest their wage income in risky projects that produce capital, or lend to a diversified pool of other investors. Investor i may start a project at cost z^i to generate κ^h or κ^l units of capital at date $t + 1$, with probability η^h and η^l, respectively. The capital trades at price q_{t+1} before the productivity shock is revealed, and it fully depreciates at the end of the period.

Lenders consume when young and old. They can store consumption goods at the gross real interest rate, R, or lend to investors. Since there are only few investors relative to lenders, the latter always store part of their wage income and the risk-free gross interest rate therefore always equals R. Note that this setup maps into the costly state verification model analyzed before, with $R^h = \kappa^h q_{t+1}$ and $R^l = \kappa^l q_{t+1}$.

Absent frictions, all investors with low project costs, $z^i \leq q_{t+1}(\eta^h \kappa^h + \eta^l \kappa^l)/R$, would invest in equilibrium. Since the productivity shock is i.i.d., the price of capital, and thus the return characteristics of investment projects, would be constant over time and the economy would invest a time-invariant amount, independently of the history of productivity shocks. Both capital, k_t, and its price, q_t, would not fluctuate over time.

With asymmetric information, in contrast, costly state verification generates agency costs. Capital accumulation is reduced because the external finance premium discourages some investors that would have started a project if information were symmetric. Moreover, since the number of projects initiated depends on the net worth of investors there is an *accelerator effect*: When the incentive compatibility constraints of investors bind, a lower wage due to a negative productivity shock increases the external finance premium; this leads to fewer project starts and thus a lower capital stock in the subsequent period; and this feeds, on average, into lower future wages. Vice versa, a positive shock persistently fosters capital formation. A *productivity shock* thus has *persistent effects*, in contrast with the frictionless case.

In fact, the effect of a *productivity shock* is not only persistent but also *asymmetric*. When investors are just unconstrained, a positive shock does not increase capital formation because it has no effect on agency costs. A negative shock, in contrast, does raise the external finance premium and reduces investment.

8.3.2   Collateral and Asset Prices

8.3.2.1   Collateral   When investors own productive assets, the price of these assets affects outside financing and project starts through three channels. First, a change in the price makes the asset more or less affordable. Second, it alters investor net worth and thus access to external financing. And third, future asset prices can affect the tightness of the investor's borrowing constraint (see subsection 2.2.1) when holding the asset improves the investor's incentives at the time when the loan comes due.

To study these channels we consider a modified source of financial friction. Rather than assuming asymmetric information about the project outcome, we posit symmetric information but assume that an investor cannot be forced to repay a loan; the legal system only enables the lender to obtain the investor's capital when repayment is overdue. In equilibrium, an investor therefore needs to hold capital in order to secure a loan. This capital serves as *collateral*; it provides the investor with incentives to repay rather than default when the loan comes due. (See section 13.4 for different forms of collateral.)

Formally, consider an investor with net worth nw_t that purchases capital, k_{t+1}, at price q_t. The price of capital in the subsequent period is given by q_{t+1}. When the required gross rate of return on the loan equals R, lenders are willing to extend a loan, $z_t - nw_t$, as long as $R(z_t - nw_t) \leq q_{t+1}k_{t+1}$. Rearranging, this *collateral constraint* can be expressed as

$$z_t - nw_t \leq \frac{q_{t+1}k_{t+1}}{R};\tag{8.15}$$

that is, the maximal loan size is given by the discounted collateral value. When the constraint binds, *credit* is *rationed*: The investor would be willing to borrow more but the lender refuses to extend a larger loan, even at a higher interest rate. Note that less net worth requires more collateral to support a given project size, z_t; more valuable collateral or a lower interest rate support a larger loan for given net worth.

The investor's outlays are given by the cost of capital purchases, $z_t = q_t k_{t+1}$. A fraction of these outlays must be financed out of internal funds. The *down payment* required to purchase one unit of capital equals the price net of the external financing that can be obtained when the unit is collateralized. Substituting $z_t = q_t k_{t+1}$ into the constraint (8.15) yields

$$k_{t+1}\left(q_t - \frac{q_{t+1}}{R}\right) \leq nw_t\tag{8.16}$$

and implies that the down payment equals $\tilde{v}_t \equiv q_t - q_{t+1}/R$. When the capital price is anticipated to grow at a strictly lower rate than the interest rate, the downpayment is strictly positive and an investor with net worth nw_t can maximally purchase $nw_t/\tilde{v}_t$ units of capital.

Let b_t denote the loan that matures at date t and suppose that the investor borrows the maximal amount such that condition (8.16) holds with equality. Capital held by the investor pays a dividend y per unit, which constitutes a component of net worth. Since $nw_t = (q_t + y)k_t - b_t R$, condition (8.16) (with equality) implies

$$k_{t+1} = \frac{1}{\tilde{v}_t}((q_t + y)k_t - b_t R).\tag{8.17}$$

Condition (8.17) identifies the three channels mentioned before. First, an increase of q_t renders capital purchases more expensive; this is reflected in a higher down payment that tightens the constraint. Second, a higher price raises net worth and allows the investor to expand capital purchases. The size of this effect depends on *leverage*, the extent of external finance: A price increase by one percent raises net worth by φ_t percent, where $\varphi_t \equiv q_t k_t / nw_t$ denotes the share of capital's market value in net worth. This share exceeds one when the investor is leveraged, $yk_t < b_t R$. When the collateral constraint was already binding at date $t-1$ such that $q_t k_t = b_t R$, then $\varphi_t = q_t/y$. Finally, an increase of next period's price, q_{t+1}, lowers the down payment, relaxes the collateral constraint, and increases capital purchases and leverage. When both q_t and q_{t+1} experience the same relative increase, then k_{t+1} increases as long as the investor is leveraged because net worth increases by more than the down payment.

8.3.2.2   Amplification of Net Worth Shocks

We now embed the collateral constraint in a general equilibrium model. We assume that investors are long-lived, such that they own capital when seeking external finance; this exposes them to the effects discussed above. In addition, their capital accumulation affects prices in general equilibrium. We focus on the feedback effects between investment, asset prices, and net worth.

There are two groups of infinitely lived households, investors and lenders, both of mass one. All households have linear utility functions. The aggregate stock of capital, K, is fixed (think of land). Investors operate a linear production function: One unit of capital generates y units of output as well as e units that can only be consumed. The law of motion for capital held by an investor with maximal leverage is given by condition (8.17). Lenders operate a strictly concave production function, f. When the representative investor holds k_t units of capital, then the representative lender produces $f(K - k_t)$ units of output.

Lenders are more patient than investors; the discount factor of a lender, β, is strictly larger than the discount factor of an investor, δ. Since only investors face a collateral constraint, the risk-free gross interest rate, R, equals β^{-1}. Letting c_t^l denote consumption of a lender and b_t the loan to investors, the lender's budget constraint reads[12]

$$c_t^l + q_t(k_t - k_{t+1}) + b_{t+1} = b_t R + f(K - k_t).$$

The lender's portfolio choice problem implies that in equilibrium, the gross interest rate on a loan to investors, R, and the gross rate of return on capital, $(q_{t+1} + f'(K - k_{t+1}))/q_t$, are equal to each other. The *user cost* of capital, namely the price net of the discounted resale value, $v_t \equiv q_t - q_{t+1}/R$, thus equals the discounted marginal product,

$$R = \frac{q_{t+1} + f'(K - k_{t+1})}{q_t} \quad \Leftrightarrow \quad v_t = \frac{f'(K - k_{t+1})}{R} \equiv v(k_{t+1}).$$

A higher user cost is associated with a higher marginal product of capital employed by lenders, and thus with less capital held by lenders and more by investors. Note that under our assumption about the collateral constraint the user cost, v_t, equals the down payment, $\tilde{v}_t$.

Iterating the definition of user costs, $q_t = v_t + q_{t+1}/R$, forward and ruling out a price bubble implies that the price of capital equals the discounted sum of future user costs. Substituting the equilibrium relationship between k_{t+1+s} and v_{t+s}, $v(k_{t+1+s})$, into the dis-

---

[12] Recall that k_t denotes capital held by investors.

counted sum yields

$$q_t = \sum_{s=0}^{\infty} \frac{v(k_{t+1+s})}{R^s}.$$ (8.18)

Equation (8.17) with $\tilde{v}_t$ replaced by $v(k_{t+1})$ and equation (8.18) characterize the quantity and price dynamics of capital conditional on an initial k_t and b_t.

Suppose that the economy is in steady state at date $t = 0$ and the investor is collateral constrained, $qk = bR$. Equations (8.17) and (8.18) then imply

$$\frac{f'(K-k)}{R} = v = y = q\frac{R-1}{R}, \quad b(R-1) = yk.$$

To prove that this steady state exists, we need to establish that investors choose maximal leverage as we have assumed in the derivation of condition (8.17). Since $\delta R < 1$, and under the condition that $e > y(\delta^{-1} - 1)$, this can be shown to be true.

Consider now the implications of a small, temporary, unexpected productivity shock that increases output y at date $t = 0$ by $\hat{y}$ percent. Approximating conditions (8.17) (with $\tilde{v}_t = v(k_{t+1})$) and (8.18) around the steady state yields the linearized system

$$\hat{k}_1\left(1 + \frac{1}{\varepsilon}\right) = \hat{q}_0\frac{R}{R-1} + \hat{y},$$ (8.19)

$$\hat{k}_{t+1}\left(1 + \frac{1}{\varepsilon}\right) = \hat{k}_t, \; t \geq 1,$$ (8.20)

$$\hat{q}_0 = \frac{R-1}{R}\frac{1}{\varepsilon}\sum_{t=0}^{\infty}\frac{\hat{k}_{t+1}}{R^t},$$ (8.21)

where circumflexes denote relative deviations from steady state and ε denotes the elasticity of lenders' capital supply with respect to the user cost,

$$\varepsilon \equiv \frac{1/k}{v'(k)/v} = -\frac{f'(K-k)}{f''(K-k)}\frac{1}{k}.$$

This elasticity is large when f'' is close to zero—that is, when the production function f is nearly linear; in this case, small changes in user cost induce lenders to adjust their capital holdings by a large amount.

Equation (8.19) characterizes the price and quantity effects on impact. The right-hand side of the equation represents the change in net worth. If the shock does not affect q_0, then net worth increases by $\hat{y}$ percent because steady-state net worth equals yk. When q_0 also changes, net worth may rise more than proportionally. Recall that the effect of an increase of q_0 on net worth depends on the share of capital's market value in net worth, φ. Due to leverage, and since the collateral constraint binds before the price increase, $\varphi = q/y = R/(R-1)$. If the shock leads to a price increase (as we will establish below) and $R > 1$, net worth thus increases by more than $\hat{y}$ percent.

According to the left-hand side of equation (8.19), higher net worth is reflected in higher capital purchases, $\hat{k}_1 > 0$. If $\varepsilon = \infty$ such that user costs are independent of k_1, then the down payment is constant as well and purchases grow by the same rate as net worth. If $\varepsilon < \infty$, in contrast, the user cost must increase to induce lenders to sell capital; the higher user cost drives up the down payment; and this reduces the magnitude of the effect of net worth on capital purchases by investors.

Equation (8.20) characterizes the persistence of these effects. Starting at date $t = 1$, productivity returns to its steady-state value and the collateral constraint is tight ($q_t k_t = b_t R$). Net worth therefore exceeds its steady-state value only when capital exceeds its steady-state value. Unless lenders' capital supply is completely inelastic ($\varepsilon = 0$), the expansionary effect of the productivity shock on investors' capital holdings is persistent. Finally, equation (8.21) relates the initial price change to the user costs, and thus to capital reallocations. More capital purchases by investors drive up the user costs and this increases the price of capital at date $t = 0$.

The three conditions jointly pin down the equilibrium path of prices and investor capital holdings. Substituting equation (8.20) into equation (8.21) yields

$$\hat{q}_0 = \frac{R-1}{R}\frac{1}{\varepsilon}\hat{k}_1 \sum_{s=0}^{\infty}\frac{1}{R^s(1+\varepsilon^{-1})^s} = \frac{R-1}{R}\frac{1}{\varepsilon}\frac{R(1+\varepsilon)}{R(1+\varepsilon)-\varepsilon}\hat{k}_1.$$

Note the importance of the persistence of the increase in investor capital holdings. If investors expanded capital holdings only temporarily, then future user costs would remain unchanged and the multiplier $R(1+\varepsilon)/(R(1+\varepsilon)-\varepsilon)$ would collapse to one.

Substituting the expression for the price change into equation (8.19) yields

$$\hat{q}_0 = \frac{\hat{y}}{\varepsilon},$$

$$\hat{k}_1 = \frac{1}{1+\frac{1}{\varepsilon}}\left(1+\frac{1}{\varepsilon}\frac{R}{R-1}\right)\hat{y}.$$

We have established that the capital purchased by investors increases relatively more strongly than productivity, $\hat{k}_1 > \hat{y}$, when the interest rate is positive and the supply elasticity finite.

This *amplification* of the temporary *productivity shock* reflects static and dynamic feedback effects. The static amplification channel operates through $k_1, v_1,$ and q_0: Higher productivity increases net worth and enables investors to buy more capital; keeping future prices constant, this pushes up the user cost and thus the price of capital; and this increases net worth further (because of leverage). Formally, if future prices and thus future user costs remained unchanged, condition (8.21) would read $\hat{q}_0 = (R-1)\hat{k}_1/(R\varepsilon)$; the $R/(R-1)$ terms in equations (8.19) and (8.21) would balance;[13] and the effects on the price and capital

---

[13] In condition (8.19), the term $R/(R-1)$ reflects leverage; in equation (8.21), the term $(R-1)/R$ reflects user costs relative to the price of capital.

purchases, respectively, would reduce to

$$\hat{q}_0 = \frac{R-1}{R}\frac{\hat{y}}{\varepsilon},$$

$$\hat{k}_1 = \hat{y}.$$

Intertwined with this static channel is a dynamic amplification mechanism that operates through future capital holdings and user costs: Since the expansion of capital holdings and user costs is persistent, the price of capital rises much more strongly and this fuels the amplification.

Conversely, a shock that tightens the collateral constraint reduces investors' borrowing capacity and forces them to sell capital and deleverage. Since the price of capital is determined by the marginal unconstrained buyer, which is a lender in this case, and since lenders employ capital less productively than investors, the *fire sale* of capital (further) depresses the price below the fundamental value for the constrained investor, fueling the amplification.

The expansion (reduction) of investors' capital holdings after a positive (negative) net worth shock is mirrored by a persistent increase (decline) in output because capital employed by financially constrained investors is more productive. If investors were not borrowing constrained (the first-best case), a productivity shock would be reflected in output but the price of capital would not be affected.

8.3.3 Pecuniary Externalities and Constrained Inefficiency

A fire sale of capital by distressed investors is inefficient because it reallocates capital from more to less productive users and misaligns their marginal rates of transformation. The inefficiency is a consequence of market incompleteness; if investors could obtain insurance against negative net worth shocks or borrow more against future income, then the reallocation would be unnecessary. We have encountered similar sources of inefficiency in the context of households' savings and insurance choices when market incompleteness impedes consumption smoothing across time and histories, and causes marginal rates of substitution to be misaligned (see subsections 2.2.1, 4.1.1, and 4.2.1).

When an equilibrium allocation is inefficient because of borrowing, collateral, or other financial constraints, we may ask whether it is also *constrained* inefficient—that is, whether subject to the financial constraints, a feasible, Pareto superior allocation could be implemented. To address this question, we analyze the welfare effects of portfolio choices when markets are incomplete and we show that these effects generally are not fully internalized in equilibrium. We then ask whether a social planner subject to the same financial constraints as the private sector could improve on the equilibrium allocation. We argue that this is generally the case; that is, the decentralized equilibrium allocation generally is constrained inefficient.

Consider a stochastic economy with heterogeneous groups of households, indexed by h. Each group has a mass one of members. At date t, the representative household in group h has an endowment $w_t^{hn}(\epsilon^t)$ of good n and consumes $c_t^{hn}(\epsilon^t)$ units thereof. The price of good n is denoted $p_t^n(\epsilon^t)$. Preferences are time and state additive, with discount factor β and strictly concave period utility function, u^h. A household in group h maximizes $\sum_t \beta^t \mathbb{E}_0[u^h(c_t^h(\epsilon^t))]$ where $c_t^h(\epsilon^t)$ denotes the consumption vector at date t.

Assets are indexed by j. The representative household in group h holds $a_{t+1}^{hj}(\epsilon^t)$ units of asset j between dates t and $t+1$. The dividend and price of asset j, respectively, are denoted $d_t^j(\epsilon^t)$ and $p_t^j(\epsilon^t)$. The dynamic budget constraint of a group-h household thus reads

$$\sum_n p_t^n(\epsilon^t)\left(w_t^{hn}(\epsilon^t) - c_t^{hn}(\epsilon^t)\right) + \sum_j a_t^{hj}(\epsilon^{t-1})d_t^j(\epsilon^t) = \sum_j p_t^j(\epsilon^t)\left(a_{t+1}^{hj}(\epsilon^t) - a_t^{hj}(\epsilon^{t-1})\right).$$

Households may face financial constraints. We represent constraints for group h at date t, history ϵ^t by means of functions

$$\Gamma_t^h\left(\{a_{t+1}^{hj}(\epsilon^t)\}_j; \{p_t^j(\epsilon^t)\}_j, \epsilon^t\right).$$

For example, a borrowing constraint at date t can be represented as $\Gamma_t^h(\cdot, \epsilon^t) \geq 0$ with $\Gamma_t^h(\cdot, \epsilon^t) \equiv \sum_j p_t^j(\epsilon^t)a_{t+1}^{hj}(\epsilon^t)$.

Let $\lambda_t^h(\epsilon^t)$ and $\gamma_t^h(\epsilon^t)$ denote the normalized multipliers associated with the budget constraint and the financial constraint, respectively. The first-order condition with respect to $c_t^{hn}(\epsilon^t)$ is given by $u_n^h(c_t^h(\epsilon^t)) = \lambda_t^h(\epsilon^t)p_t^n$ and the first-order condition for $a_{t+1}^{hj}(\epsilon^t)$ reads

$$\lambda_t^h(\epsilon^t)p_t^j(\epsilon^t) = \beta\mathbb{E}_t\left[\lambda_{t+1}^h(\epsilon^{t+1})\left(d_{t+1}^j(\epsilon^{t+1}) + p_{t+1}^j(\epsilon^{t+1})\right)\right] + \gamma_t^h(\epsilon^t)\frac{\partial\Gamma_t^h(\cdot, \epsilon^t)}{\partial a_{t+1}^{hj}(\epsilon^t)},$$

indicating that a financial friction distorts the household's intertemporal choice.

An individual household takes prices as given when choosing its portfolio and consumption. In the aggregate, however, actions taken by households affect equilibrium prices and the representative household in each group therefore exerts a *pecuniary externality* on other households. This externality affects the allocation twofold: by directly changing the budget sets of others, and by tightening or relaxing financial constraints if these constraints depend on prices.

Suppose that a marginal portfolio change by households in group 1 causes equilibrium price changes $\{dp_t^n(\epsilon^t)\}_n$ and $\{dp_t^j(\epsilon^t)\}_j$ at date t, and let θ^h denote the social valuation of group h relative to group 1. From the budget and financial constraints, the marginal welfare effect due to the pecuniary externalities then equals

$$\sum_h \theta^h \lambda_t^h(\epsilon^t) \left\{ \sum_n dp_t^n(\epsilon^t) \left(w_t^{hn}(\epsilon^t) - c_t^{hn}(\epsilon^t) \right) + \sum_j dp_t^j(\epsilon^t) \left(a_t^{hj}(\epsilon^{t-1}) - a_{t+1}^{hj}(\epsilon^t) \right) \right\}$$

$$+ \sum_h \theta^h \gamma_t^h(\epsilon^t) \left\{ \sum_j dp_t^j(\epsilon^t) \frac{\partial \Gamma_{t,\epsilon^t}^h}{\partial p_t^j(\epsilon^t)} \right\}. \tag{8.22}$$

The terms multiplying $\theta^h \lambda_t^h(\epsilon^t)$ in the first line of (8.22) represent the income effects that a household in group h experiences as a consequence of altered prices: When the household consumes less of good n than its endowment, or when it sells asset j, then it benefits from a rise in $p_t^n(\epsilon^t)$ or $p_t^j(\epsilon^t)$, and vice versa. The term multiplying $\theta^h \gamma_t^h(\epsilon^t)$ in the second line represents the extent to which the financial constraint of a household in group h tightens or relaxes when asset prices change.

The sum of the income effects over all households equals zero because one household's gain corresponds to another household's loss. Formally, for every good n or asset j, market clearing implies

$$\sum_h (w_t^{hn}(\epsilon^t) - c_t^{hn}(\epsilon^t)) = 0 \text{ and } \sum_h a_t^{hj}(\epsilon^{t-1}) = \sum_i a_{t+1}^{hj}(\epsilon^t) = 0;$$

as a consequence, the income effects cancel each other. In contrast, the sum of the income effects weighted by their social valuation, $\theta^h \lambda_t^h(\epsilon^t)$, generally differs from zero; the sign of this sum depends on the covariance across groups between the income effect and the social valuation. The sum of the changes of the financial constraints as well as the sum of these changes weighted by their social valuation also generally differ from zero.

Expression (8.22) indicates that pecuniary externalities generally have first-order welfare implications, by redistributing income and altering financial constraints. When financial constraints are absent (or not binding) then the welfare effects only reflect income effects (given in the first line of (8.22)). Under specific conditions, even these effects vanish.

Most importantly, this is the case when markets are complete. To establish this result we use the first welfare theorem, according to which a complete markets allocation is Pareto optimal and thus solves a social planner problem. The planner maximizes utility of group 1, subject to the resource constraint as well as minimum utility requirements for the other groups. Letting θ^h denote the multiplier associated with the minimum utility requirement for group h, the planner's first-order conditions imply (see also subsection 4.2.1) $\theta^h u_n^h(c_t^h(\epsilon^t)) = u_n^1(c_t^1(\epsilon^t))$. Since in the decentralized equilibrium, marginal utility equals the shadow value of income times the price of a good, $u_n^h(c_t^h(\epsilon^t)) = \lambda_t^h(\epsilon) p_t^n$, we conclude that $\theta^h \lambda_t^h(\epsilon^t)$ is independent of h in the complete markets decentralized equilibrium,

$$\theta^h \lambda_t^h(\epsilon^t) = \lambda_t^1(\epsilon^t).$$

From the market clearing conditions, expression (8.22) then collapses to zero: When markets are complete, pecuniary externalities do not have first-order welfare effects. First-order welfare effects also are absent when there are no transactions; for example, because there is just one group of households or because the endowment allocation is Pareto optimal.

Returning to the general case with nonzero welfare effects from pecuniary externalities we analyze *constrained inefficiency*. Suppose that households face binding financial constraints which imply that the decentralized equilibrium allocation is not Pareto optimal. Can a social planner facing the same financial constraints do better—is the equilibrium allocation constrained inefficient—or does the private sector optimally make use of the limited options it has?

Addressing this question is conceptually difficult because a social planner problem does not involve prices, while prices are at the heart of the equilibrium conditions and the pecuniary externalities. Therefore, distinguishing between social planner interventions that go beyond what the private sector could achieve and those that do not is delicate.

Against this background, we assess constrained efficiency by restricting the admissible planner interventions to feasible consumption and portfolio choices at date $t = 0$; that is, we only allow the planner to choose $\{c_0^{hn}\}_{h,n}$ and $\{a_1^{hj}\}_{h,j}$ subject to the date-$t = 0$ resource and asset market clearing conditions. Starting from date $t = 1$, the allocation is determined by the equilibrium conditions. The intervention at date $t = 0$ enables the planner to internalize welfare effects due to pecuniary externalities in subsequent periods. When, as a consequence of this internalization, the planner implements an allocation that Pareto dominates the decentralized equilibrium allocation, then the latter is constrained inefficient.

Formally, let $V^h(\epsilon^1)$ denote lifetime welfare of a household in group h at date $t = 1$, history ϵ^1, in the competitive equilibrium; $V^h(\epsilon^1)$ is a function of $\{a_1^{hj}\}_{h,j}$ because these portfolio holdings determine the household's budget set both directly and indirectly, as they affect prices in general equilibrium. The social planner maximizes $u^1(c_0^1) + \beta \mathbb{E}_0[V^1(\epsilon^1)]$ subject to the constraints

$$\sum_h w_0^{hn} = \sum_h c_0^{hn}, \quad \sum_h a_1^{hj} = 0,$$
$$u^h(c_0^h) + \beta \mathbb{E}_0[V^h(\epsilon^1)] \geq \bar{V}^h, \ h \geq 1,$$

where $\bar{V}^h$ denotes the minimum utility requirement for group h. The planner's choice of consumption and portfolios at date $t = 0$ redistributes across groups and changes equilibrium prices, which has the welfare implications discussed previously. The planner's choice also induces responses by households who adjust their consumption and portfolio choices in subsequent periods, but envelope conditions imply that these responses do not have first-order welfare effects.

When markets are complete, the equilibrium allocation is Pareto efficient and thus also *constrained efficient*. This follows from two observations. First, the direct welfare effects from the planner's intervention amount to redistribution, not to a Pareto improvement. And second, the welfare effects due to pecuniary externalities at date $t = 1$ and later wash out when markets are complete, as shown above.

When markets are incomplete, in contrast, then the equilibrium allocation almost always is constrained inefficient—an appropriate social planner intervention at date $t = 0$ changes equilibrium prices and this increases the welfare of all households in the economy. Exceptionally, constrained efficiency prevails when prices do not enter the financial constraints and income effects are absent; for example, because there is just one group of households (such that there are no transactions); all groups of households have identical, homothetic preferences (such that equilibrium prices are independent of the wealth distribution); or the economy lasts for just two periods and there is only one good (such that there are no relative prices that can change).[14]

8.4 Bibliographic Notes

Jorgensen (1963) presents the neoclassical theory of investment; Tobin (1969) discusses the relative price of installed capital; and Hayashi (1982) analyzes the relation between marginal and average *q*. Lucas and Prescott (1971), Baldwin and Meyer (1979), McDonald and Siegel (1986), and Dixit (1989, chapters 1–2) study risky investment decisions and the option value of waiting.

Diamond (1982), Mortensen (1982), and Pissarides (1985) develop the search and matching model of the labor market. Pissarides (1990; 2000) describes the baseline model and reviews the literature. The presentation of the model with capital in the text follows Shimer (2010), who builds on Merz (1995). Hosios (1990) analyzes constrained efficiency and Hall (2005) proposes the model of individually rational sticky wages.

The costly state verification model is due to Townsend (1979); Bernanke and Gertler (1989) embed it in a general equilibrium framework; see also Carlstrom and Fuerst (1997) and Bernanke et al. (1999). Shleifer and Vishny (1992) analyze the fire-sale feedback loop between asset prices and asset sales of an investor in financial distress. Kiyotaki and Moore (1997) analyze collateral constraints in general equilibrium. Hart (1975), Stiglitz (1982), and Geanakoplos and Polemarchakis (1986) analyze pecuniary externalities and their efficiency implications in models with incomplete markets; Dávila and Korinek (2018) categorize pecuniary externalities.

---

[14] When markets at date $t = 0$ are complete but households are financially constrained starting at date $t = 1$, then the equilibrium allocation also is constrained efficient.

Related Topics and Additional References   Dixit and Pindyck (1994) cover models of irreversible, risky investment.

McCall (1970) analyzes job search in partial equilibrium. Lucas and Prescott (1974) study a general equilibrium model of spatially separated, competitive labor markets subject to persistent productivity shocks; workers in markets with low productivity optimally move to other markets with higher expected demand, at the cost of temporary (frictional) unemployment.

Modigliani and Miller (1958) show that the *value of a firm* is independent of its liability structure, a consequence of *value additivity* (see also Fisher, 1930; Williams, 1938). Incentive problems and other frictions undermine this result; see Tirole (2006) for a textbook treatment.

Stiglitz and Weiss (1981) analyze credit rationing due to adverse selection (Akerlof, 1970); in their model, raising the interest rate would worsen the pool of investors that seek funding and the profit-maximizing choice for lenders thus is to charge a non-market-clearing interest rate and to ration funding.

Hart and Moore (1994; 1998) propose micro-foundations for collateral constraints, including renegotiation in the face of incomplete contracts, the inalienability of human capital, or output diversion by investors.

Building on Holmström (1983) and Thomas and Worrall (1988) (in the context of wage contracts), Marcet and Marimon (1992; 2019), Kehoe and Levine (1993), and Kocherlakota (1996) analyze the conflict between insurance provision and incentive compatibility when an off-equilibrium breach of contract triggers financial autarky; they show that equilibrium consumption typically increases faster when the incentive constraint binds (see also section 13.4). Recursive formulations of the contracting problem rely on a *promised value* or the cumulative sum of multipliers associated with binding incentive constraints as a state variable; see Ljungqvist and Sargent (2018, chapters 21–22) for a textbook treatment. Alvarez and Jermann (2000) analyze the asset pricing implications of borrowing constraints due to lack of commitment.

Greenwald and Stiglitz (1986) analyze pecuniary externalities in models with incentive constraints. Caballero and Krishnamurthy (2003), Lorenzoni (2008), and Stein (2012), respectively, analyze financial market frictions and pecuniary externalities in the context of insufficient domestic insurance against exchange rate shocks, inefficient credit booms, and excessive safe asset creation. Dávila et al. (2012) analyze constrained efficiency in the neoclassical growth model with uninsurable income risk.

Brunnermeier and Sannikov (2014) analyze endogenous risk, nonlinear amplification effects, and the *volatility paradox*—lower exogenous risk induces leverage and more volatility during crises.

Brunnermeier et al. (2012) and Walsh (2017, sections 10.6–10.7) cover macroeconomic models with financial frictions. Magill and Quinzii (1996) cover equilibrium in economies with incomplete financial markets and heterogeneous agents (see their § 25 for an analysis of constrained inefficiency). Golosov et al. (2016) cover recursive contracts.

See also subsection 4.1.1 on incomplete markets and section 13.4 on sovereign debt.

9 Money

In the competitive equilibria we have analyzed so far, agents optimize subject to given relative prices and they trade in a centralized market or a sequence of such markets. A payment system is absent or rudimentary at best. Now we introduce *money*, an object that performs three functions. First, it serves as the unit of account in which prices are quoted. Second, it serves as the store of value for savings. Third, it serves as the medium of exchange or means of payment that helps reduce frictions due to the lack of a *double coincidence of wants*: Suppose an agent seeking to exchange good A for good B meets another agent seeking to exchange good C for good A. The first agent can sell A in exchange for money to the second agent, and money in exchange for B to a third party. The second agent can act similarly, in cooperation with a fourth party that in turn may trade with the third or other parties. Without money, all agents involved in these exchanges would have to meet at the same time and place in order to barter, or they would have to extend credit. Note that the means-of-payment function requires that money also serves as a store of value, at least temporarily.

Money can take the form of intrinsically worthless *fiat money*, like a bank note; it can be convertible into valuable objects like gold or silver; or it can be *commodity money* that provides a consumption value (or contributes to production) beyond serving as money. Money issued by the government constitutes *outside money* because it is a net asset for the private sector. In contrast, bank deposits constitute *inside money* because they are both a private sector asset (for deposit holders) and liability (for banks).

We introduce intrinsically worthless money that serves as a unit of account in the household's consumption–saving problem, and we analyze equilibrium prices, returns, and exchange rates. Subsequently, we study bubbly money that serves as a store of value although it does not pay interest. Finally, we analyze environments where frictions create a role for money as medium of exchange, and we derive the implications of the latter role for the value of money.

9.1   Unit of Account

Consider a generalization of the saving problem under risk studied in subsection 4.1.3. The infinitely lived household may invest both in real assets, $\{a_{t+1}^l(\epsilon^t)\}_l$, whose prices and returns are quoted in terms of the consumption good, and in nominal assets, $\{B_{t+1}^j(\epsilon^t)\}_j$, whose prices and returns are quoted in terms of money. The household may also invest in money, $M_{t+1}(\epsilon^t)$, which does not pay interest. Let $P_t(\epsilon^t)$ denote the *price level*; that is, the price of the consumption good in terms of money, which serves as the *unit of account*. Money has value if the price level is finite.

The household's dynamic budget constraint at date t reads

$$\sum_l a_{t+1}^l(\epsilon^t) + \frac{\sum_j B_{t+1}^j(\epsilon^t) + M_{t+1}(\epsilon^t)}{P_t(\epsilon^t)} = \tag{9.1}$$

$$w_t(\epsilon^t) + \frac{W_t(\epsilon^t)}{P_t(\epsilon^t)} - c_t(\epsilon^t) + \sum_l a_t^l(\epsilon^{t-1})R_t^l(\epsilon^t) + \frac{\sum_j B_t^j(\epsilon^{t-1})I_t^j(\epsilon^t) + M_t(\epsilon^{t-1})}{P_t(\epsilon^t)},$$

where $w_t(\epsilon^t)$, $W_t(\epsilon^t)$, and $c_t(\epsilon^t)$ denote real and nominal exogenous incomes as well as consumption, respectively. The gross real rate of return on asset l is denoted by $R_t^l(\epsilon^t)$, and the gross nominal rate of return on asset j by $I_t^j(\epsilon^t) \equiv 1 + i_t^j(\epsilon^t)$. To convert nominal incomes, returns, or asset purchases into real terms we divide by the price level.

The household maximizes $\sum_{t=0}^{\infty} \beta^t \mathbb{E}_0[u(c_t(\epsilon^t))]$, the discounted expected utility flows from consumption, subject to (9.1), a no-Ponzi-game condition, and the condition that money cannot be shorted, $M_{t+1} \geq 0$. Differentiating with respect to $a_{t+1}^l(\epsilon^t)$, $B_{t+1}^j(\epsilon^t)$, and $c_t(\epsilon^t)$, and letting $m_{t+1}(\epsilon^{t+1})$ denote the household's stochastic discount factor, we arrive at the stochastic Euler equation for real assets (see section 5.1) and a parallel condition for nominal assets,

$$1 = \mathbb{E}_t\left[m_{t+1}(\epsilon^{t+1})R_{t+1}^l(\epsilon^{t+1})\right] = \mathbb{E}_t\left[m_{t+1}(\epsilon^{t+1})\frac{I_{t+1}^j(\epsilon^{t+1})}{\Pi_{t+1}(\epsilon^{t+1})}\right]; \tag{9.2}$$

the latter contains the nominal return adjusted for inflation, $\Pi_{t+1}(\epsilon^{t+1}) \equiv P_{t+1}(\epsilon^{t+1})/P_t(\epsilon^t)$. In equilibrium, condition (9.2) holds for all nonmonetary assets in the household's portfolio. In section 9.2, we study the first-order condition with respect to $M_{t+1}(\epsilon^t)$.

9.1.1   Fisher Equation

Consider a real bond with risk-free gross real rate of return, $R_{t+1}(\epsilon^t)$, and a nominal bond with risk-free gross nominal rate of return, $I_{t+1}(\epsilon^t)$. If the household invests in both bonds, condition (9.2) implies

$$\begin{aligned} I_{t+1}^{-1}(\epsilon^t) &= \mathbb{E}_t\left[m_{t+1}(\epsilon^{t+1})\Pi_{t+1}^{-1}(\epsilon^{t+1})\right] \\ &= R_{t+1}^{-1}(\epsilon^t)\mathbb{E}_t\left[\Pi_{t+1}^{-1}(\epsilon^{t+1})\right] + \mathbb{C}\mathrm{ov}_t\left[m_{t+1}(\epsilon^{t+1}), \Pi_{t+1}^{-1}(\epsilon^{t+1})\right]. \end{aligned}$$

This is a stochastic version of the *Fisher equation*, which links inflation, real, and nominal interest rates.

In the absence of inflation risk, the covariance term equals zero and the Fisher equation reduces to

$$I_{t+1} = R_{t+1}\Pi_{t+1};$$

that is, the gross nominal interest rate equals the gross real rate times gross inflation. With risk, in contrast, the nominal interest rate reflects both the real rate, average (inverse) inflation, and a (positive or negative) inflation risk premium. Suppose, for example, that the covariance term is positive; that is, inverse inflation covaries positively with the stochastic discount factor, or inflation covaries positively with consumption at date $t + 1$. Then,

$$I_{t+1}^{-1}(\epsilon^t) > R_{t+1}^{-1}(\epsilon^t)\mathbb{E}_t\left[\Pi_{t+1}^{-1}(\epsilon^{t+1})\right].$$

Intuitively, the inflation-adjusted return on the nominal bond covaries negatively with future consumption in this case—the nominal bond is a good hedge—and this lowers the nominal interest rate (see section 5.2).

Combining the Fisher equation with the term structure of real interest rates (see section 5.4), we may also derive the *term structure of nominal interest rates*.

9.1.2   Interest Parity and Nominal Exchange Rate

Condition (9.2) also relates returns on assets that are denominated in different currencies. Let $E_t(\epsilon^t)$ denote the *nominal exchange rate*; that is, the price of one unit of foreign currency expressed in terms of domestic currency, and let a star denote foreign variables. The gross real rate of return on a foreign currency investment then equals

$$\frac{P_t(\epsilon^t)}{E_t(\epsilon^t)}I_{t+1}^{\star}(\epsilon^{t+1})\frac{E_{t+1}(\epsilon^{t+1})}{P_{t+1}(\epsilon^{t+1})} = \frac{I_{t+1}^{\star}(\epsilon^{t+1})}{E_t(\epsilon^t)}\frac{E_{t+1}(\epsilon^{t+1})}{\Pi_{t+1}(\epsilon^{t+1})},$$

because one unit of the good buys $P_t(\epsilon^t)$ units of domestic currency and thus, $P_t(\epsilon^t)/E_t(\epsilon^t)$ units of foreign currency. We conclude that, when the household invests in the foreign-currency-denominated asset, the equilibrium condition

$$1 = \mathbb{E}_t\left[m_{t+1}(\epsilon^{t+1})\frac{I_{t+1}^{\star}(\epsilon^{t+1})}{\Pi_{t+1}(\epsilon^{t+1})}\frac{E_{t+1}(\epsilon^{t+1})}{E_t(\epsilon^t)}\right]$$

holds.

Consider a domestic- and a foreign-currency-denominated bond with risk-free gross nominal rates of return $I_{t+1}(\epsilon^t)$ and $I_{t+1}^{\star}(\epsilon^t)$, respectively. When the household invests in both bonds, condition (9.2) and the previous equation imply the indifference condition

$$\mathbb{E}_t\left[\frac{m_{t+1}(\epsilon^{t+1})}{\Pi_{t+1}(\epsilon^{t+1})}\right]I_{t+1}(\epsilon^t) = \mathbb{E}_t\left[\frac{m_{t+1}(\epsilon^{t+1})}{\Pi_{t+1}(\epsilon^{t+1})}E_{t+1}(\epsilon^{t+1})\right]\frac{I_{t+1}^{\star}(\epsilon^t)}{E_t(\epsilon^t)}.$$

Suppose first that it is known at date t that the exchange rate at date $t + 1$ will equal $E_{t+1}(\epsilon^t)$; for example, because the household engages in a forward contract. The indifference condition then reduces to the *covered interest parity* condition,

$$E_t(\epsilon^t) = E_{t+1}(\epsilon^t) \frac{I^\star_{t+1}(\epsilon^t)}{I_{t+1}(\epsilon^t)},$$

which states that the foreign-currency interest rate exceeds the domestic-currency interest rate in proportion to the foreign-currency depreciation between dates t and $t+1$. Intuitively, when investments in the two currencies expose the household to identical risks, then the returns on the two strategies, expressed in domestic currency terms, must be identical; otherwise the household would not hold both bonds.

Suppose next that the exchange rate at date $t + 1$ is not known at date t. The indifference condition can then be expressed as

$$E_t(\epsilon^t) = \left(\mathbb{E}_t \left[E_{t+1}(\epsilon^{t+1}) \right] + \mathbb{C}\text{ov}_t \right) \frac{I^\star_{t+1}(\epsilon^t)}{I_{t+1}(\epsilon^t)},$$

where $\mathbb{C}\text{ov}_t$ denotes a covariance term. When we abstract from this term, we arrive at the *uncovered interest parity* condition. It states that a foreign-currency interest rate premium is associated with an *expected* depreciation of the foreign currency.

According to the *law of one price*, identical goods have the same price internationally as long as transportation costs and other impediments to trade are negligible. When all goods are tradable and the law of one price applies, then the real exchange rate equals one (see section 7.2) and (absolute) *purchasing power parity* holds; that is, the nominal exchange rate reflects differences in international price levels,

$$E_t(\epsilon^t) = P_t(\epsilon^t)/P^\star_t(\epsilon^t).$$

When prices only respond sluggishly to macroeconomic shocks (e.g., because of price rigidities; see chapter 10), then purchasing power parity only holds in the long run, after price levels have adjusted. In contrast, interest parity always holds, otherwise asset markets would not clear. The interplay between the two parities can give rise to nonmonotone and volatile exchange rate dynamics. Consider a domestic monetary expansion that temporarily lowers the interest rate and raises the domestic price level in the long run. Interest parity implies an expected exchange rate appreciation—a falling exchange rate—during the period of lower interest rates. At the same time, purchasing power parity implies that in the long run, the increased price level is reflected in a higher exchange rate. These two requirements can only jointly be satisfied if the exchange rate *overshoots* in the short run to an even higher level than in the long run. With inflexible prices, a monetary expansion thus gives rise to a strong depreciation of the domestic currency, which is partly undone during the transition to the new, long-run exchange rate.

9.2 Store of Value

So far, we have only analyzed the household's demand for nonmonetary assets. Consider now the first-order condition with respect to $M_{t+1}(\epsilon^t)$ in the savings problem laid out in section 9.1. Since money pays no interest and cannot be shorted, this is given by

$$1 \geq \mathbb{E}_t \left[m_{t+1}(\epsilon^{t+1}) \frac{1}{\Pi_{t+1}(\epsilon^{t+1})} \right],$$

with equality if the household chooses to hold money as a *store of value*. Comparing this condition with condition (9.2) and abstracting for simplicity from risk, we conclude that the household holds intrinsically worthless money with zero interest as a store of value only if $\Pi_{t+1}^{-1} = R_{t+1}$; that is, if money is a *bubble* whose price, $1/P_t$, grows at the real rate of interest. For such a bubble to be sustained in a rational expectations equilibrium, the economy's growth rate must exceed the real interest rate, as is the case in an inefficient overlapping generations economy (see subsection 5.3.2). We turn to this case next.

9.2.1 Overlapping Generations

Consider an overlapping generations endowment economy. Absent money, the steady-state life cycle consumption profile of each household equals its endowment profile, $(c_1, c_2) = (w_1, w_2)$, and the gross real interest rate equals the marginal rate of substitution,

$$R = \frac{u'(w_1)}{\beta u'(w_2)}.$$

Suppose that the gross population growth rate, v, strictly exceeds R; that is, the autarky equilibrium is inefficient.

Then there exists a Pareto superior equilibrium with valued, bubbly money that supports the efficient allocation with intergenerational transfers analyzed in subsection 3.2.7. In this superior equilibrium, the old cohort creates M units of intrinsically worthless money per capita of the young at date $t = 0$, which they sell to the young at price $1/P_0 < \infty$ in exchange for goods. At date $t = 1$, the then-old households sell the money at price $1/P_1 = v/P_0$ to the young of cohort 1. Since there are v young households per old household, the money market clears, and since the price level has fallen by the factor v, the gross real rate of return on money equals $P_0/P_1 = v$. The same pattern repeats in all subsequent periods.

The old at date $t = 0$ benefit from this arrangement because they receive goods in exchange for the money they create. To see that the young benefit as well, let $z \equiv M/P_0$ denote *real balances* at date $t = 0$. Under the monetary arrangement, welfare of a young household equals $u(w_1 - z) + \beta u(w_2 + zv)$; this exceeds $u(w_1) + \beta u(w_2)$ to the first order because

$$(u(w_1 - z) + \beta u(w_2 + zv)) - (u(w_1) + \beta u(w_2))$$
$$\approx -zu'(w_1) + z\beta v u'(w_2) > -zu'(w_1) + z\beta R u'(w_2) = 0.$$

Intuitively, money enables intergenerational transfers that help improve the allocation of consumption across cohorts, and thus over the life cycle (see subsection 3.2.7).

Note that there exists another equilibrium in which money is not valued. If the young at date t anticipate $P_{t+1} = \infty$, then money does not serve them as a store of value and accordingly, they do not give up resources in exchange for it, $P_t = \infty$. In an efficient economy, only the equilibrium without valued money exists.

9.2.2   Borrowing Constrained, Infinitely Lived Households

Consider next a model with two groups of infinitely lived representative households. Households in the first or "even" group receive a high endowment, $\bar{w}$, at even dates, starting at date $t = 0$, and a low endowment, $\underline{w}$, at odd dates; that is, their endowment stream is given by $\{\bar{w}, \underline{w}, \bar{w}, \ldots\}$. Households in the second or "odd" group, which has the same size, receive the same endowment stream shifted by one period, $\{\underline{w}, \bar{w}, \underline{w}, \ldots\}$. All households have the same CIES preferences. Let superscripts e and o denote variables of a typical household in the even or odd group, respectively.

Suppose first that markets are complete such that households can trade with each other. In a competitive equilibrium, a household in the even group solves

$$\max_{\{c_t^e, a_{t+1}^e\}_{t=0}^{\infty}} \sum_{t=0}^{\infty} \beta^t u(c_t^e) \ \text{ s.t. } \ c_t^e = w_t^e + a_t^e R_t - a_{t+1}^e, \ \ a_0^e = 0,$$

and a no-Ponzi-game condition. Here, c_t^e and a_t^e denote consumption and assets; R_t is the gross real interest rate; and w_t^e is high (low) in even (odd) periods. Households in the odd group solve a parallel program. The resource constraint is given by

$$c_t^e + c_t^o = w_t^e + w_t^o = \underline{w} + \bar{w}.$$

The households' Euler equations imply

$$\frac{u'(c_{t+1}^e)}{u'(c_t^e)} = \frac{u'(c_{t+1}^o)}{u'(c_t^o)}.$$

Since aggregate resources are constant over time, this implies that households in the even (odd) group consume the constant amount c^e (c^o). Market clearing then requires $R_t = \beta^{-1}$. Note that households in the even (odd) group carry assets (liabilities) from even to odd periods, $a_1^e = -a_1^o = a_3^e = -a_3^o = \ldots > 0$. In contrast, members of both groups carry zero assets or liabilities from odd to even periods. At each date, $a_{t+1}^e + a_{t+1}^o = 0$. The complete markets equilibrium is Pareto optimal.

Suppose next that households face borrowing constraints that prevent negative asset positions. A household in the even group then solves

$$\max_{\{c_t^e, a_{t+1}^e\}_{t=0}^{\infty}} \sum_{t=0}^{\infty} \beta^t u(c_t^e) \ \text{ s.t. } \ c_t^e = w_t^e + a_t^e R_t - a_{t+1}^e, \ \ a_0^e = 0, \ \ a_{t+1}^e \geq 0,$$

and its first-order and complementary slackness conditions read

$$u'(c_t^e) = \beta R_{t+1} u'(c_{t+1}^e) + \mu_t^e, \quad \mu_t^e a_{t+1}^e = 0,$$

where μ_t^e denotes the nonnegative multiplier attached to the borrowing constraint. Households in the odd group solve a parallel program.

One equilibrium in the incomplete markets environment is the autarkic equilibrium satisfying $c_t^e = w_t^e$, $c_t^o = w_t^o$, and $a_{t+1}^e = a_{t+1}^o = 0$ in all periods. The interest rate in this autarkic equilibrium is constant and satisfies

$$u'(\bar{w}) = \beta R u'(\underline{w}).$$

Another equilibrium, which we focus on, supports a bubble. As in the autarkic equilibrium, there is no lending and borrowing between members of the two groups. But unlike in the autarkic equilibrium, aggregate asset holdings are strictly positive, $a_{t+1}^e + a_{t+1}^o > 0$, and invested in a bubble. Households in the even (odd) group buy the bubble in even (odd) periods from members of the odd (even) group and sell it back in the subsequent period. When they buy the bubble, households satisfy the Euler equation subject to $\mu_t = 0$; and when they sell it they are borrowing constrained ($\mu_t > 0$). Letting a denote savings invested in the bubble, the equilibrium satisfies

$$
\begin{aligned}
u'(\bar{w} - a) &= \beta R u'(\underline{w} + aR), \\
u'(\underline{w} + aR) &\geq \beta R u'(\bar{w} - a), \quad a \geq 0.
\end{aligned}
$$

Goods market clearing requires aggregate consumption, $(\bar{w} - a) + (\underline{w} + aR)$, to equal the aggregate endowment, $\bar{w} + \underline{w}$, implying $R = 1$.

Note that the bubble size is limited in equilibrium; if the bubble were large, households could smooth consumption and the constraint would no longer be binding. But this would require $R = \beta^{-1}$, which is ruled out by market clearing.

To motivate the borrowing constraints, note that the equilibrium conditions in the bubbly equilibrium exactly mimic the conditions in the overlapping generations model analyzed in subsection 9.2.1 (for $w_1 = \bar{w}$, $w_2 = \underline{w}$, $z = a$, and $v = 1$). Although households in the even and odd groups are infinitely lived, the binding borrowing constraints divide their budget sets into two-period subsets that resemble the budget sets of short-lived cohorts. Another motivation relates the borrowing constraints to spatially separated trading posts. Envision a turnpike that extends to infinity in both directions. Households in the even (odd) group travel eastward (westward) along the turnpike and stop in each period at subsequent trading posts. A household therefore never meets another household more than once during its infinite lifetime, and no pair of households shares a trading partner in the past or the future. While this rules out any form of private lending and borrowing in a centralized market, it does admit trading of a bubble.

In parallel to the overlapping generations economy, the bubble in the *turnpike model* can be interpreted as real money balances. The gross interest rate on real balances in the turnpike model equals unity; that is, the price level is constant over time, reflecting the constant population size.

9.3   Medium of Exchange

When intrinsically worthless money is not a bubble—that is, when its price grows at a rate smaller than the rate of interest—this money will only be held if it generates benefits in addition to serving as a low-return store of value. The key additional benefit is that money serves as a *medium of exchange*—it lubricates trade. We analyze this function of money in three models; the first emphasizes micro-foundations, the other two tractability.

9.3.1   Matching Frictions

Consider an economy with a continuum of infinitely lived households of measure one. Since households are anonymous, private lending and borrowing is ruled out and all trade is *quid pro quo*.

Households are risk neutral and discount the future at factor β. They produce consumption goods at no cost and derive utility from the consumption of goods produced by a share $\gamma \in (0, 1)$ of the other households. Conditional on meeting a potential trading partner, which occurs with probability $\theta \in (0, 1)$, the probability of a double coincidence of wants therefore equals γ^2. Goods can be stored at no cost and are indivisible. Accepting a good in trade generates a small cost, ε, and consuming the preferred sort of good generates utility, u. Upon consuming, a household immediately produces a new good. In a monetary equilibrium, households thus always hold one good or one unit of money.

We conjecture that an equilibrium with valued money and constant price level, $P_t = 1$, exists. In such an equilibrium, a share $M \in (0, 1)$ of households hold money; households weakly prefer holding money over holding goods; and potential trading partners that hold a good therefore accept money with positive probability, $\hat{\eta} > 0$. Note that the medium of exchange role of money is coupled with a store of value role because money does not immediately change hands. Since accepting a good in trade has a small cost, no household with money buys a good except for its own consumption.

Three types of transactions may occur: A household might exchange a good against another good or sell it against money, or a household with money may buy a good. Let η denote the household's optimal probability of accepting money in exchange for goods—the household's best response to $\hat{\eta}$. The value of holding a good, V, and of holding money,

W, solve the Bellman equations

$$
\begin{aligned}
V &= \theta(1 - M)\gamma^2(u - \varepsilon + \beta V) + \theta M\gamma \max_\eta \beta[\eta W + (1 - \eta)V] \\
&\quad + (1 - \theta(1 - M)\gamma^2 - \theta M\gamma)\beta V \\
&= \beta V + \theta\gamma\left((1 - M)\gamma(u - \varepsilon) + M\beta \max_\eta[\eta(W - V)]\right), \\
W &= \theta(1 - M)\gamma\hat{\eta}(u - \varepsilon + \beta V) + (1 - \theta(1 - M)\gamma\hat{\eta})\beta W \\
&= \beta W + \theta(1 - M)\gamma\hat{\eta}(u - \varepsilon + \beta(V - W)).
\end{aligned}
$$

Intuitively, the value of holding the good derives from three sources: The possibility of exchanging the good against the preferred consumption good; the possibility of exchanging it against money if this improves the continuation value; and the continuation value if no trading partner is met. The value of holding money derives from the possibility that other households accept it in exchange for the preferred consumption good, and from the continuation value.

The first Bellman equation implies that the household's optimal response only depends on the difference between V and W: If $W > V$ then $\eta = 1$; if $W < V$ then $\eta = 0$; and if $W = V$ then $\eta \in [0, 1]$. From the second Bellman equation, $\hat{\eta} = 0$ implies $W = 0$; when other households do not accept money, then holding money has no value. Finally, combining the two Bellman equations yields the result that $\hat{\eta} < \gamma$ implies $W < V$, and thus $\eta = 0$; $\hat{\eta} > \gamma$ implies $W > V$, and thus $\eta = 1$; and $\hat{\eta} = \gamma$ implies $W = V$, and thus $\eta \in [0, 1]$. We conclude that conditional on $M \in (0, 1)$, monetary equilibria exist: They require $\hat{\eta} = \eta \geq \gamma$.

The optimal monetary equilibrium under the *veil of ignorance*; that is, before households know their initial endowment, maximizes $(1 - M)V + MW$ subject to $\hat{\eta} = \eta \geq \gamma$. Suppose that initially, a third party offers to exchange at most $\bar{M}$ units of money against the same number of goods. When households anticipate $\hat{\eta} > \gamma$ such that $W > V$, then all households that have the possibility to do so accept this offer. In the aggregate, this does not only lubricate trade, which has a positive effect on welfare, but it also reduces the number of goods available for consumption, which has a negative effect. This puts an upper bound on the optimal $\bar{M}$.

When households anticipate $\hat{\eta} = \gamma$ (such that $W = V$), in contrast, then the economy is better off in a nonmonetary equilibrium because money does not lubricate trade beyond what the exchange of goods achieves.

9.3.2   Money in the Utility Function

Suppose next that a household that purchases consumption goods does not only spend income but also *shopping time*, which reduces the time available for leisure consumption. Real balances, $z_{t+1}(\epsilon^t) \equiv M_{t+1}(\epsilon^t)/P_t(\epsilon^t)$, provide *transactions services* and reduce the required shopping time per unit of consumption, rendering real balances and shopping time partial substitutes. We assume that purchasing $c_t(\epsilon^t)$ units of consumption goods requires $\ell(c_t(\epsilon^t), z_{t+1}(\epsilon^t))$ units of time, where function ℓ strictly increases in the transactions volume and decreases in real balances. Household utility increases in consumption and leisure, $\tilde{u}(c_t(\epsilon^t), x_t(\epsilon^t))$. Substituting the time constraint, $1 = x_t(\epsilon^t) + \ell(c_t(\epsilon^t), z_{t+1}(\epsilon^t))$, into the utility function $\tilde{u}$, we arrive at the reduced form *money-in-the-utility-function* specification

$$u(c_t(\epsilon^t), z_{t+1}(\epsilon^t)).$$

We assume that u is strictly increasing in consumption and, up to some point, in real balances (reflecting restrictions on the functions ℓ and $\tilde{u}$). We also assume that u is strictly concave with positive cross-partial derivatives.

The household maximizes $\sum_{t=0}^{\infty} \beta^t \mathbb{E}_0[u(c_t(\epsilon^t), z_{t+1}(\epsilon^t))]$ subject to (9.1), a no-Ponzi-game condition, and the constraint that money cannot be shorted. The first-order conditions are given by (9.2) for all assets other than money, and the additional condition

$$u_z(c_t(\epsilon^t), z_{t+1}(\epsilon^t)) = u_c(c_t(\epsilon^t), z_{t+1}(\epsilon^t)) - \beta \mathbb{E}_t \left[\frac{u_c(c_{t+1}(\epsilon^{t+1}), z_{t+2}(\epsilon^{t+1}))}{\Pi_{t+1}(\epsilon^{t+1})} \right]. \tag{9.3}$$

Intuitively, the marginal utility of consumption that the household forgoes when buying a unit of real balances is equalized with the marginal benefit of holding real balances for transactions services, plus the discounted expected marginal utility of consuming what the real balances buy in the subsequent period. Note that the right-hand side of the equality can be expressed as the product of the marginal utility of consumption, $u_c(c_t(\epsilon^t), z_{t+1}(\epsilon^t))$, and the cost of holding a unit of real balances overnight,

$$1 - \mathbb{E}_t[m_{t+1}(\epsilon^{t+1}) \Pi_{t+1}^{-1}(\epsilon^{t+1})].$$

When the market clearing nominal interest rate is positive, this cost is positive as well (see equation (9.2)).

Combining conditions (9.2) and (9.3) and assuming a risk-free nominal interest rate, we arrive at

$$\frac{u_z(c_t(\epsilon^t), z_{t+1}(\epsilon^t))}{u_c(c_t(\epsilon^t), z_{t+1}(\epsilon^t))} = 1 - \mathbb{E}_t[m_{t+1}(\epsilon^{t+1}) \Pi_{t+1}^{-1}(\epsilon^{t+1})] = \frac{i_{t+1}(\epsilon^t)}{I_{t+1}(\epsilon^t)}. \tag{9.4}$$

This represents a *money demand* function; it states that the demand for real balances is positively related to the transactions volume (consumption), and negatively to the opportunity cost of holding money (the nominal interest rate). Stated differently, conditional on consumption, real balances depend negatively on the nominal interest rate and the *velocity of money*, $c_t(\epsilon^t)/z_{t+1}(\epsilon^t)$, thus depends positively on it.

The left equality in condition (9.4) also can be expressed as an asset pricing equation: Dividing condition (9.3) by $P_t(\epsilon^t)$ and iterating forward yields

$$\frac{u_c(c_t(\epsilon^t), z_{t+1}(\epsilon^t))}{P_t(\epsilon^t)} = \sum_{s=0}^{\infty} \beta^s \mathbb{E}_t \left[\frac{u_z(c_{t+s}(\epsilon^{t+s}), z_{t+s+1}(\epsilon^{t+s}))}{P_{t+s}(\epsilon^{t+s})} \right].$$

The condition states that the price of a unit of nominal balances, $1/P_t(\epsilon^t)$, equals the discounted value of a dividend stream from nominal balances, normalized by the marginal utility of consumption. The dividend, in turn, is given by the transaction services provided by a unit of real balances, divided by the price level. Note that absent transaction services from money, the price of money equals zero. Unlike in the models studied in section 9.2 and subsection 9.3.1, however, money can have strictly positive value even if it is not valued in the infinite future.

Consider for simplicity the deterministic case with no exogenous nominal income and with a single (real) asset other than money. We can then express condition (9.1) as

$$d_{t+1} = d_t R_t + w_t - c_t - z_t(R_t - \Pi_t^{-1}) = d_t R_t + w_t - c_t - z_t R_t i_t / I_t,$$

where we define $d_{t+1} \equiv a_{t+1} + z_{t+1}$. For a given level of financial assets, d_t, the return on the household's portfolio decreases in the level of real balances, z_t, unless the nominal interest rate equals zero. This reflects the cost of holding money. Iterating the budget constraint forward and imposing a transversality condition yields

$$d_0 R_0 + \sum_{t=0}^{\infty} \frac{w_t}{R_1 \cdots R_t} = \sum_{t=0}^{\infty} \frac{c_t}{R_1 \cdots R_t} + \sum_{t=0}^{\infty} \frac{z_t i_t}{R_1 \cdots R_{t-1} I_t},$$

indicating that wealth (on the left-hand side of the equation) equals consumption outlays and the cost of holding money.

In steady state, all real variables including real balances are constant; nominal balances and the price level grow at a constant gross rate, say μ. Condition (9.2) thus implies $R = \beta^{-1}$ and $I = \mu\beta^{-1}$: The money growth rate determines the inflation rate and affects the nominal interest rate but it has no effect on the real interest rate.

To derive the effect of μ on steady-state capital, income, and consumption, we embed the household's problem in the representative agent general equilibrium environment studied in section 3.1. The condition $R = \beta^{-1}$ then determines the capital–labor ratio. Suppose first that the representative household's labor supply is fixed at unity (i.e., the time endowment available for leisure and shopping time is measured net of the time spent working). This implies that the representative household's capital and labor income are independent of μ. The budget constraint (9.1) thus reduces to $c = f(k, 1) - \delta k - (M_{t+1} - M_t)/P_t = f(k, 1) - \delta k - (1 - \mu^{-1})z$. We conclude that money is *neutral*: The steady-state allocation is not affected by a level change in nominal balances, which is reflected in an equiproportional change in the price level. The growth rate of money, however, does affect the allocation (it reduces consumption).

Assume, in addition, that the steady-state income loss that the household experiences from holding nominal balances, $(1 - \mu^{-1})z$, is compensated by an equal-sized transfer income from the newly injected money; that is, there is a *helicopter drop* of money. Or suppose alternatively that the household's real balances are negligible in size; that is, the economy is in the *cashless limit*. In either case, steady-state consumption is independent not only of the level of nominal balances but also of their growth rate, μ; that is, money is *superneutral*: Its growth rate does not affect the steady-state allocation except that real balances fall if μ, and thus inflation and the nominal interest rate, increase.

Outside of steady state, monetary neutrality prevails in the cashless limit, provided that utility is separable between consumption and real balances such that the first-order conditions characterizing the household's choices of real variables are independent of nominal balances and prices. If utility is nonseparable, money generally is not neutral because real balances affect the marginal utility of consumption.

Suppose next that labor supply is endogenous. When working time enters preferences, the interaction between the marginal disutility of working and the marginal utility of real balances creates a link between μ and steady-state labor supply, and thus consumption, even in the cashless limit. In general, money therefore is neither neutral nor superneutral.

9.3.3   Cash-in-Advance Constraint

Consider finally an environment in which only real balances provide transactions services. At the beginning of date t, asset markets open and the household rebalances its portfolio and replenishes money holdings, $M_{t+1}(\epsilon^t)$. Subsequently, it purchases consumption goods against money subject to the *cash-in-advance constraint*

$$\frac{M_{t+1}(\epsilon^t)}{P_t(\epsilon^t)} \geq c_t(\epsilon^t),$$

which stipulates that consumption purchases cannot exceed the real balances the household has acquired at the beginning of the period.

Nominal income in the form of cash, $W_{t-1}(\epsilon^{t-1})$, cannot be spent in the period when it is earned; the cash must rather be carried into the following period. The dynamic budget constraint (9.1) thus is replaced by the condition

$$\sum_l a_{t+1}^l(\epsilon^t) + \frac{\sum_j B_{t+1}^j(\epsilon^t) + M_{t+1}(\epsilon^t)}{P_t(\epsilon^t)} = w_t(\epsilon^t) + \sum_l a_t^l(\epsilon^{t-1}) R_t^l(\epsilon^t) \qquad (9.5)$$

$$+ \frac{\sum_j B_t^j(\epsilon^{t-1}) I_t^j(\epsilon^t) + W_{t-1}(\epsilon^{t-1}) + M_t(\epsilon^{t-1}) - c_{t-1}(\epsilon^{t-1}) P_{t-1}(\epsilon^{t-1})}{P_t(\epsilon^t)}.$$

The three right-most terms in the constraint represent real balances carried into the period, which originate from two sources: Cash income generated at date $t - 1$, and real balances acquired on the asset market at the beginning of date $t - 1$, which were not spent on consumption.

The household maximizes $\sum_{t=0}^{\infty} \beta^t \mathbb{E}_0[u(c_t(\epsilon^t))]$ subject to the cash-in-advance constraint, the budget constraint (9.5), and a no-Ponzi-game condition. The first-order conditions for this problem are given by (9.2) for all nonmonetary assets, as well as

$$\xi_t(\epsilon^t) = u'(c_t(\epsilon^t)) - \beta \mathbb{E}_t \left[\frac{u'(c_{t+1}(\epsilon^{t+1}))}{\Pi_{t+1}(\epsilon^{t+1})} \right] = u'(c_t(\epsilon^t)) \frac{i_{t+1}(\epsilon^{t+1})}{I_{t+1}(\epsilon^{t+1})}, \qquad (9.6)$$

where $\xi_t(\epsilon^t)$ denotes the normalized multiplier associated with the cash-in-advance constraint.

Note the close parallels between the first-order conditions (9.3) and (9.6). Both in the money-in-the-utility-function and the cash-in-advance-constraint model, the means-of-payments benefit provided by money (which is represented by the multiplier in the case of the cash-in-advance-constraint model) is equalized with the financial loss that the household bears when holding money. Note also that a strictly positive nominal interest rate implies that the multiplier $\xi_t(\epsilon^t)$ is strictly positive as well, such that real balances equal consumption; that is, the velocity of money equals one. With a strictly positive nominal interest rate, the budget constraint (9.5) thus reduces to

$$\sum_l a_{t+1}^l(\epsilon^t) + \frac{\sum_j B_{t+1}^j(\epsilon^t)}{P_t(\epsilon^t)} =$$

$$w_t(\epsilon^t) - c_t(\epsilon^t) + \sum_l a_t^l(\epsilon^{t-1}) R_t^l(\epsilon^t) + \frac{\sum_j B_t^j(\epsilon^{t-1}) I_t^j(\epsilon^t) + W_{t-1}(\epsilon^{t-1})}{P_t(\epsilon^t)}.$$

Naturally, the parallels between conditions (9.3) and (9.6) extend to the asset pricing representation. Dividing the first equality in (9.6) by $P_t(\epsilon^t)$ and iterating forward yields

$$\frac{u'(c_t(\epsilon^t))}{P_t(\epsilon^t)} = \sum_{s=0}^{\infty} \beta^s \mathbb{E}_t \left[\frac{\xi_{t+s}(\epsilon^{t+s})}{P_{t+s}(\epsilon^{t+s})} \right].$$

The condition states that the price of a unit of nominal balances is strictly positive as long as the cash-in-advance constraint binds in the present or the future.

With a different timing convention, the velocity of money may differ from unity. Suppose that the asset market opens at the end of a period, after uncertainty has been revealed and consumption goods have been purchased. Households then choose money holdings before they know the state of nature in the subsequent period when they spend the money, and depending on the state of nature, the cash-in-advance constraint may be slack.

Formally, with the modified timing convention the cash-in-advance constraint reads

$$\frac{M_t(\epsilon^{t-1})}{P_t(\epsilon^t)} \geq c_t(\epsilon^t)$$

and the budget constraint is given by (9.1). The cash-in-advance constraint now drives a wedge between the marginal utility of consumption and the marginal utility of wealth, $\lambda_t(\epsilon^t)$, because holding money to purchase consumption goods in the subsequent period implies that interest income is forgone: $u'(c_t(\epsilon^t)) = \lambda_t(\epsilon^t) + \xi_t(\epsilon^t)$. As a consequence, condition (9.2) only holds in modified form, with the marginal utility of consumption replaced by the shadow value of income, $\lambda_t(\epsilon^t)$. Also, from the first-order condition with respect to money holdings, condition (9.6) is replaced by

$$\frac{\beta \mathbb{E}_t \left[\xi_{t+1}(\epsilon^{t+1}) \Pi_{t+1}^{-1}(\epsilon^{t+1}) \right]}{\lambda_t(\epsilon^t)} = \frac{i_{t+1}(\epsilon^{t+1})}{I_{t+1}(\epsilon^{t+1})},$$

reflecting the fact that the benefit of investing in money—relaxing the cash-in-advance constraint in the subsequent period—is stochastic under the modified timing convention.

9.4   The Price of Money

In subsections 9.3.2 and 9.3.3, we related the price of money, $1/P_t(\epsilon^t)$, to the expected present value of services that nominal balances provide. In the money-in-the-utility-function framework, these services derive from the marginal utility of real balances, and in the model with a cash-in-advance constraint they reflect the shadow value of relaxing that constraint. We now offer a modified representation.

We consider a general setup with money as a medium of exchange. The nominal gross interest rate on money, $I_t^M(\epsilon^t)$, may differ from unity.[15] Letting $z_{t+1}(\epsilon^t) \equiv M_{t+1}(\epsilon^t)/P_t(\epsilon^t)$ denote real balances, the dynamic budget constraint reads

$$\ldots + z_{t+1}(\epsilon^t) = z_t(\epsilon^{t-1}) \frac{I_t^M(\epsilon^t)}{\Pi_t(\epsilon^t)} \ldots,$$

where we suppress all terms that do not involve money. The equality generalizes condition (9.1), which follows in the special case of $I_t^M(\epsilon^t) = 1$.

A second constraint captures frictions that give rise to a role for money as a medium of exchange. We represent this constraint as

$$\psi_t(z_{t+1}(\epsilon^t), \ldots) \geq (=)\, 0,$$

where we suppress terms other than real balances. The constraint states that the household's real balances and other variables (indicated by dots) satisfy certain cross restrictions. For example, with a cash-in-advance constraint, function ψ_t is given by the difference between real balances and consumption, and the constraint requires this difference to be positive. With a shopping-time specification, function ψ_t relates the household's time endowment, leisure, consumption, and real balances; and the constraint is specified as an equality. Since the shopping-time friction is isomorphic to a money-in-the-utility-function friction (see subsection 9.3.2), the ψ_t constraint can equally represent the latter, as well as many other frictions.

---

[15] If the "money" also paid a real dividend, then the price of money derived below would additionally contain a fundamental value component (see subsection 5.3.1).

Let $\lambda_t(\epsilon^t)$ and $\mu_t(\epsilon^t)$ denote the nonnegative, normalized (by the probability of history ϵ^t) multipliers attached to the ψ_t and budget constraints at date t, respectively. The household's first-order condition with respect to real balances,

$$\mu_t(\epsilon^t) = \mathbb{E}_t\left[\mu_{t+1}(\epsilon^{t+1})\frac{I_{t+1}^M(\epsilon^{t+1})}{\Pi_{t+1}(\epsilon^{t+1})}\right] + \lambda_t(\epsilon^t)\frac{\partial\psi_t(z_{t+1}(\epsilon^t),\ldots)}{\partial z_{t+1}(\epsilon^t)},$$

states that a household investing in real balances equalizes the financial cost, represented on the left-hand side, and the payoff as well as the benefit of relaxing the ψ_t constraint, represented on the right-hand side. Note that conditions (9.3) and (9.6) are instances of this condition because the stochastic discount factor satisfies $m_{t+1}(\epsilon^{t+1}) = \mu_{t+1}(\epsilon^{t+1})/\mu_t(\epsilon^t)$.

Dividing by $\mu_t(\epsilon^t)P_t(\epsilon^t)$ yields

$$\frac{1}{P_t} = \mathbb{E}_t\left[m_{t+1}\frac{I_{t+1}^M}{P_{t+1}}\right] + \frac{1}{P_t}\frac{\lambda_t}{\mu_t}\frac{\partial\psi_t(z_{t+1},\ldots)}{\partial z_{t+1}},$$

where we suppress histories to improve legibility. Collecting terms, we find

$$\frac{1}{P_t} = \mathbb{E}_t\left[m_{t+1}\Lambda_{t+1}\frac{I_{t+1}^M}{P_{t+1}}\right], \tag{9.7}$$

where we define the "*liquidity discount factor*"

$$\Lambda_{t+1} \equiv \left(1 - \frac{\lambda_t}{\mu_t}\frac{\partial\psi_t(z_{t+1},\ldots)}{\partial z_{t+1}}\right)^{-1}.$$

Note that $\Lambda_{t+1} > 1$ when the ψ_t constraint binds ($\lambda_t > 0$) and real balances relax the constraint. Equation (9.7) states that the medium-of-exchange role of money alters the effective discount factor.

Iterating condition (9.7) forward yields

$$\frac{1}{P_t} = \lim_{T\to\infty}\mathbb{E}_t\left[m_{t,t+T}\Lambda_{t,t+T}I_{t,t+T}^M\frac{1}{P_{t+T}}\right],$$

where $m_{t,t+s} \equiv \prod_{j=1}^s m_{t+j}$ denotes the multiperiod stochastic discount factor, and similarly $\Lambda_{t,t+s} \equiv \prod_{j=1}^s \Lambda_{t+j}$ and $I_{t,t+s}^M \equiv \prod_{j=1}^s I_{t+j}^M$. According to this forward solution valued money is a bubble where the discount factor reflects the stochastic discount factor, the liquidity discount factor, and the nominal interest rate on money. In the following, we let $I_{t,t+T}^M = 1$; whether a money-bubble is sustainable then depends on the properties of $m_{t,t+T}$ and $\Lambda_{t,t+T}$ (see subsection 5.3.2).

If money does not have a medium-of-exchange role such that $\Lambda_{t,t+T} = 1$ and if its price is stable across histories (money is a safe asset), then the forward solution reduces to $P_t^{-1} = \lim_{T\to\infty}\mathbb{E}_t[m_{t,t+T}]P_{t+T}^{-1}$. When $m_{t,t+T}$ is very volatile, for instance because the household faces large uninsurable risks, then the long-term gross risk-free interest rate may be sufficiently low to sustain a money bubble, $1/\mathbb{E}_t[m_{t,t+T}] < 1$. When money also has a medium-of-exchange role and $\Lambda_{t,t+T}$ exceeds unity sufficiently strongly, then a money bubble may be sustainable even if the real interest rate is high; that is, even if money is an unattractive store of value.

A bank that issues money in exchange for interest bearing assets earns rents because it sells a bubble. Although the bubble does not produce fundamental payoffs, it is valuable for the buyer because it relaxes the ψ_t constraint. While the issuer's assets and liabilities have the same market value, the former yield higher fundamental payoffs than the latter; the discounted fundamental payoff difference contributes to the issuer's *franchise value*, which is reflected in its equity market value.

9.5 Bibliographic Notes

Hahn's problem—the difficulty of rationalizing why intrinsically worthless money has strictly positive value in general equilibrium—is spelled out in Hahn (1965). Fisher (1896) discusses the effect of inflation on interest rates; see also Fisher (1930). Keynes (1923) and Cassel (1918) discuss the interest parity and purchasing power parity conditions, respectively. The overshooting model is due to Dornbusch (1976).

Samuelson (1958), Shell (1971), and Wallace (1980) analyze money in the overlapping generations model. The turnpike model is due to Townsend (1980); see also Woodford (1990).

The model in subsection 9.3.1 follows Kiyotaki and Wright (1993). Sidrauski (1967) analyzes the effects of money in the utility function. Baumol (1952) and Tobin (1956) study the demand for money when the latter serves transaction purposes and portfolio rebalancing is costly. The shopping-time specification is due to Saving (1971) and McCallum and Goodfriend (1987); Feenstra (1986) and Croushore (1993) relate it to specifications with money in the utility function. The cash-in-advance constraint is due to Clower (1967); Grandmont and Younes (1972), Lucas (1980; 1982), and Svensson (1985) analyze models with cash-in-advance constraints. Lucas and Stokey (1987) study a model with *cash goods* (purchases of which are subject to a cash-in-advance constraint) and *credit goods* (which are not); substitution between the two types of goods renders the velocity of money interest elastic.

Bewley (1980) analyzes money demand in a stochastic incomplete markets environment, where households hold (bubbly) money to self-insure (see also sections 4.4 and 5.6). Brunnermeier and Sannikov (2016) analyze financial intermediation in such an environment. Section 9.4 follows Brunnermeier and Niepelt (2019); Brunnermeier and Niepelt (2019) also analyze the macroeconomic role of inside vs. outside money.

Related Topics and Additional References Kareken and Wallace (1981) establish nominal exchange rate indeterminacy in an overlapping generations economy with multiple fiat monies serving as stores of value. A version of *Gresham's law* holds: The money injected at the fastest rate drives out the other monies.

Kiyotaki and Wright (1989) study the emergence of specific commodities as commodity monies. Lagos and Wright (2005) develop a tractable matching model of monetary exchange.

Walsh (2017) covers monetary economics. Rocheteau and Nosal (2017) review the *New Monetarist* approach to monetary economics and finance in the tradition of Kiyotaki and Wright (1989; 1993) and Lagos and Wright (2005).

10 Price Setting and Price Rigidity

We have assumed so far that firms take prices as given (except in section 8.2, where we modeled firms and workers as bargaining over wages). We now modify this assumption and introduce market power. This opens up the possibility that firms actively set prices and by implication, that they set prices at levels that differ from those in the frictionless benchmark case.

We analyze the decisions of a firm with pricing power under two assumptions: That prices can be adjusted costlessly, or that the adjustment is subject to frictions. We analyze the distortions and aggregate demand externalities associated with price setting, and we study the implications of infrequent price adjustment—price rigidity—in general equilibrium.

10.1 Price Setting

Consider an environment with a continuum of *intermediate good* producers and a continuum of *final good* producers. Final good producers are competitive. Intermediate good producers, in contrast, are *monopolistic competitors*: They produce differentiated goods for which there are no perfect substitutes from other producers. Accordingly, the monopolistically competitive firms face a finite price elasticity of demand—they have pricing power—and they charge a price above marginal cost.

Formally, intermediate good producer j employs a constant-returns-to-scale technology to produce intermediate good variety j, $y_t(j, \epsilon^t)$, which it sells at price $P_t(j, \epsilon^t)$ to final good producers. The latter combine the varieties to produce the final good, $y_t(\epsilon^t)$. Their production function is given by

$$y_t(\epsilon^t) = \left(\int_0^1 y_t(j, \epsilon^t)^{\frac{\epsilon-1}{\epsilon}} \, dj \right)^{\frac{\epsilon}{\epsilon-1}}, \tag{10.1}$$

where $\epsilon > 1$ denotes the constant elasticity of substitution (see subsection 1.2.3).

A final good producer takes the intermediate good prices, $\{P_t(j, \epsilon^t)\}_{j \in [0,1]}$, as given and maximizes final good production subject to a given level of input costs, say Z. The Lagrangian associated with this program reads

$$\mathcal{L} = \left(\int_0^1 y_t(j,\epsilon^t)^{\frac{\varepsilon-1}{\varepsilon}} dj \right)^{\frac{\varepsilon}{\varepsilon-1}} - \lambda \left(\int_0^1 y_t(j,\epsilon^t) P_t(j,\epsilon^t) dj - Z \right).$$

Note that the unit cost, and thus the price of the final good, is given by

$$P_t(\epsilon^t) = \frac{\int_0^1 y_t(j,\epsilon^t) P_t(j,\epsilon^t) dj}{y_t(\epsilon^t)}.$$

From the Lagrangian, marginally raising Z increases the optimal final good output by λ. Moreover, by definition, $Z = y_t(\epsilon^t) P_t(\epsilon^t)$. This implies $\lambda^{-1} = P_t(\epsilon^t)$.

Differentiating the Lagrangian with respect to $y_t(j,\epsilon^t)$ yields

$$y_t(j,\epsilon^t)^{-\frac{1}{\varepsilon}} y_t(\epsilon^t)^{\frac{1}{\varepsilon}} = \lambda P_t(j,\epsilon^t),$$

which can be expressed as

$$y_t(j,\epsilon^t) = \left(\frac{P_t(j,\epsilon^t)}{P_t(\epsilon^t)} \right)^{-\varepsilon} y_t(\epsilon^t). \tag{10.2}$$

Condition (10.2) determines the relative demand for varieties; higher substitutability (higher ε) renders the relative demand more price elastic. Substituting condition (10.2) into the spending constraint yields

$$P_t(\epsilon^t) y_t(\epsilon^t) = Z = \int_0^1 y_t(j,\epsilon^t) P_t(j,\epsilon^t) dj = y_t(\epsilon^t) P_t(\epsilon^t)^\varepsilon \int_0^1 P_t(j,\epsilon^t)^{1-\varepsilon} dj,$$

which reduces to

$$P_t(\epsilon^t) = \left(\int_0^1 P_t(j,\epsilon^t)^{1-\varepsilon} dj \right)^{\frac{1}{1-\varepsilon}}. \tag{10.3}$$

Condition (10.3) defines the final good price index.

Turn next to intermediate good firms and their *price setting* problem. A producer of variety j maximizes profits subject to the demand curve represented by (10.2). Since the intermediate goods technology exhibits constant returns to scale, the producer's marginal and average cost is independent of the quantity produced, and thus the same for all intermediate good producers. Letting $\psi_t(\epsilon^t)$ denote marginal cost expressed in units of the final good, an intermediate good producer maximizes

$$\left(\frac{P_t(j,\epsilon^t)}{P_t(\epsilon^t)} - \psi_t(\epsilon^t) \right) y_t(j,\epsilon^t) \text{ s.t. (10.2),}$$

taking $P_t(\epsilon^t)$ and $y_t(\epsilon^t)$ as given. The first-order condition of this program with respect to $P_t(j,\epsilon^t)$ reduces to

$$P_t(j,\epsilon^t) = \psi_t(\epsilon^t) P_t(\epsilon^t) \frac{\varepsilon}{\varepsilon-1};$$

that is, an intermediate good producer sets its price as a *markup* over nominal marginal cost. Higher substitutability (higher ε) reduces pricing power and implies a lower markup. In the limit where $\varepsilon \to \infty$, the markup disappears and price equals nominal marginal cost. In an equilibrium where all producers adjust their prices every period, $P_t(j, \epsilon^t) = P_t(\epsilon^t)$ and $1 = \psi_t(\epsilon^t)\varepsilon/(\varepsilon - 1)$.

Monopolistic competition depresses output below the first-best level. If the intermediate and final good producers were to jointly optimize, they would maximize final good output net of input costs for intermediate good production,

$$\left(\int_0^1 y_t(j, \epsilon^t)^{\frac{\varepsilon-1}{\varepsilon}} \, dj \right)^{\frac{\varepsilon}{\varepsilon-1}} - \int_0^1 y_t(j, \epsilon^t)\psi_t(\epsilon^t) \, dj.$$

Accordingly, they would satisfy the first-order condition

$$y_t(j, \epsilon^t)^{-\frac{1}{\varepsilon}} y_t(\epsilon^t)^{\frac{1}{\varepsilon}} = \psi_t(\epsilon^t).$$

Efficiency requires that the marginal product of an intermediate good in final good production (represented by the term on the left-hand side of the equation) equals that good's marginal cost (on the right-hand side). In equilibrium, this efficiency condition is violated because the marginal product exceeds marginal cost by the markup (see condition (10.2) and the markup condition). The wedge reflects the fact that intermediate good producers maximize profits without internalizing that these profits constitute input costs for final good producers.

Since marginal costs are constant across varieties, efficiency also requires that the same quantity of each variety is produced. In the equilibrium with flexible prices that we have considered so far, this condition is satisfied. When intermediate good firms charge different prices, and thus supply different quantities, however, then the second efficiency condition is (also) violated in equilibrium. We return to this point in section 10.2.

Suppose that intermediate good producers incur *menu costs* when publishing an updated price list after a price adjustment. This gives rise to *nominal rigidity* or *price rigidity*: After a small shock that drives a producer's actual price from the profit-maximizing one, the producer may not adjust the price immediately because the second-order profit loss from the deviation falls short of the first-order menu costs, even if the latter are small.[16] How large a deviation the producer accepts before adjusting depends on the underlying *real rigidity*—the cost of satisfying higher or lower demand at unchanged prices. When the marginal cost of supplying additional output is small (supply is elastic), then the producer accepts larger deviations and as a consequence, nominal rigidity is more pronounced.

The second-order loss for an individual producer from not adjusting its price contrasts with first-order, potentially large gains for the economy as a whole. Consider a small

---

[16] The envelope condition implies that the profit loss from a small price deviation is of second order.

shock that drives the actual prices charged by intermediate good producers slightly below the profit-maximizing ones (conditional on $P_t(\epsilon^t)$ and $y_t(\epsilon^t)$). When all intermediate good producers refrain from raising their prices—for example, because of small menu costs—then the final good becomes cheaper and the quantity of final good output rises. This brings first-order benefits for all producers because equilibrium output was inefficiently low to start with (due to the markups); when they do not adjust their prices, the intermediate good producers thus exert a positive *aggregate demand externality*.

10.2   Staggered Price Setting

Price rigidity reflects a producer's tradeoff between the costs and benefits of price adjustment. A *state dependent* price setting strategy resolves this tradeoff by conditioning price adjustment on the producer's state, in parallel to the investment strategies studied in section 8.1. Under a *time dependent* strategy, prices are reset after specific time intervals. We focus on a tractable reduced-form specification of time dependent pricing, without modeling the actual costs of price adjustment or other determinants of the time intervals.

Suppose that after exogenously determined random durations, the intermediate good producers analyzed in section 10.1 reset their prices optimally. In each period, a fraction $\theta \in (0, 1)$ of producers must keep their prices unchanged, while a fraction $1 - \theta$ gets the opportunity to reset prices. The probability that a producer resets its price for the first time after h periods thus equals $\theta^{h-1}(1-\theta)$, and the expected duration of a price equals $(1-\theta)^{-1}$.

Producers are committed to supplying whatever quantity is demanded at the set price. Since a producer may not be able to reset its price in the following period, the firm's program is a dynamic one, in contrast to the program studied in section 10.1. Let $m_{t,t+h}(\epsilon^{t+h})$ denote the stochastic discount factor which the producer at date t uses to discount payoffs at date $t + h$. Taking $\{y_{t+h}(\epsilon^{t+h}), \psi_{t+h}(\epsilon^{t+h}), P_{t+h}(\epsilon^{t+h}), m_{t,t+h}(\epsilon^{t+h})\}_{h=0}^{\infty}$ as given, the producer chooses $P_t(j, \epsilon^t)$ to maximize

$$\mathbb{E}_t \sum_{h=0}^{\infty} \theta^h m_{t,t+h}(\epsilon^{t+h}) \left(\frac{P_t(j, \epsilon^t)}{P_{t+h}(\epsilon^{t+h})} - \psi_{t+h}(\epsilon^{t+h}) \right) \left(\frac{P_t(j, \epsilon^t)}{P_{t+h}(\epsilon^{t+h})} \right)^{-\varepsilon} y_{t+h}(\epsilon^{t+h}),$$

where we use condition (10.2) to express demand for variety j in terms of its relative price.

Letting $\rho_t(j, \epsilon^t) \equiv P_t(j, \epsilon^t)/P_t(\epsilon^t)$ denote the relative price chosen by producer j when a reset is possible, the program can equivalently be expressed as

$$\mathbb{E}_t \sum_{h=0}^{\infty} \theta^h m_{t,t+h}(\epsilon^{t+h}) \left(\frac{\rho_t(j, \epsilon^t) P_t(\epsilon^t)}{P_{t+h}(\epsilon^{t+h})} - \psi_{t+h}(\epsilon^{t+h}) \right) \left(\frac{\rho_t(j, \epsilon^t) P_t(\epsilon^t)}{P_{t+h}(\epsilon^{t+h})} \right)^{-\varepsilon} y_{t+h}(\epsilon^{t+h}).$$

Differentiating with respect to $\rho_t(j, \epsilon^t)$ yields the first-order condition

$$\mathbb{E}_t \sum_{h=0}^{\infty} \theta^h m_{t,t+h}(\epsilon^{t+h}) y_{t+h}(\epsilon^{t+h}) \left(\frac{P_t(\epsilon^t)}{P_{t+h}(\epsilon^{t+h})} \right)^{1-\varepsilon} \times$$

$$\left(\rho_t(j, \epsilon^t) - \psi_{t+h}(\epsilon^{t+h}) \frac{\varepsilon}{\varepsilon - 1} \frac{P_{t+h}(\epsilon^{t+h})}{P_t(\epsilon^t)} \right) = 0. \quad (10.4)$$

Intuitively, the producer aims at an average markup of $\varepsilon/(\varepsilon - 1)$ over the duration of the set price. When prices can be reset every period ($\theta \to 0$) we recover the solution of the static program, $\rho_t(j, \epsilon^t) = \psi_t(\epsilon^t)\varepsilon/(\varepsilon - 1)$. Note that all producers that adjust the price in a period reset it to the same value.

As mentioned in section 10.1, asynchronized price adjustments induce *price dispersion* and the associated output differences across intermediate good varieties imply a waste of resources. To see this, recall from condition (10.2) that

$$\int_0^1 y_t(j, \epsilon^t) dj = y_t(\epsilon^t) \int_0^1 \left(\frac{P_t(j, \epsilon^t)}{P_t(\epsilon^t)} \right)^{-\varepsilon} dj \equiv y_t(\epsilon^t) \Delta_t(\epsilon^t),$$

where $\Delta_t(\epsilon^t)$ is a measure of price dispersion. When all producers set the same price, then $\Delta_t(\epsilon^t) = 1$ and $\int_0^1 y_t(j, \epsilon^t) dj = y_t(\epsilon^t)$. Otherwise, $\Delta_t(\epsilon^t) > 1$ and $\int_0^1 y_t(j, \epsilon^t) dj > y_t(\epsilon^t)$. Intuitively, price differences imply that final good producers demand—and intermediate good producers supply—high (low) quantities of relatively cheap (expensive) varieties, although their marginal contribution to final good output is relatively small (large).

When producers adjust their prices infrequently, the rigidity or *stickiness* of prices at the firm level is reflected in aggregate price level rigidity; the distribution of prices in the previous period is a state variable. This distribution is nondegenerate because producers reset prices at different times. However, because the price setting opportunity is i.i.d. among firms and since all firms that do reset their price in a given period reset it to the same level, $\rho_t(j, \epsilon^t) = \rho_t(\epsilon^t)$, the aggregate price level only depends on this common choice as well as on the aggregate price level in the previous period. Formally, condition (10.3) implies

$$P_t(\epsilon^t)^{1-\varepsilon} = \int_0^1 P_t(j, \epsilon^t)^{1-\varepsilon} dj = \theta \int_0^1 P_{t-1}(j, \epsilon^{t-1})^{1-\varepsilon} dj + (1 - \theta)(\rho_t(\epsilon^t) P_t(\epsilon^t))^{1-\varepsilon}.$$

Dividing by $P_t(\epsilon^t)^{1-\varepsilon}$, this yields a relationship between gross inflation and the optimally chosen relative price,

$$1 = \theta \Pi_t(\epsilon^t)^{\varepsilon-1} + (1 - \theta)\rho_t(\epsilon^t)^{1-\varepsilon}. \quad (10.5)$$

10.3   Price Rigidity in General Equilibrium

To analyze the implications of price rigidity in general equilibrium, we augment the real business cycle model studied in section 6.3.1 with a monopolistically competitive intermediate goods sector and money.

10.3.1   Firms

Competitive final good producers purchase varieties from monopolistically competitive intermediate good firms (see sections 10.1 and 10.2). The latter solve the dynamic price-setting problem studied above, as well as the static problem of optimally renting capital and labor from households to produce output with the constant-returns-to-scale technology, f. Producer j's output is given by

$$y_t(j, \epsilon^t) = A_t(\epsilon^t) f(k_t(j, \epsilon^t), L_t(j, \epsilon^t)),$$

where $A_t(\epsilon^t)$, $k_t(j, \epsilon^t)$, and $L_t(j, \epsilon^t)$ denote productivity, capital, and labor input, respectively.

Intermediate good producers choose the minimum-cost capital–labor ratio. Due to constant returns to scale, this ratio is the same for all producers. The Lagrangian associated with the cost minimization program is given by

$$\mathcal{L} = r_t(\epsilon^t) k_t(j, \epsilon^t) + w_t(\epsilon^t) L_t(j, \epsilon^t) - \lambda \Big(A_t(\epsilon^t) f(k_t(j, \epsilon^t), L_t(j, \epsilon^t)) - y_t(j, \epsilon^t) \Big),$$

where $r_t(\epsilon^t)$ and $w_t(\epsilon^t)$ denote the rental rate and the wage, respectively. Differentiating with respect to the factor inputs and positing a Cobb-Douglas production function with capital share α, we find

$$\psi_t(\epsilon^t) \quad = \quad \frac{1}{A_t(\epsilon^t)} \left(\frac{r_t(\epsilon^t)}{\alpha} \right)^{\alpha} \left(\frac{w_t(\epsilon^t)}{1 - \alpha} \right)^{1-\alpha}, \tag{10.6}$$

$$\frac{k_t(j, \epsilon^t)}{L_t(j, \epsilon^t)} \quad = \quad \frac{\alpha}{1 - \alpha} \frac{w_t(\epsilon^t)}{r_t(\epsilon^t)}. \tag{10.7}$$

Condition (10.6) gives the marginal costs of a producer that employs the minimum-cost capital–labor ratio given in condition (10.7).

While intermediate goods producers always choose the minimum-cost factor input combination, they do not necessarily supply the profit-maximizing quantity of output. This is a consequence of infrequent price adjustment and the fact that firms supply whatever quantity is demanded at the set price. Optimal price setting implies the equilibrium conditions (10.4) and (10.5).

10.3.2   Households

The representative household maximizes $\sum_{t=0}^{\infty} \beta^t \mathbb{E}_0[u(c_t(\epsilon^t), x_t(\epsilon^t))]$ where u is strictly increasing and concave, and $c_t(\epsilon^t)$ and $x_t(\epsilon^t)$ denote consumption and leisure. The household also demands real balances; money demand is decreasing in the nominal interest rate. For simplicity, we assume that money holdings are negligible as far as their effect on the household's budget constraint or marginal utility of consumption and leisure is concerned; for example, because the economy is in the cashless limit (see subsection 9.3.2).

The household works, consumes, and saves. Its portfolio includes capital, $k_{t+1}(\epsilon^t)$, nominal bonds, $B_{t+1}(\epsilon^t)$, and negligible real balances. The gross real rate of return on capital equals $R_{t+1}(\epsilon^{t+1}) \equiv 1 - \delta + r_{t+1}(\epsilon^{t+1})$, where δ denotes the depreciation rate. The nominally risk-free gross rate of return on bonds equals $I_{t+1}(\epsilon^t)$. The household's dynamic budget constraint is given by condition (9.1), with just one type of nominal bond, no real bonds, negligible real balances, and firm profits as an additional source of household income.

Maximizing with respect to $k_{t+1}(\epsilon^t)$, $B_{t+1}(\epsilon^t)$, $c_t(\epsilon^t)$, and $x_t(\epsilon^t)$ and simplifying yields the first-order conditions (see section 6.3.1 and condition (9.2))

$$u_c(c_t(\epsilon^t), x_t(\epsilon^t)) = \beta \mathbb{E}_t \left[u_c(c_{t+1}(\epsilon^{t+1}), x_{t+1}(\epsilon^{t+1})) R_{t+1}(\epsilon^{t+1}) \right], \tag{10.8}$$

$$u_c(c_t(\epsilon^t), x_t(\epsilon^t)) = \beta \mathbb{E}_t \left[u_c(c_{t+1}(\epsilon^{t+1}), x_{t+1}(\epsilon^{t+1})) \frac{I_{t+1}(\epsilon^t)}{\Pi_{t+1}(\epsilon^{t+1})} \right], \tag{10.9}$$

$$u_x(c_t(\epsilon^t), x_t(\epsilon^t)) = w_t(\epsilon^t) u_c(c_t(\epsilon^t), x_t(\epsilon^t)). \tag{10.10}$$

10.3.3   Market Clearing

Market clearing on the markets for labor and capital requires

$$1 - x_t(\epsilon^t) = \int_0^1 L_t(j, \epsilon^t) dj,$$

$$k_t(\epsilon^{t-1}) = \int_0^1 k_t(j, \epsilon^t) dj.$$

Firm optimality and labor market clearing implies that the capital–labor ratio of each intermediate good producer equals $k_t(\epsilon^{t-1})/L_t(\epsilon^t)$ with $L_t(\epsilon^t) = 1 - x_t(\epsilon^t)$. Due to constant returns to scale, this implies

$$\int_0^1 y_t(j, \epsilon^t) dj = A_t(\epsilon^t) \int_0^1 f(k_t(j, \epsilon^t), L_t(j, \epsilon^t)) dj = A_t(\epsilon^t) f(k_t(\epsilon^{t-1}), L_t(\epsilon^t)).$$

Accordingly, the economy's resource constraint satisfies

$$c_t(\epsilon^t) + k_{t+1}(\epsilon^t) - k_t(\epsilon^{t-1})(1 - \delta) = y_t(\epsilon^t) = \frac{1}{\Delta_t(\epsilon^t)} A_t(\epsilon^t) f(k_t(\epsilon^{t-1}), L_t(\epsilon^t)), \tag{10.11}$$

where $\Delta_t(\epsilon^t)$ denotes the price dispersion measure defined in section 10.2. Price dispersion enters the resource constraint in the same way as lower productivity.

The nominal bond is in zero net supply, $B_t(\epsilon^t) = 0$, as all households are alike.

10.3.4   General Equilibrium

To simplify the analysis, we linearly approximate the equilibrium conditions around the steady state associated with constant productivity (normalized to one) and zero inflation, $A = \Pi = 1$. Let a circumflex denote relative deviations from the steady state.

In equilibrium, the firms' discount factor equals the stochastic discount factor of the household because the latter owns the firms. Since in steady state, $m_{t,t+h}(\epsilon^{t+h}) = \beta^h$, $\psi \varepsilon / (\varepsilon -$

1) = 1, and $\rho(j) = 1$, the price setting condition (10.4) implies

$$\sum_{h=0}^{\infty} \theta^h \beta^h \mathbb{E}_t \left[\hat{\rho}_t(\epsilon^t) - \hat{\psi}_{t+h}(\epsilon^{t+h}) - \hat{P}_{t+h}(\epsilon^{t+h}) + \hat{P}_t(\epsilon^t) \right] = 0$$

or

$$\hat{\rho}_t(\epsilon^t) + \hat{P}_t(\epsilon^t) = (1 - \theta\beta) \sum_{h=0}^{\infty} \theta^h \beta^h \mathbb{E}_t \left[\hat{\psi}_{t+h}(\epsilon^{t+h}) + \hat{P}_{t+h}(\epsilon^{t+h}) \right].$$

That is, the deviation of producer j's newly set price (on the left-hand side) and the discounted sum of deviations of nominal marginal costs (on the right-hand side) are equalized. We may reexpress this condition as a first-order difference equation,

$$\hat{\rho}_t(\epsilon^t) + \hat{P}_t(\epsilon^t) = (1 - \theta\beta)\left(\hat{\psi}_t(\epsilon^t) + \hat{P}_t(\epsilon^t) \right) + \theta\beta\mathbb{E}_t \left[\hat{\rho}_{t+1}(\epsilon^{t+1}) + \hat{P}_{t+1}(\epsilon^{t+1}) \right],$$

for which we seek a stationary solution. Since the inflation rate, $\pi_{t+1}(\epsilon^{t+1})$, equals $\hat{P}_{t+1}(\epsilon^{t+1}) - \hat{P}_t(\epsilon^t)$, the difference equation can equivalently be written as

$$\hat{\rho}_t(\epsilon^t) = (1 - \theta\beta)\hat{\psi}_t(\epsilon^t) + \theta\beta\mathbb{E}_t \left[\hat{\rho}_{t+1}(\epsilon^{t+1}) + \pi_{t+1}(\epsilon^{t+1}) \right].$$

From condition (10.5), the linearized law of motion for inflation is given by

$$(1 - \theta)\hat{\rho}_t(\epsilon^t) = \theta\hat{\Pi}_t(\epsilon^t) = \theta\pi_t(\epsilon^t).$$

Combining this condition with the difference equation yields the *New Keynesian Phillips curve*,

$$\pi_t(\epsilon^t) = \frac{(1 - \theta)(1 - \theta\beta)}{\theta} \hat{\psi}_t(\epsilon^t) + \beta\mathbb{E}_t[\pi_{t+1}(\epsilon^{t+1})]. \tag{10.12}$$

The Phillips curve relates inflation to marginal costs because firms target a desired markup, and to future inflation because firms take into account that they might not be able to reset their price quickly. With more price rigidity or patience (a higher θ or β), inflation responds less strongly to marginal costs.

Since there are no first-order effects on the price dispersion index, $\hat{\Delta}_t(\epsilon^t) = 0$, the resource constraint (10.11) can be expressed as

$$\hat{c}_t(\epsilon^t)\frac{c}{y} + \left(\hat{k}_{t+1}(\epsilon^t) - (1 - \delta)\hat{k}_t(\epsilon^{t-1}) \right)\frac{k}{y} =$$
$$\hat{y}_t(\epsilon^t) = \hat{A}_t(\epsilon^t) + \alpha\hat{k}_t(\epsilon^{t-1}) + (1 - \alpha)\hat{L}_t(\epsilon^t). \tag{10.13}$$

From condition (10.7),

$$r_t(\epsilon^t) - r = r\left(\hat{w}_t(\epsilon^t) + \hat{L}_t(\epsilon^t) - \hat{k}_t(\epsilon^{t-1}) \right). \tag{10.14}$$

Combining conditions (10.6) and (10.7) and using the resource constraint (10.13) to simplify yields

$$\hat{\psi}_t(\epsilon^t) = \hat{w}_t(\epsilon^t) + \hat{L}_t(\epsilon^t) - \hat{y}_t(\epsilon^t). \tag{10.15}$$

Finally, turning to the household's first-order conditions, equations (10.8)–(10.10), we assume that preferences are additively separable in consumption and leisure. Defining the positive inverse elasticities $\sigma \equiv -u_{cc}(c, x)c/u_c(c, x)$ and $\eta \equiv -u_{xx}(c, x)(1 - x)/u_x(c, x)$, we find[17]

$$-\sigma \hat{c}_t(\epsilon^t) = -\sigma \mathbb{E}_t \left[\hat{c}_{t+1}(\epsilon^{t+1}) \right] + \mathbb{E}_t[r_{t+1}(\epsilon^{t+1}) - r], \tag{10.16}$$

$$-\sigma \hat{c}_t(\epsilon^t) = -\sigma \mathbb{E}_t \left[\hat{c}_{t+1}(\epsilon^{t+1}) \right] + \mathbb{E}_t \left[i_{t+1}(\epsilon^t) - \pi_{t+1}(\epsilon^{t+1}) - (r - \delta) \right], \tag{10.17}$$

$$\eta \hat{L}_t(\epsilon^t) = \hat{w}_t(\epsilon^t) - \sigma \hat{c}_t(\epsilon^t). \tag{10.18}$$

Equation (10.17)—the *dynamic IS equation*—relates contemporaneous activity (consumption) to the nominal interest rate, similarly to a Keynesian aggregate demand relationship. Unlike in the standard Keynesian model, however, the dynamic IS equation also contains expectations of future activity and inflation.

Conditions (10.12)–(10.18) constitute a system of eight equations in eight endogenous variables $(\pi_t(\epsilon^t), \hat{\psi}_t(\epsilon^t), \hat{c}_t(\epsilon^t), \hat{k}_{t+1}(\epsilon^t), \hat{y}_t(\epsilon^t), \hat{L}_t(\epsilon^t), r_t(\epsilon^t), \hat{w}_t(\epsilon^t))$ and two exogenous variables $(\hat{A}_t(\epsilon^t), i_{t+1}(\epsilon^t))$.

10.3.5   Analysis

To build intuition for the workings of the model, consider first the case with perfectly flexible prices, $\theta = 0$. As discussed earlier, relative prices and real marginal costs are constant in this case,

$$\rho_t(j, \epsilon^t) = 1 = \psi_t(\epsilon^t)\varepsilon/(\varepsilon - 1),$$

and the Phillips curve (10.12) collapses to the condition $\hat{\psi}_t(\epsilon^t) = 0$. It follows from conditions (10.14) and (10.15) that $\hat{y}_t(\epsilon^t) - \hat{w}_t(\epsilon^t) + \hat{L}_t(\epsilon^t) = \hat{k}_t(\epsilon^{t-1}) + \hat{r}_t(\epsilon^t)$. The resource constraint (10.13) is unchanged.

The modified linearized equilibrium conditions thus parallel the conditions in the real business cycle model (see subsection 6.3.1), with two differences. First, the modified conditions characterize deviations from a distorted (due to monopolistic competition) steady state, rather than from the nondistorted steady state in the real business cycle model. Second, the modified conditions include one equation, condition (10.17), that is not present in the real business cycle model. This additional equation combined with condition (10.16) yields the Fisher equation,

$$\mathbb{E}_t \left[r_{t+1}(\epsilon^{t+1}) \right] - \delta = i_{t+1}(\epsilon^t) - \mathbb{E}_t \left[\pi_{t+1}(\epsilon^{t+1}) \right],$$

---

[17] Totally differentiating condition (10.8), we have $\sigma \mathbb{E}_t \left[\hat{c}_{t+1}(\epsilon^{t+1}) - \hat{c}_t(\epsilon^t) \right] = \mathbb{E}_t[\hat{R}_{t+1}(\epsilon^{t+1})]$. Using the fact that $\hat{R}_{t+1}(\epsilon^{t+1}) \approx \ln(1 + \hat{R}_{t+1}(\epsilon^{t+1})) = \ln(R_{t+1}(\epsilon^{t+1})/R) = \ln(R_{t+1}(\epsilon^{t+1})) - \ln(R)$ and $\ln(R_{t+1}(\epsilon^{t+1})) = \ln(1 + r_{t+1}(\epsilon^{t+1}) - \delta) \approx r_{t+1}(\epsilon^{t+1}) - \delta$, condition (10.16) follows. A parallel approximation implies condition (10.17).

which equates the expected real interest rate (on the left-hand side) and the inflation-adjusted nominal rate (on the right-hand side). Conditional on the rental rates on capital associated with the equilibrium allocation as well as on a nominal interest rate, the condition pins down expected inflation (but not, in the presence of risk, the actually realized inflation in each history). In conclusion, the model with flexible prices resembles the real business cycle model; the allocation in the model is independent of inflation; the nominal interest rate pins down expected inflation; and with risk, realized *inflation* and thus, the realized *price level* are *indeterminate*.

With price rigidity, $\theta > 0$, this *classical dichotomy* between the real allocation and nominal variables breaks down. On the one hand, the Phillips curve (10.12) links inflation to marginal costs, and thus the allocation. On the other hand, the nominal interest rate affects the allocation through the dynamic IS equation, condition (10.17). Because the Phillips curve constrains inflation, a change in $i_{t+1}(\epsilon^t)$ translates into a change in the inflation-adjusted nominal interest rate. From the Euler equations, this induces consumption and investment responses that in turn feed into wages, rental rates, and marginal costs. In the long run, consumption and capital return to their steady-state values and the classical dichotomy holds.

Independently of the degree of price rigidity, the nominal interest rate is linked to a money market equilibrium condition that is left implicit because we have not spelled out the household's money demand. (We have assumed that real balances are negligible as far as their effect on the budget constraint or marginal utility is concerned.) As long as this demand is interest elastic, a (possibly tiny) adjustment in the supply of real balances is associated with a change in the market clearing nominal interest rate. The indifference conditions underlying the term structure of interest rates (see section 5.4) also hold independently of the degree of price stickiness. Anticipated future changes in nominal interest rates affect the nominal term structure and, over horizons over which the classical dichotomy does not apply, also the real term structure. The Fisher equation links nominal and real rates as well as inflation.

When there is no capital, $\alpha = k_t(\epsilon^{t-1}) = 0$, the *New Keynesian model* simplifies substantially. Conditions (10.14) and (10.16) are superfluous in this case, and the resource constraint, intratemporal first-order condition, and marginal cost condition, respectively, reduce to

$$\hat{c}_t(\epsilon^t) = \hat{y}_t(\epsilon^t) = \hat{A}_t(\epsilon^t) + \hat{L}_t(\epsilon^t),$$

$$\hat{w}_t(\epsilon^t) = (\eta + \sigma)\hat{y}_t(\epsilon^t) - \eta\hat{A}_t(\epsilon^t),$$

$$\hat{\psi}_t(\epsilon^t) = (\eta + \sigma)\hat{y}_t(\epsilon^t) - (\eta + 1)\hat{A}_t(\epsilon^t).$$

The two core equations, the Phillips curve and the dynamic IS equation, respectively, are given by

$$\pi_t(\epsilon^t) = \frac{(1-\theta)(1-\theta\beta)}{\theta}\left((\eta+\sigma)\hat{y}_t(\epsilon^t) - (\eta+1)\hat{A}_t(\epsilon^t)\right) + \beta\mathbb{E}_t[\pi_{t+1}(\epsilon^{t+1})],$$

$$\hat{y}_t(\epsilon^t) = \mathbb{E}_t\left[\hat{y}_{t+1}(\epsilon^{t+1})\right] - \frac{1}{\sigma}\mathbb{E}_t\left[i_{t+1}(\epsilon^t) - \pi_{t+1}(\epsilon^{t+1}) + \ln(\beta)\right],$$

where $\ln(\beta)$ equals the negative of the steady-state real interest rate.

The output deviations in the conditions above represent deviations from steady state. We can alternatively express these conditions in terms of *output gaps*; that is, deviations of output from the level under flexible prices, or *natural level of output*, $y_t^n(\epsilon^t)$. Letting $\chi_t(\epsilon^t)$ denote the output gap and using the fact that the steady-state output levels y^n and y are identical, we have

$$\chi_t(\epsilon^t) \equiv \hat{y}_t(\epsilon^t) - \hat{y}_t^n(\epsilon^t) = \frac{y_t(\epsilon^t) - y_t^n(\epsilon^t)}{y}.$$

Recall that with flexible prices, real marginal costs are constant such that $(\eta+\sigma)\hat{y}_t^n(\epsilon^t) = (\eta+1)\hat{A}_t(\epsilon^t)$. It follows that we can rewrite the two core equations as

$$\pi_t(\epsilon^t) = \kappa\chi_t(\epsilon^t) + \beta\mathbb{E}_t[\pi_{t+1}(\epsilon^{t+1})], \tag{10.19}$$

$$\chi_t(\epsilon^t) = \mathbb{E}_t\left[\chi_{t+1}(\epsilon^{t+1})\right] - \frac{1}{\sigma}\mathbb{E}_t\left[i_{t+1}(\epsilon^t) - \pi_{t+1}(\epsilon^{t+1}) - r_{t+1}^n(\epsilon^{t+1})\right], \tag{10.20}$$

where $\kappa \equiv (1-\theta)(1-\theta\beta)(\eta+\sigma)/\theta$ and

$$r_{t+1}^n(\epsilon^{t+1}) \equiv -\ln(\beta) + \sigma(\mathbb{E}_t[\hat{y}_{t+1}^n(\epsilon^{t+1})] - \hat{y}_t^n(\epsilon^t))$$

denotes the real interest rate in the flexible price economy—the *natural rate of interest*.[18] Conditional on bounded sequences $\{i_{t+1}(\epsilon^t), r_{t+1}^n(\epsilon^{t+1})\}_{t=0}^{\infty}$, bounded inflation and output gap sequences $\{\pi_t(\epsilon^t), \chi_t(\epsilon^t)\}_{t=0}^{\infty}$ that satisfy conditions (10.19) and (10.20) constitute equilibria in the sticky price economy without capital.

The difference equation system (10.19)–(10.20) has one stable and one unstable eigenvalue. Since both the inflation rate and the output gap are nonpredetermined variables, this implies the existence of multiple equilibria. For given sequences of nominal and natural interest rates, the unstable eigenvalue and the requirement that system dynamics be non-explosive imposes one restriction on the contemporaneous inflation and output gap (see section 11.5 and appendix B.5); that is, the model only determines a linear combination of the two variables. Moreover, conditional on inflation and the output gap at date t and on known interest rates in subsequent periods, the model only determines the expected

---

[18] Note that $r_{t+1}^n(\epsilon^{t+1})$ denotes a real interest rate, not a rental rate of capital. The relationship between flexible price output (or consumption) growth and the natural rate of interest corresponds to the Euler equation or dynamic IS equation in the flexible price economy.

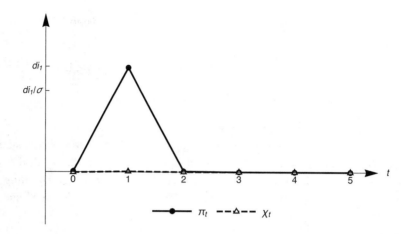

Figure 10.1
Effects of a temporary interest rate hike: $\theta \approx 0$.

inflation- and output-gap paths (not the history-contingent sequences) because the same type of indeterminacy also is present in the future.

We eliminate this indeterminacy by imposing the arbitrary restriction that the model solution does not reflect the eigenvector associated with the stable eigenvalue. Subject to this restriction, the model predicts price stability and no output gaps when the nominal and natural interest rates are at their steady-state values.

Figures 10.1–10.3 illustrate the economy's response to a temporary interest rate hike. We assume that at date $t = 0$, the nominal interest rate rises by di_1 before it falls back to its steady-state value. Figure 10.1 shows the response when prices effectively are flexible ($\theta \approx 0$). Inflation at date $t = 1$ increases by di_1 while the output gap remains at its steady-state value; that is, the classical dichotomy holds.

Figure 10.2 shows the response in the diametrically opposed case where prices effectively are fixed ($\theta \approx 1$). The interest rate hike translates into an equal-sized rise of the real interest rate in this case, which in turn gives rise to an increasing path for consumption and output: The output gap at date $t = 1$ exceeds the gap at date $t = 0$ by di_1/σ. The reversal of the nominal interest rate at date $t = 2$ and the fixed price level imply a drop of the real interest rate as well as flat consumption and output after date $t = 1$.

Finally, figure 10.3 illustrates the intermediate case ($\theta = 0.5$). Inflation at date $t = 1$ rises, but by less than one-to-one. Accordingly, the real interest rate rises as well and the output gap increases between dates $t = 0$ and $t = 1$ before reverting to its steady-state value. Positive output gaps push up marginal costs. Since inflation reflects both marginal costs and future inflation rates, it increases already at date $t = 0$ and gradually declines after date $t = 1$.

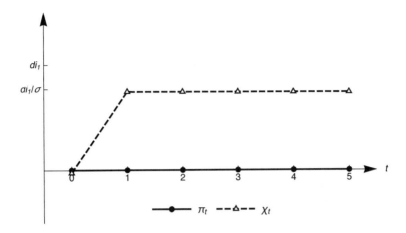

Figure 10.2
Effects of a temporary interest rate hike: $\theta \approx 1$.

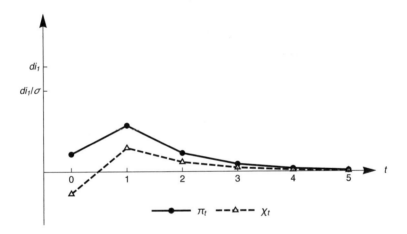

Figure 10.3
Effects of a temporary interest rate hike: $\theta \approx 0.5$.

In subsequent chapters we analyze this model further.

10.4 Bibliographic Notes

The model with monopolistically competitive intermediate good producers builds on Dixit and Stiglitz (1977). Akerlof and Yellen (1985), Mankiw (1985), and Blanchard and Kiyotaki (1987) analyze monetary models with distortions due to price setting; they show that second-order private benefits of adjustment contrast with first-order social benefits; see also Cooper and John (1988). Farhi and Werning (2016b) and Korinek and Simsek (2016) analyze aggregate demand externalities and contrast them with pecuniary externalities (see sections 8.3 and 8.4).

Calvo (1983) proposes the stochastic price adjustment specification adopted in section 10.2.

Yun (1996), King and Wolman (1996), and Goodfriend and King (1997) formulate and analyze the New Keynesian business cycle model.

Related Topics and Additional References   Fischer (1977) and Taylor (1979) consider deterministic, staggered price adjustment mechanisms; see also Chari et al. (2000). Rotemberg (1982) derives the New Keynesian Phillips curve under the assumption that firms face quadratic costs of price adjustment. Dotsey et al. (1999), Gertler and Leahy (2008), and Golosov and Lucas (2007) study the implications of state-dependent price setting. Mankiw and Reis (2002) analyze price setting in a model with flexible prices but slow information diffusion (*sticky information*).

Erceg et al. (2000) introduce wage in addition to price stickiness.

Obstfeld and Rogoff (1995) and Kollmann (2001) analyze price stickiness in open economy models.

Auclert (2019), Kaplan et al. (2018), and Broer et al. (2019) analyze the effect of household and asset heterogeneity on the monetary transmission mechanism.

Woodford (2003b), Galí (2015), and Walsh (2017) cover models of economies with sticky prices and wages.

11 The Government

We have so far abstracted from the public sector. Now we introduce a government whose policy instruments affect budget constraints, change incentives, and require resources. Our equilibrium concept remains unchanged—households and firms optimize and markets clear—but requires refinement: We assume that agents in the private sector take the government's policy as given; we require that the government also satisfies a budget constraint; and we account for the government's resource use when specifying market clearing conditions. A policy is *feasible* when it implements an equilibrium.

We analyze the macroeconomic implications of fiscal policy including taxation, government consumption, debt, and social security. Thereafter, we identify conditions under which policy changes do not alter the equilibrium allocation. Finally, we study how monetary and fiscal policy jointly affect inflation and output.

11.1 Taxation and Government Consumption

Consider the representative agent economy analyzed in section 3.1, augmented by a government sector. The government levies income taxes on labor, at rate τ_t^w, and on financial assets or capital, at rate τ_t^k.[19] The budget constraint of a household reads

$$a_{t+1} = a_t R_t (1 - \tau_t^k) + w_t (1 - \tau_t^w) - c_t$$

and household optimization thus implies the Euler equation

$$u'(c_t) = \beta R_{t+1} (1 - \tau_{t+1}^k) u'(c_{t+1}).$$

The tax on capital income reduces the net return on household saving (or borrowing). A higher τ_{t+1}^k therefore induces the same type of income and substitution effects as a lower R_{t+1} (see subsection 2.1.1), and it discourages saving. In contrast, the labor income tax

---

[19] To simplify the notation, we assume that the capital income tax is levied on the gross rather than the net return; that is, the principal is taxed as well. This is without loss of generality; each tax rate τ_t^k is associated with a tax rate on net capital income.

does not induce a substitution effect because labor is supplied inelastically; it only reduces household wealth.

Taxes finance government consumption, g_t. We assume that household preferences are separable between private and government consumption (or that households do not value g_t), such that the household's first-order conditions are unaffected by g_t. For now, we also abstract from government deficits or surpluses; that is, we assume that the government runs a *balanced budget* policy. This implies the government budget constraint

$$g_t = a_t R_t \tau_t^k + w_t \tau_t^w.$$

Substituting into the household's constraint yields

$$a_{t+1} = a_t R_t + w_t - c_t - g_t,$$

indicating that the tax-financed government consumption reduces the household's disposable income.

Combining the budget constraints of households, firms, and the government and imposing the market clearing and equilibrium conditions discussed in section 3.1 yields the core equilibrium conditions

$$k_{t+1} = k_t(1 - \delta) + f(k_t, 1) - c_t - g_t, \tag{11.1}$$

$$u'(c_t) = \beta(1 + f_K(k_{t+1}, 1) - \delta)(1 - \tau_{t+1}^k)u'(c_{t+1}). \tag{11.2}$$

Compared to the core conditions in the model without government, (3.8) and (3.9), the resource constraint (or GDP identity) now accounts for government consumption, and the tax rate on capital income enters the Euler equation.

In steady state,

$$c = f(k, 1) - \delta k - g,$$

$$1 = \beta(1 + f_K(k, 1) - \delta)(1 - \tau^k).$$

Since replacement investment, δk, and total consumption, $c + g$, sum to output, private consumption falls when government consumption rises, conditional on k_t. Moreover, since the after-tax return on savings equals β^{-1}, a tax on capital income reduces the capital stock, unlike a labor income tax. Accordingly, steady-state private consumption is maximal (conditional on g) if the government only levies labor income taxes.

Off steady state, capital income taxation also generates inferior outcomes. To see this, we compare the equilibrium allocation with the allocation in a Robinson Crusoe economy. Robinson Crusoe's program corresponds to the program studied in subsection 3.1.6, except that the additional term $-g_t$ enters the resource constraint. The optimality conditions then are given by (11.1) and (11.2), subject to $\tau_{t+1}^k = 0$. We conclude that the decentralized equilibrium allocation is Pareto optimal if and only if capital income taxes equal zero at all times.

Capital income taxes *distort* the allocation because they drive a wedge, $1 - \tau_{t+1}^k$, between the private and social marginal rates of transformation. An individual household takes tax rates as given and equalizes the marginal rate of substitution between consumption at dates t and $t + 1$, with the private marginal rate of transformation, $R_{t+1}(1 - \tau_{t+1}^k)$. This privately optimal choice does not account for the fact that the tax-induced substitution toward consumption at date t has a social cost because individual tax avoidance requires a higher equilibrium tax rate for everybody else. From a societal point of view, the marginal rate of transformation equals R_{t+1} even if the return on savings partly is appropriated by the government. The substitution effect associated with the tax wedge therefore causes a *deadweight loss*.

The substitution effect also implies that the tax revenue increases less than proportionally with the tax rate: As the tax rate rises, the *tax base* shrinks. The fall in the tax base may (eventually) be so pronounced that the revenue declines although the rate further increases. Tax revenue as a function of the tax rate thus may be inverse-U shaped, displaying a *Laffer curve* relationship.

In the Robinson Crusoe economy, deadweight losses are absent because the decision maker internalizes that government consumption needs to be funded. Deadweight losses also are absent in the decentralized equilibrium of an economy with *lump-sum taxes*; that is, taxes whose amount the household cannot affect. With lump-sum taxes, T_t, the household's budget constraint reads

$$a_{t+1} = a_t R_t + w_t - c_t - T_t$$

and the equilibrium conditions coincide with the conditions in the economy with labor but no capital income taxes (since $T_t = g_t$ in equilibrium). This is not surprising; with exogenous labor supply, a tax on labor income does not induce substitution effects and therefore is a lump-sum tax.

These findings generalize. Not only does government consumption reduce household wealth, but its financing by means of taxes that induce substitution effects gives rise to welfare-reducing tax distortions. Abstracting from distributive considerations, taxes that induce substitution effects (here, capital income taxes) therefore generate Pareto inferior outcomes compared to taxes that do not induce such effects (here, labor income taxes).

In endogenous growth models of the type considered in subsection 6.2.2, a tax-induced reduction in the after-tax interest rate can lower the economy's equilibrium *growth rate*, with potentially large welfare consequences.

11.2   Government Debt and Social Security

Next, we introduce *government debt* as a source of funding. We abstract from distortions and assume that taxes only are levied on labor income, at rate τ_t. Allowing for population growth at the gross rate v, the resource constraint is given by

$$vk_{t+1} = f(k_t, 1) + k_t(1 - \delta) - c_t - g_t,$$

where capital as well as private and government consumption are expressed in per-worker terms.

Government debt allows for the intertemporal decoupling of tax collections and government spending. The *dynamic government budget constraint* reads

$$vb_{t+1} = b_t R_t + g_t - \tau_t w_t,$$

where b_t denotes the stock of government debt per worker. The constraint states that a *primary deficit*, $g_t - \tau_t w_t > 0$, must be financed by debt issuance in excess of debt service (repayment of principal plus interest); when the government runs a *primary surplus*, in contrast, then debt is repaid on net. Equivalently, a *deficit*, $b_t(R_t - 1) + g_t - \tau_t w_t > 0$, increases the government's indebtedness, and a *surplus* reduces it. Note that we do not distinguish between the interest rates on government debt and capital. Market clearing requires that households are indifferent between the two assets and thus, absent risk, that the interest rates coincide.

Along a balanced growth path with constant per-capita values, the government budget constraint reads

$$vb = bR + g - \tau w.$$

Absent population growth, taxes equal government consumption and interest payments on debt. With strictly positive population growth, in contrast, taxes fall short of these spending items because new debt is issued in each period.

Let $q_0 \equiv 1$ and $q_t \equiv (R_1 \cdots R_t)^{-1}$. The no-Ponzi-game condition with equality, $\lim_{t\to\infty} q_t v^{t+1} b_{t+1} = 0$, and the dynamic budget constraints imply the *intertemporal government budget constraint*

$$0 = b_0 R_0 + \sum_{t=0}^{\infty} q_t v^t (g_t - \tau_t w_t).$$

It states that the value of government consumption spending and the value of tax revenues balance intertemporally, correcting for initial government indebtedness.

11.2.1   Government Debt with a Representative Agent

Consider first an economy with a representative household that maximizes $\sum_{t=0}^{\infty} \beta^t v^t u(c_t)$, subject to its dynamic budget constraint and a no-Ponzi-game condition. The Euler equation and dynamic and intertemporal budget constraints are given by

$$u'(c_t) = \beta R_{t+1} u'(c_{t+1}),$$

$$v a_{t+1} = a_t R_t + w_t (1 - \tau_t) - c_t,$$

$$0 = a_0 R_0 + \sum_{t=0}^{\infty} q_t v^t (w_t (1 - \tau_t) - c_t).$$

Suppose the government initially balances its budget in each period such that $b_t = 0$ and $\tau_t w_t = g_t$, implying $k_t = a_t$. Consider a change of policy that alters the timing of tax collections while holding its present value (at the initial interest rates) constant. For example, suppose that the government reduces tax collections at date t by Δ per capita and increases taxes at date $t + 1$ by $R_{t+1}\Delta/v$ per capita. The government also issues debt Δ per capita at date t and fully services it in the subsequent period out of the additional tax revenue.

Capital accumulation, consumption, interest rates, and wages are not affected by this policy change. To establish this result, we conjecture that wages and interest rates indeed remain unchanged and verify that the initial capital and consumption sequences continue to satisfy all equilibrium conditions. Under the conjecture, the representative household's budget set is unaffected by the policy change because the wealth effects of the tax cut at date t and the tax hike at date $t + 1$ cancel each other out,

$$-\Delta + \frac{\Delta R_{t+1}}{v} \frac{v}{R_{t+1}} = 0.$$

The initial consumption sequence therefore remains optimal for the household. From the household's dynamic budget constraint, this implies that the household increases saving when the government runs a deficit, by exactly the same amount. Since $a_{t+1} = b_{t+1} + k_{t+1}$, capital accumulation, and thus wages and interest rates, remain unchanged. Since the government's budget constraints are satisfied as well, the conjecture is verified. We conclude that the equilibrium allocation remains unaltered although the tax and government debt paths change.

This result is an instance of the *Ricardian equivalence* proposition. The proposition states that for a given government consumption sequence (and thus, present value of taxes) the timing of tax collections does not affect the equilibrium allocation. Note that the proposition makes a statement about changes in government financing, not government consumption. The proposition holds under three key conditions, all of which are satisfied in the environment studied here. First, households and the government save or borrow at the same interest rates. Second, the policy change does not shift the tax burden from one group to another. And third, taxes are nondistorting. These conditions guarantee that a change in government financing does not alter budget sets in the private sector.

11.2.2   Government Debt with Overlapping Generations

Consider next an economy with two-period lived overlapping generations. In general equilibrium,

$$u'(c_{1,t}) = \beta R_{t+1} u'(c_{2,t+1}),$$
$$v(b_{t+1} + k_{t+1}) = w_t(1 - \tau_t) - c_{1,t},$$
$$c_{2,t+1} = v(b_{t+1} + k_{t+1})R_{t+1},$$

where $c_{1,t}$ and $c_{2,t}$ denote consumption by a young and old household at date t, respectively. Note that we have imposed the market clearing condition, $a_{t+1} = b_{t+1} + k_{t+1}$.

In this economy, Ricardian equivalence does not hold. Reducing taxes at date t and increasing them at date $t + 1$ shifts the tax burden from workers in cohort t to those in the subsequent cohort. The debt that the government issues to finance its deficit constitutes net wealth for the workers who acquire it, in the sense that they do not have to contribute future resources to servicing it. Because of the tax cut's positive wealth effect on cohort t, the cohort increases saving by less than the amount of the tax cut, raising consumption.

Capital accumulation therefore slows down: Government debt *crowds out* capital. As a consequence, interest rates rise and wages fall in the subsequent period. Cohort t does not only benefit from a lighter tax burden but also from a higher return on savings, while cohort $t + 1$ bears a heavier tax burden and receives lower wages.

Recall that along a balanced growth path, the government budget constraint reads $vb = bR + g - \tau w$. If the economy is inefficient, $R < v$, then the revenue raised from additional debt issuance exceeds interest payments and the government may purchase goods without ever collecting taxes, simply by holding the debt-to-worker ratio constant ($g > 0, \tau = 0, b > 0$; note that this violates the no-Ponzi-game condition). Debt is welfare increasing in this case because it reduces capital overaccumulation. Moreover, debt is a *bubble*: While it never generates dividends (tax revenues), it is rolled over forever at a positive price.

11.2.3   Pay-as-You-Go Social Security

Maintaining the overlapping generations structure, consider finally a *pay-as-you-go social security system* in which workers contribute resources that finance contemporaneous benefits for retirees. Each old household at date t receives a transfer, $T_t v$, that is fully financed by labor income taxes levied at rate τ_t^s, such that $T_t = w_t \tau_t^s$. Abstracting from debt and government consumption, equilibrium is characterized by the conditions

$$u'(c_{1,t}) = \beta R_{t+1} u'(c_{2,t+1}),$$
$$vk_{t+1} = w_t(1 - \tau_t^s) - c_{1,t},$$
$$c_{2,t+1} = vk_{t+1}R_{t+1} + T_{t+1}v.$$

For any feasible social security policy $\{\tau^s_t, T_t\}_{t\geq 0}$, there exists an *equivalent* tax-and-debt policy $\{\tau_t, b_{t+1}\}_{t\geq 0}$ of the type considered in subsection 11.2.2, which implements the same equilibrium allocation. To see this, note first that under the social security policy, the intertemporal budget constraint of a household in cohort t is given by

$$c_{1,t} + \frac{c_{2,t+1}}{R_{t+1}} = w_t(1 - \tau^s_t) + \frac{T_{t+1}v}{R_{t+1}},$$

while under the tax-and-debt policy, the constraint reads

$$c_{1,t} + \frac{c_{2,t+1}}{R_{t+1}} = w_t(1 - \tau_t).$$

Given the equilibrium prices supported by the social security policy, the budget sets characterized by the two constraints are identical if the present value of taxes net of transfers under the social security policy, $w_t\tau^s_t - T_{t+1}v/R_{t+1}$, equals taxes under the tax-and-debt policy, $w_t\tau_t$. Since $T_{t+1} = w_{t+1}\tau^s_{t+1}$, this implies the equivalence condition

$$\tau_t = \tau^s_t - \frac{w_{t+1}\tau^s_{t+1}v}{w_t R_{t+1}},$$

which maps the sequence of social security tax rates into a sequence of tax rates.

A second equivalence condition follows from the requirement that the dynamic budget constraints of the government (or households) be satisfied. The requirement that two policies pay the same amount of funds to the old at date t,

$$vb_t R_t = vw_t\tau^s_t,$$

relates the sequence of social security tax rates to a debt sequence. Since neither policy affects the resource constraint or the factor price conditions, we conclude that the two equivalence conditions map any feasible social security policy into a tax-and-debt policy that implements the same equilibrium allocation and prices. Absent restrictions on the available tax and transfer instruments, similar mappings can be derived in environments where social security taxes are distorting, households long-lived and heterogeneous within a cohort, or outcomes stochastic.

Intuitively, under the social security policy, households save little because they receive transfers in old age. Under the equivalent tax-and-debt policy, they save more because they pay lower taxes when young but do not receive transfers when old. The difference in saving exactly corresponds to the debt the government issues under the tax-and-debt policy. In light of this equivalence, one refers to the present value of the already committed future social security benefits as the *implicit debt* of the pay-as-you-go financed social security system.

Since implicit debt associated with a social security policy or other government program and explicit debt entail the same financial commitments, focusing on the latter and disregarding the former can be misleading. Explicit debt (net of government assets) does not comprehensively measure the fiscal burden a policy imposes on future generations because these generations also have to contribute resources to service the implicit debt. Generational accounts, in contrast, do provide a comprehensive measure. The *generational account* of a group is the present value of the group's remaining lifetime taxes net of received transfers. From the government's intertemporal budget constraint, the sum of all generational accounts equals the present value of current and future government consumption plus the outstanding government debt.

Suppose that at date $t = 0$ a pay-as-you-go social security system $\{\tau_t^s, T_t\}_{t \geq 0}$ is introduced. The effect on the budget set of an old household at date $t = 0$ and on the budget set of a member of cohort $t \geq 0$, respectively, are given by

$$w_0 \tau_0^s \nu \quad \text{and} \quad -w_t \tau_t^s + \frac{w_{t+1} \tau_{t+1}^s \nu}{R_{t+1}}.$$

The first generation receiving social security benefits clearly is made better off. Whether subsequent generations benefit or lose depends on whether the equilibrium is efficient or not. Along an inefficient balanced growth path ($R < \nu$ such that $-w\tau^s + w\tau^s\nu/R > 0$), subsequent generations also benefit; along an efficient path, they are harmed. Using the relations derived earlier, we can equivalently represent the introduction of the social security system as a policy that finances a transfer to the old at date $t = 0$ out of taxes and debt, which subsequent cohorts service over time; see table 11.1.

In stochastic environments, a history-contingent social security policy (or equivalent tax-and-debt policy with history-contingent returns on government debt) can contribute to intergenerational risk sharing. This may be valuable because, absent such policies, overlapping generations cannot implement all ex-ante beneficial insurance arrangements (see section 4.4). A social security policy that provides annuities may also contribute to intragenerational risk sharing by insuring longevity risk.

A pay-as-you-go social security system contrasts with a *fully funded* system with individual accounts, where households contribute resources in young age and consume the return on their contributions in old age. In equilibrium, the contributions fund capital accumulation. Changes in the contribution rate do not have macroeconomic effects as long as households can undo them by adjusting their savings outside of the system. That is, mandatory saving in a fully funded system is irrelevant as long as the desired saving of households exceeds the mandatory saving.

11.3   Equivalence of Policies

The Ricardian equivalence proposition discussed in subsection 11.2.1 describes *equivalence classes* of fiscal policies, whose members implement the same equilibrium allocation; that is, the same sequences for consumption, capital, wages, and interest rates but not necessarily for financial assets like government debt. Our discussion of equivalent pay-as-you-go social security and tax-and-debt policies in subsection 11.2.3 identified an-

	Pay-as-you-go		Explicit debt
Effect on household budget at date t			
lifetime net taxes:	τ_t	$=$	τ_t
+ taxes on young households	τ_t^s	$>$	τ_t
− discounted old age benefits	$\frac{T_{t+1}v_{t+1}}{R_{t+1}}$	$>$	0
Effect on government budget at date t			
cash flow, $t = 0$:	0	$=$	0
+ total cash inflow	$N_0\tau_0^s$	$=$	$N_0\tau_0^s$
+ taxes on young households	$N_0\tau_0^s$	$>$	$N_0\tau_0$
+ debt issued	0	$<$	$N_0 b_1 v_1$
− total cash outflow	$N_0 T_0$	$=$	$N_0\theta_0$
− transfer to old households	$N_0 T_0$	$=$	$N_0\theta_0$
cash flow, $t > 0$:	0	$=$	0
+ total cash inflow	$N_t\tau_t^s$	$=$	$N_t\tau_t^s$
+ taxes on young households	$N_t\tau_t^s$	$>$	$N_t\tau_t$
+ debt issued	0	$<$	$N_t b_{t+1} v_{t+1}$
− total cash outflow	$N_t T_t$	$=$	$N_t b_t R_t$
− transfer to old households	$N_t T_t$	$>$	0
− debt service	0	$<$	$N_t b_t R_t$

Notes: N_t denotes the size of cohort t and $v_{t+1} \equiv N_{t+1}/N_t$, the possibly time-varying growth rate. Wages are normalized to one. Equivalence then requires $v_{t+1}b_{t+1} = \tau_t^s - \tau_t$ and $T_{t+1} = b_{t+1}R_{t+1}$. In the economy with government debt, the transfer to the initial old households, θ_0, corresponds with the transfer paid under the pay-as-you-go system. A "+" or "−" indicates positive or negative contributions.

Table 11.1
Equivalence of implicit and explicit government debt: Pay-as-you-go social security and explicit government debt.

other type of equivalence classes. We now unify these discussions and consider additional applications.

11.3.1   General Equivalence Result

Let μ denote the state at the initial date and let φ denote a policy. Equivalence classes relate pairs of policies and states. A pair (μ, φ) and another pair $(\bar{\mu}, \bar{\varphi})$ belong to the same equivalence class if and only if both pairs implement the same equilibrium allocation.[20]

A direct approach to establishing that (μ, φ) and $(\bar{\mu}, \bar{\varphi})$ belong to the same equivalence class relies on characterizing the equilibrium allocations implemented by each pair (if they exist) and showing that they are identical. An indirect approach relies on establishing that the *choice sets* of households and firms are not affected by the change of policy. Suppose a pair (μ, φ) implements an equilibrium and suppose that another pair, $(\bar{\mu}, \bar{\varphi})$, satisfies the following conditions:

  i. μ and $\bar{\mu}$ encode identical production possibilities, and restrictions on inputs and/or outputs of firms are identical across policies;
 ii. households' choice sets are identical if evaluated at the equilibrium prices;
iii. at the equilibrium allocation and prices, $(\bar{\mu}, \bar{\varphi})$ satisfies the government's dynamic budget constraints.

Then, the two pairs belong to the same equivalence class.

This can be seen as follows: Conjecture that equilibrium prices under (μ, φ) and $(\bar{\mu}, \bar{\varphi})$ are the same. With household choice sets unchanged, household demand functions are unaltered because preferences do not depend on policy. With constraints on production unaffected, firm net supply functions are unaltered. The original household and firm choices (except possibly for financial assets) thus remain optimal and clear markets. Private sector choices and the government's new policy also satisfy all budget constraints. Given that the equilibrium allocation under (μ, φ) and $(\bar{\mu}, \bar{\varphi})$ is the same, the conjecture is verified.

11.3.2   Applications

The reasoning underlying the general equivalence result parallels the argument that we made to establish Ricardian equivalence, as well as the equivalence of pay-as-you-go social security and tax-and-debt policies. There, the choice set of a household is the set of affordable consumption allocations over the household's lifetime, and condition i. is trivially satisfied because the initial capital stock that corresponds to μ is held constant. But the result holds much more broadly, as the following examples show.

11.3.2.1   Heterogeneity   Suppose that taxes are nondistorting but households are heterogeneous within cohorts. An equivalence class (conditional on some initial state) then consists of policies that satisfy the government budget constraints and impose on each household a given household-specific present value of taxes.

---

[20] For simplicity, we disregard issues related to multiplicity of equilibria.

11.3.2.2 Tax Distortions Suppose that households value consumption and leisure such that labor income taxes are distorting. The choice set of a household then is given by the set of affordable consumption and leisure combinations. An equivalence class (conditional on the initial state) consists of policies that satisfy the government budget constraints and impose on each household a given household-specific lifetime *tax function* that specifies the present value of taxes as a function of the household's choices. For example, one tax policy in such an equivalence class might tax labor income at date t at rate τ_t^w, while another policy in the same class might tax labor income at date t at rate $\tau_t^w R_{t+1}$ but collect the tax only in the subsequent period. Since both policies have the same effect on the household's choice set, an equilibrium allocation implemented by the former policy also constitutes an equilibrium allocation under the latter. As with standard Ricardian equivalence, however, the two policies are associated with different levels of government debt.

11.3.2.3 Multiple Tax Instruments Suppose that the government taxes consumption expenditures at rate τ_t^c, capital income at rate τ_t^k, and labor income at rate τ_t^w. The household's dynamic budget constraint reads

$$a_{t+1} = a_t R_t (1 - \tau_t^k) + w_t (1 - x_t)(1 - \tau_t^w) - c_t (1 + \tau_t^c),$$

where x_t denotes leisure. Iterating the dynamic budget constraint and imposing a no-Ponzi-game condition yields the intertemporal budget constraint

$$a_0 R_0 (1 - \tau_0^k) + \sum_{t=0}^{\infty} q_t \kappa_t \left(w_t (1 - x_t)(1 - \tau_t^w) - c_t (1 + \tau_t^c) \right) = 0,$$

where we define $\kappa_0 \equiv 1$ and $\kappa_t \equiv ((1 - \tau_1^k) \cdots (1 - \tau_t^k))^{-1}, t > 0$. Letting $\xi_t \equiv (1 + \tau_t^c)/(1 + \tau_0^c)$, we can rewrite this as

$$\frac{a_0 R_0 (1 - \tau_0^k)}{1 + \tau_0^c} + \sum_{t=0}^{\infty} q_t \kappa_t \xi_t \left(w_t (1 - x_t) \frac{1 - \tau_t^w}{1 + \tau_t^c} - c_t \right) = 0.$$

From the household's perspective, the price of leisure relative to consumption equals $w_t (1 - \tau_t^w)/(1 + \tau_t^c)$ and the price of consumption at date $t + 1$ relative to consumption at date t equals $q_{t+1} \kappa_{t+1} \xi_{t+1}/(q_t \kappa_t \xi_t) = (1 + \tau_{t+1}^c)/(R_{t+1}(1 - \tau_{t+1}^k)(1 + \tau_t^c))$. That is, the *tax wedges*

$$\frac{1 - \tau_t^w}{1 + \tau_t^c} \quad \text{and} \quad \frac{1 + \tau_{t+1}^c}{(1 - \tau_{t+1}^k)(1 + \tau_t^c)}$$

distort the consumption–leisure and consumption–saving choices, respectively.

If $a_0 R_0 = 0$, then the three tax rates affect the household's budget set only through the two tax wedges. Feasible tax sequences generating the same wedge sequences constitute an equivalence class in this case. For example, a feasible tax policy employing all three tax instruments is equivalent to another policy that only relies on a specific combination of capital and labor income taxes.

If $a_0 R_0 \neq 0$, then the budget set also depends on $(1 - \tau_0^k)/(1 + \tau_0^c)$. A (nondistorting) tax levied on date-$t = 0$ financial wealth, $\tau_0^k > 0$, can be replicated by a change in consumption and labor income taxes. To see this, suppose for simplicity that the initial policy imposes no taxes except for capital income taxes at date $t = 0$, $\tau_0^k > 0$. This is equivalent to a policy with no capital income taxes but a positive consumption tax at date $t = 0$, which satisfies $1 + \tau_0^c = (1 - \tau_0^k)^{-1}$; positive consumption taxes in all other periods, $\tau_t^c = \tau_0^c$, to keep intertemporal wedges unchanged; and subsidies for labor supply in all periods, $\tau_t^w = -\tau_t^c$, to keep relative prices between consumption and leisure unchanged.

11.4   Fiscal-Monetary Policy Interaction

When a government issues nominal liabilities such as nominal debt and central bank money, then the government's budget constraint includes fiscal and monetary policy instruments as well as the price level. Accordingly, fiscal and monetary policy must be coordinated in equilibrium and their interplay affects inflation.

11.4.1   Consolidated Government Budget Constraint

Suppose that the government redeems *real* and *nominal debt*, $b_t(\epsilon^{t-1})$ and $B_t(\epsilon^{t-1})$ respectively; and issues new debt as well as additional money balances, $b_{t+1}(\epsilon^t)$, $B_{t+1}(\epsilon^t)$, and $M_{t+1}(\epsilon^t) - M_t(\epsilon^{t-1})$. Liabilities issued at date t and maturing at date $t + 1$ are indexed by the history ϵ^t. Real or *inflation indexed debt* pays the potentially history-contingent gross rate of return $R_{t+1}(\epsilon^{t+1})$, expressed in real terms; nominal debt pays the gross rate of return $I_{t+1}(\epsilon^{t+1})$, expressed in nominal terms, which translates into the real rate of return $I_{t+1}(\epsilon^{t+1})\Pi_{t+1}^{-1}(\epsilon^{t+1})$, where $\Pi_{t+1}(\epsilon^{t+1})$ denotes gross inflation. Throughout, debt positions should be interpreted as net debt positions of the government.

Let $\{m_{t+1}(\epsilon^{t+1})\}_{t \geq 0}$ denote the stochastic discount factor and $P_t(\epsilon^t)$ the aggregate price level. Standard asset pricing (see equation (5.1) in section 5.3 and equation (9.2) in section 9.1) implies that the equilibrium price of real and nominal debt equals unity and $P_t^{-1}(\epsilon^t)$, respectively. To see the latter, rewrite the Euler equation for nominal debt as

$$1 = \mathbb{E}_t\left[m_{t+1}(\epsilon^{t+1})\frac{I_{t+1}(\epsilon^{t+1})}{\Pi_{t+1}(\epsilon^{t+1})}\right] = \mathbb{E}_t\left[m_{t+1}(\epsilon^{t+1})\frac{I_{t+1}(\epsilon^{t+1})/P_{t+1}(\epsilon^{t+1})}{1/P_t(\epsilon^t)}\right]$$

and note that $I_{t+1}(\epsilon^{t+1})/P_{t+1}(\epsilon^{t+1})$ is the real payoff of nominal debt. It follows that the equilibrium price of nominal debt equals $1/P_t(\epsilon^t)$.

Also, when issuing one unit of money, the government receives $1/P_t(\epsilon^t)$ units of the good in exchange. The *consolidated government budget constraint* therefore reads

$$b_t(\epsilon^{t-1})R_t(\epsilon^t) + \frac{B_t(\epsilon^{t-1})I_t(\epsilon^t)}{P_t(\epsilon^t)} = \tag{11.3}$$

$$\tau_t(\epsilon^t) - g_t(\epsilon^t) + b_{t+1}(\epsilon^t) + \frac{B_{t+1}(\epsilon^t)}{P_t(\epsilon^t)} + \frac{M_{t+1}(\epsilon^t) - M_t(\epsilon^{t-1})}{P_t(\epsilon^t)},$$

where $\tau_t(\epsilon^t) - g_t(\epsilon^t)$ denotes the primary surplus. Condition (11.3) states that the government funds maturing debt including interest (on the left-hand side) with its primary surplus and the revenue from new debt and money issuance (on the right-hand side).[21] Note that the real value of maturing government debt may be history-contingent for two reasons: Because of contingent interest rates or—with nominal debt—due to a stochastic price level.

Solving the dynamic budget constraint forward (using the Euler equation) and imposing a no-Ponzi-game condition yields the *intertemporal government budget constraint*

$$b_t(\epsilon^{t-1})R_t(\epsilon^t) + \frac{B_t(\epsilon^{t-1})I_t(\epsilon^t)}{P_t(\epsilon^t)} = \tag{11.4}$$

$$\sum_{j=0}^{\infty} \mathbb{E}_t \left[(m_{t+1}(\epsilon^{t+1}) \cdots m_{t+j}(\epsilon^{t+j})) \times \right.$$

$$\left. \left(\tau_{t+j}(\epsilon^{t+j}) - g_{t+j}(\epsilon^{t+j}) + \frac{M_{t+1+j}(\epsilon^{t+j}) - M_{t+j}(\epsilon^{t+j-1})}{P_{t+j}(\epsilon^{t+j})} \right) \right].$$

Condition (11.4) states that the market value of outstanding debt equals the present value of current and future primary surpluses, including *seignorage* revenues, where seignorage is defined as the resources that the government collects in exchange for the money it issues.

When we rewrite the dynamic budget constraint as

$$b_t(\epsilon^{t-1})R_t(\epsilon^t) + \frac{B_t(\epsilon^{t-1})I_t(\epsilon^t)}{P_t(\epsilon^t)} + \frac{M_t(\epsilon^{t-1})}{P_t(\epsilon^t)} =$$

$$\tau_t(\epsilon^t) - g_t(\epsilon^t) + b_{t+1}(\epsilon^t) + \frac{B_{t+1}(\epsilon^t)}{P_t(\epsilon^t)} + \frac{M_{t+1}(\epsilon^t)}{P_t(\epsilon^t)},$$

the left-hand side comprises a broader measure of government liabilities that includes both debt and outstanding money balances. Solving this equation forward yields

$$b_t(\epsilon^{t-1})R_t(\epsilon^t) + \frac{B_t(\epsilon^{t-1})I_t(\epsilon^t)}{P_t(\epsilon^t)} + \frac{M_t(\epsilon^{t-1})}{P_t(\epsilon^t)} =$$

$$\sum_{j=0}^{\infty} \mathbb{E}_t \left[(m_{t+1}(\epsilon^{t+1}) \cdots m_{t+j}(\epsilon^{t+j})) \times \right.$$

$$\left. \left(\tau_{t+j}(\epsilon^{t+j}) - g_{t+j}(\epsilon^{t+j}) + \frac{m_{t+1+j}(\epsilon^{t+1+j}) M_{t+1+j}(\epsilon^{t+j}) i_{t+1+j}(\epsilon^{t+1+j})}{P_{t+1+j}(\epsilon^{t+1+j})} \right) \right].$$

The last term on the right-hand side represents an alternative measure of seignorage, namely the cost reduction for the government due to the fact that money, unlike debt, does not pay interest. Owing money rather than debt reduces the government's interest payments at date $t + j + 1$ by $M_{t+1+j}(\epsilon^{t+j})i_{t+1+j}(\epsilon^{t+1+j})$; the real value as of date $t + j$ of this reduction is the

---

[21] We assume that all debt is short-term; that is, it matures after one period. With longer-term debt, the right-hand side of condition (11.3) would include changes in debt positions.

reduction times $m_{t+1+j}(\epsilon^{t+1+j})/P_{t+1+j}(\epsilon^{t+1+j})$. Note that the cost reduction enters the budget constraint in parallel to a tax revenue.

If money paid interest (see subsection 12.3.1), then no such seignorage term would be present.

11.4.2   Seignorage Needs as Driver of Inflation

Consider a deterministic economy without debt and with fixed taxes and government consumption, $g - \tau > 0$. For an equilibrium to exist, seignorage revenue then must be sufficient to balance the budget. Specifically, equation (11.3) requires that

$$g - \tau = \frac{M_{t+1} - M_t}{P_t} = \frac{M_{t+1} - M_t}{M_t} \frac{P_{t-1}}{P_t} \frac{M_t}{P_{t-1}}.$$

The right-hand side of the equation indicates that seignorage is proportional to the money growth rate; inverse inflation; and the private sector's money demand, M_t/P_{t-1}. The last-mentioned dependence implies that the government is constrained in its ability to raise seignorage revenue.

Assume that M_t grows at the constant gross rate γ_M and the private sector's demand for real balances depends negatively on the nominal interest rate, and thus (from the Fisher equation) expected inflation. Expected and actual inflation are equal to each other and to the money growth rate, reflecting a quantity theory relationship. The budget constraint can then be expressed as

$$g - \tau = \frac{\gamma_M - 1}{\gamma_M} \cdot \text{money demand}(\gamma_M).$$

The right-hand side of this equation is the product of an increasing and a decreasing function of γ_M: On the one hand, higher money growth increases the *inflation tax* that households pay when acquiring additional money in order to keep real balances constant; but on the other hand, households reduce real balances, and thus the base of the inflation tax in response to higher inflation and nominal interest rates. The two counteracting effects give rise to a *seignorage Laffer curve*—a hump-shaped relationship between the inflation-tax rate, γ_M, and the seignorage revenue. Except for too high levels of seignorage revenue, there exist at least two money growth rates that generate that revenue—a low and a high one.

The turnpike model analyzed in subsection 9.2.2 provides micro-foundations for an inflation-elastic money demand function. Consider an equilibrium in which nonconstrained households buy the bubble $a = M_{t+1}/P_t$ and sell it at value M_{t+1}/P_{t+1} in the subsequent period; the gross return on the bubble thus equals the inverse gross inflation rate, Π^{-1}. The difference between bubble purchases (by nonconstrained households) and sales (by constrained households) in a period, $a(1 - \Pi^{-1})$, corresponds to the new bubble sales by the government. To satisfy the government budget constraint, these sales have to equal the primary deficit,

$$g - \tau = a(1 - \Pi^{-1}) = a\pi/\Pi,$$

where π denotes the net inflation rate.

Let $\bar{c} \equiv \bar{w} - a$ and $\underline{c} \equiv \underline{w} + a\Pi^{-1}$ denote equilibrium consumption of a household with high and low endowment, respectively. The resource constraint is given by $\bar{c} + \underline{c} = \bar{w} + \underline{w} - g$; the Euler equation of a household investing in the bubble reads

$$u'(\bar{c}) = \beta \Pi^{-1} u'(\underline{c});$$

and the borrowing constraint implies the condition $1 \geq u'(\bar{c})/u'(\underline{c})$, which is necessarily satisfied when $a \geq 0$ and $g - \tau > 0$.

For a given inflation rate, the Euler equation pins down the demand for real balances, a, and thus seignorage revenue, $a\pi/\Pi$. Note that inflation affects seignorage revenue twofold. On the one hand, it gives rise to income and substitution effects on the demand for the bubble (see subsection 2.1.2); with logarithmic utility and $\underline{w} = 0$, these effects cancel. On the other hand, higher inflation increases the tax on bubble holdings as well as new bubble sales. When the bubble demand is sufficiently elastic, seignorage is a hump-shaped function of the inflation rate.

11.4.3   Inflation Effects of Government Financing

Consider an endowment economy inhabited by an infinitely lived representative household that owns a history-contingent endowment sequence, $\{w_t(\epsilon^t)\}_{t \geq 0}$; and a government with history-contingent resource requirement $\{g_t(\epsilon^t)\}_{t \geq 0}$. Households may not consume their own endowments, and consumption goods can only be sold to, and bought from, other households against cash (see subsection 9.3.3). The government also must use cash to purchase goods. The economy's resource constraint reads $w_t(\epsilon^t) = c_t(\epsilon^t) + g_t(\epsilon^t)$. The households' and government's cash-in-advance constraints (which bind because of positive interest rates) are given by $c_t(\epsilon^t) = M^h_{t+1}(\epsilon^t)/P_t(\epsilon^t)$ and $g_t(\epsilon^t) = M^g_{t+1}(\epsilon^t)/P_t(\epsilon^t)$, respectively. Let $M_{t+1}(\epsilon^t) \equiv M^h_{t+1}(\epsilon^t) + M^g_{t+1}(\epsilon^t)$. Securities are traded and money holdings chosen after the state of nature is realized, before cash transactions take place.

The household's dynamic budget constraint reads

$$\tau_t(\epsilon^t) + b_{t+1}(\epsilon^t) + \frac{B_{t+1}(\epsilon^t)}{P_t(\epsilon^t)} + \frac{M^h_{t+1}(\epsilon^t)}{P_t(\epsilon^t)} =$$

$$b_t(\epsilon^{t-1})R_t(\epsilon^t) + \frac{B_t(\epsilon^{t-1})I_t(\epsilon^t)}{P_t(\epsilon^t)} + \frac{M^h_t(\epsilon^{t-1})}{P_t(\epsilon^t)} + \frac{w_{t-1}(\epsilon^{t-1}) - c_{t-1}(\epsilon^{t-1})}{\Pi_t(\epsilon^t)},$$

where the last term on the right-hand side represents the real value of cash inflows from endowment sales, net of cash outflows for consumption purchases in the previous period.

Since the cash-in-advance constraint binds, this collapses to

$$\tau_t(\epsilon^t) + b_{t+1}(\epsilon^t) + \frac{B_{t+1}(\epsilon^t)}{P_t(\epsilon^t)} + c_t(\epsilon^t) =$$

$$b_t(\epsilon^{t-1})R_t(\epsilon^t) + \frac{B_t(\epsilon^{t-1})I_t(\epsilon^t)}{P_t(\epsilon^t)} + w_{t-1}(\epsilon^{t-1})\Pi_t^{-1}(\epsilon^t).$$

Since the revenue from endowment sales accrues in cash that must be carried into the next period, inflation or even low deflation $(\Pi_t^{-1}(\epsilon^t) < R_t(\epsilon^t))$ acts as a (nondistorting) tax on sales.

The initial state in the economy is $\mu = (M_0^h, M_0^g, b_0 R_0, B_0 I_0)$ and a policy is given by

$$\varphi \equiv \{\tau_t(\epsilon^t), g_t(\epsilon^t), b_{t+1}(\epsilon^t), R_{t+1}(\epsilon^{t+1}), B_{t+1}(\epsilon^t), I_{t+1}(\epsilon^{t+1}), M_{t+1}(\epsilon^t)\}_{t \geq 0}.$$

The endogenous variables are $\{c_t(\epsilon^t), P_t(\epsilon^t), m_{t+1}(\epsilon^{t+1}), M_{t+1}^h(\epsilon^t), M_{t+1}^g(\epsilon^t)\}_{t \geq 0}$. Equilibrium conditional on (μ, φ) requires

$$c_t(\epsilon^t) = w_t(\epsilon^t) - g_t(\epsilon^t),$$

$$m_{t+1}(\epsilon^{t+1}) = \beta \frac{u'(w_{t+1}(\epsilon^{t+1}) - g_{t+1}(\epsilon^{t+1}))}{u'(w_t(\epsilon^t) - g_t(\epsilon^t))},$$

$$\frac{M_{t+1}^h(\epsilon^t)}{M_{t+1}^g(\epsilon^t)} = \frac{w_t(\epsilon^t) - g_t(\epsilon^t)}{g_t(\epsilon^t)},$$

$$1 = \mathbb{E}_t\left[m_{t+1}(\epsilon^{t+1})R_{t+1}(\epsilon^{t+1})\right],$$

$$1 = \mathbb{E}_t\left[m_{t+1}(\epsilon^{t+1})I_{t+1}(\epsilon^{t+1})\Pi_{t+1}^{-1}(\epsilon^{t+1})\right],$$

$$P_t(\epsilon^t) = \frac{M_{t+1}(\epsilon^t)}{w_t(\epsilon^t)},$$

as well as the government budget constraints, conditions (11.3) and (11.4). Walras's law implies that the household budget constraints then are satisfied as well.

We are interested in policies that implement the same allocation. Such policies include the same government consumption sequence but they might differ from each other with respect to taxes, debt instruments, money balances, or nominal interest rates. Our objective is to understand whether, and how, changes in these policy instruments alter the equilibrium price level sequence.

11.4.3.1   Irrelevance of Debt Composition   Note first a neutrality result: A feasible change in the *composition* of *government debt* between real and nominal debt accompanied by no change in taxes or money supply does not alter inflation. Such a policy change neither affects total indebtedness in real terms nor total debt issuance. For example, a feasible policy φ with positive real and nominal debt implements the same equilibrium inflation as a modified policy $\bar{\varphi}$ with zero nominal debt and

$$
\begin{aligned}
\bar{b}_t(\epsilon^{t-1})\bar{R}_t(\epsilon^t) &= b_t(\epsilon^{t-1})R_t(\epsilon^t) + \frac{B_t(\epsilon^{t-1})I_t(\epsilon^t)}{P_t(\epsilon^t)}, \ t \geq 1, \\
1 &= \mathbb{E}_t\left[m_{t+1}(\epsilon^{t+1})\bar{R}_{t+1}(\epsilon^{t+1})\right].
\end{aligned}
$$

Throughout the subsection, we therefore abstract from nominal debt, without loss of generality.

11.4.3.2   Policy Mixes   We consider feasible policy changes that affect taxes, seignorage, and debt subject to (11.3) and (11.4), the asset pricing condition, and the cash-in-advance constraint. To satisfy the equilibrium conditions, the policies before and after the change, φ and $\bar{\varphi}$ respectively, and the associated price level sequences, $\{P_t\}_{t\geq 0}$ and $\{\bar{P}_t\}_{t\geq 0}$, must be related as follows:

$$
\begin{aligned}
\bar{\tau}_t(\epsilon^t) &+ \frac{\bar{M}_{t+1}(\epsilon^t) - \bar{M}_t(\epsilon^{t-1})}{\bar{P}_t(\epsilon^t)} + \bar{b}_{t+1}(\epsilon^t) - \bar{b}_t(\epsilon^{t-1})\bar{R}_t(\epsilon^t) \\
&= \tau_t(\epsilon^t) + \frac{M_{t+1}(\epsilon^t) - M_t(\epsilon^{t-1})}{P_t(\epsilon^t)} + b_{t+1}(\epsilon^t) - b_t(\epsilon^{t-1})R_t(\epsilon^t), \\
\bar{P}_t(\epsilon^t) &= \bar{M}_{t+1}(\epsilon^t)/w_t(\epsilon^t), \\
0 &= \mathbb{E}_t\left[m_{t+1}(\epsilon^{t+1})(\bar{R}_{t+1}(\epsilon^{t+1}) - R_{t+1}(\epsilon^{t+1}))\right].
\end{aligned}
$$

The new policy must also satisfy condition (11.4). We consider several special cases of such policy changes.

11.4.3.3   Current vs. Future Taxes   Delaying taxation and financing the temporary revenue shortfall by issuing government debt leaves the money supply unchanged. The equilibrium price level sequence then is unchanged as well. For example, altering taxes and debt issuance according to

$$
\begin{aligned}
\bar{\tau}_0(\epsilon^0) &= \tau_0(\epsilon^0) - \Delta, \\
\bar{b}_1(\epsilon^0) &= b_1(\epsilon^0) + \Delta, \\
\bar{\tau}_1(\epsilon^1) &= \tau_1(\epsilon^1) + R_1(\epsilon^1)\Delta,
\end{aligned}
$$

where $\Delta > 0$, has no effect on price levels.

11.4.3.4   Seignorage vs. Future Taxes   A one-time change in the composition of government liabilities between money and debt, coupled with a subsequent change in taxes but no further changes in seignorage, has a permanent effect on the price level. Formally, let

$$\bar{\tau}_0 = \tau_0,$$

$$\bar{b}_1(\epsilon^0) + \frac{\bar{M}_1(\epsilon^0) - M_0}{\bar{P}_0(\epsilon^0)} = b_1(\epsilon^0) + \frac{M_1(\epsilon^0) - M_0}{P_0(\epsilon^0)},$$

$$\bar{P}_0(\epsilon^0) = \bar{M}_1(\epsilon^0)/w_0(\epsilon^0),$$

where the two seignorage terms differ. Since the policy $\bar{\varphi}$ does not involve further changes in seignorage, the effect on the price level is permanent.[22] The change in debt issuance at date $t = 0$ implies $\bar{b}_1(\epsilon^0)\bar{R}_1(\epsilon^1) \neq b_1(\epsilon^0)R_1(\epsilon^1)$ for some history ϵ^1. Long-term budget balance therefore requires an appropriate adjustment of taxes subsequent to ϵ^1. With this adjustment, all equilibrium conditions are met.

The example illustrates that monetary policy interventions that change the government's portfolio do not only affect the price level but also have fiscal consequences. An *open market operation* in which the government purchases government debt from households against cash constitutes an example of such an intervention.

11.4.3.5   Current vs. Future Seignorage   A debt-financed reduction of seignorage that is accompanied by a subsequent increase of seignorage permanently alters the price level. In fact, such a monetary contraction coupled with a subsequent expansion implies a higher price level in the long run.

For a simple example, consider a deterministic environment with constant endowment, w, and gross interest rate, $R > 1$. Feasible policy φ involves no seignorage revenues, $M_t = M$, such that $P_t = P = M/w$. Under the modified policy, $\bar{\varphi}$, money balances are reduced at date $t = 0$ and kept constant until date $t = T - 1$, when they are increased again. That is,

$$\bar{M}_{t+1} = M - \Delta_1, \; t = 0, \ldots, T - 2,$$

$$\bar{M}_{t+1} = M - \Delta_1 + \Delta_T, \; t = T - 1, T, \ldots.$$

The cash-in-advance constraints imply

$$\bar{P}_t = (M - \Delta_1)/w, \; t = 0, \ldots, T - 2,$$

$$\bar{P}_t = (M - \Delta_1 + \Delta_T)/w, \; t = T - 1, T, \ldots.$$

Under $\bar{\varphi}$, seignorage revenues at date $t = 0$ and date $t = T - 1$, respectively, equal $-\Delta_1 w/(M - \Delta_1)$ and $\Delta_T w/(M - \Delta_1 + \Delta_T)$. To satisfy the budget constraint (11.4), the

---

[22] To see this, consider the deterministic case.   The cash-in-advance constraint implies $\{\bar{M}_{t+1}/\bar{P}_t\}_{t\geq 0} = \{M_{t+1}/P_t\}_{t\geq 0}$. $(\bar{M}_1 - M_0)/\bar{P}_0 \neq (M_1 - M_0)/P_0$ implies $\bar{P}_0 \neq P_0$ and $\bar{M}_1 \neq M_1$. $(\bar{M}_2 - \bar{M}_1)/\bar{P}_1 = (M_2 - M_1)/P_1$ implies $\bar{M}_1/\bar{P}_1 = M_1/P_1$ and thus, $\bar{P}_1 \neq P_1$ and $\bar{M}_2 \neq M_2$. The argument extends to subsequent periods.

present value of these revenues must equal zero, implying

$$\frac{\Delta_T w}{M - \Delta_1 + \Delta_T} = R^{T-1} \frac{\Delta_1 w}{M - \Delta_1} \implies \frac{\Delta_T}{\Delta_1} = R^{T-1} \frac{M - \Delta_1 + \Delta_T}{M - \Delta_1}.$$

This implies that $\Delta_T > \Delta_1$, both since $R > 1$ and $\bar{P}_{T-1} > \bar{P}_0$. That is, following a monetary contraction at date $t = 0$, money balances and thus the price level *increase* in the long run because the monetary contraction generates a revenue shortfall, which requires higher future inflation to balance the budget. A postponement of the expansionary policy increases the long-run price level (P_T increases in T).

This so-called *unpleasant monetarist arithmetic* illustrates how the fiscal implications of a monetary policy intervention force an eventual policy reversal when fiscal policy does not accommodate the intervention; and that the inflationary effects of the reversal can dominate those of the intervention.

11.4.4   Game of Chicken

When monetary and fiscal policy are controlled by separate authorities—a central bank on the one hand and a fiscal authority on the other—then the institutional structure governing the policy coordination can have important macroeconomic implications.

Suppose the fiscal authority moves first in the sense of committing to history-contingent tax and government consumption sequences before the monetary authority chooses the money supply. By moving first, the fiscal authority shifts responsibility for implementing an equilibrium to the monetary authority; the latter must generate sufficient seignorage to satisfy the intertemporal budget constraint. In this *game of chicken* the central bank's choice set is restricted by the actions of the fiscal authority. Although the central bank may wish to conduct a monetary policy aimed at stabilizing the price level, say, its second mover status can frustrate this plan.

Threats to price stability of this kind can be countered by instituting an arrangement that guarantees *central bank independence* and assigns the first mover advantage to the monetary authority. An independent central bank is relieved of the responsibility for intertemporally balancing the budget; that responsibility lies with the fiscal authority.

11.4.5   Fiscal Theory of the Price Level

When nominal debt is outstanding at date $t = 0$, the government's intertemporal budget constraint (11.4) may not only be balanced by appropriate choices of government consumption, taxes, or seignorage revenues, but also by a revaluation of nominal debt through a change in the price level. The *fiscal theory of the price level* emphasizes this possibility. It views the intertemporal budget constraint (11.4) not as a constraint on government actions but as an equilibrium condition that determines the price level.

To motivate the theory, consider a static model. Suppose that nominal liabilities $B_0 I_0$ are outstanding at date $t = 0$, which is the last period; both money balances and seignorage are negligible; and there is no real debt. Suppose further that the choice of fiscal policy is *non-Ricardian*: Rather than balancing the government's budget by setting $\tau_0 - g_0 = B_0 I_0 / P_0$ for whatever equilibrium price level is realized (as would be the case in the *Ricardian* case), the government sets $\tau_0 - g_0$ independently of P_0. For an equilibrium to exist, P_0 must adjust to $B_0 I_0 / (\tau_0 - g_0)$; the price level is fiscally determined.[23]

For a more detailed analysis, consider the model introduced in subsection 11.4.3. We abstract from real debt and assume that the nominal interest rate is risk-free such that $B_{t+1}(\epsilon^t) I_{t+1}(\epsilon^t)$ is constant across all histories ϵ^{t+1} subsequent to history ϵ^t. Accordingly, the dynamic budget constraint of the government reads

$$\frac{B_t(\epsilon^{t-1}) I_t(\epsilon^{t-1})}{P_t(\epsilon^t)} = \tau_t(\epsilon^t) - g_t(\epsilon^t) + \frac{B_{t+1}(\epsilon^t)}{P_t(\epsilon^t)} + \frac{M_{t+1}(\epsilon^t) - M_t(\epsilon^{t-1})}{P_t(\epsilon^t)},$$

and the intertemporal budget constraint at date $t = 0$ is given by

$$\frac{B_0(\epsilon^{-1}) I_0(\epsilon^{-1}) + M_0(\epsilon^{-1})}{P_0(\epsilon^0)} =$$

$$\sum_{j=0}^{\infty} \mathbb{E}_0 \left[(m_1(\epsilon^1) \cdots m_j(\epsilon^j)) \left(\tau_j(\epsilon^j) - g_j(\epsilon^j) + \frac{m_{j+1}(\epsilon^{j+1}) M_{j+1}(\epsilon^j) i_{j+1}(\epsilon^j)}{P_{j+1}(\epsilon^{j+1})} \right) \right].$$

The remaining equilibrium conditions are

$$1 = \mathbb{E}_t \left[m_{t+1}(\epsilon^{t+1}) I_{t+1}(\epsilon^t) \Pi_{t+1}^{-1}(\epsilon^{t+1}) \right],$$

$$P_t(\epsilon^t) = \frac{M_{t+1}(\epsilon^t)}{w_t(\epsilon^t)},$$

where $m_{t+1}(\epsilon^{t+1})$ is pinned down by the resource constraint.

A *policy regime* is a mapping. With each strictly positive price level sequence, it associates a policy (or set of policies); the price level sequence and policy satisfy the above equilibrium conditions, except possibly the intertemporal budget constraint. A policy regime is Ricardian if for each price level sequence, this sequence and the associated policy also satisfy the intertemporal budget constraint. Otherwise, the policy regime is non-Ricardian: there exist some price level sequences and associated policies that do not satisfy the intertemporal budget constraint. Since in equilibrium, the government must balance its budget, a non-Ricardian regime rules out certain price level sequences if they are associated with policies that do not satisfy the intertemporal budget constraint. That is, a non-Ricardian policy regime imposes restrictions on equilibrium price levels, which a Ricardian regime does not impose.

---

[23] There is an even simpler mechanism without debt to fiscally determine the price level. It relies on the government setting government consumption in real terms and tax revenue in nominal terms. The budget balance requirement pins down the price level.

Consider for simplicity a deterministic environment with constant endowments, $w_t = w$, and government consumption, $g_t = g$, implying $m_{t+1} = \beta$. A (Ricardian or non-Ricardian) policy regime imposes the following restrictions on policy:

$$
\begin{aligned}
M_{t+1} &= P_t w, \\
I_{t+1} &= \Pi_{t+1}/\beta, \\
B_{t+1} &= B_t I_t - P_t \left(\tau_t - g + w - \Pi_t^{-1} w \right).
\end{aligned}
$$

If the regime is Ricardian, then policy also satisfies the intertemporal budget constraint for any strictly positive P_0; that is, policy satisfies

$$
\frac{B_0 I_0 + M_0}{P_0} = \sum_{j=0}^{\infty} \beta^j \left(\tau_j - g + \frac{w \, i_{j+1}}{I_{j+1}} \right),
$$

where $i_t \equiv I_t - 1$. If the regime is non-Ricardian, in contrast, then policy need not satisfy the latter restriction for arbitrary price level sequences. The non-Ricardian regime rules out price level sequences that in combination with the associated policy do not satisfy the restriction.

Suppose that $B_0 I_0 + M_0 \neq 0$ and monetary policy fixes the nominal interest rate at value I. Equilibrium inflation then is constant at value $\Pi = \beta I$ and money supply grows at the gross rate Π, implying $P_t = P_0 \Pi^t$ and $M_{t+1} = P_0 \Pi^t w$. We consider fiscal policy regimes that relate positive price level sequences that grow at a constant rate to fiscal policies, $\{\tau_t, g, B_{t+1}\}_{t \geq 0}$. In any fiscal policy regime, fiscal policy satisfies

$$
B_{t+1} = B_t I - P_0 \Pi^t \left(\tau_t - g + w - \Pi^{-1} w \right).
$$

If the fiscal policy regime is Ricardian, then for any $P_0 > 0$, policy also satisfies

$$
\frac{B_0 I_0 + M_0}{P_0} = \sum_{j=0}^{\infty} \beta^j \left(\tau_j - g + w \frac{I - 1}{I} \right);
$$

that is, P_0 imposes a constraint on fiscal policy. Since there is no other condition to determine the initial price level, P_0 is *indeterminate* (see section 11.5). Under a non-Ricardian fiscal policy regime, in contrast, fiscal policy is not constrained by the latter condition; as a consequence, it may determine the price level.

Suppose alternatively that monetary policy fixes the money supply at date t at value M_{t+1} such that the equilibrium price level equals $P_t = M_{t+1}/w$. Under a non-Ricardian fiscal policy regime, the price level now is overdetermined; except for knife-edge cases, only a Ricardian fiscal policy regime is consistent with equilibrium.

That a non-Ricardian policy regime may determine the initial price level and thereby revalue initially outstanding nominal debt does not mean that the government can choose primary surpluses and seignorage revenues arbitrarily. Standard asset pricing and rational expectations imply that, when nominal debt is issued for the first time (before date

$t = 0$), the government cannot raise more resources in present value terms than it repays in the future. Accordingly, the intertemporal budget constraint binds at the time of debt issuance. This can also be seen by noting that at the "truly initial" date $t = -1$, say, when $B_{-1}I_{-1} + M_{-1} = 0$, the price level P_{-1} cannot revalue outstanding liabilities. A non-Ricardian policy regime therefore does not allow the government to escape long-run budget balance. Similarly, a non-Ricardian policy regime does not provide a *nominal anchor*—it does not determine the price level—before nominal liabilities have been issued for the first time; it may only contribute, in a stochastic environment, to determining history-contingent inflation rates.

11.4.6   Stability under Policy Rules

Mechanically, a non-Ricardian policy regime determines the equilibrium price level conditional on outstanding nominal debt because only a specific price level prevents explosive debt dynamics: The equilibrium conditions without the intertemporal budget constraint determine the path of government debt in real terms, conditional on its starting value, and this path satisfies the government's no-Ponzi-game condition (or the household's transversality condition) only for a specific starting value, and thus a specific initial price level.

The same mechanism may be at work when a policy regime prescribes ad hoc policy rules; for example, rules specifying how the interest rate and taxes are set in response to inflation and the stock of outstanding debt. Consider a deterministic setting. Suppose the policy regime prescribes that the nominal interest rate responds to inflation, and taxes net of government consumption respond to the stock of real debt at the end of the previous period,

$$
\begin{aligned}
I_{t+1} &= \alpha \Pi_t, \\
\tau_t - g_t &= \gamma \frac{B_t}{P_{t-1}},
\end{aligned}
$$

where α and γ are fixed parameters.[24] Suppose also, as before, that the equilibrium gross real interest rate equals β^{-1}. The Fisher equation, $I_{t+1} = \Pi_{t+1}/\beta$, and the interest rate rule then imply

$$
\Pi_{t+1} = \alpha \beta \Pi_t.
$$

We allow for a cash-in-advance constraint or a money demand function that depends on the interest rate; in either case, $M_{t+1}/P_t = w_t \zeta(I_{t+1})$ for some function ζ. The dynamic

---

[24] We disregard additive constant terms since they are irrelevant for the argument.

budget constraint thus can be expressed as

$$\frac{B_{t+1}}{P_t} = \frac{B_t}{P_{t-1}}\left(\frac{I_t}{\Pi_t} - \gamma\right) - \frac{M_{t+1} - M_t}{P_t}$$

$$= \frac{B_t}{P_{t-1}}(\beta^{-1} - \gamma) - \chi(w_t, w_{t-1}, \Pi_t)$$

for some function χ, where the second equality uses the Fisher equation, the money demand function, the interest rate rule, and the equilibrium condition $\Pi_{t+1} = \alpha\beta\Pi_t$.

Linearizing the two dynamic equations yields a linear difference equation system in two endogenous variables, the deviation of Π_t from its steady-state value and the deviation of B_t/P_{t-1} from its steady-state value. The latter variable is predetermined, the former is not. The matrix determining the stability of the system is given by

$$\begin{bmatrix} \alpha\beta & 0 \\ \xi & \beta^{-1} - \gamma \end{bmatrix}$$

for some constant ξ; its eigenvalues equal $\alpha\beta$ and $\beta^{-1} - \gamma$.

Since we study a linear approximation around the system's steady state, we restrict attention to bounded solutions.[25] Three cases may be distinguished; see appendix B.5. First, if both eigenvalues of the matrix are unstable, then no bounded solution exists. Second, if both eigenvalues are stable, then any initial inflation rate together with the predetermined real debt value gives rise to a bounded solution. As a consequence, sunspot shocks may buffet the system. Finally, if exactly one eigenvalue is stable, then the system is saddle-path stable and the two policy rules pin down a unique inflation rate conditional on the predetermined real debt level.

Specifically, if $|\alpha\beta| > 1$ (*active monetary policy*), inflation in the initial period must equal a specific value to guarantee stable inflation dynamics (the difference equation for inflation is solved forward to yield a bounded solution). But in this case, debt dynamics only are bounded if $|\beta^{-1} - \gamma| < 1$ (*passive fiscal policy*). The situation parallels the one in the fiscal theory of the price level when the policy regime is Ricardian.

Alternatively, if $|\beta^{-1} - \gamma| > 1$ (*active fiscal policy*), inflation (and thus the price level) in the initial period must adjust to guarantee stable debt dynamics. Stable inflation dynamics then require $|\alpha\beta < 1|$ (*passive monetary policy*). The situation is akin to a non-Ricardian policy regime in the fiscal theory of the price level when the government fixes the nominal interest rate.

---

[25] This is a more stringent stability requirement than the no-Ponzi-game condition in the fiscal theory of the price level.

11.5   Determinate Inflation and Output

In the model with flexible prices discussed in subsection 10.3.5, risk renders inflation indeterminate when the government sets the nominal interest rate. In the fiscal theory of the price level analyzed in subsection 11.4.5, a Ricardian policy regime may render the price level and the real value of government debt indeterminate. And in the model with ad hoc policy rules considered in subsection 11.4.6, sufficiently passive rules also render inflation and real debt indeterminate.

We now study the source of price level indeterminacy in more detail and analyze the role of monetary policy in the determination of the price level. We first consider a flexible price environment before turning to rigid prices. Throughout the analysis, we assume that fiscal policy is Ricardian. Since we analyze linearized equilibrium conditions, we are looking for bounded solutions.

11.5.1   Flexible Prices

Consider the model with flexible prices analyzed in subsection 10.3.5, in which the classical dichotomy holds: The nominal interest rate or the money supply do not affect the real allocation; the real interest rate equals the natural interest rate, $r_t^n(\epsilon^t)$; and inflation is determined by the Fisher equation that reads, in linearized form,

$$\mathbb{E}_t[r_{t+1}^n(\epsilon^{t+1})] = i_{t+1}(\epsilon^t) - \mathbb{E}_t[\pi_{t+1}(\epsilon^{t+1})].$$

We assume that the natural interest rate follows a stationary process, and thus is bounded.

Suppose first that the government determines a history-contingent sequence of nominal interest rates that is independent of the values of other, endogenous variables. Such an *interest rate peg* only pins down expected inflation, not the actually realized inflation (see subsection 10.3.5). That is, inflation, and thus the price level (and, for a given money demand function, nominal balances) are indeterminate. The source of the indeterminacy is that the nominal and natural interest rate sequences only constrain the price level's expected change. The consequence is that inflation might respond to sunspot shocks; see appendix B.5.

Suppose next that rather than pegging the interest rate the government follows an *interest rate rule* that specifies the interest rate as a function of inflation. In particular, consider the rule $i_{t+1}(\epsilon^t) = \bar{\imath}_{t+1}(\epsilon^t) + \phi\pi_t(\epsilon^t)$, where $\phi > 0, \phi \neq 1$ and $\{\bar{\imath}_{t+1}(\epsilon^t)\}_{t\geq 0}$ is a stationary sequence (for example, a constant sequence). In line with our assumption that the steady-state inflation rate equals zero, we impose that in steady state, $\bar{\imath} = r^n$. Substituting the rule into the Fisher equation yields

$$\mathbb{E}_t[r_{t+1}^n(\epsilon^{t+1})] = \bar{\imath}_{t+1}(\epsilon^t) + \phi\pi_t(\epsilon^t) - \mathbb{E}_t[\pi_{t+1}(\epsilon^{t+1})].$$

When $\phi < 1$, $\lim_{T\to\infty} \mathbb{E}_t[\pi_{t+T}(\epsilon^{t+T})]$ is bounded irrespective of the value of $\pi_t(\epsilon^t)$. Conditional on $\{r_{t+1}^n(\epsilon^{t+1}), \bar{\imath}_{t+1}(\epsilon^t)\}_{t\geq 0}$, the difference equation and the boundedness requirement therefore do not pin down $\pi_t(\epsilon^t)$, similarly to the case when ϕ equals zero. That is, inflation again is indeterminate and might respond to sunspot shocks.

When $\phi > 1$, in contrast, *inflation* is *determinate*. Conditional on information at date t, the only inflation rate that satisfies the difference equation and the boundedness requirement is given by (see appendix B.5)

$$\pi_t^\star(\epsilon^t) = \sum_{s=1}^{\infty} \phi^{-s} \mathbb{E}_t[r_{t+s}^n(\epsilon^{t+s}) - \bar{\imath}_{t+s}(\epsilon^{t+s-1})].$$

Any other level of inflation would imply that expected future inflation diverges, violating the boundedness requirement. Intuitively, when the government raises the nominal interest rate by more than one-to-one in response to higher inflation ($\phi > 1$), it introduces an unstable root in the law of motion for equilibrium inflation and effectively threatens to let inflation diverge, unless $\pi_t(\epsilon^t) = \pi_t^\star(\epsilon^t)$. This property of the rule—the *Taylor principle*—in combination with the boundedness requirement pins down $\pi_t(\epsilon^t)$.

A potential problem with this argument concerns the assumption that the policy rule is linear. When savers have access to cash, nominal interest rates cannot be lowered (substantially) below zero because this would trigger portfolio shifts out of interest-bearing assets into cash. The nominal interest rate therefore is constrained by a *zero lower bound* or more realistically, an *effective lower bound* that falls short of zero because cash holdings generate transaction and storage costs. In the presence of such a lower bound, the interest rate rule cannot be globally linear.

Suppose, then, that the interest rate rule is given by

$$i_{t+1}(\epsilon^t) = \max[\underline{i}, \bar{\imath}_{t+1}(\epsilon^t) + \phi \pi_t(\epsilon^t)],$$

where $\underline{i}$ denotes the effective lower bound and $\phi > 1$. Substituting this modified rule into the Fisher equation and assuming that $\underline{i} < r^n$, we find that there are two steady-state inflation rates. The first, unstable steady state corresponds to the solution derived previously, $\pi^\star = (r^n - \bar{\imath})/(\phi - 1) = 0$. The second, stable steady state, $\underline{\pi}$, satisfies $\underline{\pi} = \underline{i} - r^n < 0$. Around this second, deflationary steady state the dynamics are stable. Conditional on information at date t, any inflation rate $\pi_t(\epsilon^t) \in [\underline{\pi}, \pi^\star)$ and associated expected inflation sequence (satisfying the Fisher equation and the interest rate rule) thus constitutes an equilibrium outcome.

Suppose finally that the government pegs the money supply. Let $p_t(\epsilon^t) \equiv \ln(P_t(\epsilon^t))$ denote the logarithm of the price level such that approximately, $\pi_{t+1}(\epsilon^{t+1}) = p_{t+1}(\epsilon^{t+1}) - p_t(\epsilon^t)$. Moreover, approximate the money demand function (9.4) derived in subsection 9.3.2 by the relationship

$$\ln(M_{t+1}(\epsilon^t)) - p_t(\epsilon^t) = -\eta i_{t+1}(\epsilon^t),$$

where $\eta > 0$.[26] Substituting this relationship into the Fisher equation and defining $z_{t+s}(\epsilon^{t+s}) \equiv (\eta r^n_{t+s}(\epsilon^{t+s}) + \ln(M_{t+s}(\epsilon^{t+s-1})))/(1 + \eta)$ yields

$$p_t(\epsilon^t) = \mathbb{E}_t[z_{t+1}(\epsilon^{t+1})] + \frac{\eta}{1+\eta}\mathbb{E}_t[p_{t+1}(\epsilon^{t+1})].$$

Iterating forward, we arrive at

$$p_t(\epsilon^t) = \sum_{s=0}^{\infty}\left(\frac{\eta}{1+\eta}\right)^s \mathbb{E}_t[z_{t+1+s}(\epsilon^{t+1+s})],$$

where we rule out hyperinflation. Since the government pegs the money supply and the natural interest rate is exogenous, we conclude that the *price level* is *determinate*. This conclusion is not necessarily robust to relaxing the assumption of a linear money demand function or to allowing for hyperinflation.

11.5.2   Rigid Prices

Suppose now that prices are rigid and output is demand determined. The New Keynesian Phillips curve and dynamic IS equation, respectively, are given by

$$\pi_t(\epsilon^t) = \kappa\chi_t(\epsilon^t) + \beta\mathbb{E}_t[\pi_{t+1}(\epsilon^{t+1})],$$
$$\chi_t(\epsilon^t) = \mathbb{E}_t\left[\chi_{t+1}(\epsilon^{t+1})\right] - \frac{1}{\sigma}\mathbb{E}_t\left[i_{t+1}(\epsilon^t) - \pi_{t+1}(\epsilon^{t+1}) - r^n_{t+1}(\epsilon^{t+1})\right],$$

where $\chi_t(\epsilon^t)$ denotes the output gap, and the parameters κ, β, σ are positive and $\beta < 1$ (see equations (10.19) and (10.20) in subsection 10.3.5).

We consider linear policy rules that map inflation, the output gap, and a stationary *monetary policy shock*, $\zeta_t(\epsilon^t)$, into the nominal interest rate,

$$i_{t+1}(\epsilon^t) = \bar{\imath}_{t+1}(\epsilon^t) + \phi_\pi\pi_t(\epsilon^t) + \phi_\chi\chi_t(\epsilon^t) + \zeta_t(\epsilon^t),$$

where the coefficients ϕ_π and ϕ_χ are strictly positive. Substituting the rule into the dynamic IS equation, we arrive at a difference equation system in two nonpredetermined endogenous variables, inflation and the output gap, as well as three exogenous variables, the intercept of the policy rule, the natural rate of interest, and the monetary policy shock.

The system is saddle-path stable if and only if the condition

$$\phi_\pi + \frac{1-\beta}{\kappa}\phi_\chi > 1$$

is satisfied. In particular, for $\phi_\pi = \phi_\chi = 0$ the system is not saddle-path stable and inflation and output are indeterminate (see subsection 10.3.5). To gain intuition for this restriction, consider a deterministic environment with constant intercept and natural rate, $\bar{\imath} = r^n$. We

---

[26] Since we consider the case where the real allocation is independent of monetary policy, we suppress the dependence of money demand on transactions volume (e.g., consumption).

know that in this case, one equilibrium is given by zero inflation and a zero output gap at all times. Suppose there exists another equilibrium with a constant, nonzero inflation rate, say $\bar{\pi}$. From the Phillips curve, this requires that the output gap is constant as well, at level $\bar{\chi} = (1-\beta)\bar{\pi}/\kappa$; and from the dynamic IS equation, this implies the restriction $\phi_\pi\bar{\pi}+\phi_\chi\bar{\chi} = \bar{\pi}$, which corresponds to the above condition with the inequality sign replaced by an equality. We conclude that when the above condition is just violated, then there exists a continuum of equilibria with constant, nonzero inflation and output gaps.

When the condition is met, in contrast, then the interest rate rule satisfies the *Taylor principle*, and inflation and *output* are *determinate*: A hypothetical rise in inflation would increase the nominal interest rate by more than one-to-one, and this would imply explosive dynamics. There is a unique inflation rate and associated output gap that place the system on the saddle path in this case.

11.6   Real Effects of Monetary Policy

11.6.1   Flexible Prices

Even when prices are perfectly flexible, a monetary policy shock can affect the allocation if frictions other than price rigidity prevent an immediate adjustment of the price level to its frictionless level. Imperfect information and market segmentation constitute two examples of such frictions.

Consider first *imperfect information*. Envision an overlapping generations economy without capital or storage; as in the model analyzed in subsection 9.2.1, young households only save by holding money. Unlike in that model, however, young households produce output. How much they optimally produce depends on the expected return on savings, and thus on the current and expected future price level. The price level in turn is affected by two shocks: First, a monetary policy shock; absent information frictions, this shock would be neutral—it would not lead to changes in production. And second, a real shock with asymmetric effects on different subgroups among the young; groups favored by the shock optimally increase their production.

Households do not observe the two shocks but imperfectly infer them from the observed equilibrium price level (see the discussion of rational expectations equilibrium in section 1.3). Households thus solve a *signal extraction problem*. When the price level rises, the solution to this problem leads households to rationally attach positive probability both to a favorable real shock and an expansionary monetary shock. As a consequence, all households expand production in response to an increased price level, even if the increase was triggered purely by a monetary shock. Under perfect information, the same shock would have been neutral.

Consider next *market segmentation* due to restrictions on specific types of financial transactions. When these restrictions give rise to distinct valuations of money in different markets or for different groups of agents, then a monetary policy shock may not be neutralized by a price level adjustment, unlike in the case without segmentation.

Suppose, for example, that firms and households are subject to a cash-in-advance constraint (see subsection 9.3.3). At the beginning of a period, before observing the monetary policy shock, households deposit money at banks. Banks, in turn, lend the money to firms that need to prepay inputs into production. Once households have chosen their portfolio, the government transfers new money to banks. When this transfer is larger than expected, the equilibrium price level rises by more than anticipated and households' real balances do not suffice to pay for the planned consumption. Banks, on the other hand, hold more cash than planned and lend it at cheaper rates to firms—the monetary expansion triggers a *liquidity effect* and this stimulates production. The real allocation therefore varies with the monetary policy shock. If the money injection symmetrically benefited banks and households, or if banks and households could trade money after the monetary policy shock, neutrality would prevail.

11.6.2   Rigid Prices

When prices are rigid, a change in the nominal interest rate affects the allocation (see subsection 10.3.5). By extension, this also holds true when the government sets the interest rate according to a policy rule. The exact *transmission mechanism* depends on the characteristics of this rule.

Consider the framework analyzed in subsection 11.5.2 and assume that policy is Ricardian; the condition for determinacy is satisfied ($\phi_\pi \kappa + (1 - \beta)\phi_\chi > \kappa$); and the intercept of the policy rule and the natural rate of interest are constant. Since inflation and the output gap are not predetermined, $\pi_t(\epsilon^t)$ and $\chi_t(\epsilon^t)$ are functions of $\zeta_t(\epsilon^t)$ only (see equation (B.4) in appendix B.5). Specifically, when the policy shock $\zeta_t(\epsilon^t)$ follows a first-order autoregressive process with coefficient $\rho \in [0, 1)$, then

$$\pi_t(\epsilon^t) = -\kappa \omega \zeta_t(\epsilon^t),$$
$$\chi_t(\epsilon^t) = -(1 - \beta\rho)\omega \zeta_t(\epsilon^t),$$

where $\omega \equiv ((1 - \beta\rho)(\sigma(1 - \rho) + \phi_\chi) + \kappa(\phi_\pi - \rho))^{-1}$ is strictly positive. Substituting these results into the dynamic IS equation and the interest rate rule yields expressions for the real and nominal interest rates, respectively, as functions of the policy shock:

$$\mathbb{E}_t\left[i_{t+1}(\epsilon^t) - \pi_{t+1}(\epsilon^{t+1})\right] = r^n + \sigma(1 - \rho)(1 - \beta\rho)\omega \zeta_t(\epsilon^t),$$
$$i_{t+1}(\epsilon^t) = \bar{\iota} + (\sigma(1 - \rho)(1 - \beta\rho) - \kappa\rho)\omega \zeta_t(\epsilon^t).$$

Following a positive monetary policy shock, $\zeta(\epsilon^t) > 0$, the nominal interest rate exceeds the level implied by the systematic part of the interest rate rule. This leads to lower inflation, a lower output gap, and (since the natural level of output is unaffected by the nominal interest rate) lower output. When $\rho > 0$, these effects are persistent, otherwise they are temporary.

Associated with the output contraction is an increase in the real interest rate. Paradoxically, however, the nominal interest rate need not rise; for sufficiently high values of ρ, the response of $i_{t+1}(\epsilon^t)$ to $\pi_t(\epsilon^t)$ and $\chi_t(\epsilon^t)$ through the systematic part of the policy rule may more than offset the direct positive effect of the policy shock. Intuitively, when ρ is sufficiently high, the policy shock generates expectations of negative inflation in subsequent periods and this lowers the nominal relative to the real interest rate.

Recall that κ, the coefficient on the output gap in the Phillips curve, depends on the frequency of price adjustments by firms, $1 - \theta$. As $\theta \to 0$ (perfectly flexible prices), $\kappa \to \infty$ and the effect of the policy shock on the output gap is zero. The marginal effect on inflation equals $-(\phi_\pi - \rho)^{-1}$, and the marginal effect on the nominal interest rate as well as on expected inflation in the subsequent period equals $-\rho(\phi_\pi - \rho)^{-1}$; accordingly, the real interest rate is not affected. Consistent with the results in subsection 11.5.1, we thus find that expected inflation and the nominal interest rate move in tandem; and the impact effect of the monetary policy shock on inflation is determined by the restriction that the expected inflation sequence under the policy rule be bounded.

For $\theta \to 1$ (completely rigid prices), in contrast, $\kappa \to 0$ and inflation is unaffected by the shock. The marginal effect on the output gap equals $-(\phi_\chi + \sigma(1 - \rho))^{-1}$ because, with zero inflation, it is determined by the difference equation

$$\chi_t(\epsilon^t) = \mathbb{E}_t \left[\chi_{t+1}(\epsilon^{t+1}) \right] - \frac{1}{\sigma} \mathbb{E}_t \left[\phi_\chi \chi_t(\epsilon^t) + \zeta_t(\epsilon^t) \right]$$

and the requirement that expected future output gaps remain bounded. The marginal effect of the policy shock on both the nominal and the real interest rate equals $\sigma(1-\rho)(\phi_\chi + \sigma(1 - \rho))^{-1}$. A higher persistence of the shock implies a stronger output effect but potentially a weaker interest rate response. When the persistence is very high ($\rho \to 1$), interest rates do not respond at all.

11.7 Bibliographic Notes

Baxter and King (1993) and Barro (1990) analyze tax-financed government consumption or investment in the neoclassical growth model and the *Ak* model, respectively.

The modern formulation of the Ricardian equivalence proposition is due to Barro (1974). Diamond (1965) studies debt in the overlapping generations model. Auerbach et al. (1994) discuss generational accounting, Breyer (1989) and Rangel (1997) analyze equivalent social security reforms, and Ball and Mankiw (2007) analyze risk sharing properties of social security systems.

Classic statements of neutrality results are due to Wallace (1981) and Bryant (1983); see also Gonzalez-Eiras and Niepelt (2015). Bassetto and Kocherlakota (2004) derive the neutrality result for policy changes that involve distorting taxes.

Cagan (1956) analyzes need-for-seignorage-driven (hyper)inflation. The unpleasant monetarist arithmetic is due to Sargent and Wallace (1981). Subsection 11.4.3 follows Sargent (1987, section 5.4). Leeper (1991) analyzes active and passive policy rules. The fiscal theory of the price level is due to Sims (1994) and Woodford (1995); see also Aiyagari and Gertler (1985) and Kocherlakota and Phelan (1999). For critiques, see Bassetto (2002), Buiter (2002), and Niepelt (2004a).

Sargent and Wallace (1975) establish price level indeterminacy under an interest rate rule. Interest rate rules often are referred to as *Taylor rules*, after Taylor (1993). Taylor (1999) and Woodford (2001) discuss the Taylor principle and Bullard and Mitra (2002) analyze the conditions for price level determinacy; see also Atkeson et al. (2010). Benhabib et al. (2002) analyze determinacy under interest rate rules in the presence of an effective lower bound. Brock (1974) and Obstfeld and Rogoff (1983) analyze determinacy when the government pegs the money supply.

Following Friedman (1968) and Phelps (1970), Lucas (1972) analyzes a model with imperfect information and real effects of monetary policy shocks. Grossman and Weiss (1983), Rotemberg (1984), and Lucas (1990) analyze models with segmented markets; see also Alvarez et al. (2002) on endogenous segmentation.

Related Topics and Additional References   Farhi and Werning (2016a) analyze *fiscal multipliers*—the effects of increased government consumption on private consumption and output over time—in the New Keynesian model.

Woodford (1990) analyzes how public debt increases private sector liquidity and helps relax borrowing constraints; see also Holmström and Tirole (1998) and Aiyagari and Mc-Grattan (1998). On bubbly debt, see Domeij and Ellingsen (2018) and section 9.5.

Wallace (1981) and Chamley and Polemarchakis (1984) derive neutrality results in economies with money as a store of value.

Del Negro and Sims (2015) and Hall and Reis (2015) study implications for monetary policy and *central bank insolvency* when the fiscal and monetary authorities satisfy separate budget constraints.

Poole (1970) assesses how interest and money supply targets stabilize output and prices.

Woodford (2003a) analyzes how lack of common knowledge gives rise to monetary nonneutrality; see also Mankiw and Reis (2002). For an overview over models with *incomplete information*, see Angeletos and Lian (2016).

Woodford (2003b, chapter 4), Galí (2015, chapter 3), and Walsh (2017, chapter 8) cover the stability properties of the New Keynesian model and its transmission mechanism. Walsh (2017, chapter 5) covers models of monetary policy under imperfect information and with segmented markets.

12 Optimal Policy

When policy affects the equilibrium allocation, preferences over allocations induce preferences over policies. The *Ramsey program* consists of choosing the *optimal* or *Ramsey policy*, which implements the *Ramsey allocation*. A Ramsey policy must be feasible—it must implement an equilibrium—and it must be *admissible*—it may only use policy instruments at the government's disposal. Both requirements are costly; a social planner that directly chooses among feasible allocations does at least as well as a *Ramsey government* that chooses among feasible allocations that can be implemented as an equilibrium given the set of admissible instruments.

We analyze how a government optimally chooses deficits and taxes over time when it is attentive to the welfare costs of tax distortions and the wealth distribution. Thereafter, we study how social insurance undermines private incentives and how the resulting tradeoff affects the optimal taxation of savings. Finally, we analyze the characteristics of optimal monetary policy, both under flexible and rigid prices. Many of the findings are instances of fundamental results from public finance, which we review in appendix B.6.

12.1 Tax Smoothing

The public finance problem of which goods to optimally tax, and at what rate, in order to minimize distortions or negative distributive implications (see appendix B.6), corresponds to the macroeconomic problem of *when* to tax. Since a decoupling of taxation from government spending relies on government debt (see section 11.2), the Ramsey policy determines the optimal sequence of government indebtedness.

12.1.1 Complete Markets

Consider a representative household economy without capital. The household is endowed with one unit of time per period which can be transformed into $w_t(\epsilon^t)$ units of the good. Household preferences over consumption, c, and leisure, x, are represented by the utility function $\sum_{t=0}^{\infty} \beta^t \mathbb{E}_0[u(c_t(\epsilon^t), x_t(\epsilon^t))]$, where u is strictly concave and increasing and β denotes the discount factor.

To finance a given stream of government consumption, $\{g_t(\epsilon^t)\}_{t\geq 0}$, the government taxes labor income at rates $\{\tau_t(\epsilon^t)\}_{t\geq 0}$ and issues Arrow securities of arbitrary maturity; markets are complete. Without loss of generality, taxes on consumption are normalized to zero (see the discussion in subsection 11.3.2).

Variable $_tb_s(\epsilon^{t-1}, \epsilon^s)$, $s \geq t$, denotes claims vis-à-vis the government held at date t, given that history ϵ^{t-1} occurred; one claim entitles to one unit of the consumption good at date s after history ϵ^s. The marginal distribution of ϵ^t is denoted by $H_t(\epsilon^t)$ and its density by $h_t(\epsilon^t)$; the conditional distribution of ϵ^s given ϵ^t, $s \geq t$, is denoted $H_s(\epsilon^s|\epsilon^t)$.

The benevolent government maximizes household welfare subject to the resource constraint,

$$c_t(\epsilon^t) + g_t(\epsilon^t) = w_t(\epsilon^t)(1 - x_t(\epsilon^t)),$$

and the equilibrium conditions that characterize household choices. The latter are given by the household's (complete markets) intertemporal budget constraint,

$$\sum_{t=0}^{\infty} \int q_t(\epsilon^t)[c_t(\epsilon^t) - (1 - \tau_t(\epsilon^t))w_t(\epsilon^t)(1 - x_t(\epsilon^t)) - {_0b_t}(\epsilon^{-1}, \epsilon^t)]d\epsilon^t = 0,$$

and the first-order conditions,

$$u_c(c_0, x_0)q_t(\epsilon^t) = \beta^t h_t(\epsilon^t)u_c(c_t(\epsilon^t), x_t(\epsilon^t)),$$
$$u_c(c_t(\epsilon^t), x_t(\epsilon^t))w_t(\epsilon^t)(1 - \tau_t(\epsilon^t)) = u_x(c_t(\epsilon^t), x_t(\epsilon^t)).$$

Variable $q_t(\epsilon^t)$ denotes the price at date $t = 0$ of the good at date t, history ϵ^t, and $\{_0b_t(\epsilon^{-1}, \epsilon^t)\}_{t=0}^{\infty}$ are the private sector claims vis-à-vis the government that are outstanding at the initial date. The first optimality condition is the Euler equation and the second characterizes the labor–leisure tradeoff; note that taxes distort this tradeoff. The resource and budget constraint imply the government's intertemporal budget constraint.

To represent the government's constraint set more compactly, we adopt the primal approach (see appendix B.6). Substituting the first-order conditions into the budget constraint yields the *implementability constraint*,

$$\sum_{t=0}^{\infty} \int \beta^t[u_c(c_t(\epsilon^t), x_t(\epsilon^t))(c_t(\epsilon^t) - {_0b_t}(\epsilon^{-1}, \epsilon^t)) - u_x(c_t(\epsilon^t), x_t(\epsilon^t))(1 - x_t(\epsilon^t))]dH_t(\epsilon^t) = 0,$$

which comprises all equilibrium conditions in the household sector and expresses them solely in terms of the allocation, without direct reference to prices and after-tax wages. The government's problem is to maximize welfare subject to the resource constraint, the implementability constraint, and the first-order conditions. Conditional on an allocation that satisfies the resource and implementability constraint, the first-order conditions pin down prices and tax rates. The Ramsey allocation therefore solves the problem of maximizing welfare subject to the resource and implementability constraints.

Let v and $-\beta^t \mu_t(\epsilon^t) h_t(\epsilon^t)$ denote the multipliers associated with the implementability and resource constraints, respectively. Suppressing histories to improve legibility, the first-order conditions for consumption and leisure are given by

$$(1 + v)u_c(c_t, x_t) + v(u_{cc}(c_t, x_t)(c_t - {}_0b_t) - u_{xc}(c_t, x_t)(1 - x_t)) = \mu_t,$$

$$(1 + v)u_x(c_t, x_t) + v(u_{cx}(c_t, x_t)(c_t - {}_0b_t) - u_{xx}(c_t, x_t)(1 - x_t)) = \mu_t w_t,$$

respectively. The conditions state that the government accounts for three types of effects when increasing c_t or x_t. First, the direct effects on the objective function. Second, the resource costs, represented by the terms multiplying μ_t. And third, the marginal effects on the implementability constraint, represented by the terms multiplying v. The latter effects reflect both higher outlays for consumption or leisure and changes in the marginal rates of substitution—corresponding to changed inter- and intratemporal prices.

Together with the implementability and resource constraints, the first-order conditions of the government fully characterize the Ramsey allocation. Moreover, from the household's first-order conditions, the allocation implies the optimal tax rates,

$$\tau_t = 1 - \frac{u_x(c_t, x_t)}{u_c(c_t, x_t)w_t},$$

as well as prices. Finally, from the government's intertemporal budget constraint, the history-contingent sequence of taxes implies a unique sequence of optimal government indebtedness because the value of outstanding debt equals the market value of future primary surpluses (see subsection 11.4.1). Note that the level of indebtedness at date t,

$$\sum_{s=t}^{\infty} \int \frac{q_s\, {}_tb_s}{q_t} d\epsilon^s | \epsilon^t,$$

does not uniquely determine the *maturity structure* $\{{}_tb_s(\epsilon^{t-1}, \epsilon^s)\}_{s \geq t}$; that is, the composition of public debt by maturity.

We make four key observations. First, the multiplier associated with the implementability constraint, v, represents the *shadow value of public funds*—the government's valuation of public relative to private sector wealth. To see this, recall that the implementability constraint incorporates all competitive equilibrium conditions beyond the resource constraint. The multiplier associated with the constraint represents the shadow cost of the competitive equilibrium requirement and specifically, of the government's need to levy distorting taxes. A marginal lump-sum transfer from the private to the public sector (or a reduction of the government's initial indebtedness) would relax the implementability constraint and increase the value of the program by v.

Second, with complete markets, the shadow value is constant over time and across histories. This is just a restatement of the fact that the government faces a single implementability constraint with a single multiplier. Intuitively, with complete markets, households smooth the shadow value of income over time and across histories and the same holds true for the government, implying that the ratio of the shadow values, v, is constant as well. If the government did not face complete markets but, to take an extreme example, had to balance the budget at each date and history, then the single implementability constraint would be replaced by a history-contingent sequence of constraints with an associated sequence of multipliers. The government's inability to decouple tax collections and government spending would imply that the shadow cost of public funds varies over time and across histories. We return to this point in subsection 12.1.2.

Third, as established above, under the Ramsey policy government indebtedness generally differs from zero, and in stochastic environments it is stochastic as well. That is, the optimal return on the government's portfolio generally is not risk-free. This is an implication of the constancy of the shadow cost, v. In parallel to households, the government uses financial claims to shift purchasing power across periods and histories. We return to this point below.

Finally, tax rates at date t only depend on $(_0b_t, w_t, g_t)$. To see this, note that the two first-order conditions combine to an equation in $(v, _0b_t, w_t, c_t, x_t)$, while the variables (g_t, w_t, c_t, x_t) enter the resource constraint. Since the structure of either equation is not history dependent, the equilibrium allocation at a date and history is an invariant function of the exogenous state, $(_0b_t, w_t, g_t)$, as well as of the constant multiplier, v. As a consequence, the tax rates in two histories with the same state are identical. In environments with additional state variables (e.g., capital), this complete markets result generalizes.

To characterize the Ramsey tax policy in more detail, we manipulate the optimality conditions to derive two auxiliary conditions,

$$(1 + v)[u_c(c_t, x_t)(c_t - _0b_t) - u_x(c_t, x_t)(1 - x_t)] + vQ_t + (g_t + _0b_t)\mu_t = 0,$$

$$vQ + \sum_{t=0}^{\infty} \int \beta^t(g_t + _0b_t)\mu_t dH_t = 0,$$

where $Q_t < 0, Q < 0$, and $\mu_t > 0$.[27] From the resource constraint, the first condition implies that, even with no government spending in a history ($g_t = _0b_t = 0$), the tax rate is strictly positive when public funds are scarce ($v > 0$). According to the second condition, the shadow value of public funds equals zero if the market value of government consumption and initial government debt equals zero.

Suppose first that $\sum_{t=0}^{\infty} \int \beta^t u_c(c_t, x_t)(g_t + _0b_t)dH_t = 0$, for example, because $g_t + _0b_t = 0$ in all histories. As we have just seen, $v = 0$ in this case. The first-order conditions then imply that the allocation is not distorted, $u_c(c_t, x_t)w_t = u_x(c_t, x_t)$, and tax rates therefore

---

[27] The first equation results from multiplying the government's first-order conditions by $c_t - _0b_t$ and $x_t - 1$, respectively, summing them, and using the resource constraint. The second equation follows from integrating the first condition, weighting by β^t, summing over time, and using the intertemporal budget constraint.

equal zero. Intuitively, when the government's initial asset holdings (negative $_0b_t$) suffice to finance government consumption, there is no need to levy distorting taxes.

Suppose next that $v > 0$ such that the government needs to raise taxes, and that $(w_t, g_t, _0b_t)$ is constant across all histories. As shown above, (c_t, x_t) and thus tax rates then are constant as well. Accordingly, the government budget is balanced at all times. From now on, we let $_0b_t = 0$ in all histories.

Third, consider a deterministic environment with constant productivity, w, and $g_t = 0$ at all dates except at date $t = T$, when $g_T > 0$. Our findings imply that tax rates at all dates $t \neq T$ are constant and strictly positive. Intuitively, since tax distortions are convex in the tax rate, optimal tax rates vary less than government consumption—the optimal *tax smoothing* policy spreads tax collections over time to reduce average tax distortions. Accordingly, the government accumulates assets before date $t = T$ and services debt thereafter.

Next, consider the same scenario except that at date $t = T$, government consumption is stochastic and can take two values: $g_T > 0$ or $g_T = 0$. Our findings imply that tax rates are constant, except at date $t = T$ if $g_T > 0$, due to tax smoothing. Since the tax revenue before and after date $t = T$ is constant, the government's indebtedness at date $t = T + 1$ must be independent of the realization of g_T. Moreover, since the government budget at date $t = T$ is not balanced, this requires that the government's indebtedness at date $t = T$ is history-contingent: When $g_T > 0$, government debt is lower than when $g_T = 0$. That is, between $t = T - 1$ and $t = T$, the rate of return on government debt is contingent on the realization of g_T—the private sector (partially) insures the government against the high government consumption shock, letting the government smooth taxes both across time and histories.

Finally, if (w_t, g_t) follows a deterministic cycle, then (c_t, x_t) and tax rates follow a deterministic cycle as well and the government's budget is balanced over the cycle. Similarly, if (w_t, g_t) follows a stationary Markov process, then (c_t, x_t) and tax rates inherit the stochastic properties of the state.

We have seen that with complete markets and stochastic (w_t, g_t), the tax smoothing Ramsey policy relies on contingent government indebtedness. One mechanism to generate this contingency is to make the coupon payment contingent on the realization of the state. A more subtle mechanism, which works even when coupons are risk-free, relies on an appropriate choice of *maturity structure* and the fact that shocks that change the interest rate affect the market value of outstanding debt differently, depending on the debt's maturity. Suppose, for example, that a shock to productivity or government consumption alters equilibrium consumption and leads to a persistent increase in interest rates. This has no effect on the value of maturing liabilities but it devalues outstanding longer-term debt and this effect is stronger when the maturity is longer.

For a given level of indebtedness at date t, the indebtedness in the subsequent period thus depends on the choice of maturity structure at date t. Generically, the contingent government indebtedness under the complete markets Ramsey policy is spanned by the contingent term structure of interest rates associated with the Ramsey allocation. That is, the contingent indebtedness under the complete markets Ramsey policy can be generated even if the coupons on government debt are restricted to be risk-free, provided that a sufficiently rich maturity structure of government debt is admissible.

12.1.2   Incomplete Markets

12.1.2.1   Short-Term, Risk-Free Debt   Assume now that the government only issues one-period debt, with a risk-free coupon, implying that government indebtedness is non-contingent. The complete markets Ramsey allocation characterized in subsection 12.1.1 generally cannot be implemented in this case and the properties of the Ramsey policy change.

Let $b_t(\epsilon^{t-1})$ denote claims vis-à-vis the government, which are due at date t in any history subsequent to history ϵ^{t-1} (the claims are measurable with respect to ϵ^{t-1} rather than ϵ^t as before). For convenience, we assume that productivity equals unity at all times. Using the resource constraint, we adopt the shorthand notation $u_t(\epsilon^t) \equiv u(c_t(\epsilon^t), 1 - c_t(\epsilon^t) - g_t(\epsilon^t))$; $u_{c,t}(\epsilon^t) \equiv u_c(c_t(\epsilon^t), 1 - c_t(\epsilon^t) - g_t(\epsilon^t))$; and similarly for $u_{x,t}(\epsilon^t)$.

Since the government only issues debt with a risk-free return, the household faces incomplete markets. In competitive equilibrium, the household satisfies its intratemporal first-order condition and stochastic Euler equation; the household or equivalently, the government, satisfies its dynamic budget constraint; government debt or assets are bounded; and the resource constraint is met. From the intratemporal first-order condition and the resource constraint, we can express the government's primary surplus, $s_t(\epsilon^t) \equiv \tau_t(\epsilon^t)(1 - x_t(\epsilon^t)) - g_t(\epsilon^t)$, as

$$s_t(\epsilon^t) = \left(1 - \frac{u_{x,t}(\epsilon^t)}{u_{c,t}(\epsilon^t)}\right)(c_t(\epsilon^t) + g_t(\epsilon^t)) - g_t(\epsilon^t).$$

Accordingly, the government's dynamic budget constraint incorporating the household optimality conditions and the resource constraint reads

$$b_t(\epsilon^{t-1}) \le s_t(\epsilon^t) + \beta \mathbb{E}_t \left[\frac{u_{c,t+1}(\epsilon^{t+1})}{u_{c,t}(\epsilon^t)} b_{t+1}(\epsilon^t)\right],$$

where we assume that the government may pay lump-sum transfers, thus the inequality constraint.

Iterating this equation (with equality) forward, applying the law of iterated expectations, and assuming $\lim_{T \to \infty} \beta^T u_{c,T}(\epsilon^T) = 0$ almost surely, yields the implementability constraint

$$u_{c,0}b_0 = \sum_{t=0}^{\infty} \int \beta^t u_{c,t} s_t dH_t(\epsilon^t),$$

where we suppress histories to improve legibility. There are two differences between this implementability constraint and the one in subsection 12.1.1. First, the constraint here incorporates the resource constraint. Second, it is derived from the government's rather than the private sector's intertemporal budget constraint. Both differences affect the exposition but not the underlying economic structure.

However, the implementability constraint does not yet reflect the restriction that indebtedness be noncontingent (see the discussion of equation (4.1) on page 48). To incorporate this restriction, we need to impose the intertemporal budget constraint along each history. Equivalently, we require that the indebtedness at date t, and thus the present value of primary surpluses from that node onward be the same for all ϵ^t conditional on ϵ^{t-1}. This *measurability constraint* can be stated as

$$u_{c,t}b_t = \sum_{j=t}^{\infty} \int \beta^{j-t} u_{c,j} s_j dH_j(\epsilon^j | \epsilon^t) \; \forall \epsilon^t | \epsilon^{t-1}, \; t \geq 1,$$

where b_t on the left-hand side of the equation is measurable with respect to ϵ^{t-1}. Note that the measurability constraint at date $t \geq 1$ has the same form as the implementability constraint that holds at date $t = 0$. We also impose boundedness conditions, requiring that b_t, and thus the right-hand side of the measurability constraint normalized by $u_{c,t}$, lies between some bounds $\underline{M}$ and $\bar{M}$.

Let $\beta^t h_t(\epsilon^t) \gamma_t(\epsilon^t)$ denote the multiplier associated with the implementability constraint (for $t = 0$) and the measurability constraints (for $t \geq 1$) with $\gamma_0 \leq 0$; and let $\beta^t h_t(\epsilon^t) \xi_{1,t}(\epsilon^t)$ and $\beta^t h_t(\epsilon^t) \xi_{2,t}(\epsilon^t)$ denote the multipliers associated with the upper and lower bounds, respectively. The Lagrangian of the government's program reads

$$\mathcal{L} = \sum_{t=0}^{\infty} \int \beta^t \left\{ u_t + u_{c,t}(\gamma_t b_t + \xi_{1,t}\bar{M} - \xi_{2,t}\underline{M}) \right.$$

$$\left. - (\gamma_t + \xi_{1,t} - \xi_{2,t}) \left(\sum_{j=t}^{\infty} \int \beta^{j-t} u_{c,j} s_j dH_j(\epsilon^j | \epsilon^t) \right) \right\} dH_t(\epsilon^t).$$

This can be rewritten as

$$\mathcal{L} = \sum_{t=0}^{\infty} \int \beta^t \left\{ u_t + u_{c,t}(\gamma_t b_t + \xi_{1,t}\bar{M} - \xi_{2,t}\underline{M}) - u_{c,t} s_t \sum_{j=0}^{t} (\gamma_j + \xi_{1,j} - \xi_{2,j}) \right\} dH_t(\epsilon^t),$$

where the multipliers $\gamma_j, \xi_{1,j}$, and $\xi_{2,j}$ in the sum $\sum_{j=0}^{t} (\gamma_j + \xi_{1,j} - \xi_{2,j})$ denote multipliers along the branch of the event tree whose nodes precede the node ϵ^t. We thus have

$$\mathcal{L} = \sum_{t=0}^{\infty} \int \beta^t \left\{ u_t + u_{c,t}(\gamma_t b_t + \xi_{1,t}\bar{M} - \xi_{2,t}\underline{M}) - u_{c,t} s_t \nu_t \right\} dH_t(\epsilon^t)$$

$$\text{s.t.} \quad \nu_t = \nu_{t-1} + \gamma_t + \xi_{1,t} - \xi_{2,t}, \; \nu_{-1} = 0.$$

Differentiating with respect to $c_t(\epsilon^t)$ and $b_{t+1}(\epsilon^t)$ yields the first-order conditions

$$u_{c,t} - u_{x,t} - v_t((u_{cc,t} - u_{cx,t})s_t + u_{c,t}s_{c,t}) + (u_{cc,t} - u_{cx,t})(\gamma_t b_t + \xi_{1,t}\bar{M} - \xi_{2,t}\underline{M}) = 0,$$

$$\int \gamma_{t+1}u_{c,t+1}dH_{t+1}(\epsilon^{t+1}|\epsilon^t) = 0,$$

respectively. The first optimality condition relates the allocation to the level of debt as well as to time-varying multipliers $(\gamma_t, \xi_{1,t}, \xi_{2,t})$ and their cumulative sum (v_t). The second condition states that the shadow cost of the measurability constraint in utility terms, $\gamma_{t+1}u_{c,t+1}$, should equal zero on average.

To build intuition for these conditions, consider first the hypothetical complete markets case, where debt service at date t is measurable with respect to ϵ^t rather than ϵ^{t-1}, and $\xi_{1,t} = \xi_{2,t} = 0$. The second optimality condition then changes to $\gamma_{t+1} = 0$ and v_t is constant across histories; the optimality conditions thus reduce to the equivalent of the conditions in subsection 12.1.1. Intuitively, with complete markets, there is no cost associated with having to satisfy the intertemporal budget constraint after the initial period, conditional on satisfying it in the initial period. Stated differently, the optimal choice of contingent indebtedness equalizes the shadow cost of the government budget constraint across histories.

With incomplete markets, in contrast, the government cannot equalize the shadow cost across histories. With risk-free indebtedness it can only equalize this cost on average, over time. After a negative shock to the budget, the intertemporal budget constraint tightens ($\gamma_t < 0$ and v_t decreases) and going forward, the Ramsey allocation is more distorted than it would have been after a positive shock, which leads to an increase of v_t. The tightening or relaxation of the budget constraint is permanently reflected in the multiplier v, and thus in the Ramsey allocation and tax policy. In contrast to the complete markets case, tax rates therefore do not only inherit the stochastic properties of the government consumption shock but also reflect its history.

It is instructive to consider the special case of quasilinear utility, $u(c, x) = c + G(x)$, where G is increasing and concave. From the household's first-order conditions, the stochastic discount factor then equals β, and $\tau_t = 1 - G'(x)$. Tax revenue thus is a function of x_t, say

$$\rho(x_t) = (1 - G'(x_t))(1 - x_t).$$

Under standard assumptions, it is a strictly concave function on the domain $[\underline{x}, \bar{x}]$, where $\underline{x}$ denotes the undistorted level of leisure ($\rho(\underline{x}) = 0$) and $\bar{x} < 1$ denotes the level where $\rho(\bar{x})$ attains the maximum of the Laffer curve. Inverting ρ yields leisure as a strictly convex function of tax revenue, say $\chi(\rho_t)$. Function χ is defined on the domain $[0, \rho(\bar{x})]$.

Since utility at date t equals $1 - \chi(\rho_t) - g_t + G(\chi(\rho_t))$ we may formulate the Ramsey program with tax revenue and debt as the choice variables. This program reads

$$\max_{\{\rho_t(\epsilon^t), b_{t+1}(\epsilon^t)\}_{t \geq 0}} \quad -\sum_{t=0}^{\infty} \int \beta^t \mathcal{D}(\rho_t) dH_t(\epsilon^t)$$

$$\text{s.t.} \quad b_t \leq \rho_t - g_t + \beta b_{t+1},$$

$$\underline{M} \leq b_{t+1} \leq \bar{M},$$

where we define the deadweight loss $\mathcal{D}(\rho_t) \equiv \chi(\rho_t) - G(\chi(\rho_t))$. Note that $\mathcal{D}$ is strictly convex over the domain $[0, \rho(\bar{x})]$ and reaches a minimum at $\rho_t = 0$.

With quasilinear utility the optimality conditions simplify to

$$1 - G'(x_t) - v_t[1 - G'(x_t) + (1 - x_t)G''(x_t)] \;=\; 0,$$

$$v_t = v_{t-1} + \gamma_t + \xi_{1,t} - \xi_{2,t}, \; v_{-1} \;=\; 0,$$

$$\mathbb{E}_t[\gamma_{t+1}] \;=\; 0,$$

where the first condition can be expressed as $-\mathcal{D}'(\rho_t) = v_t$. Whenever the debt limits do not bind, v_t and thus the marginal deadweight loss follows a martingale. That is, the Ramsey policy keeps the expected marginal tax distortion constant over time. Compare this to the complete markets environment, where the Ramsey policy stabilizes the actual marginal tax distortion across all histories.

The Ramsey program with quasilinear utility is isomorphic to a consumption–saving problem with the utility function $-\mathcal{D}(\rho_t)$; an interest rate equal to the inverse of the time discount factor; negative income shocks (government consumption); an asset with a risk-free return; and the natural borrowing limit.[28] The difference between this saving problem and the problem analyzed in subsection 4.3.2 is that the utility function $-\mathcal{D}(\rho_t)$ has a bliss point (at $\rho_t = 0$, corresponding to no deadweight loss).

Since v_t is nonpositive and $\mathbb{E}_t[v_{t+1}] = v_t + \mathbb{E}_t[\xi_{1,t+1}] \geq v_t$, v_t is a nonpositive submartingale. Due to the bliss point of $-\mathcal{D}$, convergence of the submartingale does not require an infinite asset level, unlike in the problem analyzed in subsection 4.3.2. If the Markov process for government consumption has a nontrivial invariant distribution, then government utility converges to the bliss point; the Ramsey tax rate and v_t converge to zero; and the government accumulates a sufficiently large stock of assets to finance an infinite sequence of maximal government consumption. Whenever the realization of government consumption is lower than its maximal value, the government pays lump-sum transfers to the households.[29]

---

[28] The lower bound $\underline{M}$ does not bind, $\xi_{2,t} = 0$, because the government can pay lump-sum transfers.

[29] If the process for government consumption has an absorbing state, then v_t and taxes converge to a strictly negative and positive value, respectively. Ad hoc restrictions on asset accumulation would imply that $\xi_{2,t}$ differs from zero, undermining the convergence result.

12.1.2.2 Broader Portfolio Returning to the case with general preferences, assume next that the government holds a broader portfolio of liabilities and assets, including physical capital. Markets are incomplete.

We assume that a Markov process governs government consumption and productivity, and we formulate the Ramsey program recursively. Output $f(k_\circ, 1 - x_\circ(\epsilon_\circ), \epsilon_\circ)$ depends on the predetermined capital stock, $k_\circ$; labor input, $1 - x_\circ(\epsilon_\circ)$; and a productivity shock, reflected by $\epsilon_\circ$. To simplify the notation we let $u_c(\epsilon_\circ) \equiv u_c(c_\circ(\epsilon_\circ), x_\circ(\epsilon_\circ))$, $f_K(\epsilon_\circ) \equiv f_K(k_\circ, 1 - x_\circ(\epsilon_\circ), \epsilon_\circ)$, and so forth.

The state at the beginning of a period, before the realization of the shock, includes the economy's capital stock, $k_\circ$; the government's net liabilities, $b_\circ$; the shock in the previous period, ϵ_-; and marginal utility in the previous period, $u_c(\epsilon_-)$. The choice variables in the government's program include the gross real risk-free interest rate on government debt, $R_\circ$; government holdings of capital, $k_\circ^g$; exposures to arbitrary securities (in zero net supply), $\{e_\circ^i\}_i$, with exogenous gross returns $\{R^i(\epsilon_\circ)\}_i$; as well as variables which vary with the shock realization, namely consumption and leisure, $c_\circ(\epsilon_\circ)$ and $x_\circ(\epsilon_\circ)$; the capital stock at the beginning of the subsequent period, $k_+(\epsilon_\circ)$; government net liabilities at the beginning of the subsequent period, $b_+(\epsilon_\circ)$; and the labor income tax rate, $\tau_\circ(\epsilon_\circ)$. In the initial period, the risk-free interest rate is given.

The constraints of the government's program are given by

$$u_c(\epsilon_-) = \beta \mathbb{E}[u_c(\epsilon_\circ)R_\circ|\epsilon_-],$$

$$u_c(\epsilon_-) = \beta \mathbb{E}[u_c(\epsilon_\circ)(1 + f_K(\epsilon_\circ) - \delta)|\epsilon_-],$$

$$u_c(\epsilon_-) = \beta \mathbb{E}[u_c(\epsilon_\circ)R^i(\epsilon_\circ)|\epsilon_-],$$

$$\tau_\circ(\epsilon_\circ) = 1 - \frac{u_x(\epsilon_\circ)}{u_c(\epsilon_\circ)f_L(\epsilon_\circ)},$$

$$R_\circ b_\circ - \omega_\circ(\epsilon_\circ) + g_\circ(\epsilon_\circ) \le \tau_\circ(\epsilon_\circ)(1 - x_\circ(\epsilon_\circ))f_L(\epsilon_\circ) + b_+(\epsilon_\circ),$$

$$c_\circ(\epsilon_\circ) + g_\circ(\epsilon_\circ) + k_+(\epsilon_\circ) = (1 - \delta)k_\circ + f(\epsilon_\circ),$$

$$\underline{M}(\cdot) \le u_c(\epsilon_\circ)b_+(\epsilon_\circ) \le \bar{M}(\cdot),$$

where

$$\omega_\circ(\epsilon_\circ) \equiv \sum_i e_\circ^i(R^i(\epsilon_\circ) - R_\circ) + k_\circ^g(1 + f_K(\epsilon_\circ) - \delta - R_\circ)$$

denotes the return on the government's portfolio ($\{e_\circ^i\}_i, k_\circ^g$). The first three constraints represent the household's Euler equations for risk-free government debt, capital, and the other assets. The fourth constraint relates the labor income tax rate to the household's marginal rate of substitution. The remaining constraints represent the (government) budget constraint, the resource constraint, and the debt limits.

Using the household's first-order conditions to substitute out $\tau_o(\epsilon_o)$ and R_o and letting $\tilde{b}_o \equiv b_o u_c(\epsilon_-)$, we can express the budget constraint as

$$\left(\frac{\tilde{b}_o}{\beta\mathbb{E}[u_c(\epsilon_o)|\epsilon_-]} - \tilde{\omega}_o(\epsilon_o) + g_o(\epsilon_o)\right)u_c(\epsilon_o) \leq (u_c(\epsilon_o)f_L(\epsilon_o) - u_x(\epsilon_o))(1 - x_o(\epsilon_o)) + \tilde{b}_+(\epsilon_o),$$

where $\tilde{\omega}_o(\epsilon_o)$ differs from $\omega_o(\epsilon_o)$ in that R_o is replaced by $u_c(\epsilon_-)/(\beta\mathbb{E}[u_c(\epsilon_o)|\epsilon_-])$. The constraint set of the government is characterized by this modified budget constraint as well as the Euler equations, the resource constraint, and the debt limits. The Bellman equation reads

$$V(k_o, \tilde{b}_o, u_c(\epsilon_-), \epsilon_-) = \max \mathbb{E}[u(\epsilon_o) + \beta V(k_+(\epsilon_o), \tilde{b}_+(\epsilon_o), u_c(\epsilon_o), \epsilon_o)|\epsilon_-]$$
$$\text{s.t.} \quad \text{constraint set,}$$

and the choice variables are $k_o^g, \{e_o^i\}_i, \{c_o(\epsilon_o), x_o(\epsilon_o), k_+(\epsilon_o), \tilde{b}_+(\epsilon_o)\}_{\epsilon_o}$. Note that in accordance with our definition of the state, the value function represents the unconditional value, prior to the realization of ϵ_o.

Let $v_o(\epsilon_o) \cdot \text{prob}(\epsilon_o|\epsilon_-)$ denote the multiplier associated with the budget constraint (the shadow value of public funds) when ϵ_o is realized. The government's first-order conditions with respect to $\tilde{b}_+(\epsilon_o)$ (assuming debt limits do not bind), e_o^i, and k_o^g, respectively, are given by

$$v_o(\epsilon_o) + \beta V_b(k_+(\epsilon_o), \tilde{b}_+(\epsilon_o), u_c(\epsilon_o), \epsilon_o) = 0,$$
$$\mathbb{E}[v_o(\epsilon_o)u_c(\epsilon_o)(R^i(\epsilon_o) - R_o)|\epsilon_-] = 0,$$
$$\mathbb{E}[v_o(\epsilon_o)u_c(\epsilon_o)(1 + f_K(\epsilon_o) - \delta - R_o)|\epsilon_-] = 0,$$

and the envelope condition implies

$$V_b(k_o, \tilde{b}_o, u_c(\epsilon_-), \epsilon_-) = -\sum_{\epsilon_o} v_o(\epsilon_o)\text{prob}(\epsilon_o|\epsilon_-)\frac{u_c(\epsilon_o)}{\beta\mathbb{E}[u_c(\epsilon_o)|\epsilon_-]} = -\frac{R_o}{u_c(\epsilon_-)}\mathbb{E}[v_o(\epsilon_o)u_c(\epsilon_o)|\epsilon_-].$$

Combined, these equations yield the optimality conditions

$$v_-(\epsilon_-)u_c(\epsilon_-) = \beta\mathbb{E}[v_o(\epsilon_o)u_c(\epsilon_o)R_o|\epsilon_-],$$
$$v_-(\epsilon_-)u_c(\epsilon_-) = \beta\mathbb{E}[v_o(\epsilon_o)u_c(\epsilon_o)R^i(\epsilon_o)|\epsilon_-],$$
$$v_-(\epsilon_-)u_c(\epsilon_-) = \beta\mathbb{E}[v_o(\epsilon_o)u_c(\epsilon_o)(1 + f_K(\epsilon_o) - \delta)|\epsilon_-].$$

These conditions resemble the stochastic Euler equations characterizing a household's portfolio choice (see section 5.1). They differ insofar as marginal utility is replaced by the product of marginal utility and the shadow value of public funds. Intuitively, the Ramsey policy equalizes the return-weighted average valuation of public funds over time, exactly as a household equalizes the return-weighted average marginal utility.

Note that the first condition coincides with the result derived earlier, namely that the change in the government budget multiplier, weighted by marginal utility, equals zero on average. This follows from

$$\mathbb{E}\left[\beta R_\circ v_\circ(\epsilon_\circ)u_c(\epsilon_\circ) - v_-(\epsilon_-)u_c(\epsilon_-)|\epsilon_-\right] = \beta R_\circ \mathbb{E}\left[(v_\circ(\epsilon_\circ) - v_-(\epsilon_-))u_c(\epsilon_\circ)|\epsilon_-\right] = 0.$$

The second and third optimality condition generalize this result. For any asset or liability in the government's portfolio, the Ramsey policy satisfies

$$\beta\mathbb{E}\left[v_\circ(\epsilon_\circ)u_c(\epsilon_\circ)\left(R^i(\epsilon_\circ) - R_\circ\right)|\epsilon_-\right] = 0.$$

That is, a more diversified portfolio results in a smoother multiplier, and thus better insurance for the government. If the portfolio were sufficiently diversified for the government (and the household) to face complete markets, then the multiplier would be constant across histories.

The optimality conditions can be used to derive a *stochastic discount factor* for *government projects*. Letting $\mu_\circ(\epsilon_\circ) \cdot \text{prob}(\epsilon_\circ|\epsilon_-)$ denote the multiplier associated with the resource constraint when $\epsilon_\circ$ is realized, this discount factor is given by

$$\beta\frac{v_\circ(\epsilon_\circ)u_c(\epsilon_\circ) + \mu_\circ(\epsilon_\circ)}{v_-(\epsilon_-)u_c(\epsilon_-) + \mu_-(\epsilon_-)}.$$

12.1.3   Capital Income Taxation

12.1.3.1   Neutrality Result   Consider the model with capital of subsection 12.1.2 and assume that the government may impose state-contingent taxes on the return on capital, in addition to labor income taxes. Capital income tax rates, $\tau_\circ^k(\epsilon_\circ)$, only enter the household's Euler equation for capital and the government's budget constraint:

$$u_c(\epsilon_-) = \beta\mathbb{E}[u_c(\epsilon_\circ)(1 + (1 - \tau_\circ^k(\epsilon_\circ))(f_K(\epsilon_\circ) - \delta))|\epsilon_-],$$
$$R_\circ b_\circ - \omega_\circ(\epsilon_\circ) + g_\circ(\epsilon_\circ) \leq \tau_\circ(\epsilon_\circ)(1 - x_\circ(\epsilon_\circ))f_L(\epsilon_\circ) + \tau_\circ^k(\epsilon_\circ)k_\circ(f_K(\epsilon_\circ) - \delta) + b_+(\epsilon_\circ).$$

In the household's Euler equation, only the average tax wedge (suitably weighted) matters. In the budget constraint, effects from changes in tax rates can be neutralized by appropriately adjusting the government's portfolio when markets are complete. With complete markets, an equilibrium allocation thus can be implemented with different combinations of instruments; for instance, with state-contingent capital income taxes and risk-free-coupon bonds, or with noncontingent capital income taxes and state-contingent coupon bonds.

We have thus derived a neutrality result: Optimal state-contingent capital income tax rates are indeterminate if the government faces complete markets.

12.1.3.2   Zero Capital Income Taxation   Consider a deterministic setting and suppose that the economy is inhabited by an infinitely lived, representative agent whose date-t capital and labor incomes are taxed at rates τ_t^k and τ_t, respectively. The household's intertemporal budget constraint and first-order conditions are given by

$$0 = k_0 R_0 (1 - \tau_0^k) + \sum_{t=0}^{\infty} \tilde{q}_t \left(w_t (1 - x_t)(1 - \tau_t) - c_t \right),$$

$$\tilde{q}_t = \beta^t u_c(c_t, x_t) / u_c(c_0, x_0),$$

$$w_t(1 - \tau_t) = u_x(c_t, x_t) / u_c(c_t, x_t),$$

where we define $\tilde{q}_t \equiv (\tilde{R}_1 \cdots \tilde{R}_t)^{-1}$ and $\tilde{R}_t$ denotes the after-tax gross interest rate. In equilibrium, the latter equals $\tilde{R}_t = 1 + (1 - \tau_t^k)(f_K(k_t, 1 - x_t) - \delta)$. Substituting the first-order conditions into the intertemporal budget constraint, we arrive at the implementability constraint that is a function of $\{c_t, x_t\}_{t \geq 0}$, $k_0 R_0$, and the tax rate on the initial capital stock, τ_0^k, which we assume to be capped by an exogenous upper bound.[30] Write this constraint as

$$\iota_0(c_0, x_0, k_0 R_0, \tau_0^k) + \sum_{t=0}^{\infty} \beta^t \iota(c_t, x_t) = 0$$

for some functions ι_0 and ι. The Lagrangian associated with the Ramsey program reads

$$\mathcal{L} = \sum_{t=0}^{\infty} \beta^t \{ v(c_t, x_t, \nu) - \mu_t (c_t + g_t + k_{t+1} - (1 - \delta) k_t - f(k_t, 1 - x_t)) \} + \nu \iota_0(c_0, x_0, k_0 R_0, \tau_0^k),$$

where we define $v(c_t, x_t, \nu) \equiv u(c_t, x_t) + \nu \iota(c_t, x_t)$; ν and $\beta^t \mu_t$ denote the multipliers associated with the implementability and resource constraints, respectively.

The first-order conditions with respect to $c_t, t \geq 1$, and k_{t+1}, respectively, are given by

$$v_c(c_t, x_t, \nu) = \mu_t, \ t \geq 1,$$

$$\mu_t = \beta \mu_{t+1} (1 - \delta + f_K(k_{t+1}, 1 - x_{t+1})).$$

Combining these conditions yields the key equation of interest, which we report together with the household's Euler equation:

$$v_c(c_t, x_t, \nu) = \beta(1 - \delta + f_K(k_{t+1}, 1 - x_{t+1})) v_c(c_{t+1}, x_{t+1}, \nu), \ t \geq 1,$$

$$u_c(c_t, x_t) = \beta(1 + (1 - \tau_{t+1}^k)(f_K(k_{t+1}, 1 - x_{t+1}) - \delta)) u_c(c_{t+1}, x_{t+1}).$$

The two equations imply that under the Ramsey policy, capital income is not taxed at dates $t \geq 2$ whenever $v_c(c_t, x_t, \nu)$ and $u_c(c_t, x_t)$ grow at the same rate. Two alternative conditions guarantee such equal growth, and thus optimality of *zero capital income taxation*. The first condition relates to preferences. If preferences are separable between consumption and leisure, and homothetic, then $v_c(c_t, x_t, \nu)$ is proportional to $u_c(c_t, x_t)$. In this case, the zero capital taxation implication is an instance of the uniform commodity taxation

---

[30] Without an upper bound, the Ramsey problem would be trivial: The Ramsey policy would only tax the inelastically supplied initial capital stock.

result discussed in appendix B.6.1. Recall from subsection 11.3.2 that capital income taxation is equivalent to time-varying taxation of consumption. When consumption taxes are normalized to zero and the structure of preferences calls for uniform taxation of consumption, capital income must not be taxed. Standard CIES preferences satisfy the separability and homotheticity conditions.

The second, alternative condition relates to the economy's dynamics. If the Ramsey allocation converges to a path along which both $v_c(c_t, x_t, v)$ and $u_c(c_t, x_t)$ are constant over time (i.e., a steady state) or growing at equal rates, then the optimality of zero capital income taxation follows. In fact, it also follows in richer environments, for instance when in steady state the derivative of the implementability constraint(s) with respect to capital equal(s) zero and the multiplier(s) of the constraint(s) are constant.[31]

An upper bound on capital income tax rates, $\tau_{t+1}^k \leq \bar{\tau}^k$, which can be expressed as

$$1 - \left(\frac{u_c(c_t, x_t)}{\beta u_c(c_{t+1}, x_{t+1})} - 1 \right) / (f_K(k_{t+1}, 1 - x_{t+1}) - \delta) \leq \bar{\tau}^k,$$

introduces additional terms in the government's optimality conditions. As long as the constraint binds (forcing taxes to be spread over a longer horizon), the key equation discussed above contains additional terms, and this undermines the zero-tax-rate implication. The constraint may bind forever.

12.1.4　Heterogeneous Households

When households are homogeneous, the assumption that the government levies distorting taxes rests on weak foundations; after all, if everybody is the same such that distributive effects are not a concern, a uniformly levied lump-sum tax clearly is preferable to a distorting tax. With heterogeneous agents, in contrast, an *equity-efficiency tradeoff* might arise and this tradeoff can rationalize distorting taxation of an endogenous tax base.

Consider a variant of the economy analyzed in subsection 12.1.1 with two rather than one group of households, groups a and b with population shares η^a and $\eta^b = 1 - \eta^a$, respectively. Both groups have the same preferences but their labor productivities differ, $w_t^a \neq w_t^b$. For simplicity, we abstract from risk. The resource constraint is given by

$$\eta^a c_t^a + \eta^b c_t^b + g_t = \eta^a w_t^a (1 - x_t^a) + \eta^b w_t^b (1 - x_t^b).$$

In each period, the government has two tax instruments at its disposal: A proportional labor income tax levied at rate τ_t, and a lump-sum tax, θ_t. Importantly, the taxes cannot be differentiated across groups, for example, because the government does not observe which group a household belongs to. The government's objective function is given by the *social welfare function* $\omega \eta^a U^a + \eta^b U^b$, where U^i denotes welfare of a member of group i and ω

---

[31] This holds true, for example, in the steady state of an economy with heterogeneous households whose capital income—but not labor income—is taxed at a uniform rate.

denotes some positive weight. The intertemporal budget constraint of a household in group
i reads

$$\sum_{t=0}^{\infty} q_t[c_t^i - (1 - \tau_t)w_t^i(1 - x_t^i) + \theta_t] = 0.$$

Substituting the household first-order conditions,

$$u_c(c_0^i, x_0^i)q_t = \beta^t u_c(c_t^i, x_t^i),$$
$$u_c(c_t^i, x_t^i)w_t^i(1 - \tau_t) = u_x(c_t^i, x_t^i),$$

into the budget constraints yields the implementability constraints,

$$\sum_{t=0}^{\infty} \beta^t[u_c(c_t^i, x_t^i)(c_t^i + \theta_t) - u_x(c_t^i, x_t^i)(1 - x_t^i)] = 0, \tag{12.1}$$

$$u_c(c_t^a, x_t^a)/u_c(c_0^a, x_0^a) = u_c(c_t^b, x_t^b)/u_c(c_0^b, x_0^b), \tag{12.2}$$

$$u_c(c_t^a, x_t^a)w_t^a/u_x(c_t^a, x_t^a) = u_c(c_t^b, x_t^b)w_t^b/u_x(c_t^b, x_t^b). \tag{12.3}$$

Constraints (12.2) and (12.3) capture the restriction that households in both groups face
the same prices and tax rates.

Let ν^a and ν^b denote the multipliers associated with the implementability constraints (12.1)
for groups a and b. The optimal choice of lump-sum tax at date t satisfies

$$\nu^a u_c(c_t^a, x_t^a) + \nu^b u_c(c_t^b, x_t^b) = 0;$$

that is, the Ramsey policy sets the average multiplier equal to zero. To understand this
result, suppose first that group b did not exist, such that only the implementability constraint (12.1) for group a were present. The optimality condition for θ_t then would collapse
to $\nu^a = 0$, indicating that the competitive equilibrium constraints were not binding for the
Ramsey government. Intuitively, the Ramsey policy could implement the first best in this
case because the government could costlessly transfer resources from the private to the
public sector.

With heterogeneous households, the lump-sum tax still allows the government to extract
resources without distorting household choices. But since the lump-sum tax cannot be differentiated across groups, the government cannot in general extract resources and attain
the preferred wealth distribution without distorting household choices. Against this background, the optimal choice of θ_t "at least" equalizes the average value of the multiplier
with zero. If, by chance, the optimal lump-sum tax happens to implement the preferred
wealth distribution, then ν^a and ν^b individually equal zero as well. Otherwise, the Ramsey
policy also employs labor income taxes, at the cost of generating tax distortions.

From the implementability constraint (12.2), marginal utility grows at identical rates
across groups. This implies that all lump-sum taxes but one are redundant instruments
(their first-order conditions are multiples of each other) and a Ricardian equivalence result

holds: A change in timing of lump-sum taxes accompanied by suitable debt operations does not alter the equilibrium allocation.

To see how the timing of labor income taxes can affect the wealth distribution, let $u(c, x) \equiv \ln(c) + \gamma \ln(x)$ and disregard lump-sum taxes. The implementability constraints then read

$$\sum_{t=0}^{\infty} \beta^t [1 - \gamma(1 - x_t^i)/x_t^i] = 0,$$

$$\frac{c_0^a}{c_0^b} = \frac{c_t^a}{c_t^b} = \frac{w_t^a}{w_t^b} \frac{x_t^a}{x_t^b}$$

or, more compactly,

$$\sum_{t=0}^{\infty} \beta^t \left[1 - \gamma \left(\frac{1}{x_t^a} - 1 \right) \right] = 0,$$

$$\sum_{t=0}^{\infty} \beta^t \left[1 - \gamma \left(\frac{c_0^a}{c_0^b} \frac{w_t^b}{w_t^a} \frac{1}{x_t^a} - 1 \right) \right] = 0.$$

From the first equation, raising x_0^a requires lowering x_t^a at some other date. From the second equation, this translates into a change in relative wealth and consumption, c_0^a/c_0^b, if relative productivity varies over time, $w_0^a/w_0^b \neq w_t^a/w_t^b$. Specifically, an increase in x_0^a (corresponding to a tax hike at date $t = 0$) and corresponding decrease of x_t^a raises c_0^a/c_0^b if $w_0^a/w_0^b \leq w_t^a/w_t^b$. Wealth is redistributed for two reasons. First, collecting taxes in periods where one group is relatively more productive shifts the tax burden to that group. Second, tax-induced changes in consumption, and thus interest rates, affect debtors and creditors asymmetrically.

12.2   Social Insurance and Saving Taxation

When households are exposed to idiosyncratic income risk, the government can provide insurance by redistributing between households with high and low income realizations. But if income also depends on effort choices and if the government is unable to observe these choices, then the provision of insurance can discourage effort—an *insurance-incentives tradeoff* arises. To mitigate the consequences of this tradeoff, it may be optimal to discourage savings.

Consider a two-period economy with a continuum of measure one of ex-ante identical households, indexed by i. Household i receives an endowment w_0 in the first period, which can be consumed or saved at the gross interest rate R_1. In the second period, the household works and consumes. Labor productivity, $w_1^i(\epsilon^1)$, is random and i.i.d. across the population. Household i's preferences are given by

$$U^i \equiv u(c_0^i) + \beta \mathbb{E}_0[u(c_1^i(\epsilon^1)) + v(x_1^i(\epsilon^1))],$$

where u and v are strictly increasing and concave.

The government can observe labor income, $y_1^i(\epsilon^1) \equiv w_1^i(\epsilon^1)(1 - x_1^i(\epsilon^1))$, but not its two components, labor productivity and labor supply. An insurance scheme in the second period therefore can only be conditioned on $(c_0^i, y_1^i(\epsilon^1))$. The government maximizes the social welfare function, $\int_i U^i di$, subject to the resource constraint,

$$\left(w_0 - \int_i c_0^i di \right) R_1 + \int_i w_1^i(\epsilon^1)(1 - x_1^i(\epsilon^1)) di = \int_i c_1^i(\epsilon^1) di,$$

as well as incentive compatibility constraints. The latter reflect the fact that households respond privately optimally to government policy.

Rather than studying a particular insurance scheme, we adopt a general approach. By the revelation principle, we may without loss of generality restrict attention to direct mechanisms that induce truth telling. A mechanism maps household i's self-reported productivity level together with the observed c_0^i into consumption and labor income at date $t = 1$. It induces truth telling if all households always find it optimal to report truthfully.

Let $(c_0^\star, \{c_1^\star(w_1), y_1^\star(w_1)\}_{w_1})$ denote the equilibrium consumption and labor income profile under the optimal mechanism (using the i.i.d. assumption) and consider a marginal change of allocation that has no effect on incentives. This change consists of a reduction of first-period consumption (higher saving) by $\Delta/u'(c_0^\star)$, where Δ is small in absolute value, and a contingent increase of second-period consumption by $\Delta/(\beta u'(c_1^\star(w_1)))$; that is, the change reduces the utility from goods consumption at date $t = 0$ by Δ and increases the utility from goods consumption at date $t = 1$, for any w_1, by Δ/β. Along each history, the total utility from goods consumption thus remains unchanged and households have no incentive to modify their individually optimal reporting strategies.

Consider now the resource implications of the change of allocation: The additional saving at date $t = 0$ generates resources at date $t = 1$ equal to $\Delta/u'(c_0^\star)R_1$, while aggregate consumption rises by $\mathbb{E}_0[\Delta/(\beta u'(c_1^\star(w_1)))]$ (using the i.i.d. assumption). Since the allocation $(c_0^\star, \{c_1^\star(w_1), y_1^\star(w_1)\}_{w_1})$ is optimal, the change of allocation must not free resources; if it did free resources the government could use them to improve the allocation. Optimality of $(c_0^\star, \{c_1^\star(w_1), y_1^\star(w_1)\}_{w_1})$ thus requires

$$\frac{\Delta}{u'(c_0^\star)} R_1 = \mathbb{E}_0 \left[\frac{\Delta}{\beta u'(c_1^\star(w_1))} \right].$$

Canceling Δ, we have established that the optimal allocation satisfies a *reciprocal Euler equation*.

Without incentive problems, the government could perfectly insure consumption in the second period and $c_1^\star(w_1)$ would be deterministic. The reciprocal Euler equation would reduce to the standard Euler equation in this case. When the insurance scheme needs to provide incentives, in contrast, consumption in the second period must depend on observed labor income, and thus be random. Jensen's inequality then implies $\mathbb{E}_0[1/u'(c_1^\star(w_1))] >$

$1/\mathbb{E}_0[u'(c_1^\star(w_1))]$ and the reciprocal Euler equation therefore requires

$$u'(c_0^\star) < \beta R_1 \mathbb{E}_0 \left[u'(c_1^\star(w_1)) \right].$$

This condition differs from the Euler equation of an individual household that chooses savings unless the return on savings is taxed. We conclude that the optimal mechanism must tax the return on savings if it is decentralized in a way that lets households freely choose their savings.

Intuitively, with moral hazard, saving imposes a social cost, in addition to the cost and benefit internalized by a household. Higher assets at date $t = 1$ reduce the covariance between labor supply and consumption in the second period and this undermines incentives. The optimal policy addresses this adverse effect by discouraging saving.

12.3   Monetary Policy

12.3.1   Friedman Rule

The social marginal cost of producing fiat money essentially equals zero. This suggests that an allocation in which fiat money is scarce is inefficient because the scarcity could be reduced or even eliminated at no cost. When money is scarce, its opportunity cost—the interest forgone when holding it—is high. Accordingly, the efficiency of money supply should be reflected in the interest rate.

We formalize this argument in a deterministic version of the money-in-the-utility-function model analyzed in subsection 9.3.2. Date-t period utility depends on consumption, c_t, and real balances, z_{t+1}. Money demand satisfies a variant of condition (9.4),

$$\frac{u_z(c_t, z_{t+1})}{u_c(c_t, z_{t+1})} = \frac{i_{t+1} - i_{t+1}^M}{1 + i_{t+1}},$$

where i_{t+1} denotes the nominal interest rate on bonds, and i_{t+1}^M denotes the interest rate on money which we have previously assumed to be zero. Money demand decreases in $i_{t+1} - i_{t+1}^M$.

Suppose that for any level of consumption, there exists a *satiation level* of real balances, $z(c_t)$, at which the marginal utility of real balances equals zero, $u_z(c_t, z(c_t)) = 0$. In equilibrium, this satiation level is attained when the opportunity cost of holding money equals zero—as the *Friedman rule* stipulates. When money pays no interest, $i_{t+1}^M = 0$, then this opportunity cost equals $i_{t+1}/(1 + i_{t+1})$ and the Friedman rule requires $i_{t+1} = 0$. From the Fisher equation, this requires *deflation* at the same rate as the real rate of interest. When money does pay interest, in contrast, then full satiation can also be attained by paying *interest on money* and *reserves* at the rate $i_{t+1}^M = i_{t+1}$, thereby reducing the opportunity cost to zero.

Parallel results follow in the model with a cash-in-advance constraint, where the opportunity cost of holding money equals the multiplier associated with the constraint (see condition (9.6) in subsection 9.3.3). When the Friedman rule is satisfied (or money pays interest) the constraint does not bind. Moreover, distortions due to the fact that households substitute away from activities requiring the use of money disappear in this case.

Optimality of the Friedman rule also follows in an extension of the general equilibrium turnpike model analyzed in subsection 9.2.2. Suppose that the government periodically transfers new money, $M_{t+1} - M_t$, to money holders (such that money pays interest), and collects lump-sum taxes from even and odd households to balance the budget. Letting τ_t denote taxes, the government budget constraint reads

$$z_{t+1} + \tau_t = z_t / \Pi_t,$$

where $z_{t+1} \equiv M_{t+1}/P_t$ denotes real balances and $\Pi_t \equiv P_t/P_{t-1}$ denotes the gross inflation rate. In a stationary equilibrium with constant real balances, the budget constraint reduces to $\tau = z(\Pi^{-1} - 1)$. The real interest rate paid on money thus equals $\tau/z = \Pi^{-1} - 1$ and the gross real interest rate equals Π^{-1}.

Recall that in the equilibrium of the turnpike model, households with a high endowment buy real balances (the bubble), z. We assume that in the subsequent period, they collect the interest rate from the government and pay their share of taxes, $\tau/2$, before selling the remaining money holdings, $z + \tau - \tau/2$, to households of the other group. The latter pay their share of taxes, $\tau/2$, and hold z to the next period. Consumption of a household with high and low endowment, respectively, therefore equals

$$\begin{aligned}
\bar{c} &= \bar{w} - z - \tau/2 = \bar{w} - z(1 + \Pi^{-1})/2, \\
\underline{c} &= \underline{w} + z + \tau/2 = \underline{w} + z(1 + \Pi^{-1})/2.
\end{aligned}$$

Under the veil of ignorance; that is, before knowing one's even or odd type, households favor a policy that maximizes the average welfare of the two groups. The benevolent government therefore maximizes $u(\bar{c}) + u(\underline{c})$ subject to the Euler equation of households investing in real balances,

$$u'(\bar{c}) = \beta \Pi^{-1} u'(\underline{c}),$$

and the condition that households selling the bubble may not borrow, $1 \geq u'(\bar{c})/u'(\underline{c})$. The solution of this program is given by $\bar{c} = \underline{c}$ and thus, $\Pi = \beta$. The latter equality prescribes deflation at the real rate of interest and thus, the Friedman rule; at the optimal deflation rate, consumption of all households is constant over time. Note that the real interest rate strictly exceeds the growth rate. Nevertheless, the real-balances bubble is viable because net of taxes, it does not grow faster than the economy.

The Friedman rule may be criticized on the grounds that it abstracts from the government's need to raise revenue. When the government levies distorting taxes to finance government consumption, then it seems natural to expect that the Ramsey policy also distorts money holdings, and thus violates the Friedman rule. Whether this is indeed the case depends on the structure of preferences, among other factors. Plausible restrictions on preferences and the shopping-time technology underlying the money-in-the-utility-function model imply that the conditions for uniform commodity taxation and production efficiency (see appendix B.6) are satisfied. In this case, the marginal distortion from inflation per unit of revenue raised exceeds the marginal distortion from other taxes and as a consequence, the Friedman rule is optimal.

12.3.2   Dealing with Price Rigidity

Consider next an environment where price rigidity rather than the nonsatiation of money demand constitutes the motivation to conduct monetary policy. Following the analysis in subsections 10.3.5, 11.5.2, and 11.6.2, we study an economy without capital, in the cashless limit, subject to a Ricardian policy regime.

There are two sources of friction in this environment. First, monopolistic competition that leads producers in the intermediate goods sector to charge markups and to undersupply. The natural level of output in the final good sector, $y_t^n(\epsilon^t)$, thus falls short of the efficient level, $y_t^e(\epsilon^t)$. Second, price rigidity. When a shock buffets the economy, price rigidity causes time-varying levels of underproduction. Moreover, it gives rise to an inefficient composition of intermediate goods because producers that have adjusted their prices at different points in time supply unequal quantities to the final good sector (see equation (10.11) in subsection 10.3.3).

We assume that the distortion caused by monopolistic competition is neutralized by a time-invariant production subsidy that is financed with a nondistorting tax. Absent shocks, the natural and efficient levels of output therefore coincide. To address the distortions caused by price rigidity, the government uses monetary policy. We now study to what extent this is possible.

The New Keynesian Phillips curve and the dynamic IS equation, respectively, are given by

$$\pi_t(\epsilon^t) = \kappa\chi_t(\epsilon^t) + \beta\mathbb{E}_t[\pi_{t+1}(\epsilon^{t+1})] + \upsilon_t(\epsilon^t),$$

$$\chi_t(\epsilon^t) = \mathbb{E}_t\left[\chi_{t+1}(\epsilon^{t+1})\right] - \frac{1}{\sigma}\mathbb{E}_t\left[i_{t+1}(\epsilon^t) - \pi_{t+1}(\epsilon^{t+1}) - r_{t+1}^e(\epsilon^{t+1})\right].$$

This representation differs from equations (10.19) and (10.20) in subsection 10.3.5 because we have redefined the output gap, $\chi_t(\epsilon^t)$, as the relative deviation of output from the efficient (rather than the natural) level. Accordingly, the Phillips curve contains an additional term, the *cost push shock* $\upsilon_t(\epsilon^t) \equiv \kappa(\hat{y}_t^e(\epsilon^t) - \hat{y}_t^n(\epsilon^t))$; moreover, in the dynamic IS equation, the natural rate of interest is replaced by the *efficient rate of interest*, $r_{t+1}^e(\epsilon^{t+1})$, which differs from the natural rate (see subsection 10.3.5) only in that natural levels of output are replaced by efficient levels. The inflation rate, $\pi_t(\epsilon^t)$, and the nominal interest rate, $i_{t+1}(\epsilon^t)$, enter as in equations (10.19) and (10.20). The parameters κ, β, and σ are positive (and $\beta < 1$); and the sequence of efficient interest rates is stationary.

As long as only nominal shocks buffet the economy, the natural and efficient levels of output coincide and the two output gap measures are identical. But when a real shock—for instance, an exogenous change in firms' desired markups—drives a wedge between the natural and efficient levels of output such that $v_t(\epsilon^t) \neq 0$, then the two gap measures differ. The modified definition of the output gap is preferable for the subsequent analysis because it is directly relevant for welfare evaluations.

The government maximizes the utility of the representative household. Output deviations from the first-best level harm the household because they drive a wedge between the marginal rate of substitution (between consumption and leisure) and the marginal rate of transformation. Inflation deviations are costly because they give rise to price differences across firms, and thus an inefficient composition of intermediate inputs. As long as the deviations are small, they only cause second-order welfare losses because the steady state is efficient, due to the production subsidy. Accordingly, the government's *loss function* (the negative of its objective function) can be represented as

$$L_0 = \frac{1}{2} \sum_{t=0}^{\infty} \beta^t \mathbb{E}_0[\omega \chi_t^2(\epsilon^t) + \pi_t^2(\epsilon^t)],$$

where the strictly positive weight ω is a function of primitives: It is increasing in the curvature of the household's utility function and decreasing in the degree of price rigidity and the elasticity of substitution between intermediate inputs. Intuitively, the curvature determines how strongly output gaps translate into wedges between the marginal rates of substitution and transformation, while price rigidity and the elasticity of substitution affect how inflation alters relative price differences and the composition of intermediate goods.

12.3.2.1 No Cost Push Shocks   When there are no cost push shocks, the optimal monetary policy attains $L_0 = 0$; that is, it implements the first best with zero inflation and zero output gaps at all times.[32] To see this, observe that when $v_t(\epsilon^t) = 0$, the efficient levels of inflation and output satisfy the Phillips curve and the dynamic IS equation as long as $i_{t+1}(\epsilon^t) = \mathbb{E}_t[r_{t+1}^e(\epsilon^{t+1})]$. The government can uniquely implement this nominal interest rate and the efficient equilibrium by following the rule

$$i_{t+1}(\epsilon^t) = \mathbb{E}_t[r_{t+1}^e(\epsilon^{t+1})] + \phi_\pi \pi_t(\epsilon^t) + \phi_\chi \chi_t(\epsilon^t),$$

where the coefficients ϕ_π and ϕ_χ satisfy the Taylor principle (see section 11.5).

Intuitively, by perfectly stabilizing output at its efficient level, the optimal policy prevents inflationary or deflationary pressures from building up; and by perfectly stabilizing inflation—*strict inflation targeting*—the optimal policy makes it unnecessary for firms to

---

[32] We assume that at date $t = 0$, all firms charge the same price; that is, the initial price distribution is degenerate.

ever change their prices. As a consequence, time-varying levels of under- or overproduction and inefficient price dispersion are avoided.

This *divine coincidence* holds as long as the government observes changes in the efficient rate of interest and can adjust the intercept of the policy rule, $\mathbb{E}_t[r^e_{t+1}(\epsilon^{t+1})]$, accordingly. Otherwise, the first best allocation may not be implementable and a tradeoff between inflation and output gaps arises, which calls for *flexible inflation targeting*. Cost push shocks, which we turn to next, give rise to a similar tradeoff, even when the government can follow a flexible interest rate rule.

12.3.2.2   Cost Push Shocks   In the presence of cost push shocks, the Ramsey policy implements stationary inflation and output gap sequences that minimize L_0 subject to the Phillips curve, the dynamic IS equation, and the exogenous sequence $\{v_t(\epsilon^t)\}_{t=0}^{\infty}$. Note that the IS equation does not constitute a binding constraint in this program as long as the interest rate rule contains a time-varying intercept. Any inflation and output gap sequence that satisfies the Phillips curve also is consistent with the dynamic IS equation, subject to an appropriate choice of nominal interest rate. Therefore only the Phillips curve constrains the Ramsey policy.

To build intuition for the properties of the optimal allocation, consider first a perfect foresight example with a temporary cost push shock at date $t = 0$, $v_0 > 0$. The Phillips curves are given by

$$\pi_0 = \kappa\chi_0 + \beta\pi_1 + v_0,$$
$$\pi_t = \kappa\chi_t + \beta\pi_{t+1}, \ t \geq 1.$$

One feasible outcome involves positive inflation at date $t = 0$, $\pi_0 = v_0$; zero inflation in all subsequent periods; and zero output gaps at all times. But this outcome is suboptimal. The convexity of the loss function renders it preferable to let inflation *and* the output gap deviate from their target values ($0 < \pi_0 < v_0$ and $\chi_0 < 0$). An even better outcome is achieved when the losses are smoothed over time, by letting $\pi_1 < 0$ and thus, $\chi_1, \pi_2 < 0$, $\chi_2, \pi_3 < 0$, etc. That is, efficient smoothing of the welfare losses calls for modest inflation at the date when the shock occurs; deflation at a diminishing rate in the subsequent periods; and shrinking negative output gaps.

The same intuition applies in a stochastic setting. The Ramsey policy accommodates a cost push shock at date t by engineering a modest increase in contemporaneous inflation, coupled with downward adjustments of future inflation as well as current and future output gaps. Formally, letting $\lambda_t(\epsilon^t)$ denote the normalized multiplier attached to the Phillips curve constraint, the first-order conditions with respect to $\pi_t(\epsilon^t)$ and $\chi_t(\epsilon^t)$ read

$$\pi_t(\epsilon^t) = \lambda_t(\epsilon^t) - \lambda_{t-1}(\epsilon^{t-1}),$$
$$\omega\chi_t(\epsilon^t) = -\kappa\lambda_t(\epsilon^t),$$

respectively. At date $t = 0$, the first-order condition with respect to inflation does not contain the $\lambda_{t-1}(\epsilon^{t-1})$ term. Combining these equations yields the optimality condition

$$\chi_t(\epsilon^t) = -\frac{\kappa}{\omega}\left(\pi_0(\epsilon^0) + \cdots + \pi_t(\epsilon^t)\right) = -\frac{\kappa}{\omega}\left(p_t(\epsilon^t) - p_{-1}(\epsilon^{-1})\right). \qquad (12.4)$$

Condition (12.4) confirms the intuition developed above. It indicates that the Ramsey policy *targets* the *price level*; that is, the negative output gap evolves proportionally to the cumulative inflation rate and it disappears only when the price level has reverted to its starting value, $p_{-1}(\epsilon^{-1})$. A characterization of optimal policy in terms of relations between policy targets is referred to as a *targeting rule*. The targeting rule (12.4) implies an associated interest rate rule; when the latter satisfies the Taylor principle, then it uniquely implements the Ramsey allocation.

12.4   Bibliographic Notes

Lucas and Stokey (1983) analyze the model presented in subsection 12.1.1. Angeletos (2002) shows that a sufficiently rich maturity structure renders markets complete, even when coupons are noncontingent (see also Gale, 1990). Aiyagari et al. (2002), Werning (2003), and Farhi (2010) analyze the model presented in subsection 12.1.2. The special case with quasilinear utility provides micro-foundations for the tax-smoothing results in Barro (1979) and Bohn (1990). The indeterminacy result for optimal capital income taxes is due to Zhu (1992) and Chari et al. (1994). Chamley (1986) and Chari et al. (1994) derive the optimality of zero capital income taxes with CIES preferences. Chamley (1986) and Judd (1985) derive steady-state results and Straub and Werning (2014) clarify the conditions under which these results apply. Subsection 12.1.4 follows Werning (2007) and Niepelt (2004b).

Diamond and Mirrlees (1978), Rogerson (1985), and Golosov et al. (2003) establish that moral hazard gives rise to a nonzero optimal intertemporal wedge.

Bailey (1956) and Friedman (1969) analyze the welfare costs of inflation. Phelps (1973) questions the applicability of the Friedman rule in environments with distorting taxes; see also Chari et al. (1996), Mulligan and Sala-i-Martin (1997), and Correia and Teles (1999). Clarida et al. (1999) analyze optimal policy in the New Keynesian model, and Rotemberg and Woodford (1997) and Woodford (2003b, chapter 6) derive the loss function in that model.

Related Topics and Additional References   Bhandari et al. (2017) characterize the stationary distribution of Ramsey taxes and debt when markets are incomplete.

Aiyagari (1995) shows that the optimal long-run capital income tax is strictly positive when uninsurable idiosyncratic labor income risk leads households to excessively accumulate capital. Farhi (2010) derives optimal capital income taxes in the model discussed in subsection 12.1.2. Atkinson and Sandmo (1980) and King (1980) derive conditions for optimal capital income taxes in the overlapping generations model.

Atkeson and Lucas (1992), Phelan (2006), and Farhi and Werning (2007) study the implications of optimal social insurance in dynastic economies with private information; constrained efficient allocations display *immiseration*—inheritable and increasing welfare inequality—unless the Ramsey government values the welfare of future generations directly, not only indirectly through the altruism of their ancestors.

Siu (2004) analyzes the Ramsey policy in an environment with rigid prices when inflation serves as fiscal shock absorber, due to noncontingent, nominal debt; he finds that even a small degree of price rigidity renders optimal inflation nonvolatile and tax rates volatile. Adam and Weber (2019) study the optimal steady-state inflation rate when the productivity of firms displays experience and cohort effects.

Correia et al. (2008) establish that with sufficiently flexible tax instruments, the Ramsey policy can neutralize the effects of price rigidity; see also Correia et al. (2013).

Chari and Kehoe (1999) cover optimal taxation and Ramsey policies; see also the references in appendix B.6. Ljungqvist and Sargent (2018, chapter 20) cover models with a tradeoff between insurance and incentives, and Golosov et al. (2016) cover dynamic incentive problems. Woodford (2003b, chapters 6, 7), Galí (2015, chapters 4, 5), and Walsh (2017, chapter 8) cover optimal policy in the New Keynesian model.

13 Time Consistent Policy

Ramsey policies of the type analyzed in chapter 12 specify history-contingent values for all policy instruments. These values are optimal ex ante, from the perspective of the initial date, and they are chosen under *commitment*: Ex post, as time proceeds, the government implements the ex-ante optimal choice and does not reoptimize. An alternative specification of government behavior is that governments *sequentially* determine the values of the policy instruments, under *discretion*, at the time when the instruments actually are implemented. Governments acting under discretion perceive private sector choices in earlier periods as bygones, unlike a Ramsey government that determines all instruments before the private sector makes its choices. This alters the tradeoffs that governments face and introduces a layer of dynamic interaction between the private sector and successive governments (or selves of one and the same government), which is absent when the government acts under commitment.

We illustrate this interaction in the context of a simple two-period model. Thereafter, we study the taxation of labor and capital income when the government chooses tax rates under discretion, and we analyze public debt policy when the government cannot commit to honoring its liabilities. Finally, we study redistribution in politico-economic equilibrium and analyze how, and with what effect, discretionary monetary policy differs from a committed or rules-based policy.

13.1 Time Consistency and the Role of State Variables

Sequential policy choice introduces the possibility that the government at a date $t > 0$ chooses values for the policy instruments that differ from the preferred values of the government at date $t = 0$. This may occur for two reasons: Either because the objectives of the two governments (or of the same government at different points in time) are not dynamically consistent, similarly to the preferences of a household with nongeometrically declining discount factors (see subsection 2.2.2); or because the constraints faced by the government change over time.

To see how the passing of time can alter a government's constraint set, consider a setting with two periods. At date $t = 0$, the private sector makes a choice, say s (for instance, it saves), and at date $t = 1$, the government takes an action, τ (for example, it imposes a tax). The private sector's choice depends on the expected government action, τ^e. When the government moves first, choosing τ before the household determines s, then the choice of τ also determines τ^e and thus affects s. When the government moves second, in contrast, then its actual choice, τ, is irrelevant for s; all that matters for s is the action the private sector anticipates the government to take, τ^e. Ex post (conditional on $s(\tau^e)$), the government's choice of τ may differ from τ^e.

In equilibrium, the government's seeming degree of freedom to choose $\tau \neq \tau^e$ vanishes because the private sector rationally anticipates the government's ex-post optimal action: τ^e thus equals τ in equilibrium. In fact, the government's choice set when moving first—under commitment—is larger than when it moves second—under discretion—because only in the former case can the government steer private sector expectations away from anticipating the ex-post optimal government action.

These findings generalize. When the government cannot commit, an *equilibrium policy* satisfies two requirements: It implements an economic equilibrium and it is *time consistent*; that is, the continuation of the policy is ex-post optimal. Compared to a Ramsey policy, an equilibrium policy thus satisfies additional *incentive compatibility constraints*. The optimal policy under commitment (the Ramsey policy) is optimal in the set of feasible and admissible policies, while the optimal policy under discretion is optimal in the set of policies that are both feasible and admissible and ex-post optimal. Since the former set always is weakly larger than the latter, the ability to commit always has a nonnegative value. When the Ramsey policy is *time inconsistent*, then the ability to commit has strictly positive value.

When a government lacks commitment, other state variables may partly or even fully compensate for this deficiency. Consider again the two-period example and assume for simplicity that the government can take an action at date $t = 0$, whose only effect is to render it very costly for the government at date $t = 1$ to implement a τ that differs from $\hat{\tau}$ by more than ε. The action and the cost of implementing a τ that strongly differs from $\hat{\tau}$ constitute a state variable. When $\varepsilon = 0$, then this state variable is a perfect substitute for commitment. But even when $\varepsilon > 0$, the action is useful when it enhances the date-$t = 0$ government's *credibility*; that is, when it induces the government at date $t = 1$ to choose a policy that corresponds to the policy announcement of the date-$t = 0$ government. In a stochastic environment, stronger credibility may come at the cost of reduced flexibility: When $\hat{\tau}$ cannot be contingent, the action may limit the ability of the government at date $t = 1$ to appropriately respond to shocks.

The ideal state variable that helps implement the Ramsey allocation when the government cannot commit has two properties. Ex ante, it is neutral in the sense that it does not impose additional constraints on the equilibrium allocation. Ex post, its presence provides incentives for the government not to deviate from the ex-ante optimal policy choice. In the model discussed in section 13.2, the maturity structure of public debt constitutes such an ideal state variable.

13.2   Credible Tax Policy

Consider the complete markets tax-smoothing problem analyzed in subsection 12.1.1 and suppose that the government cannot commit to the ex-ante optimal tax policy while it can commit to repaying debt. Recall that the Ramsey allocation uniquely determines the value of government indebtedness at date t,

$$\sum_{s=t}^{\infty} \int \frac{q_s(\epsilon^s)}{q_t(\epsilon^t)} {}_t b_s(\epsilon^{t-1}, \epsilon^s) d\epsilon^s | \epsilon^t,$$

while it does not determine the *maturity structure*. This ex-ante indeterminacy can be exploited to render the Ramsey policy time consistent. There exists a unique maturity structure of debt that both supports the Ramsey policy and renders it time consistent.[33]

To see this, consider date $t = 1$ (parallel arguments apply for subsequent periods), when the government is bound to honor the outstanding promises $\{{}_1 b_t(\epsilon^0, \epsilon^t)\}_{t \geq 1}$ but free to choose any tax sequence $\{\tau_t(\epsilon^t)\}_{t \geq 1}$ satisfying the date-$t = 1$ implementability constraint, as well as the resource constraints. The government's program at date $t = 1$ resembles the program at date $t = 0$, except that the debt maturities outstanding are given by $\{{}_1 b_t(\epsilon^0, \epsilon^t)\}_{t \geq 1}$ rather than $\{{}_0 b_t(\epsilon^{-1}, \epsilon^t)\}_{t \geq 0}$. Accordingly, the first-order conditions of the date-$t = 1$ program are given by

$$(1 + \nu_1) u_c(c_t, x_t) + \nu_1 (u_{cc}(c_t, x_t)(c_t - {}_1 b_t) - u_{xc}(c_t, x_t)(1 - x_t)) = \mu_{1t},$$

$$(1 + \nu_1) u_x(c_t, x_t) + \nu_1 (u_{cx}(c_t, x_t)(c_t - {}_1 b_t) - u_{xx}(c_t, x_t)(1 - x_t)) = \mu_{1t} w_t$$

for $t \geq 1$, where we suppress histories for legibility and use the notation from subsection 12.1.1. Note that the multipliers of the date-$t = 1$ program are indexed by "1" to distinguish them from the multipliers of the date-$t = 0$ program.

If these conditions, together with the implementability constraint as of date $t = 1$ and the resource constraints, are to prescribe the same allocation as the conditions resulting from the program at date $t = 0$, then the first-order conditions of the two programs must be satisfied for the same sequences $\{c_t, x_t\}_{t \geq 1}$. From the first-order conditions of the date-$t = 0$ and date-$t = 1$ programs, this implies the restrictions

$$\nu_{1 \; 1} b_t = \nu_{\; 0} b_t + (\nu_1 - \nu) A_t, \; t \geq 1 \; \forall \epsilon^t | \epsilon^1,$$

---

[33] We assume that the Ramsey policy operates on the increasing segment of the Laffer curve.

where A_t is a function of the Ramsey allocation.[34] For every history ϵ^1, the multiplier v and the sequences $\{A_t\}_{t\geq 1}$ and $\{_0 b_t\}_{t\geq 1}$ are given; the above restrictions and the implementability constraint as of date $t = 1$ thus pin down v_1 and $\{_1 b_t\}_{t\geq 1}$. We conclude that the Ramsey allocation, the multiplier v, and the initial maturity structure $\{_0 b_t\}_{t\geq 1}$ uniquely determine a maturity structure of debt issued at date $t = 0$ and outstanding at date $t = 1$ that renders the Ramsey policy time consistent.

Intuitively, the choice of maturity structure at date $t = 0$ affects the tradeoffs faced by the government at date $t = 1$ because the extent to which changes in the allocation, and thus the stochastic discount factor, affect the intertemporal budget constraint depend on the debt positions, $\{_1 b_t\}_{t\geq 1}$. By appropriately structuring these positions, the government at date $t = 0$ can ensure that the preferred tax sequences as of date $t = 0$ and date $t = 1$ coincide from date $t = 1$ onward. The choice of maturity structure at date $t = 0$ thus allows the government to effectively tie its hands, as if it had commitment.

13.3   Capital Income Taxation

Capital and capital income constitute elastic tax bases ex ante when households adjust their saving and investment in response to anticipated capital income tax rates, but a completely inelastic tax base ex post when no such adjustment is possible any more. Ex ante, capital income taxes thus are distorting, while they are nondistorting ex post. This renders capital income taxation particularly exposed to problems of time inconsistency.

Consider an infinite horizon economy with two subperiods at each date t, a "morning" and an "evening." In the morning, the representative household is endowed with w units of the good that it may consume, c_{1t}, or invest in capital, k_t,

$$w = c_{1t} + k_t.$$

In the evening, capital yields the exogenous return $R > 1$ and depreciates thereafter. Households supply labor, $1 - x_t$, whose productivity equals unity; consume leisure, x_t; and consume their after-tax capital and labor income. Capital income is taxed at rate $\tau_t^k \leq 1$ and labor income, $1 - x_t$, is taxed at rate $\tau_t \leq 1$. Consumption in the evening, c_{2t}, thus equals

$$c_{2t} = k_t R(1 - \tau_t^k) + (1 - x_t)(1 - \tau_t).$$

Households discount the future at the factor $\beta \in (0, 1)$. Their period utility function, u, is strictly increasing and concave in consumption and leisure. For simplicity, we assume that c_{1t} and c_{2t} are perfect substitutes such that utility from consumption and leisure at

---

[34] To derive the restriction, multiply the first-order condition with respect to c_t by w_t; subtract the first-order condition with respect to x_t from the resulting equality; follow the same steps with the first-order conditions from the date-$t = 0$ program; and collect terms. We have $A_t \equiv (w_t u_c(c_t, x_t) - u_x(c_t, x_t) + c_t(w_t u_{cc}(c_t, x_t) - u_{cx}(c_t, x_t)) + (1 - x_t)(u_{xx}(c_t, x_t) - w_t u_{cx}(c_t, x_t)))/(w_t u_{cc}(c_t, x_t) - u_{cx}(c_t, x_t))$.

date t equals $u(c_{1t} + c_{2t}, x_t)$. The government is benevolent, faces an exogenous revenue requirement, g, in the evening, and does not issue debt. The government budget constraint thus reads

$$g = k_t R \tau_t^k + (1 - x_t)\tau_t.$$

We start by characterizing the Ramsey policy before studying time consistent policies in the absence of commitment.

13.3.1 Commitment Benchmark

Since capital immediately depreciates and the government issues no debt, the Ramsey problem consists of a sequence of subproblems, one for each date. Focusing on the problem at date t, consider the savings choice of a household. When the after-tax return on a unit of capital exceeds unity; that is, when $\tau_t^k \leq (R-1)/R$, then the household saves its first-period endowment in full and the capital income tax is nondistorting. The tax rate affects the tax revenue in this case, but not the tax base. When the after-tax return is strictly smaller than unity, in contrast, then the savings rate equals zero and the government collects no capital income taxes. The maximal capital income tax revenue thus is attained for $\tau_t^k = (R-1)/R$ and equals $w(R-1)$.

We assume that $g > w(R-1)$, such that the Ramsey tax rate on capital income equals $(R-1)/R$ and the Ramsey policy also taxes labor income. The tax rate τ_t and equilibrium labor supply, $1 - x_t$, then solve

$$\frac{u_x(w + (1-x_t)(1-\tau_t), x_t)}{u_c(w + (1-x_t)(1-\tau_t), x_t)} = 1 - \tau_t,$$
$$w(R-1) + (1-x_t)\tau_t = g.$$

The first condition equates the household's marginal rate of substitution between consumption and leisure with the marginal rate of transformation, and the second condition represents the government budget constraint. Both conditions are evaluated at the equilibrium household choices $c_{1t} = 0$, $k_t = w$, and $c_{2t} = w + (1-x_t)(1-\tau_t)$. Let u^R denote the period utility under the Ramsey policy.

13.3.2 No Commitment

Suppose next that the government cannot commit. Households choose their saving in the morning before the government fixes the tax rates that are imposed in the evening.

13.3.2.1 Static Equilibrium For now, we also assume that there are no state variables other than capital. Since the capital income tax is nondistorting ex post, while the labor income tax does distort labor supply, the government's optimal policy choice in the evening amounts to taxing capital income as much as possible (and needed). That is, for any level of k_t that the household saves, the government sets $\tau_t^k = \min[1, g/(k_t R)]$.

Anticipating this ex-post optimal policy choice, households do not save at all and the government is forced to collect all revenue from labor income taxes.[35] Labor supply and the labor income tax rate in this *static time consistent equilibrium* satisfy

$$\frac{u_x(w + (1 - x_t)(1 - \tau_t), x_t)}{u_c(w + (1 - x_t)(1 - \tau_t), x_t)} = 1 - \tau_t,$$

$$(1 - x_t)\tau_t = g.$$

The allocation in the static time consistent equilibrium gives strictly lower utility than the Ramsey allocation.[36] Intuitively, both the Ramsey policy and the static time consistent policy implement a competitive equilibrium but only the latter satisfies the incentive compatibility constraint that the policy choice be ex-post optimal. This additional constraint is costly. Let u^s denote the period utility in the static equilibrium and let $V^s \equiv u^s/(1 - \beta)$ denote the continuation value in a static equilibrium.

If the government announced any tax rate $\tau_t^k \leq (R - 1)/R$ (e.g., the Ramsey tax rate) and households believed the announcement and accumulated capital, the government could always do better than following the announcement by imposing $\tau_t^k = \min[1, g/(k_t R)]$ instead and levying low labor income taxes. The period utility for households (and the government) of inducing capital accumulation k_t and deviating from the announcement ex post, $u^d(k_t)$ say, would exceed the utility from not deviating—a policy of taxing capital at a low rate therefore is not time consistent.

Note that the time inconsistency of policies with $\tau_t^k \leq (R - 1)/R$ reflects a *lack of instruments*. If the government had access to a nondistorting tax, it would use this instrument rather than the labor income tax and the Ramsey policy would be time consistent.

13.3.2.2 History as a State Variable

Consider now the effect of introducing a new state variable—the *history* of preceding policy choices. We let $\pi_t \equiv (\tau_t^k, \tau_t)$ denote the choice of tax rates at date t, and π^t the history of such choices up to and including date t. When households and the government condition their decisions on π^t, this introduces a dynamic link across periods which has not been present so far. Moreover, when this link provides incentives for the government not to overburden capital ex post, then this opens the possibility for time consistent equilibria that Pareto dominate the static equilibrium.

To explore this possibility, we study an *equilibrium* of *household* and *government plans*, ϕ and ψ respectively. The timing of events at date t is as follows. First, each household chooses the morning allocation according to the date-t morning component of the household plan, ϕ_{1t}, which maps the history π^{t-1} into (c_{1t}, k_t); moreover, the household

---

[35] Note that $g/(k_t R) \geq g/(wR) > w(R - 1)/(wR) = (R - 1)/R$.

[36] The conditions characterizing (x_t, τ_t) in the static time consistent equilibrium coincide with the equilibrium conditions under the Ramsey policy when the government faces a larger revenue requirement, namely $g + w(R - 1)$ rather than g. This implies that $u^R > u^s$.

determines a continuation plan for future choices contingent on future histories. Second, the government chooses feasible tax rates according to the date-t component of the government plan, ψ_t, which maps the history π^{t-1} into the policy choice π_t, and it determines a continuation plan. And finally, each household chooses the evening allocation according to the evening component of the household plan, ϕ_{2t}, which maps the history $\pi^t = (\pi^{t-1}, \pi_t)$ into (c_{2t}, x_t), and determines a continuation plan.

Note that conditional on history π^{t-1}, a government plan of feasible policies induces the history $\pi^t = (\pi^{t-1}, \psi_t(\pi^{t-1}))$, $\pi^{t+1} = (\pi^t, \psi_{t+1}(\pi^t))$, and so forth. Jointly, the household and government plans therefore induce a continuation utility for the household (and the government) from date t onward, which we denote by $V_t(\pi^{t-1}, \phi, \psi)$. We are interested in plans that implement an equilibrium with higher continuation value than in the static equilibrium, V^s.

Household and government plans perform two functions. On the one hand, they steer household expectations. On the other hand, they render it advantageous for the government to act in accordance with these expectations ex post by letting noncompliance trigger a change of expectations that implies worse outcomes in the future. An optimal plan leads households to expect sufficiently low capital income tax rates, and thus to accumulate capital while at the same time assuring ex-post incentive compatibility on the part of the government. Since the incentive to comply derives from the desire to avert worse outcomes in the future, the mechanism can only work if the economy has an infinite horizon.

A *sustainable equilibrium* is a pair of incentive-compatible *sustainable plans*, ϕ and ψ, which induce a policy that implements a competitive equilibrium: Given ψ, the continuation of ϕ in the morning and the evening of date t is optimal for the household for any history π^{t-1} and π^t, respectively; and given ϕ, the continuation of ψ at date t is feasible and optimal for the government for any history π^{t-1}. To find the *best sustainable equilibrium* we first determine the *worst* one because the threat of a reversal to the latter incentivizes the government to implement the former.

The worst sustainable equilibrium is given by the static equilibrium characterized above. The static equilibrium is sustainable because given the expectation of a high capital income tax rate, households optimally do not save; and given zero savings in the present and the future, the government is indifferent between setting a high or low capital income tax rate. It is the worst sustainable equilibrium because any feasible policy balances the government budget and in the static equilibrium the government levies taxes in the least efficient manner, relying exclusively on labor income taxes.

We have established that plans which implement the static equilibrium are incentive compatible and that they implement the worst sustainable equilibrium. Plans that trigger a reversion to the static equilibrium in response to noncompliance by the government thus provide the strongest possible incentive for the government to remain compliant. This implies that a pair of plans constitutes a sustainable equilibrium as long as the value of complying with the plans exceeds the value from deviating and implementing the static equilibrium forever after.

Formally, consider plans $\phi^\star$ and $\psi^\star$ that prescribe the policy $\pi_t = \pi^\star$ as long as the government only chose $\pi^\star$ in the past; and the policy implementing the static equilibrium in all future periods once the government has deviated from $\pi^\star$. The plans form a sustainable equilibrium if

$$V_t(\pi^{t-1}, \phi^\star, \psi^\star) \geq u^d(k_t) + \beta V^s.$$

In this case, infinite repetition of the policy choice $\pi^\star$ constitutes a *credible policy*.

Note that the static equilibrium is a sustainable equilibrium because $V^s \geq u^d(0) + \beta V^s$. But due to the dynamic link introduced by the state variable π^t, equilibria with strictly positive capital accumulation are sustainable as well, as long as the long-term loss from reverting to the static equilibrium outweighs the short-term gain from imposing a high tax rate on the capital income tax base ex post. For a sufficiently high discount factor, even the Ramsey allocation can be sustained: As $\beta \to 1$, the sustainability condition

$$\frac{u^R}{1-\beta} \geq u^d(w) + \beta \frac{u^s}{1-\beta}$$

necessarily is satisfied.

13.4   Sovereign Debt and Default

When a debtor-creditor pair engages in borrowing and lending, both parties benefit from gains of trade (see section 7.3). Once the debt comes due, however, their interests are no longer aligned because debt repayment constitutes a transfer from the debtor to the creditor. If the prospective debtor lacks commitment, this ex-post conflict of interest can undermine the viability of the arrangement ex ante. For if the lender foresees that the borrower would not repay, then the lender does not enter into the credit relationship in the first place (see also section 8.3).

We study a benevolent government that issues *sovereign debt* to a representative, competitive, risk neutral international investor. The government levies lump-sum taxes or pays lump-sum transfers to the representative domestic household that does not have access to international financial markets and makes no decisions. Unlike the investor, the government cannot commit. Rather than making contractually agreed payments to the investor, it might choose to *default*.

13.4.1   Insurance

Consider first a static model. The country's endowment is risky. It takes the value $w_1(\epsilon^1)$ with probability $\eta(\epsilon^1)$. Since the household's period utility function, u, is strictly concave but the investor is risk neutral, the investor and the benevolent government agree on an insurance contract that stipulates (positive or negative) contingent payments, $T(\epsilon^1)$, from the country to the investor. In equilibrium, the investor must break even on average; that is, the contract must satisfy the investor's participation constraint (or the country's budget constraint), $\sum_{\epsilon^1} \eta(\epsilon^1)T(\epsilon^1) \geq 0$.

Violating the contract ex post triggers exogenous default costs, $L(\epsilon^1) \geq 0$, which are born by the domestic household whose consumption equals $w(\epsilon^1) - T(\epsilon^1) - L(\epsilon^1)$. Since the government lacks commitment, it cannot credibly promise to make a positive payment to the investor unless the amount is smaller than the costs the country would have to bear in case of default. Incentive compatibility therefore requires that, in addition to the participation constraint, the contract satisfies the incentive constraints $L(\epsilon^1) \geq T(\epsilon^1)$. Note that the commitment outcome can be implemented in equilibrium when the default costs are sufficiently large such that the incentive constraints never bind. When $L(\epsilon^1) = 0$ in all histories, in contrast, then insurance is not viable because the government cannot credibly promise to make any payments to the investor.

In equilibrium, the country never defaults. If it did, the insurance contract could be improved by lowering the contractual payment to the investor in the history with default to the value of the default costs; this would lower the expected cost for the domestic household and weakly increase the expected payments to the investor. Letting λ and $\eta(\epsilon^1)\mu(\epsilon^1)$ denote the multipliers attached to the participation and incentive compatibility constraints, respectively, the optimal contracting program thus can be represented by the Lagrangian

$$\mathcal{L} = \sum_{\epsilon^1} \eta(\epsilon^1)u(w(\epsilon^1) - T(\epsilon^1)) + \lambda \left(\sum_{\epsilon^1} \eta(\epsilon^1)T(\epsilon^1) \right) + \sum_{\epsilon^1} \eta(\epsilon^1)\mu(\epsilon^1)(L(\epsilon^1) - T(\epsilon^1)),$$

where the first sum on the right-hand side is expected utility and the other terms represent the constraints. The first-order condition with respect to $T(\epsilon^1)$ is given by

$$u'(w(\epsilon^1) - T(\epsilon^1)) + \mu(\epsilon^1) = \lambda.$$

The condition states that the equilibrium contract provides insurance across all histories in which the incentive constraint does not bind ($\mu(\epsilon^1) = 0$). In histories where the constraint does bind ($\mu(\epsilon^1) > 0$), marginal utility is lower and thus consumption higher than in the insured histories. If the constraint never binds, as would be the case with commitment, then consumption is perfectly insured (see subsection 4.2.1).

Intuitively, in histories with a binding incentive constraint, the government cannot pay as much to the investor as perfect insurance would require because a high payment would violate incentive compatibility. From the budget constraint, the investor thus pays less to the country in some other histories than it would pay if the government could commit. Compared with the Ramsey allocation, the country therefore consumes more in histories with high endowments and a binding incentive constraint, and less in histories with low endowments.

13.4.2   Borrowing with Contingent Debt

Suppose next that the country borrows an amount b at date $t = 0$ and repays the contingent amount $T(\epsilon^1)$ at date $t = 1$. The household's discount factor is β and the investor requires an expected gross interest rate R. We assume that either R or the endowment at date $t = 0$, w_0, is sufficiently low such that the government has a borrowing motive. The Lagrangian associated with this modified program reads

$$\mathcal{L} = \beta^{-1}u(w_0 + b) + \sum_{\epsilon^1}\eta(\epsilon^1)u(w(\epsilon^1) - T(\epsilon^1)) + \lambda\left(\sum_{\epsilon^1}\eta(\epsilon^1)T(\epsilon^1) - Rb\right)$$
$$+ \sum_{\epsilon^1}\eta(\epsilon^1)\mu(\epsilon^1)(L(\epsilon^1) - T(\epsilon^1)),$$

where the objective (expected utility over two periods) is divided by β to ease the comparison with the program analyzed before. The first-order conditions derived in the insurance case continue to apply; they are augmented by the first-order condition with respect to b, namely $u'(w_0 + b) = \lambda\beta R$. Combined, the conditions yield the Euler equation

$$u'(w_0 + b) = \beta R(u'(w(\epsilon^1) - T(\epsilon^1)) + \mu(\epsilon^1)),$$

which states that marginal utility declines by more in histories where the incentive constraint binds ($\mu(\epsilon^1) > 0$). The intuition parallels the one from the insurance case.

The explicitly history-contingent payment, $T(\epsilon^1)$, can be interpreted as the payment on a bond with notionally risk-free return that is *renegotiated* ex post. To see this, focus on the set of histories in which the incentive constraint binds and disregard all other histories. According to the interpretation, the bond has *face value* $b\rho = \max[T(\epsilon^1)]$ in the second period, where ρ denotes the contractual interest rate. When $L(\epsilon^1)$ is revealed and is smaller than $b\rho$, the government threatens to default and the parties agree to lower the payment to the amount the country would forfeit in case of default, $T(\epsilon^1) = L(\epsilon^1)$; this helps both the country and the investor. Note that while the default costs serve as a threat point during the renegotiation, they do not materialize in equilibrium.

13.4.3   Borrowing with Noncontingent Debt

When both explicitly history-contingent payments and renegotiation are ruled out, for example because the investor cannot verify the realization of the default costs, then the government only has a choice between repaying the noncontingent face value in full or defaulting; in contrast to the case with renegotiation, default costs therefore generally materialize in equilibrium.

Let $b\rho$ denote the face value of debt at date $t = 1$. Since the government chooses to default when $b\rho \geq L(\epsilon^1)$, the contracting program reads

$$\mathcal{L} = \beta^{-1}u(w_0 + b) + \sum_{\epsilon^1 \in \mathcal{E}^r} \eta(\epsilon^1)u(w(\epsilon^1) - b\rho) + \sum_{\epsilon^1 \notin \mathcal{E}^r} \eta(\epsilon^1)u(w(\epsilon^1) - L(\epsilon^1))$$
$$+ \lambda \left(\sum_{\epsilon^1 \in \mathcal{E}^r} \eta(\epsilon^1)b\rho - Rb \right),$$

where $\mathcal{E}^r$ denotes the (endogenous) set of repayment histories in which $L(\epsilon^1) \geq b\rho$. The first-order condition with respect to b implies a stochastic Euler equation,[37]

$$u'(w_0 + b) = \beta\rho \sum_{\epsilon^1 \in \mathcal{E}^r} \eta(\epsilon^1)u'(w(\epsilon^1) - b\rho),$$

which relates the marginal utility gain from debt issuance in the first period to marginal utility losses in histories in which the country services the debt. From the participation constraint, which holds with equality, $\rho = R / \sum_{\epsilon^1 \in \mathcal{E}^r} \eta(\epsilon^1)$.

Since the government repays in full if it repays, the country receives no insurance across histories $\epsilon^1 \in \mathcal{E}^r$. In the other histories, the country bears default costs in equilibrium, reflected in the $-L(\epsilon^1)$ terms in the sum $\sum_{\epsilon^1 \notin \mathcal{E}^r} \eta(\epsilon^1)u(w(\epsilon^1) - L(\epsilon^1))$. These costs are a *social loss* because they constitute a cost for the borrower without corresponding benefit for the investor. Without renegotiation, the default costs thus generate an *external finance premium* (see subsection 8.3.1).

13.4.4   Loan Size Determinants

To study the role of social losses and the determinants of equilibrium loan size in more detail, we focus on the interaction between b, ρ, and L. We assume that default costs are continuously distributed according to a smooth cumulative distribution function, H, and we take into account that a marginal change of b affects the probability of repayment. For tractability, we simplify the model along other dimensions.

Suppose that the government raises investor funds for a project whose return (including nondepreciated capital) is determined by a neoclassical production function, f. Both the investor and the household represented by the government are risk neutral; the investor's required expected gross rate of return equals R. If the government could commit it would borrow $b^\star$, invest that amount, and repay $b^\star R$ where $f'(b^\star) = R$. Since the government cannot commit, however, it only repays when this is in the country's interest ex post.

We consider four scenarios that are distinguished along two dimensions. One dimension relates to the fact whether the government and the investor can renegotiate or not. With renegotiation (case R), default costs do not materialize in equilibrium but they affect the

---

[37] We assume that at the margin, changing b does not affect $\mathcal{E}^r$. More on this below.

size of the payment to the investor. Without renegotiation (case N), default costs do materialize in equilibrium, and because they constitute a social loss they drive a wedge between what the country pays and what the investor receives.

The other dimension relates to the fact whether the government takes the *loan supply schedule* or rather the *contractual interest rate* as given. The former case (case S) can be interpreted as a form of credit rationing because any given contractual interest rate is linked to a particular loan size, which caps what the country can borrow. In the latter case (case I), the government perceives the contractual interest rate to be independent of the loan size it chooses.

With renegotiation (case R), a loan of size b with contractual gross interest rate ρ yields the expected investor return

$$(1 - H(b\rho))b\rho + \int_0^{b\rho} L \, dH(L). \tag{13.1}$$

The first term represents the probability of repayment in full (which occurs when L exceeds the contractual obligation) times the contractual obligation; and the second term represents the payments in histories where only $L < b\rho$ is paid, weighted by their probability. Note that a marginal increase of $b\rho$ changes the expected return by

$$1 - H(b\rho) - H'(b\rho)b\rho + b\rho H'(b\rho),$$

which equals $1 - H(b\rho)$. The two terms that cancel each other reflect the slightly reduced probability of repayment in full and the slightly increased probability of partial repayment when partial equals full repayment.

In equilibrium, the expected return given in (13.1) must equal bR. This equilibrium condition traces a loan supply schedule, $\rho(b)$. Totally differentiating the equilibrium condition, we find that

$$\rho'(b) = \frac{R - \rho(1 - H(b\rho))}{b(1 - H(b\rho))} > 0. \tag{13.2}$$

Intuitively, a larger loan size reduces both the probability of repayment in full and the payment per unit of debt when repayment is partial. To guarantee the required rate of return to the investor, the contractual interest rate therefore must rise with the loan size.

Without renegotiation (case N), the investor's expected return amounts to

$$(1 - H(b\rho))b\rho \tag{13.3}$$

and a marginal increase of $b\rho$ changes the expected return by

$$1 - H(b\rho) - H'(b\rho)b\rho.$$

The modified expected return gives rise to a modified loan supply schedule with slope

$$\rho'(b) = \frac{H'(b\rho)\rho^2}{1 - H(b\rho) - H'(b\rho)b\rho}. \tag{13.4}$$

We now turn to the four scenarios. Suppose first that renegotiation is possible and the government internalizes the loan supply schedule (13.2) (scenario R-S). The government then solves

$$\max_b f(b) - (1 - H(b\rho(b)))b\rho(b) - \int_0^{b\rho(b)} L \, dH(L).$$

Differentiating with respect to b yields the first-order condition

$$f'(b) = (1 - H(b\rho(b)))(\rho(b) + b\rho'(b)) = R,$$

where the second equality follows from condition (13.2). Note that the government chooses the first-best loan size.

Suppose next that the government perceives the contractual interest rate to be independent of b (scenario R-I). It then solves

$$\max_b f(b) - (1 - H(b\rho))b\rho - \int_0^{b\rho} L \, dH(L)$$

while the investor sets ρ to guarantee the required return. The equilibrium conditions thus are given by

$$f'(b) = (1 - H(b\rho))\rho,$$
$$R = (1 - H(b\rho))\rho + \frac{1}{b} \int_0^{b\rho} L \, dH(L),$$

implying that $f'(b) < R$ in equilibrium. Intuitively, the government *overborrows* because it does not internalize the effect of an increase in b on the equilibrium interest rate.

In scenario N-S, the government's program is the same as in scenario R-S, except that the supply schedule is given by (13.4) rather than (13.2). Using condition (13.4), the first-order condition of this program can be expressed as

$$f'(b) = R \frac{1 - H(b\rho(b))}{1 - H(b\rho(b)) - H'(b\rho(b))b\rho(b)} > R,$$

implying *underborrowing* relative to the benchmark. Intuitively, when L constitutes a social loss rather than a transfer to the investor and the government fully internalizes this, it chooses to borrow less.

Finally, in scenario N-I, the government solves the same program as in scenario R-I but the contractual interest rate reflects the expected investor return given in (13.3) rather than (13.1). The equilibrium conditions therefore reduce to

$$f'(b) = (1 - H(b\rho))\rho,$$
$$R = (1 - H(b\rho))\rho,$$

implying that the equilibrium loan size equals $b^\star$. On the one hand, the social losses from default induce the government to borrow less than in the case with renegotiation. On the other hand, the perception that the interest rate is independent of the loan size induces the government to borrow more than when it internalizes the loan supply schedule. The two effects exactly cancel each other.

13.4.5   Debt Laffer Curve and Debt Overhang

Default risk can give rise to a *debt Laffer curve*, namely an inverse-U shaped relationship between the contractual debt obligation and the funds the government actually raises. To see this, consider the N-S scenario analyzed above where the government raises funds b and promises the contractual repayment or face value $d \equiv b\rho$. The breakeven requirement of the investor relates b to the face value, the distribution function, H, and the risk-free gross interest rate, R. Expressing b as a function of d, (13.3) implies

$$b(d) = R^{-1}(1 - H(d))d.$$

Note that $R^{-1}(1 - H(d))$ equals the equilibrium price of one unit of face value of debt. Differentiating with respect to d, we find

$$b'(d) = R^{-1}(1 - H(d) - H'(d)d).$$

A marginal increase in the face value thus has two effects on the funds raised: A positive one, $R^{-1}(1 - H(d))$, reflecting the price of the marginal unit of face value; and a negative one, $-R^{-1}H'(d)d$, representing the marginal price reduction due to additional debt issuance, multiplied by the inframarginal units of face value. As d increases, the positive effect diminishes. When the negative effect outweighs the positive effect, the marginal revenue from debt issuance equals zero and a maximum of the debt Laffer curve is reached.[38]

Let $\bar{d}$ denote the face value associated with the top of the debt Laffer curve, $b'(\bar{d}) = 0$, and suppose that the country finds itself in a situation with $d > \bar{d}$; for example, because an ex ante unlikely event has changed the distribution function H and rendered low L realizations much more likely. The country then faces a situation of *debt overhang*. Conditional on H, the investor would benefit from *reducing* the face value of debt because this would *increase* the expected debt return, $(1 - H(d))d$. The country would benefit from a *debt write-down* as well because this would reduce the sum of expected debt repayment and default costs,

$$(1 - H(d))d + \int_0^d L\, dH(L).$$

In a richer model with endogenous output, the case for a debt write-down may be even stronger. For example, lowering the face value might induce the government to undertake actions that favorably affect H (reduce default risk) and simultaneously increase output.

---

[38] A sufficient condition for a unique maximum of the debt Laffer curve is that the hazard rate $H'(d)/(1 - H(d))$ be nondecreasing.

13.4.6   Multiple Equilibria

We have assumed so far that the government chooses the face value of second-period debt, d, subject to the price schedule, $R^{-1}(1 - H(d))$. For a given distribution function, H, the optimal choice satisfies $d \le \bar{d}$ in this case because placing the country on the declining segment of the debt Laffer curve generates higher costs and smaller benefits. The equilibrium loan size, b, and contractual interest rate, $\rho = d/b$, both are unique.

This changes when the government chooses b, which we assume to be smaller than the maximum of the debt Laffer curve, and lets the competitive representative investor determine ρ and thus, $d = b\rho$. With this modified protocol, the equilibrium contractual *interest rate* is *indeterminate* because multiple values for ρ and d yield the same funding level, $b = d/\rho$. For example, when the debt Laffer curve is strictly concave, then there exist two such contractual interest rates and associated face values, corresponding to the two solutions of the equilibrium condition

$$\rho(1 - H(b\rho)) = R.$$

The indeterminacy of equilibrium reflects different degrees of investor *confidence*. When the investor expects a low default risk and therefore requires a low contractual interest rate, then the face value of maturing debt and thus default risk is small as well, in line with investor expectations. In contrast, expectations of high default risk imply a high contractual interest rate and this drives up the face value, and thus the actual default risk.

The equilibria can be Pareto ranked. The low risk equilibrium dominates the high risk outcome because both equilibria produce the same funds in the first period, the investor always breaks even, and the expected default costs in the high risk equilibrium exceed those in the low risk equilibrium. Accordingly, the country may benefit from institutional restrictions such as an *interest rate cap* in the *debt auction*, which prevent the investor from selecting the high risk equilibrium.

13.4.7   Financial Autarky as Deterrent

Beyond income losses, a default may have other detrimental effects for the borrowing country or its government. In particular, it might trigger exclusion from international financial markets, undermining the country's ability to smooth consumption in the future. When the country is risk averse and its income is volatile, then it is costly to lose the possibility to smooth consumption; a credible threat of financial autarky therefore can be sufficient to deter default.

Importantly, the disciplining effect of financial autarky relies on the ability to exclude the defaulting country from both borrowing and lending. If a defaulting country could continue to lend, then the strategy of servicing the outstanding debt to preserve the option to borrow in the future would be dominated by an alternative strategy of defaulting, lending the amount due to a third party rather than repaying it to the investor, and consuming the return on the loan in the future. The threat of exclusion from borrowing markets alone therefore cannot deter a default. More generally, whether the threat of financial autarky is sufficient to sustain sovereign borrowing in the absence of commitment depends on the outside options for consumption smoothing after a default.

13.5   Redistribution in Politico-Economic Equilibrium

With heterogeneous groups of households, the policy choices of successive governments reflect the sequential aggregation of preferences in the political process. A natural benchmark is the case where the *political objective function* maximized by the government in place at a certain time represents a weighted average of the indirect utility functions of all households alive at that date. The weights reflect relative political influence, which in turn depends on the political environment.

13.5.1   Probabilistic Voting

Consider a setting with two competing candidates and associated policy proposals, among which the electorate chooses by majority vote. When each household votes for the candidate that promotes the household's preferred economic *policy platform* (and under some regularity conditions), the political objective function reflects the *median voter* household's indirect utility function. That is, the government's policy choice is the median preferred choice across voters.

When the election outcome is stochastic, in contrast, because the strength of political support depends on both a candidate's economic policy platform and exogenous shocks— that is, in a *probabilistic voting* setting—then (under some regularity conditions) the political objective function attaches strictly positive weight to the interests of all voters; see appendix B.7 for foundations of the probabilistic voting model. The broader representation of household preferences implies that changes in economic or demographic fundamentals give rise to a smoother equilibrium policy response than in a median voter setting.

In the following, we adopt the probabilistic-voting assumption and consider an overlapping generations economy with v_t young relative to old households at date t. The political objective function pursued by the date-t government therefore equals $\Omega_t \equiv \omega U_t^o + v_t U_t^y$, subject to the economic and political equilibrium conditions described below. Here, U_t^o and U_t^y denote utility of an old and a young household, respectively, and $\omega > 0$ denotes the relative per-capita political influence of the old.

13.5.2   Politico-Economic Equilibrium

We embed our analysis of the time consistent resolution of political conflict in the model of pay-as-you-go funded social security studied in subsection 11.2.3. At the beginning of date t, the nonnegative tax rate, τ_t, is determined in a probabilistic voting game. Subsequently, each worker inelastically supplies labor at wage w_t and pays social security taxes, $w_t \tau_t$. Disposable income is allocated to consumption, $c_{1,t}$, and saving, s_t, which pays the gross interest rate R_{t+1}. Retired households consume the return on their savings as well as the social security contributions, $c_{2,t} = s_{t-1}R_t + w_t\tau_t\nu_t$. The period utility function, u, is strictly increasing and concave, and the discount factor of households is denoted β. Capital fully depreciates over a period and output per worker is strictly increasing in the capital–labor ratio, k_t.

A *politico-economic equilibrium* comprises a competitive equilibrium conditional on the equilibrium policy sequence, and a political equilibrium. The competitive equilibrium conditions for a given sequence of policy instruments, $\{\tau_t\}_{t\geq0}$, are standard (see subsection 11.2.3): Factor prices are determined competitively and thus correspond to marginal products; that is, the wage and the gross interest rate are given by $w_t = w(k_t)$ and $R_t = R(k_t)$, respectively, where the former is strictly increasing and the latter strictly decreasing in the capital–labor ratio; households optimize subject to their budget constraints and taking factor prices and policy instruments as given,

$$
\begin{aligned}
u'(c_{1,t}) &= \beta R_{t+1}u'(c_{2,t+1}), \\
w_t(1 - \tau_t) &= c_{1,t} + s_t, \\
c_{2,t+1} &= s_t R_{t+1} + w_{t+1}\tau_{t+1}\nu_{t+1};
\end{aligned}
$$

and markets clear,

$$
k_t = s_{t-1}/\nu_t.
$$

Political equilibrium requires that the tax rate at date t represents the winning policy platform in that date's vote. Since each voter's preferred tax rate is a function of the economy's state, z_t say, the equilibrium tax choice also is a function of z_t, $\tau_t = \mathcal{T}_t(z_t)$. The equilibrium *policy functions*, $\{\mathcal{T}_t\}_{t\geq0}$, constitute key objects of politico-economic equilibrium.

When evaluating a policy platform, voters rationally account for its general equilibrium implications and for the consequences of these implications for future policy choices. Specifically, voters internalize that capital accumulation affects factor prices in the subsequent period and may also affect the tax rate (when $\mathcal{T}_{t+1}$ depends on k_{t+1}). The state determining the policy choice at date $t + 1$, z_{t+1}, may in general include both the *fundamental, payoff-relevant state variables*, namely the capital–labor ratio and the demographic structure, and *nonfundamental state variables*; for instance, the history of policy choices in earlier periods (see the discussion in section 13.3). Here, we restrict attention to *Markov equilibria*; that is, we rule out nonfundamental state variables.[39]

The economic and political equilibrium requirements imply *fixed-point* conditions. Consider first economic equilibrium. On the one hand, the saving choice of an individual

---

[39] In a finite horizon economy, this restriction is without loss of generality because the policy choice in the last period only reflects the fundamental state; since this is anticipated, the same holds true in the last period but one, and so forth. In an infinite horizon economy, in contrast, the exclusion of nonfundamental state variables is restrictive, as discussed in section 13.3.

worker, say S_t^i, is a function of after-tax labor income as well as factor prices and the tax rate in the subsequent period,

$$S_t^i(w_t(1 - \tau_t), R_{t+1}, w_{t+1}, \tau_{t+1}).$$

On the other hand, the average saving per worker determines these factor prices,

$$R_{t+1} = R(s_t/v_{t+1}) \quad \text{and} \quad w_{t+1} = w(s_t/v_{t+1}).$$

In competitive equilibrium, average and individual saving coincide. The aggregate saving function, say S_t^a, which is a function of after-tax labor income and the tax rate in the subsequent period, thus is a fixed point of the functional equation

$$S_t^a(y, \tau_{t+1}) = S^i\left(y, R(S_t^a(y, \tau_{t+1})/v_{t+1}), w(S_t^a(y, \tau_{t+1})/v_{t+1}), \tau_{t+1}\right)$$

for all levels of disposable labor income, y.

In political equilibrium, τ_{t+1} is a function of the next period's state, and thus generally also depends on the level of saving,

$$\tau_{t+1} = \mathcal{T}_{t+1}(s_t/v_{t+1}, \hat{z}_{t+1}),$$

where $\hat{z}_{t+1}$ denotes state variables other than k_{t+1}. This implies a modified aggregate saving function, say S_t, of after-tax labor income and conditional on the tax *function* in the subsequent period. The saving function is a fixed point of the functional equation

$$S_t(y, \mathcal{T}_{t+1}) = $$
$$S^i\left(y, R(S_t(y, \mathcal{T}_{t+1})/v_{t+1}), w(S_t(y, \mathcal{T}_{t+1})/v_{t+1}), \mathcal{T}_{t+1}(S_t(y, \mathcal{T}_{t+1})/v_{t+1}, \hat{z}_{t+1})\right)$$

for all levels of disposable labor income, y.

In a finite horizon economy, the saving and tax functions, $\{S_t, \mathcal{T}_t\}_{t=0}^T$, can be found by backward induction. In the last period, at date $t = T$, the saving function is identically equal to zero, $S_T(w_T(1 - \tau_T), 0) = 0$, and the political objective function is given by

$$\Omega_T(z_T, \tau_T) \equiv \omega u(c_{2,T}) + v_t u(c_{1,T}),$$

subject to the factor price conditions and the budget constraints described above. The equilibrium policy function, $\mathcal{T}_T$, gives the tax rate τ_T that maximizes Ω_T conditional on z_T. At any date $t < T$, the competitive equilibrium conditions encapsulated in the saving function S_t^a and the policy function $\mathcal{T}_{t+1}$ imply the saving function S_t. The political objective function is given by

$$\Omega_t(z_t, \tau_t) \equiv \omega u(c_{2,t}) + v_t \left(u(c_{1,t}) + \beta u(c_{2,t+1})\right),$$

subject to the factor price conditions; the budget constraints; the saving function, $s_t = S(w(k_t)(1 - \tau_t), \mathcal{T}_{t+1})$; and the policy function in the subsequent period, $\mathcal{T}_{t+1}$. The tax rate τ_t that maximizes Ω_t conditional on z_t defines $\mathcal{T}_t$.

In an infinite horizon economy, when the environment is time-invariant conditional on z_t (for instance, because the state follows a Markov process), the policy and objective functions are time-invariant as well, $\mathcal{T}_t = \mathcal{T}$ and $\Omega_t = \Omega$. The latter is defined as

$$\Omega(z_t, \tau_t) \equiv \omega u(c_{2,t}) + v_t \left(u(c_{1,t}) + \beta u(c_{2,t+1}) \right),$$

subject to the factor price conditions; the budget constraints; the restriction $s_t = \mathcal{S}(w(k_t)(1 - \tau_t), \mathcal{T})$; and the policy function that governs the policy choice in the subsequent period. Since in equilibrium, the anticipated mapping from the state to the equilibrium policy choice corresponds to the actual mapping, the policy function $\mathcal{T}$ is the fixed point of the functional equation

$$\mathcal{T}(z_t) = \arg \max_{\tau_t \geq 0} \Omega(z_t, \tau_t)$$

for all values of the state, z_t.

13.5.3   Support for Redistribution

Differentiating the political objective function with respect to the tax rate, the first-order condition characterizing τ_t is given by

$$w_t v_t \left(\omega u'(c_{2,t}) - u'(c_{1,t}) \right) + v_t \mathcal{B}_t \leq 0,$$

with equality when $\tau_t > 0$. The first two terms on the left-hand side of the condition reflect the direct political benefit and cost of higher taxes, respectively. Retirees benefit from a marginal increase in τ_t because it increases social security benefits and thus, retirees' consumption by $w_t v_t$. Workers, in contrast, who pay for the benefits, marginally lose w_t units of disposable income. In the political objective function, the benefit per retiree is multiplied by the relative political weight of retirees, ω, and the cost per worker is weighted by the number of workers per retiree, v_t.

The third term in the first-order condition, $v_t \mathcal{B}_t$, reflects the welfare implications for workers of the policy-induced change in aggregate saving. An increase in the tax rate reduces aggregate saving and this increases next period's return, R_{t+1}, but lowers wages, w_{t+1}; the former effect benefits current workers and the latter hurts them because it reduces social security benefits. Lower saving may also affect the equilibrium tax rate in the subsequent period, $\mathcal{T}(z_{t+1})$. When $\mathcal{B}_t$ is positive, the political cost of taxing workers is lower than what their direct income loss would suggest. Intuitively, the fact that the tax allows workers to collectively change intertemporal prices in their favor (by raising R_{t+1}), and thus to shift part of the cost of taxation to the next generation (by lowering w_{t+1}), reduces the political resistance against a tax hike because those suffering most from lower future wages (workers in the next period) are not yet represented in the political process.

To characterize politico-economic equilibrium in closed form, we assume that household preferences are logarithmic, $\ln(c_{1,t}) + \beta \ln(c_{2,t+1})$, and the production function is Cobb-Douglas, $w(k_t) = (1 - \alpha)k_t^\alpha$ and $R(k_t) = \alpha k_t^{\alpha-1}$, where α denotes the capital share. From the household's Euler equation, competitive equilibrium then implies

$$\frac{1}{w_t(1 - \tau_t) - s_t} = \beta R_{t+1} \frac{1}{s_t R_{t+1} + w_{t+1}\tau_{t+1}v_{t+1}} = \beta \frac{\alpha}{s_t(\alpha + (1 - \alpha)\tau_{t+1})},$$

where we use the fact that $v_{t+1}w_{t+1} = s_t R_{t+1}(1 - \alpha)/\alpha$. Letting $e_t \equiv \alpha/(\alpha + (1 - \alpha)\tau_{t+1})$, this yields

$$s_t = w_t(1 - \tau_t)\frac{\beta e_t}{1 + \beta e_t}, \qquad (13.5)$$

which corresponds to the saving function S_t^a discussed earlier. Using the budget constraints, the factor price conditions, and the market clearing condition for capital, we conclude that in competitive equilibrium

$$c_{1,t} = (1 - \alpha)\left(\frac{s_{t-1}}{v_t}\right)^\alpha (1 - \tau_t)\left(\frac{1}{1 + \beta e_t}\right),$$

$$c_{2,t} = s_{t-1}^\alpha v_t^{1-\alpha}(\alpha + (1 - \alpha)\tau_t).$$

We conjecture, and later verify, that the capital–labor ratio is not an argument of the equilibrium tax function. Accordingly, the marginal effect of a tax hike on the logarithm of aggregate saving, $d \ln(s_t)/d\tau_t$, is independent of the equilibrium tax rate in the subsequent period (see condition (13.5)), rendering the political optimization problem tractable. Omitting terms independent of the policy instrument, τ_t, the political objective function reduces to

$$\Omega(z_t, \tau_t) \simeq \omega \ln(\alpha + (1 - \alpha)\tau_t) + v_t \left(\ln(1 - \tau_t) + \beta \ln((1 - \tau_t)^\alpha)\right),$$

and the marginal effect of a change of tax rate on the political objective function is given by

$$\frac{d\Omega(z_t, \tau_t)}{d\tau_t} = \frac{\omega(1 - \alpha)}{\alpha + (1 - \alpha)\tau_t} - v_t \frac{1 + \alpha\beta}{1 - \tau_t}.$$

This marginal effect equals zero when

$$\tau_t = \hat{\mathcal{T}}(v_t) \equiv \frac{\omega(1 - \alpha) - v_t(1 + \alpha\beta)\alpha}{\omega(1 - \alpha) + v_t(1 + \alpha\beta)(1 - \alpha)}.$$

When $\hat{\mathcal{T}}(v_t)$ violates the nonnegativity constraint, then the constrained maximum of Ω is attained for $\tau_t = 0$ because the objective function is strictly concave. The equilibrium tax rate therefore equals $\mathcal{T}(v_t) = \max[\hat{\mathcal{T}}(v_t), 0]$, and the equilibrium policy function is independent of k_t, as conjectured.

The equilibrium tax rate increases in ω and decreases in α, β, and v_t. Intuitively, the political benefit of taxation increases with the relative weight the political process attaches to retirees (ω), while the political cost of taxes and depressed capital accumulation increases with the weight attached to the future (β) and to those who care about the future (v_t). A decrease in the capital share (α) raises the marginal benefit of transfers for retirees and decreases the marginal cost of taxation for workers, thereby increasing the equilibrium tax rate. When the capital share α approaches zero, the economy collapses to an endowment economy without capital.[40] The general equilibrium effect, $\mathcal{B}_t$, equals zero in this case; the equilibrium tax rate reduces to $\omega/(\omega + \nu_t)$; and the equilibrium consumption ratio, $c_{2,t}/c_{1,t}$, equals ω. Intuitively, in the absence of capital accumulation, social security only has a direct, redistributive effect. Under probabilistic voting, the equilibrium ratio of marginal utilities therefore corresponds to the relative political weight of transfer recipients and tax-payers, ω.

Pensions as a share of GDP, $(w_t \mathcal{T}(\nu_t)\nu_t)/(w_t \nu_t + R_t s_{t-1}) = (1 - \alpha)\mathcal{T}(\nu_t)$, are decreasing in the number of workers relative to the number of retirees. The relationship between the share of the elderly and public pension payments per retiree, $w_t \mathcal{T}(\nu_t)\nu_t$, is inverse-U shaped.

13.6   Monetary Policy

13.6.1   Stabilization Bias

Recall the Ramsey policy in the New Keynesian model analyzed in subsection 12.3.2, where prices are rigid and the Phillips curve relates current and future values of inflation, $\pi_t(\epsilon^t)$, to the contemporaneous output gap, $\chi_t(\epsilon^t)$, and cost push shock. Since the Ramsey government controls the complete sequence of policy instruments, it also controls the private sector's rational expectations of future policy. The Ramsey policy exploits this feature in order to smooth the welfare losses from inflation deviations and output gaps over time, and this manifests itself in price level targeting.

Suppose now that the government cannot commit but sequentially chooses the policy instruments ex-post optimally; it therefore has no control over (expectations of) future policy. The date-t government's first-order conditions then have the same structure as the conditions in the program with commitment for the policy instruments in the initial period, namely

$$\pi_t(\epsilon^t) = \lambda_t(\epsilon^t),$$
$$\omega\chi_t(\epsilon^t) = -\kappa\lambda_t(\epsilon^t),$$

where ω and κ denote strictly positive parameters (see subsection 12.3.2). The optimality condition (12.4) in the program with commitment thus is replaced by the equilibrium condition

$$\chi_t(\epsilon^t) = -\frac{\kappa}{\omega}\pi_t(\epsilon^t).$$

Without commitment, the government is unable to smooth welfare losses over time because it cannot control expectations of future policy. It may only smooth welfare losses within a period, by trading off output gaps and deviations of inflation from target. In con-

---

[40] In the limit, we have $w_t = 1$, $R_t = 0$, $c_{1,t} = 1 - \tau_t$, and $c_{2,t} = \nu_t \tau_t$.

trast to the Ramsey policy, output and inflation deviate from their target values only as long as a cost push shock is present. That is, without commitment, the reversion of output and inflation to their long-run target values occurs faster than under the Ramsey policy—the discretionary policy exhibits a *stabilization bias*. Related, and also in contrast to the Ramsey policy, the price level does not revert to its starting value.

In both the program with and without commitment, inflation and the output gap eventually return to their long-run values of zero. This is a consequence of the assumption that at $\chi_t(\epsilon^t) = \pi_t(\epsilon^t) = 0$, the government does not have an incentive to drive inflation up or down. We turn next to a model where such an incentive is present.

13.6.2   Inflation Bias

Consider an infinite horizon economy with no exogenous shocks. The government at date t chooses contemporaneous inflation, π_t, to minimize the reduced-form loss function

$$L_t = \sum_{j=0}^{\infty} \beta^j \ell_{t+j} \text{ with } \ell_{t+j} = \frac{\alpha}{2}\pi_{t+j}^2 - \gamma(\pi_{t+j} - \pi_{t+j}^e),$$

where $\beta \in (0, 1)$ denotes the discount factor; α and γ are strictly positive parameters; and π_{t+j}^e denotes private sector inflation expectations. The loss components ℓ_{t+j} reflect the assumption that deviations of inflation from zero generate costs, while unexpectedly high inflation rates generate benefits. The costs arise, for example, because inflation distorts relative prices (see section 10.2). The benefits may derive from the fact that an inflation surprise stimulates output (due to a Phillips curve relationship in the background, see subsection 10.3.5) or reduces the real value of public debt, and thus the need to levy distorting taxes (see subsection 11.4.1).

Absent commitment, the government at date t chooses π_t after the private sector has formed inflation expectations. The equilibrium inflation rate under discretion therefore solves $\partial L_t / \partial \pi_t = 0$ for given inflation expectations and it equals $\bar{\pi} \equiv \gamma/\alpha$. Anticipating this ex-post optimal policy choice, the private sector forms expectations $\pi_t^e = \bar{\pi}$ and the loss at date t (and in all future periods) equals $\ell_t = \gamma^2/(2\alpha)$.

The discretionary outcome is suboptimal because strictly positive inflation generates costs but no benefits when it is anticipated. If the government was able to commit, it could control both inflation and inflation expectations and improve outcomes; specifically, the Ramsey policy amounts to $\pi_{t+j} = \pi_{t+j}^e = 0$ in all periods and generates losses $\ell_{t+j} = 0$. Absent commitment, however, inflation expectations are beyond the government's control and since $\gamma > 0$, the ex-post optimal choice is the discretionary one. As a consequence, the economy suffers from an *inflation bias*.

If the government announced a policy rule to implement the Ramsey policy, then this announcement would not be credible. For if the private sector believed the announcement and formed expectations accordingly, $\pi_{t+j}^e = 0$, then the ex-post optimal policy choice would still be given by $\bar{\pi}$ and would generate a negative loss, $\ell_t = -\gamma^2/(2\alpha)$; that is, after announcing that it would follow the rule, the government would be tempted to renege on the announcement, in particular if the private sector believed the announcement.

13.6.2.1   Trigger Strategy
The situation changes and certain announced rules $\pi^\star$ become credible in spite of the government's lack of commitment when we introduce an additional state variable. Suppose that the government and the private sector play a *trigger strategy*, conditioning expectations on the history of equilibrium outcomes (see subsection 13.3.2). Specifically, the private sector expects the announced policy, $\pi^\star$, if expected and actual inflation in the previous period coincided; and the discretionary policy, $\bar{\pi}$, if this was not the case:

$$\pi_t^e = \begin{cases} \pi^\star & \text{if } \pi_{t-1} = \pi_{t-1}^e \\ \bar{\pi} & \text{if } \pi_{t-1} \neq \pi_{t-1}^e \end{cases}.$$

With these expectations (which are validated in equilibrium), a deviation of the government's choice from $\pi^\star$ triggers a one-period punishment phase, where the private sector expects the discretionary outcome and the government optimally responds accordingly. The expectation formation mechanism thus links the contemporaneous policy choice to the constraints (private sector expectations) the government faces in the subsequent period. As a consequence, some rules that dominate discretion become credible.

Conditional on the announced rule $\pi^\star$, the government's *temptation* to deviate from the rule and implement the discretionary outcome is given by

$$-\left(\frac{\alpha}{2}\bar{\pi}^2 - \gamma(\bar{\pi} - \pi^\star)\right) + \left(\frac{\alpha}{2}\pi^{\star 2} - \gamma(0)\right),$$

which equals the difference between $-\ell_t$ when deviating from the rule and when following it. Note that as long as $\pi^\star < \bar{\pi}$, the government is tempted to deviate—this is the source of the inflation bias discussed earlier. At the same time, the fact that a deviation affects expectation formation provides incentives not to deviate. The strength of this incentive—the *enforcement*—equals

$$\beta \left\{ -\left(\frac{\alpha}{2}\pi^{\star 2} - \gamma(0)\right) + \left(\frac{\alpha}{2}\bar{\pi}^2 - \gamma(0)\right) \right\},$$

namely the discounted difference between $-\ell_t$ when following the rule (and this is expected) and implementing the discretionary policy (and this is expected).

An announced rule is credible if enforcement exceeds temptation; that is, if

$$\beta\frac{\alpha}{2}\left(\bar{\pi}^2 - \pi^{\star 2}\right) \geq \frac{\alpha}{2}\left(\pi^{\star 2} - \bar{\pi}^2\right) + \gamma(\bar{\pi} - \pi^\star) = \frac{\alpha}{2}\left(\bar{\pi} - \pi^\star\right)^2.$$

The best enforceable rule is given by the smallest $\pi^\star$ that satisfies this condition, namely

$$\underline{\pi} = \frac{\gamma(1 - \beta)}{\alpha(1 + \beta)}.$$

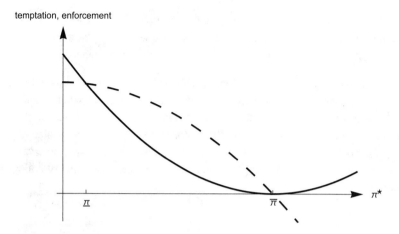

Figure 13.1
Time consistent monetary policy: Temptation and enforcement.

Note that for $\beta \to 0$, the best credible rule reduces to the discretionary outcome because enforcement equals zero in this case. For $\beta \to 1$, the best credible rule approaches the Ramsey policy.

Figure 13.1 plots temptation and enforcement, represented by the solid and dashed lines respectively, against the announced rule, $\pi^\star$. The two schedules intersect at the discretionary inflation rate, $\bar{\pi}$, and the lower inflation rate $\underline{\pi}$ (because the figure is plotted for $\beta > 0$), which represents the optimal rule.

13.6.2.2 Delegation Irrevocable *delegation* of decision power introduces an alternative state variable that can help reduce the inflation bias. If it is possible to delegate monetary policy to a bureaucrat whose appointment cannot be overturned ex post, because of *central bank independence*, then the bureaucrat's preferences constitute a state variable under the control of the appointing government. When the government appoints a *conservative*— that is, inflation averse—*central bank governor*, then future policy choices, and thus the private sector's inflation expectations, reflect this aversion.

Suppose, for example, that preferences of the government and of society at large are represented by the parameters α and γ in the government's loss function, while preferences of the central bank governor are represented by $\hat{\alpha}$ and $\hat{\gamma}$. When $\hat{\gamma}/\hat{\alpha} < \gamma/\alpha$, that is, when the governor attaches more weight to the cost of inflation than society, then the nonrevocable appointment reduces the inflation bias. In the extreme case where $\hat{\gamma} = 0$, the discretionary policy choice of the governor supports the Ramsey policy.

When all agents in society have identical preferences, delegation per se cannot solve the time inconsistency problem. But a nonrevocable contract that makes the central bank governor's salary depend negatively on realized inflation effectively changes the governor's preferences and therefore achieves the same goal.

13.6.2.3   Reputation   Endogenous beliefs constitute yet another state variable that can affect government behavior. Suppose that the government may have two types—a committed one that always implements $\pi^\star$, and a noncommitted or opportunistic one that always behaves ex-post optimally. The private sector does not observe the government's type but rationally infers it based on Bayes's rule from the observed inflation choices.

The government's *reputation* is the probability that the private sector assigns to the event that the government is committed. In equilibrium, high reputation leads the private sector to expect low inflation, and vice versa. When the remaining horizon is sufficiently long— not necessarily infinitely long—the opportunistic type therefore *mimics* the committed type and implements low inflation in order to build or maintain good (high) reputation, and thus support low inflation expectations. As the final period approaches, however, the opportunistic type eventually surprises the private sector with higher than expected inflation and destroys its reputation.

13.7   Bibliographic Notes

Kydland and Prescott (1977) emphasize that private sector decisions depend on expectations about ex-post optimal policy choices; they discuss examples of Ramsey policies that are not time consistent. Calvo (1978) analyzes time inconsistency in an environment where the government may devalue money ex post using inflation.

Section 13.2 follows Lucas and Stokey (1983). Debortoli et al. (2018) show that access to a rich maturity structure may not suffice to render the Ramsey policy time consistent when this policy operates on the declining segment of the Laffer curve.

Fischer (1980) analyzes time consistent capital income taxation. Section 13.3 follows Chari and Kehoe (1990), who relate sustainable plans to game theoretic equilibrium notions; see also Stokey's (1989; 1991) credible policies. Abreu, Pearce, and Stacchetti (1986; 1990) use recursive methods to identify the worst and best sustainable equilibrium in infinite horizon economies; see Ljungqvist and Sargent (2018, chapter 24) for a textbook treatment.

Eaton and Gersovitz (1981) study the sovereign debt model with incomplete markets. Subsection 13.4.4 follows Eaton and Fernandez (1995, section 3.1). Calvo (1988) analyzes multiplicity of equilibrium in a model where the government chooses loan size rather than face value of maturing debt. Bulow and Rogoff (1989) and Grossman and Han (1999) analyze the conditions under which financial autarky constitutes a credible threat.

Krusell and Ríos-Rull (1996) and Krusell et al. (1997) define dynamic politico-economic equilibrium. The analysis in section 13.5 follows Gonzalez-Eiras and Niepelt (2008).

Clarida et al. (1999) analyze equilibrium policy in the New Keynesian model. The model in subsection 13.6.2 is due to Barro and Gordon (1983). Rogoff (1985) and Walsh (1995) analyze delegation and the provision of incentives to a central banker. Backus and Driffill (1985) analyze the sequential equilibrium with reputation in the Barro and Gordon (1983) setup.

Related Topics and Additional References   Chang (1998) and Phelan and Stacchetti (2001) extend the approach proposed by Abreu, Pearce and Stacchetti (1986; 1990) to economies with fundamental state variables; see Ljungqvist and Sargent (2018, 25) for a textbook treatment. For the theory of repeated games, see Fudenberg and Maskin (1986) and Abreu (1988); for sequential equilibrium, see Kreps and Wilson (1982).

Myers (1977) and Krugman (1989) analyze debt overhang when the debtor must be incentivized.

Gonzalez-Eiras and Niepelt (2015) derive conditions for *politico-economic equivalence* in environments where policy is endogenous and chosen sequentially; a set of political institutions and a state are equivalent to another such pair if both pairs give rise to the same allocation in politico-economic equilibrium.

Woodford (2003b, chapter 6) derives the government's loss function in the New Keynesian model in the presence of small steady-state distortions; Benigno and Woodford (2005) propose a solution method for models with large steady-state distortions. Dixit and Lambertini (2003) analyze games between fiscal and monetary authorities under commitment and discretion.

Ljungqvist and Sargent (2018, chapter 21) cover models with two-sided lack of commitment. Mueller (1989) and Persson and Tabellini (2000) cover models of public choice and politico-economic equilibrium. Woodford (2003b, chapter 7), Galí (2015, chapter 5), and Walsh (2017, chapters 6, 8) cover discretionary policy in the New Keynesian model.

A Mathematical Tools

A.1 Constrained Optimization

Consider a maximization problem with one equality constraint and one inequality constraint,

$$\max_{x} f(x) \text{ s.t. } g(x) = 0, \ h(x) \leq 0,$$

where the functions f, g, and h are continuous and differentiable and $x \in \mathbb{R}^n$. Form the *Lagrangian*

$$\mathcal{L}(x, \lambda, \mu) \equiv f(x) - \lambda g(x) - \mu h(x),$$

where λ and μ denote scalars.

Suppose that $x^\star \in \mathbb{R}^n$ is a local maximizer of f on the constraint set. Suppose furthermore that the Jacobian matrix (the matrix of first-order partial derivatives) at $x^\star$ of the binding constraints has full rank. Mathematical results imply that in this case, there exist multipliers $\lambda^\star$ and $\mu^\star$ such that

$$\partial \mathcal{L}(x^\star, \lambda^\star, \mu^\star)/\partial x_i = 0, \ i = 1, \ldots, n,$$
$$g(x^\star) = 0,$$
$$\mu^\star \geq 0, \ h(x^\star) \leq 0, \ \mu^\star h(x^\star) = 0.$$

The last equality is referred to as the *complementary slackness condition*.

We conclude that these equalities and inequalities are necessary conditions for a local maximum. The result generalizes to the case with multiple constraints.

Note that the equalities and inequalities are not sufficient conditions for a local maximum. Whether a point satisfying the equalities and inequalities is a local maximizer (or minimizer) depends on second-order conditions. In a maximization program with a concave objective function and no constraints, the necessary conditions for a local maximum are sufficient conditions for a global maximum.

A.2 Infinite-Horizon Dynamic Programming

Using the notation of subsection 2.1.3, define the *sequence problem* as

$$V^\star(a_0) = \max_{\{a_{t+1}\}_{t \geq 0}} \sum_{t=0}^{\infty} \beta^t u(a_t R + w - a_{t+1}) \text{ s.t. } a_0 \text{ given, } a_{t+1} \in A(a_t). \tag{SP}$$

Rather than imposing a no-Ponzi-game condition, we require the choice variable, a_{t+1}, to lie in the set described by the correspondence $A(a_t)$. A lower bound on this set implies that debt cannot be rolled over forever (if interest rates are strictly positive), and thus rules out Ponzi games.

The *Bellman equation* associated with the sequence problem reads

$$V(a_t) = \max_{a_{t+1} \in A(a_t)} \{u(a_t R + w - a_{t+1}) + \beta V(a_{t+1})\} \text{ for all } a_t \in \mathcal{A}. \tag{BE}$$

Since the problem is time-autonomous, the time indices of the state and the control variable in (BE) do not carry significance. $\mathcal{A}$ denotes the state space.

A.2.1   Principle of Optimality

We assume that the set $A(a_t)$ is nonempty for all $a_t \in \mathcal{A}$. We also assume that for all sequences $\{a_{t+1}\}_{t \geq -1}$ that start with $a_0 \in \mathcal{A}$ and satisfy $a_{t+1} \in A(a_t)$, the infinite sequence in (SP) exists and is finite. Under these conditions, the *Principle of Optimality* applies: $V^\star(a_t) = V(a_t)$ for all $a_t \in \mathcal{A}$; moreover, a plan $\{a_{t+1}\}_{t \geq 0}$ conditional on $a_0 \in \mathcal{A}$ that attains $V^\star(a_0)$ in (SP) also solves (BE), and the reverse statement holds as well.

The principle follows from the fact that, if the infinite sum in (SP) exists and is finite, then it can be expressed as the sum of a contemporaneous payoff and a continuation payoff, similarly to the two terms on the right-hand side of (BE).

A.2.2   Uniqueness of V

If in addition, the set $\mathcal{A}$ is bounded and complete; $A(a_t)$ is nonempty, bounded, and complete for all $a_t \in \mathcal{A}$; and A and u are continuous, then a unique continuous and bounded function V satisfying (BE) as well as an optimal plan $\{a_{t+1}\}_{t \geq 0}$ solving (SP) or (BE) exist.

Uniqueness follows from results on *contractions*. Note that the right-hand side of (BE) constitutes an operator on the value function, say $T(V)$: For any value function V on the right-hand side of (BE), the operator returns a value function on the left-hand side. The solution to (BE) then satisfies $V = T(V)$ and the function V constitutes a fixed point of the operator T. Under the maintained assumptions, the maximization problem on the right-hand side of (BE) has a solution such that T exists, and in fact is continuous. The operator T therefore maps a set of continuous functions into the same set. Moreover, it satisfies Blackwell's sufficient conditions for a contraction.[41] But if an operator constitutes a contraction, then it has a unique fixed point. Moreover, repeated application of the operator generates a sequence of functions that converges to the fixed point.

We conclude that for an arbitrary continuous function V_0, repeated application of the operator generates a sequence of functions, $V_0, T(V_0), T(T(V_0)), T(T(T(V_0))), \ldots$, that converges to the fixed point V.

A.2.3   Properties of V

If in addition, u is concave and A convex, then the value function V in (BE) is strictly concave and the optimal plan $\{a_{t+1}\}_{t \geq 0}$ solving (SP) or (BE) is unique.

---

[41] A metric space $(\mathcal{M}, d)$ is a set $\mathcal{M}$ whose elements can be added, multiplied by scalars, and for pairs of which a norm or distance d is defined. An operator T that maps the metric space into itself is a contraction if there exists a $\rho \in [0, 1)$ such that $d(T(m), T(n)) \leq \rho d(m, n)$ for all $m, n \in \mathcal{M}$.

If in addition, u is strictly increasing in the state and A is monotone, then the value function V in (BE) is strictly increasing.

If in addition, u is continuously differentiable on the interior of its domain, then the value function V in (BE) is differentiable.

A.3   Systems of Linear Difference Equations

Consider a *system* of two *difference equations* in the variables x_t and y_t,

$$z_{t+1} = M z_t \text{ with } z_t \equiv \begin{bmatrix} x_t \\ y_t \end{bmatrix}, \ M \equiv \begin{bmatrix} a & b \\ c & d \end{bmatrix},$$

where a, b, c, and d are scalars. If M is diagonal (i.e., $b = c = 0$), then the two equations are uncoupled, $x_{t+1} = a x_t$ and $y_{t+1} = d y_t$, and we can solve them independently of each other to find $x_t = a^t x_0$ and $y_t = d^t y_0$ for arbitrary x_0, y_0. If M is not diagonal, then we can use eigenvalues and -vectors to transform the system and render the equations uncoupled, as we show next.

Suppose that M has two distinct and real eigenvalues, ρ_1 and ρ_2, with associated eigenvectors, v_1 and v_2, satisfying

$$M[v_1 \ v_2] = [v_1 \ v_2] \begin{bmatrix} \rho_1 & 0 \\ 0 & \rho_2 \end{bmatrix} \text{ or } MV = VP.$$

Premultiplying the original system $z_{t+1} = M z_t$ by V^{-1} yields a transformed, uncoupled system in the vector $Z \equiv V^{-1} z$ with diagonal matrix entries equal to the eigenvalues of M:

$$Z_{t+1} = V^{-1} M z_t = V^{-1} M V Z_t = P Z_t \text{ and therefore } Z_t = \begin{bmatrix} \rho_1 & 0 \\ 0 & \rho_2 \end{bmatrix}^t Z_0.$$

Using $z_t = V Z_t$, the latter equation can be transformed back to yield

$$z_t = V \begin{bmatrix} \rho_1 & 0 \\ 0 & \rho_2 \end{bmatrix}^t Z_0 = V \begin{bmatrix} \rho_1 & 0 \\ 0 & \rho_2 \end{bmatrix}^t V^{-1} z_0.$$

Note that M^t is given by $V P^t V^{-1}$. Letting $\varphi_0 \equiv V^{-1} z_0$, we conclude that

$$z_t = V \begin{bmatrix} \rho_1^t & 0 \\ 0 & \rho_2^t \end{bmatrix} \varphi_0 \text{ or } z_t = \varphi_{0[1]} \rho_1^t v_1 + \varphi_{0[2]} \rho_2^t v_2.$$

This first-order difference equation system in z_t has a family of solutions with two degrees of freedom, corresponding to the two elements of z_0 or φ_0. For a definite solution, we need two restrictions. An initial condition for an element of z_0 constitutes such a restriction. If an eigenvalue is unstable, then the requirement that system dynamics be stable also implies a restriction; for example, $\rho_1 > 1$ and system stability imply $\varphi_{0[1]} = 0$.

Similar solution strategies are available when the eigenvalues of M are complex or not distinct. The extension to the case with more than two variables is immediate.

A.4   Bibliographic Notes

Simon and Blume (1994, chapters 17–19), Mas-Colell et al. (1995, section M.K), and Acemoglu (2009, section A.11) review optimization and Lagrangian methods.

Stokey and Lucas (1989, chapters 3, 4) and Acemoglu (2009, chapter 6) cover dynamic programming. Acemoglu (2009, example 6.5) covers the savings problem and discusses an approach to guaranteeing compactness of $\mathcal{A}$ in that program.

Simon and Blume (1994, chapter 23) cover linear difference equations, including the case of repeated or complex eigenvalues.

Related Topics and Additional References   Stokey and Lucas (1989, chapters 7–9) and Acemoglu (2009, chapter 16) cover stochastic dynamic programming.

B Technical Discussions

B.1 Transversality Condition in Infinite-Horizon Saving Problem

Using the notation of subsection 2.1.3, the household's program is given by

$$\max_{\{a_{t+1}\}_{t\geq 0}} \sum_{t=0}^{\infty} \beta^t u(a_t R_t + w_t - a_{t+1}) \text{ s.t. } a_0 \text{ given, } \lim_{T\to\infty} q_T a_{T+1} \geq 0.$$

Let $\hat{a} \equiv \{\hat{a}_{t+1}\}_{t\geq 0}$ denote a plan that satisfies the Euler equation at all times, as well as the *transversality condition*, $\lim_{T\to\infty} q_T \hat{a}_{T+1} = 0$. Let $\bar{a} \equiv \{\bar{a}_{t+1}\}_{t\geq 0}$ denote an alternative plan that satisfies $\lim_{T\to\infty} q_T \bar{a}_{T+1} \geq 0$. We want to show that the former dominates the latter.

For brevity, let $\hat{u}_t \equiv u(\hat{a}_t R_t + w_t - \hat{a}_{t+1})$ and $\hat{u}'_t \equiv u'(\hat{a}_t R_t + w_t - \hat{a}_{t+1})$ and similarly for $\bar{u}_t$ and $\bar{u}'_t$. Strict concavity of u and positive marginal utility imply $\hat{u}_t + R_t \hat{u}'_t (\bar{a}_t - \hat{a}_t) - \hat{u}'_t (\bar{a}_{t+1} - \hat{a}_{t+1}) > \bar{u}_t$ if $\hat{a}_t \neq \bar{a}_t$ or $\hat{a}_{t+1} \neq \bar{a}_{t+1}$. If $\hat{a}_{t+1} \neq \bar{a}_{t+1}$ for some $t \in \{0, \ldots, T\}$, we thus have

$$\sum_{t=0}^{T} \beta^t (\bar{u}_t - \hat{u}_t) < \sum_{t=0}^{T} \beta^t \{R_t \hat{u}'_t (\bar{a}_t - \hat{a}_t) - \hat{u}'_t (\bar{a}_{t+1} - \hat{a}_{t+1})\} = \beta^T \hat{u}'_T (\hat{a}_{T+1} - \bar{a}_{T+1}),$$

where we use $\hat{a}_0 = \bar{a}_0$ and $\hat{u}'_t = \beta R_{t+1} \hat{u}'_{t+1}$. From the Euler equation, $\beta^T \hat{u}'_T = \hat{u}'_0 q_T$. If $\hat{a}$ is not identical to $\bar{a}$, it follows that

$$\lim_{T\to\infty} \sum_{t=0}^{T} \beta^t (\bar{u}_t - \hat{u}_t) < \lim_{T\to\infty} \hat{u}'_0 q_T (\hat{a}_{T+1} - \bar{a}_{T+1}) = \lim_{T\to\infty} -\hat{u}'_0 q_T \bar{a}_{T+1} \leq 0,$$

such that $\sum_{t=0}^{\infty} \beta^t \hat{u}_t > \sum_{t=0}^{\infty} \beta^t \bar{u}_t$. Satisfying $\lim_{T\to\infty} q_T \hat{a}_{T+1} = 0$ therefore is optimal.

B.2 Representative Household

According to the *Sonnenschein-Mantel-Debreu theorem*, aggregate demand functions possess less structure than the underlying demand functions of individual households. While both aggregate and individual demand functions are homogeneous of degree zero and satisfy Walras's law, the former generally do not satisfy the restrictions imposed by individual rationality; for example, consistency with the weak axiom of revealed preference and symmetry of the Slutsky matrix. This is a consequence of the fact that aggregate demand blends household-specific wealth effects (of price changes), which may differ when endowments and preferences are heterogeneous.

Since aggregate demand functions cannot generally be viewed as representing the demand of a single, fictional decision maker, we need to impose additional assumptions if we want to interpret macroeconomic aggregates through the lens of demand theory. One strategy is to assume that all households in the economy literally are alike, such that average outcomes are identical to the individual choices of the typical, *representative household*. Other strategies require that we restrict household preferences or the wealth distribution. We consider two examples.

Suppose first that preferences of each household h admit an indirect utility function, v^h, of the *Gorman form*,

$$v^h(p, w^h) = a^h(p) + b(p)w^h,$$

where p denotes the price vector; w^h denotes household wealth; and a^h and b are differentiable functions. Using *Roy's Identity*, household h's (vector valued) demand function, $x^h(p, w^h)$, satisfies

$$x^h(p, w^h) = -\frac{\partial v^h(p, w^h)/\partial p}{\partial v^h(p, w^h)/\partial w^h} = -\frac{(\partial a^h(p)/\partial p) + (\partial b(p)/\partial p)w^h}{b(p)}.$$

Accordingly, aggregate demand is given by

$$\sum_h x^h(p, w^h) = -\frac{\sum_h \partial a^h(p)/\partial p}{b(p)} - \frac{\partial b(p)/\partial p}{b(p)}w,$$

where $w \equiv \sum_h w^h$.

Note that aggregate demand does not depend on the distribution of wealth because the function $b(p)$ is identical across households; that is, all households have parallel, straight Engel curves.[42] As a consequence, aggregate demand can be viewed as solving the program of a fictional, rational household—a *positive representative household*—with indirect utility function

$$v(p, w) = \sum_h a^h(p) + b(p)w.$$

By Roy's Identity, the demand of this fictional household satisfies

$$-\frac{\partial v(p, w)/\partial p}{\partial v(p, w)/\partial w} = -\frac{\sum_h \partial a^h(p)/\partial p}{b(p)} - \frac{\partial b(p)/\partial p}{b(p)}w,$$

which corresponds to aggregate demand.

Suppose next that each household h has generalized CIES preferences,

$$\sum_{t=0}^{\infty} \beta^t \frac{(\phi + \chi c_t^h)^{1-\sigma}}{1-\sigma},$$

where $\sigma > 0, \phi \geq 0, \chi > 0$; β denotes the discount factor; and c_t^h denotes consumption. Let p_t denote the price of consumption at date t with $p_0 = 1$. The Euler equation and intertemporal budget

---

[42] The reverse implication holds as well: If aggregate demand is to be independent of the wealth distribution for any price vector, then households must have preferences that admit indirect utility functions of the Gorman form with identical $b(p)$. Identical, homothetic, or quasilinear preferences satisfy this restriction.

constraint of household h imply

$$(\phi + \chi c_t^h) = (\beta^{-t} p_t)^{-\frac{1}{\sigma}} (\phi + \chi c_0^h),$$

$$\sum_{t=0}^{\infty} c_t^h p_t = w^h.$$

Due to market completeness and the functional form assumption for preferences, the equilibrium conditions can be summed across households.[43] Letting $c_t \equiv \sum_h c_t^h$, we have

$$(\phi + \chi c_t) = (\beta^{-t} p_t)^{-\frac{1}{\sigma}} (\phi + \chi c_0),$$

$$\sum_{t=0}^{\infty} c_t p_t = w,$$

which constitute the optimality conditions of a positive representative household that chooses aggregate consumption subject to the aggregate budget constraint.

An economy admits a *normative representative household* when it admits a positive representative household whose preference relation constitutes a meaningful welfare measure. Suppose that there exists a wealth distribution rule which maps prices and aggregate wealth into household wealth, $\{w^h(p, w)\}_h$, such that aggregate demand, $\sum_h x^h(p, w^h(p, w))$, solves the program of a positive representative household. Moreover, suppose that for some social welfare function, W, the wealth distribution is optimal; that is, for any (p, w) the wealth distribution rule solves the program

$$\max_{\{w^h\}_h} W\left(\{v^h(p, w^h)\}_h\right) \text{ s.t. } \sum_h w^h = w.$$

The positive representative household then is a normative representative household and the social welfare function is the utility function of the normative representative household.

When preferences admit indirect utility functions of the Gorman form, then the positive representative household is a normative one. This follows from the fact that any wealth distribution is optimal with respect to the *utilitarian social welfare function* which gives equal weight to all households.[44]

B.3   Transversality Condition in Infinite-Horizon Planner Problem

Using the notation of subsection 3.1.6, let $g(k_t) \equiv k_t(1 - \delta) + f(k_t, 1)$. Note that the function g is strictly concave. The program is given by

$$\max_{\{k_{t+1}\}_{t \geq 0}} \sum_{t=0}^{\infty} \beta^t u(g(k_t) - k_{t+1}) \text{ s.t. } k_0 \text{ given, } k_{t+1} \geq 0.$$

Let $\hat{k} \equiv \{\hat{k}_{t+1}\}_{t \geq 0}$ denote a plan that satisfies the Euler equation and complementary slackness condition, $\hat{u}'_t = \beta g'(\hat{k}_{t+1}) \hat{u}'_{t+1} + \hat{\mu}_t$ and $\hat{\mu}_t \hat{k}_{t+1} = 0$ respectively, at all times, as well as $\lim_{T \to \infty} \beta^T \hat{u}'_T \hat{k}_{T+1} = 0$.

---

[43] Market completeness implies that all households share the same marginal rates of substitution. The functional form assumption implies that the Euler equation is linear in consumption. The budget constraint also is linear in consumption.

[44] Since $b(p)$ is the same for all households, changes in the wealth distribution do not affect social welfare when the social welfare function is utilitarian.

Let $\bar{k} \equiv \{\bar{k}_{t+1}\}_{t\geq0}$ denote an alternative plan that satisfies the Euler equation and complementary slackness condition as well as $\lim_{T\to\infty} \beta^T \bar{u}'_T \bar{k}_{T+1} \geq 0$. Here, we let $\hat{u}_t \equiv u(g(\hat{k}_t) - \hat{k}_{t+1})$ and $\hat{u}'_t \equiv u'(g(\hat{k}_t) - \hat{k}_{t+1})$ and similarly for $\bar{u}_t$ and $\bar{u}'_t$. We want to show that $\hat{k}$ dominates $\bar{k}$.

Strict concavity of u and g and positive marginal utility imply $\hat{u}_t + \hat{u}'_t g'(\hat{k}_t)(\bar{k}_t - \hat{k}_t) - \hat{u}'_t(\bar{k}_{t+1} - \hat{k}_{t+1}) > \bar{u}_t$ if $\hat{k}_t \neq \bar{k}_t$ or $\hat{k}_{t+1} \neq \bar{k}_{t+1}$. If $\hat{k}_{t+1} \neq \bar{k}_{t+1}$ for some $t \in \{0, \ldots, T\}$, we thus have

$$\sum_{t=0}^{T} \beta^t(\bar{u}_t - \hat{u}_t) \quad < \quad \sum_{t=0}^{T} \beta^t\{\hat{u}'_t g'(\hat{k}_t)(\bar{k}_t - \hat{k}_t) - \hat{u}'_t(\bar{k}_{t+1} - \hat{k}_{t+1})\}$$

$$= \quad \beta^T \hat{u}'_T(\hat{k}_{T+1} - \bar{k}_{T+1}) - \sum_{t=0}^{T-1} \beta^t \hat{\mu}_t \bar{k}_{t+1},$$

where we use $\hat{k}_0 = \bar{k}_0$, the Euler equation, and the complementary slackness condition. If $\hat{k}$ is not identical to $\bar{k}$, it follows that

$$\lim_{T\to\infty} \sum_{t=0}^{T} \beta^t(\bar{u}_t - \hat{u}_t) \quad < \quad \lim_{T\to\infty} \left\{ \beta^T \hat{u}'_T(\hat{k}_{T+1} - \bar{k}_{T+1}) - \sum_{t=0}^{T-1} \beta^t \hat{\mu}_t \bar{k}_{t+1} \right\}$$

$$= \quad -\lim_{T\to\infty} \left\{ \beta^T \hat{u}'_T \bar{k}_{T+1} + \sum_{t=0}^{T-1} \beta^t \hat{\mu}_t \bar{k}_{t+1} \right\} \leq 0,$$

since marginal utility, the capital stock, and the multiplier are all weakly positive. We conclude that $\sum_{t=0}^{\infty} \beta^t \hat{u}_t > \sum_{t=0}^{\infty} \beta^t \bar{u}_t$. Satisfying $\lim_{T\to\infty} \beta^T \hat{u}'_T \hat{k}_{T+1} = 0$ therefore is optimal.

B.4   Nonexpected Utility

Let U_t denote the utility derived from a consumption sequence starting at date t, $\{c_t(\epsilon^t), c_{t+1}(\epsilon^{t+1}), \ldots\}$. For legibility, we omit the reference to histories when there is no danger of confusion. We consider *recursive preference* specifications of the form

$$U_t = \mathcal{A}\left(c_t, \mathcal{B}^{-1}\left(\mathbb{E}_t[\mathcal{B}(U_{t+1})]\right)\right),$$

where the function $\mathcal{A}$ is homogeneous of degree one and the functions $\mathcal{A}$ and $\mathcal{B}$ are increasing and concave. Note that $\mathcal{B}^{-1}(\mathbb{E}_t[\mathcal{B}(U_{t+1})])$ is the *certainty equivalent* of the random variable U_{t+1}, conditional on information at date t. That is,

$$\mathcal{B}(\text{CE}_t[U_{t+1}]) = \mathbb{E}_t[\mathcal{B}(U_{t+1})],$$

where CE_t denotes the certainty equivalent operator.

We adopt the functional form assumptions

$$\mathcal{A}(c, C) \quad \equiv \quad \left((1-\beta)c^{1-\sigma} + \beta C^{1-\sigma}\right)^{\frac{1}{1-\sigma}}, \quad \beta \in (0,1), \sigma > 0, \sigma \neq 0,$$

$$\mathcal{B}(U) \quad \equiv \quad \frac{U^{1-\gamma}}{1-\gamma}, \quad \gamma > 0, \gamma \neq 0,$$

implying

$$U_t = \left((1-\beta)c_t^{1-\sigma} + \beta\left(\mathbb{E}_t\left[U_{t+1}^{1-\gamma}\right]\right)^{\frac{1-\sigma}{1-\gamma}}\right)^{\frac{1}{1-\sigma}}. \tag{B.1}$$

Since $\mathcal{B}^{-1}(\mathbb{E}_t[\mathcal{B}(U_{t+1})])$ is the certainty equivalent of U_{t+1}, γ represents a measure of risk aversion. In contrast, σ is an (inverse) measure of the intertemporal elasticity of substitution. To see this, suppose that the consumption sequence is deterministic. Equation (B.1) then reduces to

$$U_t = \left((1-\beta)c_t^{1-\sigma} + \beta U_{t+1}^{1-\sigma}\right)^{\frac{1}{1-\sigma}}$$

or, defining $\bar{U}_t \equiv U_t^{1-\sigma}$,

$$\bar{U}_t = (1-\beta)c_t^{1-\sigma} + \beta\bar{U}_{t+1} = (1-\beta)\sum_{s=t}^{\infty}\beta^{s-t}c_s^{1-\sigma}.$$

Absent risk, U_t thus exhibits a constant intertemporal elasticity of substitution, σ^{-1}.

When $\gamma = \sigma$, we recover standard expected utility. Equation (B.1) then implies

$$U_t = \left((1-\beta)c_t^{1-\sigma} + \beta\mathbb{E}_t\left[U_{t+1}^{1-\sigma}\right]\right)^{\frac{1}{1-\sigma}}$$

or

$$\bar{U}_t = (1-\beta)\sum_{s=t}^{\infty}\beta^{s-t}\mathbb{E}_t\left[c_s^{1-\sigma}\right].$$

We conclude that relative to the benchmark specification with $\gamma = \sigma$, the more general *nonexpected utility* specification (B.1) decouples risk aversion and the intertemporal elasticity of substitution.

Differences between γ and σ imply a preference for early or late resolution of risk. To establish this, we consider an environment with a single source of risk, namely a permanent shock to consumption at date $t = 1$. We assume that consumption at date $t = 0$ is certain and equals c, while consumption at dates $t \geq 1$ equals either x or y, with equal probability. We compare two scenarios. In the first scenario (early resolution), risk is resolved at date $t = 0$; that is, the household learns at date $t = 0$ whether consumption starting at date $t = 1$ equals x or y. In the second scenario (late resolution), the household only learns this at date $t = 1$.

We determine first the utility at date $t = 1$, conditional on knowing that current and future consumption equals x, U^x. Due to stationarity,

$$U^x = \left((1-\beta)x^{1-\sigma} + \beta(U^x)^{1-\sigma}\right)^{\frac{1}{1-\sigma}},$$

implying $U^x = x$. Similarly, utility conditional on knowing that consumption equals y is given by $U^y = y$. Turning next to the utility at date $t = 0$, consider first the scenario with *early resolution of risk*. Utility at date $t = 0$, conditional on learning that consumption will equal x or y, respectively, is given by

$$U_0|x = \left((1-\beta)c^{1-\sigma} + \beta x^{1-\sigma}\right)^{\frac{1}{1-\sigma}},$$

$$U_0|y = \left((1-\beta)c^{1-\sigma} + \beta y^{1-\sigma}\right)^{\frac{1}{1-\sigma}},$$

and utility before information is revealed equals the certainty equivalent of the risky utility U_0,

$$U^{\text{early}} = \left(\frac{(U_0|x)^{1-\gamma} + (U_0|y)^{1-\gamma}}{2}\right)^{\frac{1}{1-\gamma}}.$$

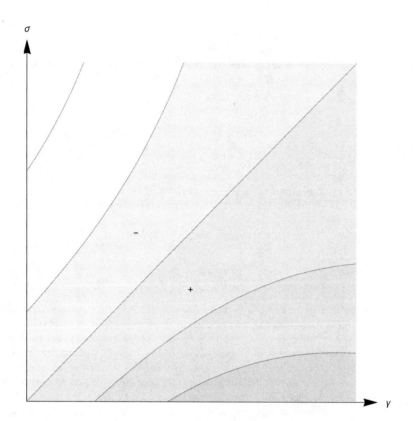

Figure B.1
Preference for early or late resolution of risk: $U^{\text{early}} - U^{\text{late}}$.

In contrast, utility at date $t = 0$ with *late resolution of risk* equals

$$U^{\text{late}} = \left((1-\beta)c^{1-\sigma} + \beta \left(\frac{x^{1-\gamma} + y^{1-\gamma}}{2} \right)^{\frac{1-\sigma}{1-\gamma}} \right)^{\frac{1}{1-\sigma}}.$$

When $\gamma = \sigma$ (the expected utility case), the timing of the resolution of risk does not affect utility, $U^{\text{early}} = U^{\text{late}}$. When $\gamma \neq \sigma$, in contrast, the timing does have welfare consequences because

$$\mathcal{A}(c, \text{CE}_0[U_1]) \neq \text{CE}_0[\mathcal{A}(c, U_1)].$$

Figure B.1 plots the level curves of $U^{\text{early}} - U^{\text{late}}$ against γ and σ; darker areas indicate higher values. Early (late) resolution is preferred when $\gamma > (<)\sigma$.

Returning to the general specification (B.1), we compute the stochastic discount factor at date t, history ϵ^t. Differentiating U_t with respect to $c_t(\epsilon^t)$ and $c_{t+1}(\epsilon^{t+1})$, respectively, yields

$$\frac{\partial U_t}{\partial c_t} = U_t^\sigma (1-\beta) c_t^{-\sigma},$$

$$\frac{\partial U_t}{\partial c_{t+1}} = U_t^\sigma \beta \left(CE_t(U_{t+1}) \right)^{\gamma-\sigma} (U_{t+1})^{-\gamma} h(\epsilon^{t+1}|\epsilon^t) \frac{\partial U_{t+1}}{\partial c_{t+1}},$$

where c_{t+1} and U_{t+1} denote consumption and continuation utility in history ϵ^{t+1}, and $h(\epsilon^{t+1}|\epsilon^t)$ denotes the probability (density) of ϵ^{t+1} conditional on ϵ^t.

We define the stochastic discount factor in the usual way, as

$$m_{t+1}(\epsilon^{t+1}) \equiv \frac{\partial U_t/\partial c_{t+1}}{\partial U_t/\partial c_t} \frac{1}{h(\epsilon^{t+1}|\epsilon^t)}.$$

Substituting the expressions for marginal utility yields

$$
\begin{aligned}
m_{t+1}(\epsilon^{t+1}) &= \frac{U_t^\sigma \beta \left(CE_t(U_{t+1}) \right)^{\gamma-\sigma} (U_{t+1})^{-\gamma} \frac{\partial U_{t+1}}{\partial c_{t+1}}}{U_t^\sigma (1-\beta) c_t^{-\sigma}} \\
&= \frac{\beta \left(CE_t(U_{t+1}) \right)^{\gamma-\sigma} (U_{t+1})^{-\gamma} U_{t+1}^\sigma (1-\beta) c_{t+1}^{-\sigma}}{(1-\beta) c_t^{-\sigma}} \\
&= \beta \left(\frac{c_{t+1}}{c_t} \right)^{-\sigma} \left(\frac{CE_t(U_{t+1})}{U_{t+1}} \right)^{\gamma-\sigma}.
\end{aligned}
$$

When $\gamma = \sigma$, this expression reduces to $m_{t+1}(\epsilon^{t+1}) = \beta(c_{t+1}/c_t)^{-\sigma}$. Otherwise, the stochastic discount factor, and thus asset prices, are a function not only of consumption in the two periods but also of the continuation value and its certainty equivalent.

B.5 Linear Rational Expectations Models

B.5.1 Single Equation Model

B.5.1.1 Backward- and Forward-Solution of a Difference Equation Consider the difference equation

$$x_{t+1} = \alpha x_t + s_t,$$

where the variable x_t is endogenous and predetermined and the variable s_t is exogenous. The sequence $\{s_t\}_{t\geq 0}$ is bounded. Iterating the equation backward yields

$$x_{t+1} = s_t + \alpha s_{t-1} + \alpha^2 s_{t-2} + \ldots + \alpha^t s_0 + \alpha^{t+1} x_0.$$

Iterating forward implies

$$x_{t+T} = \alpha^T x_t + \alpha^{T-1} s_t + \alpha^{T-2} s_{t+1} + \ldots + \alpha s_{t+T-2} + s_{t+T-1}.$$

When $|\alpha| < 1$, then $\lim_{T\to\infty} x_{t+T}$ is bounded irrespective of the value of x_t. When $|\alpha| > 1$, in contrast, this does not hold true. To see this, define

$$x_t^\star \equiv -\lim_{T\to\infty} \sum_{j=1}^{T} \frac{s_{t+j-1}}{\alpha^j}.$$

Since $\{s_t\}_{t\geq 0}$ is bounded and $|\alpha| > 1$, $x_t^\star$ is well defined. When $x_t = x_t^\star$, $\lim_{T\to\infty} x_{t+T}$ equals zero. But when $x_t = x_t^\star + \Delta$ with $\Delta \neq 0$, x_{t+T} diverges as T increases. We conclude that for $|\alpha| > 1$ there exists a unique value for x_t, namely $x_t^\star$, such that $\{x_t\}_{t\geq 0}$ is bounded.

B.5.1.2　Rational Expectations Model　Consider next a stochastic (but still bounded) sequence $\{s_t\}_{t\geq 0}$.[45] The model is given by two conditions. First, the difference equation

$$\mathbb{E}_t[y_{t+1}] = \alpha y_t + s_t \quad \text{or} \quad y_{t+1} = \alpha y_t + s_t + \delta_{t+1},$$

where the variable y_t is endogenous and nonpredetermined, and δ_{t+1} denotes a forecast error satisfying $\mathbb{E}_t[\delta_{t+1}] = 0$. And second, the restriction that $\lim_{T\to\infty} \mathbb{E}_t[y_{t+T}]$ be bounded.

Iterating forward and using the law of iterated expectations yields

$$\mathbb{E}_t[y_{t+T}] = \alpha^T y_t + \alpha^{T-1} s_t + \mathbb{E}_t[\alpha^{T-2} s_{t+1} + \ldots + \alpha s_{t+T-2} + s_{t+T-1}].$$

When $|\alpha| < 1$, then $\lim_{T\to\infty} \mathbb{E}_t[y_{t+T}]$ is bounded irrespective of the value of y_t. That is, the model restrictions do not determine the actual realization of y_t, but only its expectation, $\mathbb{E}_{t-1}[y_t] = \alpha y_{t-1} + s_{t-1}$. The model thus allows for a *sunspot shock* to affect y_t.

When $|\alpha| > 1$, in contrast, boundedness of $\lim_{T\to\infty} \mathbb{E}_t[y_{t+T}]$ requires that y_t equals

$$y_t^\star \equiv -\lim_{T\to\infty} \mathbb{E}_t \sum_{j=1}^{T} \frac{s_{t+j-1}}{\alpha^j},$$

for parallel reasons as in the deterministic case. The model determines the expectation, $\mathbb{E}_{t-1}[y_t] = \alpha y_{t-1} + s_{t-1}$, and it also determines the actual realization, $y_t = y_t^\star$. As in the case with $|\alpha| < 1$, the forecast error $\delta_t = y_t^\star - \mathbb{E}_{t-1}[y_t]$ is unpredictable. But unlike in that case, the forecast error only reflects the effect of new information about $\{s_{t+j}\}_{j\geq 0}$ on $y_t^\star$; the model does not allow for a sunspot shock to affect y_t.

B.5.2　Multiple Equation Model

The *model* consists of the system of difference equations

$$\begin{bmatrix} x_{t+1} \\ \mathbb{E}_t[y_{t+1}] \end{bmatrix} = M \begin{bmatrix} x_t \\ y_t \end{bmatrix} + N s_t \tag{B.2}$$

or equivalently,

$$\begin{bmatrix} x_{t+1} \\ {\scriptstyle (n_x \times 1)} \\ y_{t+1} \\ {\scriptstyle (n_y \times 1)} \end{bmatrix} = \underset{(n \times n)}{M} \begin{bmatrix} x_t \\ {\scriptstyle (n_x \times 1)} \\ y_t \\ {\scriptstyle (n_y \times 1)} \end{bmatrix} + \underset{(n \times n_s)(n_s \times 1)}{N \quad s_t} + \begin{bmatrix} 0 \\ {\scriptstyle (n_x \times 1)} \\ \delta_{t+1} \\ {\scriptstyle (n_y \times 1)} \end{bmatrix}.$$

There are n_x predetermined variables (including, for example, the capital stock), denoted by x_t; n_y nonpredetermined variables (e.g., consumption), denoted by y_t; and n_s exogenous bounded variables (e.g., productivity), denoted by s_t. The number of endogenous variables equals $n = n_x + n_y$, and δ_t denotes a vector of forecast errors. The model imposes the additional restriction that the endogenous variables be bounded.

---

[45] To simplify the notation, we do not index variables by history.

Using the notation of appendix A.3, matrix M can be represented as the product of matrices that contain its eigenvectors and eigenvalues,

$$M = VPV^{-1} \equiv [v_1 \; v_2 \cdots v_n] \underset{(n \times n)}{\begin{bmatrix} \rho_1 & & 0 \\ & \ddots & \\ 0 & & \rho_n \end{bmatrix}} \underset{(n \times n)}{V^{-1}} \equiv V \begin{bmatrix} \underset{(n_< \times n_<)}{P_{<<}} & \underset{(n_< \times n_>)}{0} \\ \underset{(n_> \times n_<)}{0} & \underset{(n_> \times n_>)}{P_{>>}} \end{bmatrix} V^{-1},$$

where $n_<$ $(n_>)$ denotes the number of eigenvalues whose absolute value is weakly smaller than (exceeds) unity, respectively. We assume that the eigenvalues are distinct and real and ordered in ascending absolute value, $|\rho_1| < |\rho_2| < \ldots < |\rho_n|$. Let

$$Z_t \equiv \begin{bmatrix} \underset{(n_< \times 1)}{Z_{<t}} \\ \underset{(n_> \times 1)}{Z_{>t}} \end{bmatrix} \equiv V^{-1} \begin{bmatrix} x_t \\ y_t \end{bmatrix} \quad \text{and} \quad \begin{bmatrix} \underset{(n_< \times n_s)}{N_<} \\ \underset{(n_> \times n_s)}{N_>} \end{bmatrix} \equiv V^{-1}N. \tag{B.3}$$

Premultiplying equation (B.2) by V^{-1} yields $\mathbb{E}_t[Z_{t+1}] = PZ_t + V^{-1}Ns_t$. Iterating forward, we arrive at

$$\mathbb{E}_t[Z_{t+T}] = P^T Z_t + \sum_{j=0}^{T-1} P^{T-1-j} V^{-1} N \mathbb{E}_t[s_{t+j}].$$

Boundedness ($\lim_{T \to \infty} \mathbb{E}_t[Z_{t+T}] = 0$) thus requires

$$\lim_{T \to \infty} \left((P_{>>})^T Z_{>t} + \sum_{j=0}^{T-1} (P_{>>})^{T-1-j} N_> \mathbb{E}_t[s_{t+j}] \right) = 0$$

or

$$Z_{>t}^\star = - \sum_{j=0}^{\infty} (P_{>>})^{-1-j} N_> \mathbb{E}_t[s_{t+j}].$$

That is, the requirement that system dynamics be stable imposes $n_>$ restrictions on Z_t. The initial conditions for the predetermined variables x_t impose n_x additional restrictions. We may distinguish three cases:

B.5.2.1   No Solution, $n_y < n_>$ With $n_y < n_>$ (and thus, $n_x > n_<$), the stability requirement imposes more restrictions than there are nonpredetermined variables that could adjust to satisfy them. In general, the model has *no solution* in this case.

B.5.2.2   Determinate Solution, $n_y = n_>$ With $n_y = n_>$ the stability requirement imposes as many restrictions as there are nonpredetermined variables. From condition (B.3), the nonpredetermined variables, $y_t^\star$, satisfy

$$\begin{bmatrix} Z_{<t} \\ Z_{>t}^\star \end{bmatrix} = V^{-1} \begin{bmatrix} x_t \\ y_t^\star \end{bmatrix}.$$

Since $n_y = n_>$, this equation can be solved for $y_t^\star$ as long as the relevant submatrix of V^{-1} is invertible; all endogenous variables thus are uniquely *determined*. The model dynamics satisfy

$$Z_{t+1} = \begin{bmatrix} P_{<<} & 0 \\ 0 & 0 \end{bmatrix} Z_t + \begin{bmatrix} N_< \\ 0 \end{bmatrix} s_t + \begin{bmatrix} \underset{(n_< \times n_>)}{0} \\ \underset{(n_> \times n_>)}{I} \end{bmatrix} Z_{>t+1}^\star.$$

or

$$
\begin{bmatrix} x_{t+1} \\ y_{t+1} \end{bmatrix} = V \begin{bmatrix} P_{<<} & 0 \\ 0 & 0 \end{bmatrix} V^{-1} \begin{bmatrix} x_t \\ y_t \end{bmatrix} + V \begin{bmatrix} N_< \\ 0 \end{bmatrix} s_t + V \begin{bmatrix} 0 \\ I \end{bmatrix} Z^{\star}_{>t+1}. \tag{B.4}
$$

The forecast error, $\delta_{t+1} = y_{t+1} - \mathbb{E}_t[y_{t+1}]$, reflects the effect of new information about $\{s_{t+j}\}_{j \geq 1}$ on $Z^{\star}_{>t+1}$.

B.5.2.3   Indeterminate Solution, $n_y > n_>$ With $n_y > n_>$ the stability requirement does *not pin down* all nonpredetermined variables; there are $n_y - n_>$ degrees of freedom. Suppose, for example, that $n_x = n_s = 0$ such that the model reduces to

$$
y_{t+1} = My_t + \delta_{t+1}
$$

and $Z^{\star}_{>t} = 0$. In this case, $n_<$ elements of y_t can freely be chosen in each period without triggering explosive dynamics. Although $s_t = 0$ in all periods, the forecast errors may be nonzero. In particular, y_t may respond to nonfundamental sunspot shocks.

B.6   Ramsey Taxation

Consider a complete markets economy with N goods and H households. Firms operate a constant-returns-to-scale technology; the function f characterizes the production frontier, $y_1 = f(y_2, \ldots, y_N)$, and y denotes the vector of net outputs. Firms take the vector of *producer prices*, p, as given and maximize profits. Price taking and constant returns to scale imply that profits equal zero. Alternatively, firms are price takers and all profits are fully taxed away.

Household h takes the vector of *consumer prices*, q, as given and chooses the vector of net demands, x^h, to maximize utility, u^h, subject to its budget constraint. The net demand vector includes, for example, demand for consumption or supply (negative demand) of labor. The demand function of household h for good j is denoted $x^h_j(q)$ and its demand function for all goods is denoted $x^h(q)$. The household's *indirect utility function*, v^h, is defined as

$$
v^h(q) \equiv \max_{x^h} u^h(x^h) \text{ s.t. } q \cdot x^h = 0.
$$

It maps consumer prices into maximal utility. Let $x \equiv \sum_h x^h$ and $x(q) \equiv \sum_h x^h(q)$.

The government maximizes a *social welfare function*, v, which aggregates household utilities $(u^1, \ldots, u^H)$. The government has access to a technology whose production frontier is characterized by the function g, $z_1 = g(z_2, \ldots, z_N)$; z denotes the vector of government net outputs. The government also has access to good-specific, proportional *excise taxes*; these taxes drive a wedge between consumer and producer prices, $q \neq p$.

Market clearing requires $x = y + z$. When firms and households satisfy their budget constraints and all markets clear, Walras's law implies that the government satisfies its budget constraint as well.

B.6.1   Primal Approach

We first abstract from government production and assume that the government has an exogenous resource requirement for good 1, $z_1 \leq 0$; all other components of z equal zero. In a competitive equilibrium, the first-order conditions of households and firms, the budget constraints of households, the market clearing condition, and the technological constraint are satisfied, respectively,

$$
\begin{aligned}
\frac{u_i^h(x^h)}{u_1^h(x^h)} &= \frac{q_i}{q_1}, \\
-f_i(y_2, \ldots, y_N) &= p_i/p_1, \ i > 1, \\
q \cdot x^h &= 0, \\
x &= y + z, \\
y_1 &= f(y_2, \ldots, y_N).
\end{aligned}
$$

The government chooses x, y, p, and q subject to these constraints. Note that we can normalize $p_1 = q_1 = 1$ because the equilibrium conditions only include relative producer and consumer prices (because households do not receive exogenous income).

From the first-order conditions of firms, the government can select any point on the production frontier by choosing p. This choice does not affect household demand because the government may choose q independently of p and there are no profits. Accordingly, the first-order conditions of firms do not constrain the government; they only determine the price vector p that supports a feasible y. We may therefore drop the first-order conditions of firms, and thus p, from the set of equilibrium conditions that constrain the Ramsey government.

Further simplifying these conditions, we substitute the households' marginal rates of substitution for consumer prices, thus arriving at

$$
\begin{aligned}
\frac{u_i^1(x^1)}{u_1^1(x^1)} &= \frac{u_i^h(x^h)}{u_1^h(x^h)}, \\
\sum_{i=1}^{N} u_i^h(x^h)x_i^h &= 0, \\
x_1 - z_1 &= f(x_2, \ldots, x_N).
\end{aligned}
$$

The first two conditions, the *implementability constraints*, reflect equilibrium in the household sector: Marginal rates of substitution are equal across households because all households face the same consumer prices; and each household satisfies its budget constraint with prices expressed in terms of marginal rates of substitution. The last condition imposes market clearing and the technological constraint.

Note that the equations above do not involve prices. The *Ramsey program* thus can be specified as a constrained choice of allocation; this is referred to as the *primal approach*. Note also that the constraint set is smaller than the constraint set of a social planner; the latter need not satisfy the implementability constraints. Finally, note that restrictions on the admissible tax instruments— for example that certain tax rates have to be equal to each other—would give rise to additional implementability constraints.

Suppose that $H = 1$ such that there is just one implementability constraint. The Ramsey program then reads

$$
\max_x u^1(x) \ \text{s.t.} \ \sum_{i=1}^{N} u_i^1(x)x_i = 0, \ x_1 - z_1 = f(x_2, \ldots, x_N).
$$

Letting λ and μ denote the multipliers associated with the implementability and resource constraint, respectively, the first-order conditions are given by

$$
\begin{aligned}
u_1^1(x)[1 + \lambda(1 - E_1)] &= \mu, \\
u_j^1(x)[1 + \lambda(1 - E_j)] &= -\mu f_j(x_2, \ldots, x_N), \quad j > 1,
\end{aligned}
$$

where we define

$$
E_j \equiv -\sum_{i=1}^{N} \frac{u_{ji}^1(x)x_i}{u_j^1(x)}
$$

as the sum of the elasticities of marginal utility, $u_j^1(x)$, with respect to each of the goods. A social planner not bound by the implementability constraint ($\lambda = 0$) optimally sets all marginal rates of substitution equal to the corresponding marginal rates of transformation. The Ramsey government does not have that option because equilibrium and specifically, government budget balance, require distorting taxes (unless $z_1 = 0$ such that the implementability constraint is slack).

Since $u_j^1(x) = \alpha^1 q_j$ where α^1 denotes the household's *marginal utility of income* (from the household's first-order condition), and since $p_1 = q_1 = 1$, the first-order conditions can be written as

$$
\begin{aligned}
\alpha^1[1 + \lambda(1 - E_1)] &= \mu, \\
\alpha^1 q_j[1 + \lambda(1 - E_j)] &= \mu p_j, \quad j > 1.
\end{aligned}
$$

Solving the former equation for λ and substituting into the latter yields

$$
\frac{q_j - p_j}{q_j} = 1 - \frac{\alpha^1}{\mu}[1 + \lambda(1 - E_j)] = \frac{\mu - \alpha^1}{\mu} \frac{E_j - E_1}{1 - E_1}, \quad j > 1.
$$

If $-E_1 \rightarrow \infty$ (completely inelastic demand for good 1), the term on the right-hand side of the last equality is independent of j, which implies that optimal tax rates are uniform across goods 2 to N. (Taxes on the first good are normalized to zero.) If $-E_1 \rightarrow 0$ (completely elastic demand for good 1), then there are no income effects on $x_j, j > 1$, and the optimal tax rates are proportional to E_j. If, moreover, the cross-partials of the utility function equal zero (independent demands), then E_j reduces to the inverse of the own-price elasticity and optimal tax rates are inversely proportional to the price elasticity.[46]

Suppose that $u(x) \equiv u(w(x_1, \ldots, x_n), x_{n+1}, \ldots, x_N)$ where the function w is homothetic. This implies that E_j is the same for all $j \leq n$, and thus that the first-order conditions combine to

$$
\frac{u_j^1(x)}{u_1^1(x)} = -f_j(x_2, \ldots, x_N), \quad 1 < j \leq n.
$$

Equivalently, $q_j/p_j = q_1/p_1$; that is, the optimal *ad valorem tax rates* on goods 1 to n are *uniform* (and equal to zero since we normalized the tax rate on good 1 to zero).

B.6.2   Dual Approach

For the *dual approach*, we use the indirect utility functions and specify the Ramsey program as a choice of prices and thus taxes, rather than allocation. We allow for government production and

---

[46] From $u_j^1(x) = q_j\alpha^1$, we have $u_{jj}^1(x)x_j'(q_j) = \alpha^1$ and thus, $E_j = -u_{jj}^1(x)x_j/u_j^1(x) = -x_j/[x_j'(q_j)q_j]$.

multiple households and let $v(q) \equiv v(v^1(q), \dots, v^H(q))$. Normalizing $p_1 = q_1 = 1$, the program reads

$$\max_{q_2,\dots,q_N,z_2,\dots,z_N} v(q) \text{ s.t. } x_1(q) - g(z_2,\dots,z_N) = f(x_2(q) - z_2,\dots,x_N(q) - z_N)$$

and the first-order conditions are given by

$$0 = \lambda\Big(f_j(x_2(q) - z_2,\dots,x_N(q) - z_N) - g_j(z_2,\dots,z_N)\Big),\ j > 1,$$

$$\frac{\partial v(q)}{\partial q_j} = \lambda\left(\frac{\partial x_1(q)}{\partial q_j} - \sum_{i=2}^{N} f_i \frac{\partial x_i(q)}{\partial q_j}\right),\ j > 1.$$

The first condition represents optimality of z_j. It implies that as long as resources are scarce ($\lambda \neq 0$), *production efficiency* is optimal: The marginal rates of transformation should be equalized across the private and the public sectors and more generally, across all productive sectors. Production efficiency rules out sector-specific taxes on production factors (e.g., sector-specific investment subsidies; taxes on goods used as intermediate inputs in certain sectors; sector-specific payroll taxes; or tariffs that drive a wedge between domestic and world market producer prices). Note that the production efficiency condition implies the uniform commodity taxation result.

The second condition represents optimality of q_j. Using the equilibrium expression for producer prices, $p_i = -f_i(y_2, \dots, y_N)$, and letting $t_j \equiv q_j - p_j$, it can be written as[47]

$$\frac{\partial v(q)}{\partial q_j} = \lambda \sum_{i=1}^{N} p_i \frac{\partial x_i(q)}{\partial q_j} = -\lambda \frac{\partial}{\partial t_j} \sum_{i=1}^{N} t_i x_i(p + t).$$

At the optimum, a price change thus affects the social welfare function proportionally to the resource cost of meeting the induced change in demand, or proportionally to the induced change in tax revenue. The latter result would also have followed if we had maximized the social welfare function subject to the government budget constraint (for given producer prices) rather than the resource constraint.

By Roy's Identity, $\partial v^h(q)/\partial q_j = -\alpha^h x_j^h(q)$, where α^h denotes household h's marginal utility of income. Letting $\beta^h \equiv \alpha^h \partial v(q)/\partial v^h$ denote household h's *social marginal utility of income*, the first-order condition with respect to prices can be expressed as

$$\sum_{h=1}^{H} \beta^h x_j^h(q) = \lambda \sum_{h=1}^{H} \left(x_j^h(q) + \sum_{i=1}^{N} t_i s_{ij}^h(q) - x_j^h(q) \sum_{i=1}^{N} t_i \frac{\partial x_i^h(q)}{\partial I}\right).$$

Here, s_{ij}^h denotes the derivative of household h's compensated demand for good i with respect to q_j, and $\partial x_i^h(q)/\partial I$ denotes the income effect (the decomposition uses the Slutsky equation). Finally, letting $\gamma^h \equiv \beta^h/\lambda + \sum_{i=1}^{N} t_i \partial x_i^h(q)/\partial I$ denote the *social marginal valuation of income*—the marginal valuation of h's income given that this income also generates tax revenue—the condition simplifies to the *many-person Ramsey rule*,

$$\frac{\sum_{h=1}^{H}(\gamma^h - 1)x_j^h(q)}{x_j(q)} = \frac{\sum_{h=1}^{H}\sum_{i=1}^{N} t_i s_{ij}^h(q)}{x_j(q)}.$$

---

[47] The second equality uses the household budget constraint, $\sum_i (p_i + t_i)x_i(q) = 0$.

The right-hand side of the condition constitutes a measure of the tax induced substitution effects on $x_j(q)$ (using the symmetry of the Slutzky matrix). If producer prices were constant, consumers compensated, and the derivatives of compensated demand constant, then it would equal the relative change in demand for $x_j(q)$. The left-hand side accounts for differences in the social marginal valuation of income and the expenditure shares. If γ^h is the same for all households or $x_i^h(q)/x_i(q)$ the same across goods, then the left-hand side reduces to a constant and the tax-induced substitution effects are constant across goods. Otherwise, they are not.

Suppose the government can also levy a *poll tax*—a uniform lump-sum tax on all taxpayers; an excise tax on labor supply combined with a poll tax constitutes a linear labor income tax. Optimality then requires

$$\sum_{h=1}^{H} \beta^h = \lambda \sum_{h=1}^{H} \sum_{i=1}^{N} p_i \frac{\partial x_i^h(q)}{\partial I}.$$

Since

$$\sum_{h=1}^{H} \sum_{i=1}^{N} p_i \frac{\partial x_i^h(q)}{\partial I} = \sum_{h=1}^{H} \sum_{i=1}^{N} (q_i - t_i) \frac{\partial x_i^h(q)}{\partial I} = \sum_{h=1}^{H} \left(1 - \sum_{i=1}^{N} t_i \frac{\partial x_i^h(q)}{\partial I} \right),$$

we conclude that with a poll tax, the average γ^h equals unity. Accordingly, the left-hand side of the many-person Ramsey rule equals the covariance between γ^h and $x_i^h(q)/x_i(q)$. Under the Ramsey policy, the relative change in demand for good j is proportional to this covariance: Consumption of goods in strong demand by households with high social marginal valuation of income should be discouraged less.

With just one consumer, $v = v^1$ and the many-person Ramsey rule collapses to the condition

$$\gamma^1 - 1 = \frac{\sum_{i=1}^{N} t_i s_{ij}^1(q)}{x_j(q)}.$$

That is, the tax-induced substitution effects should be constant across goods. If a poll tax is available such that $\gamma^1 = 1$, no commodity taxes are levied.

B.7   Probabilistic Voting

Suppose that two political candidates, a and b, compete for office in a democratic election. Voters are indexed by $i \in [0, I]$. Which candidate a voter supports depends both on the candidate's policy platform and on the voter's *ideological* attachment. Voter i supports candidate a if the voter's utility in the equilibrium implemented by a's proposed policy choice (and the continuation policies induced by policy functions of future decision makers) exceeds the utility resulting from b's proposal by more than a threshold value. This threshold value, which reflects the voter's ideological attachment to candidate b, is a random variable with two components: A voter specific, i.i.d. component, ξ^i; and an aggregate component, ξ. Accordingly, the outcome of the vote is *probabilistic* as well.

The voter-specific component is drawn from a uniform distribution with density ϕ^i that is symmetric around zero, $\xi^i \sim U[-1/(2\phi^i), 1/(2\phi^i)]$. A positive ξ^i reflects a permanent ideological bias of voter i in favor of candidate b. The average bias across voters equals zero. The aggregate component is drawn from a uniform distribution with density φ, $\xi \sim U[-1/(2\varphi), 1/(2\varphi)]$. It represents an aggregate shock to ideological attachment, which is realized after the candidates have proposed their policy platforms. The sum of the two components represents the total ideological bias of voter i in favor of candidate b in the current election.

Let $V^i(a)$ and $V^i(b)$ denote utility of voter i when the policy platform of candidate a or b, respectively, is implemented. Voter i supports candidate a if and only if

$$V^i(a) \geq V^i(b) + \xi + \xi^i.$$

Let $\Delta^i \equiv V^i(a) - V^i(b)$. Conditional on ξ, the probability that i supports candidate a equals[48]

$$\mathrm{prob}(\xi^i \leq \Delta^i - \xi) = \frac{1}{2} + \phi^i \times (\Delta^i - \xi)$$

and candidate a's vote share conditional on ξ therefore equals

$$\frac{1}{2} + \frac{\int_i \phi^i \times (\Delta^i - \xi)di}{I}.$$

The unconditional probability that candidate a's vote share exceeds one-half is given by

$$\mathrm{prob}\left(\frac{\int_i \phi^i \times (\Delta^i - \xi)di}{I} \geq 0\right) = \mathrm{prob}\left(\frac{\int_i \phi^i \Delta^i di}{\int_i \phi^i di} \geq \xi\right) = \frac{1}{2} + \varphi \frac{\int_i \phi^i \Delta^i di}{\int_i \phi^i di}.$$

The probability that candidate b wins the election equals one minus the former expression.

Conditional on b's platform, candidate a's vote share is a continuous function of a's platform (unlike in the median-voter setup); the optimal platform choice maximizes $\int_i \phi^i \Delta^i di$. Similarly, candidate b's optimal choice minimizes this expression conditional on a's platform. In equilibrium, the policy platforms of the two candidates coincide and maximize the weighted sum of utilities,

$$\int_i \phi^i V^i(a)di = \int_i \phi^i V^i(b)di.$$

Note that the equilibrium platform attaches larger weight to the policy preferences of voters with low variability of ideological attachment (a large value for ϕ^i); voters that care a lot about policy relative to the candidate's other characteristics thus have more political influence. Intuitively, voters whose ideological attachment is unlikely to be biased are more likely to alter their political support in response to small changes in the policy platform. In equilibrium, these groups of *swing voters* thus tilt policy in their favor. If all voters are equally responsive to changes in the policy platform, electoral competition implements the utilitarian optimum with respect to voters.

B.8 Bibliographic Notes

Gorman (1953) and Lewbel (1989) derive conditions under which aggregate demand in an economy with heterogeneous households can be represented as the demand of a fictional representative household; see also Deaton and Muellbauer (1980, chapter 6). Caselli and Ventura (2000) analyze several dimensions of heterogeneity in a growth model with generalized CIES preferences. Kirman (1992) criticizes the "pseudo-microfoundations" (p. 125) of the representative household construct.

Stokey and Lucas (1989, theorem 4.15) and Acemoglu (2009, theorem 6.10) discuss the transversality condition in the infinite-horizon planner problem.

---

[48] To keep the notation simple, we assume that probabilities are interior.

Kreps and Porteus (1978) and Epstein and Zin (1989) provide axiomatic foundations for recursive, nonexpected utility specifications. Epstein and Zin (1989) and Weil (1989) analyze the asset pricing implications of the model discussed in section B.4; see also Bansal and Yaron (2004).

Sargent and Wallace (1973) discuss the forward solution and Blanchard and Kahn (1980) propose the solution strategy for linear rational expectations models, following Vaughan (1970).

Ramsey (1927) introduces the primal approach. Atkinson and Stiglitz (1972) establish the results discussed in subsection B.6.1. Diamond and Mirrlees (1971a; 1971b) introduce the dual approach and prove the production efficiency result. The many-person Ramsey rule is due to Diamond (1975). Atkinson and Stiglitz (1976) show that commodity taxes are superfluous: with a linear labor income tax, or with a nonlinear tax (Mirrlees, 1971) if preferences are weakly separable between consumption and leisure.

The probabilistic voting model is due to Lindbeck and Weibull (1987).

Related Topics and Additional References   Baqaee and Farhi (2018) study models of disaggregated household and production sectors.

Mas-Colell et al. (1995, sections 4.B–D, 17.E) cover aggregation, including the Sonnenschein-Mantel-Debreu and Gorman aggregation theorems. Miao (2014, chapter 2) reviews solution strategies for linear rational expectations models. Atkinson and Stiglitz (1980, chapters 12–14), Stiglitz (1987), and Salanié (2003, chapters 3–5) cover optimal taxation and Ramsey policies. Persson and Tabellini (2000, chapter 3) cover the probabilistic voting model.

Bibliography

Abreu, Dilip. 1988. On the theory of infinitely repeated games with discounting. *Econometrica* 56 (2): 383–396. (Cited on p. 240.)

Abreu, Dilip, David Pearce, and Ennio Stacchetti. 1986. Optimal cartel equilibria with imperfect monitoring. *Journal of Economic Theory* 39 (1): 251–269. (Cited on pp. 239 and 240.)

Abreu, Dilip, David Pearce, and Ennio Stacchetti. 1990. Toward a theory of discounted repeated games with imperfect monitoring. *Econometrica* 58 (5): 1041–1063. (Cited on pp. 239 and 240.)

Acemoglu, Daron. 2009. *Introduction to modern economic growth*. Princeton: Princeton University Press. (Cited on pp. 87, 243, 244, and 259.)

Adam, Klaus, and Henning Weber. 2019. Optimal trend inflation. *American Economic Review* 109 (2): 702–737. (Cited on p. 214.)

Aiyagari, S. Rao. 1994. Uninsured idiosyncratic risk and aggregate saving. *Quarterly Journal of Economics* 109 (3): 659–684. (Cited on pp. 53 and 87.)

Aiyagari, S. Rao. 1995. Optimal capital income taxation with incomplete markets, borrowing constraints, and constant discounting. *Journal of Political Economy* 103 (6): 1158–1175. (Cited on p. 213.)

Aiyagari, S. Rao, and Mark Gertler. 1985. The backing of government bonds and Monetarism. *Journal of Monetary Economics* 16 (1): 19–44. (Cited on p. 190.)

Aiyagari, S. Rao, and Ellen R. McGrattan. 1998. The optimal quantity of debt. *Journal of Monetary Economics* 42 (3): 447–469. (Cited on p. 190.)

Aiyagari, S. Rao, Albert Marcet, Thomas J. Sargent, and Juha Seppälä. 2002. Optimal taxation without state-contingent debt. *Journal of Political Economy* 110 (6): 1220–1254. (Cited on p. 213.)

Akerlof, George A. 1970. The market for lemons: Qualitative uncertainty and the market mechanism. *Quarterly Journal of Economics* 84 (3): 488–500. (Cited on p. 126.)

Akerlof, George A., and Janet L. Yellen. 1985. A near-rational model of the business cycle, with wage and price inertia. *Quarterly Journal of Economics* 100 (Supplement): 823–838. (Cited on p. 159.)

Allais, Maurice. 1947. *Economie et interet*. Paris: Imprimerie Nationale. (Cited on p. 38.)

Alvarez, Fernando, and Urban J. Jermann. 2000. Efficiency, equilibrium, and asset pricing with risk of default. *Econometrica* 68 (4): 775–797. (Cited on p. 126.)

Alvarez, Fernando, and Urban J. Jermann. 2004. Using asset prices to measure the cost of business cycles. *Journal of Political Economy* 112 (6): 1223–1256. (Cited on p. 87.)

Alvarez, Fernando, Andrew Atkeson, and Patrick J. Kehoe. 2002. Money, interest rates, and exchange rates with endogenously segmented markets. *Journal of Political Economy* 110 (1): 73–112. (Cited on p. 190.)

Angeletos, George-Marios. 2002. Fiscal policy with noncontingent debt and the optimal maturity structure. *Quarterly Journal of Economics* 117 (3): 1105–1131. (Cited on p. 213.)

Angeletos, George-Marios. 2007. Uninsured idiosyncratic investment risk and aggregate saving. *Review of Economic Dynamics* 10 (1): 1–30. (Cited on p. 53.)

Angeletos, George-Marios, and C. Lian. 2016. Incomplete information in macroeconomics: Accommodating frictions in coordination. In *Handbook of macroeconomics*, eds. John B. Taylor and Harald Uhlig, Vol. 2A, 1065–1240. Amsterdam: North Holland. Chap. 14. (Cited on p. 190.)

Arrow, Kenneth J. 1953. Le rôle des valeurs boursières pour la répartition la meilleure des risques. *Économétrie, Colloques Internationaux du Centre National de la Recherche Scientifique* 11: 41–47. (Cited on pp. 8 and 53.)

Arrow, Kenneth J. 1964. The role of securities in the optimal allocation of risk-bearing. *Review of Economic Studies* 31 (2): 91–96. (Cited on pp. 8 and 53.)

Arrow, Kenneth J., and Gerard Debreu. 1954. Existence of an equilibrium for a competitive economy. *Econometrica* 22 (3): 265–290. (Cited on p. 8.)

Atkeson, Andrew, and Robert E. Lucas. 1992. On efficient distribution with private information. *Review of Economic Studies* 59: 427–453. (Cited on p. 213.)

Atkeson, Andrew, Varadarajan V. Chari, and Patrick J. Kehoe. 2010. Sophisticated monetary policies. *Quarterly Journal of Economics* 125 (1): 47–89. (Cited on p. 190.)

Atkinson, Anthony B., and Agnar Sandmo. 1980. Welfare implications of the taxation of savings. *Economic Journal* 90 (359): 529–549. (Cited on p. 213.)

Atkinson, Anthony B., and Joseph E. Stiglitz. 1972. The structure of indirect taxation and economic efficiency. *Journal of Public Economics* 1 (1): 97–119. (Cited on p. 260.)

Atkinson, Anthony B., and Joseph E. Stiglitz. 1976. The design of tax structure: Direct versus indirect taxation. *Journal of Public Economics* 6 (1–2): 55–75. (Cited on p. 260.)

Atkinson, Anthony B., and Joseph E. Stiglitz. 1980. *Lectures on public economics*. London: McGraw-Hill. (Cited on p. 260.)

Auclert, Adrien. 2019. Monetary policy and the redistribution channel. *American Economic Review* 109 (6): 2333–2367. (Cited on p. 160.)

Auerbach, Alan J., Jagadeesh Gokhale, and Laurence J. Kotlikoff. 1994. Generational accounting: A meaningful way to evaluate fiscal policy. *Journal of Economic Perspectives* 8 (1): 73–94. (Cited on p. 189.)

Azariadis, Costas. 1981. Self-fulfilling prophecies. *Journal of Economic Theory* 25 (3): 380–396. (Cited on p. 87.)

Backus, David, and John Driffill. 1985. Inflation and reputation. *American Economic Review* 75 (3): 530–538. (Cited on p. 240.)

Backus, David K., and Gregor W. Smith. 1993. Consumption and real exchange rates in dynamic economies with non-traded goods. *Journal of International Economics* 35 (3–4): 297–316. (Cited on p. 96.)

Bailey, Martin J. 1956. The welfare cost of inflationary finance. *Journal of Political Economy* 64 (2): 93–110. (Cited on p. 213.)

Balasko, Yves, and Karl Shell. 1980. The overlapping-generations model, I: The case of pure exchange without money. *Journal of Economic Theory* 23 (3): 281–306. (Cited on p. 38.)

Balassa, Bela. 1964. The purchasing-power parity doctrine: A reappraisal. *Journal of Political Economy* 72 (6): 584–596. (Cited on p. 96.)

Baldwin, Carliss Y., and Richard F. Meyer. 1979. Liquidity preference under uncertainty: A model of dynamic investment in illiquid opportunities. *Journal of Financial Economics* 7 (4): 347–374. (Cited on p. 125.)

Ball, Laurence, and N. Gregory Mankiw. 2007. Intergenerational risk sharing in the spirit of Arrow, Debreu, and Rawls, with applications to social security design. *Journal of Political Economy* 115 (4): 523–547. (Cited on p. 189.)

Bansal, Ravi, and Amir Yaron. 2004. Risks for the long run: A potential resolution of asset pricing puzzles. *Journal of Finance* 59 (4): 1481–1509. (Cited on p. 260.)

Baqaee, David Rezza, and Emmanuel Farhi. 2018. Macroeconomics with heterogeneous agents and input-output networks, Working Paper 24684, NBER, Cambridge, Massachusetts. (Cited on p. 260.)

Barbie, Martin, Marcus Hagedorn, and Ashok Kaul. 2007. On the interaction between risk sharing and capital accumulation in a stochastic OLG model with production. *Journal of Economic Theory* 137 (1): 568–579. (Cited on p. 38.)

Barro, Robert J. 1974. Are government bonds net wealth? *Journal of Political Economy* 82 (6): 1095–1117. (Cited on p. 189.)

Barro, Robert J. 1979. On the determination of the public debt. *Journal of Political Economy* 87 (5): 940–971. (Cited on p. 213.)

Barro, Robert J. 1990. Government spending in a simple model of endogenous growth. *Journal of Political Economy* 98 (5): 103–125. (Cited on p. 189.)

Barro, Robert J., and David B. Gordon. 1983. Rules, discretion, and reputation in a model of monetary policy. *Journal of Monetary Economics* 12: 101–121. (Cited on pp. 239 and 240.)

Barro, Robert J., and Herschel I. Grossman. 1971. A general disequilibrium model of income and employment. *American Economic Review* 61 (1): 82–93. (Cited on p. 8.)

Bassetto, Marco. 2002. A game-theoretic view of the fiscal theory of the price level. *Econometrica* 70 (6): 2167–2196. (Cited on p. 190.)

Bassetto, Marco, and Narayana Kocherlakota. 2004. On the irrelevance of government debt when taxes are distortionary. *Journal of Monetary Economics* 51 (2): 299–304. (Cited on p. 189.)

Baumol, William J. 1952. The transactions demand for cash. *Quarterly Journal of Economics* 67 (4): 545–556. (Cited on p. 144.)

Baumol, William J., and William G. Bowen. 1966. *Performing arts—the economic dilemma: A study of problems common to theater, opera, music and dance.* Cambridge, Massachusetts: MIT Press. (Cited on p. 96.)

Baxter, Marianne, and Robert G. King. 1993. Fiscal policy in general equilibrium. *American Economic Review* 83: 315–334. (Cited on p. 189.)

Becker, Gary S. 1965. A theory of the allocation of time. *Economic Journal* 75 (299): 493–517. (Cited on p. 86.)

Benhabib, Jess, and Roger E. A. Farmer. 1994. Indeterminacy and increasing returns. *Journal of Economic Theory* 63 (1): 19–41. (Cited on p. 87.)

Benhabib, Jess, and Roger E. A. Farmer. 1999. Indeterminacy and sunspots in macroeconomics. In *Handbook of macroeconomics*, eds. John B. Taylor and Michael Woodford, Vol. 1A, 387–448. Amsterdam: North-Holland. Chap. 6. (Cited on p. 87.)

Benhabib, Jess, Stephanie Schmitt-Grohé, and Martín Uribe. 2002. Avoiding liquidity traps. *Journal of Political Economy* 110 (3): 535–563. (Cited on p. 190.)

Benigno, Pierpaolo, and Michael Woodford. 2005. Inflation stabilization and welfare: The case of a distorted steady state. *Journal of the European Economic Association* 3 (6): 1185–1236. (Cited on p. 240.)

Bernanke, Ben S., and Mark Gertler. 1989. Agency costs, net worth, and business fluctuations. *American Economic Review* 79 (1): 14–31. (Cited on p. 125.)

Bernanke, Ben S., Mark Gertler, and Simon Gilchrist. 1999. The financial accelerator in a quantitative business cycle framework. In *Handbook of macroeconomics*, eds. John B. Taylor and Michael Woodford, Vol. 1C, 1341–1393. Amsterdam: North-Holland. Chap. 21. (Cited on p. 125.)

Bewley, Truman F. 1972. Existence of equilibria in economies with infinitely many commodities. *Journal of Economic Theory* 4 (3): 514–540. (Cited on p. 8.)

Bewley, Truman F. 1977. The permanent income hypothesis: A theoretical formulation. *Journal of Economic Theory* 16 (2): 252–292. (Cited on p. 53.)

Bewley, Truman F. 1980. The optimum quantity of money. In *Models of monetary economies*, eds. John H. Kareken and Neil Wallace, 169–210. Minneapolis: Federal Reserve Bank of Minneapolis. (Cited on pp. 53, 63, and 144.)

Bewley, Truman F. 1986. Stationary monetary equilibrium with a continuum of independently fluctuating consumers. In *Contributions to mathematical economics in honor of gerard debreu*, eds. Werner Hildenbrand and Andreu Mas-Colell, 79–102. Amsterdam: North Holland. (Cited on p. 53.)

Bhandari, Anmol, David Evans, Mikhail Golosov, and Thomas J. Sargent. 2017. Fiscal policy and debt management with incomplete markets. *Quarterly Journal of Economics* 132 (2): 617–663. (Cited on p. 213.)

Blanchard, Olivier J. 1985. Debt, deficits, and finite horizons. *Journal of Political Economy* 93 (2): 223–247. (Cited on p. 38.)

Blanchard, Olivier J., and Charles M. Kahn. 1980. The solution of linear difference models under rational expectations. *Econometrica* 48 (5): 1305–1311. (Cited on p. 260.)

Blanchard, Olivier J., and Nobuhiro Kiyotaki. 1987. Monopolistic competition and the effects of aggregate demand. *American Economic Review* 77 (4): 647–666. (Cited on p. 159.)

Bohn, Henning. 1990. Tax smoothing with financial instruments. *American Economic Review* 80 (5): 1217–1230. (Cited on p. 213.)

Borch, Karl. 1962. Equilibrium in a reinsurance market. *Econometrica* 30 (3): 424–444. (Cited on p. 53.)

Breeden, Douglas T. 1979. An intertemporal asset pricing model with stochastic consumption and investment opportunities. *Journal of Financial Economics* 7 (3): 265–296. (Cited on p. 63.)

Breyer, Friedrich. 1989. On the intergenerational Pareto efficiency of pay-as-you-go financed pension systems. *Journal of Institutional and Theoretical Economics* 145 (4): 643–658. (Cited on p. 189.)

Brock, William A. 1974. Money and growth: The case of long run perfect foresight. *International Economic Review* 15 (3): 750–777. (Cited on p. 190.)

Brock, William A., and Leonard J. Mirman. 1972. Optimal economic growth and uncertainty: The discounted case. *Journal of Economic Theory* 4 (3): 479–513. (Cited on p. 86.)

Broer, Tobias, Niels-Jakob Harbo Hansen, Per Krusell, and Erik Öberg. 2019. The New Keynesian transmission mechanism: A heterogeneous-agent perspective. *Review of Economic Studies* (forthcoming). (Cited on p. 160.)

Brunnermeier, Markus K., and Dirk Niepelt. 2019. On the equivalence of private and public money. *Journal of Monetary Economics* (forthcoming). (Cited on p. 144.)

Brunnermeier, Markus K., and Martin Oehmke. 2013. Bubbles, financial crises, and systemic risk. In *Handbook of the economics of finance*, eds. George M. Constantinides, Milton Harris, and Rene M. Stulz, Vol. 2B, 1221–1288. Amsterdam: North Holland. Chap. 18. (Cited on p. 63.)

Brunnermeier, Markus K., and Yuliy Sannikov. 2014. A macroeconomic model with a financial sector. *American Economic Review* 104 (2): 379–421. (Cited on p. 126.)

Brunnermeier, Markus K., and Yuliy Sannikov. 2016. The I theory of money, Working Paper 22533, NBER, Cambridge, Massachusetts. (Cited on p. 144.)

Brunnermeier, Markus K., Thomas M. Eisenbach, and Yuliy Sannikov. 2012. Macroeconomics with financial frictions: A survey, Working Paper 18102, NBER, Cambridge, Massachusetts. (Cited on p. 126.)

Bryant, John. 1983. Government irrelevance results: A simple exposition. *American Economic Review* 73 (4): 758–761. (Cited on p. 189.)

Buiter, Willem H. 1981. Time preference and international lending and borrowing in an overlapping-generations model. *Journal of Political Economy* 89 (4): 769–797. (Cited on p. 96.)

Buiter, Willem H. 2002. The fiscal theory of the price level: A critique. *Economic Journal* 112 (481): 459–480. (Cited on p. 190.)

Bullard, James, and Kaushik Mitra. 2002. Learning about monetary policy rules. *Journal of Monetary Economics* 49 (6): 1105–1129. (Cited on p. 190.)

Bulow, Jeremy, and Kenneth Rogoff. 1989. Sovereign debt: Is to forgive to forget? *American Economic Review* 79 (1): 43–50. (Cited on p. 239.)

Caballero, Ricardo J., and Arvind Krishnamurthy. 2003. Excessive dollar debt: Financial development and underinsurance. *Journal of Finance* 58 (2): 867–893. (Cited on p. 126.)

Cagan, Philip. 1956. The monetary dynamics of hyperinflation. In *Studies in the quantity theory of money*, ed. Milton Friedman, 25–117. Chicago: University of Chicago Press. (Cited on p. 189.)

Calvo, Guillermo A. 1978. On the time consistency of optimal policy in a monetary economy. *Econometrica* 46: 1411–1428. (Cited on p. 239.)

Calvo, Guillermo A. 1983. Staggered prices in a utility-maximizing framework. *Journal of Monetary Economics* 12 (3): 383–398. (Cited on p. 160.)

Calvo, Guillermo A. 1988. Servicing the public debt: The role of expectations. *American Economic Review* 78: 647–661. (Cited on p. 239.)

Campbell, John Y. 1986. Bond and stock returns in a simple exchange model. *Quarterly Journal of Economics* 101 (4): 785–804. (Cited on p. 63.)

Campbell, John Y. 2018. *Financial decisions and markets: A course in asset pricing.* Princeton: Princeton University Press. (Cited on p. 63.)

Cao, Dan, and Iván Werning. 2018. Saving and dissaving with hyperbolic discounting. *Econometrica* 86 (3): 805–857. (Cited on p. 24.)

Carlstrom, Charles T., and Timothy S. Fuerst. 1997. Agency costs, net worth, and business fluctuations: A computable general equilibrium analysis. *American Economic Review* 87 (5): 893–910. (Cited on p. 125.)

Carroll, Christopher D. 1997. Buffer-stock saving and the life cycle/permanent income hypothesis. *Quarterly Journal of Economics* 112 (1): 1–55. (Cited on p. 53.)

Caselli, Francesco, and Jaume Ventura. 2000. A representative consumer theory of distribution. *American Economic Review* 90 (4): 909–926. (Cited on p. 259.)

Cass, David. 1965. Optimum growth in an aggregative model of capital accumulation. *Review of Economic Studies* 32: 233–240. (Cited on p. 38.)

Cass, David. 1972. On capital overaccumulation in the aggregative, neoclassical model of economic growth: A complete characterization. *Journal of Economic Theory* 4: 200–223. (Cited on p. 38.)

Cass, David, and Karl Shell. 1983. Do sunspots matter? *Journal of Political Economy* 91 (2): 193–227. (Cited on p. 53.)

Cassel, Gustav. 1918. Abnormal deviations in international exchanges. *Economic Journal* 28 (112): 413–415. (Cited on p. 144.)

Chamberlain, Gary, and Charles A. Wilson. 2000. Optimal intertemporal consumption under uncertainty. *Review of Economic Dynamics* 3 (3): 365–395. (Cited on p. 53.)

Chamley, Christophe. 1986. Optimal taxation of capital income in general equilibrium with infinite lives. *Econometrica* 54 (3): 607–622. (Cited on p. 213.)

Chamley, Christophe, and Herakles Polemarchakis. 1984. Assets, general equilibrium and the neutrality of money. *Review of Economic Studies* 51 (1): 129–138. (Cited on p. 190.)

Chang, Roberto. 1998. Credible monetary policy in an infinite horizon model: Recursive approaches. *Journal of Economic Theory* 81 (2): 431–461. (Cited on p. 240.)

Chari, V. V., and Patrick J. Kehoe. 1990. Sustainable plans. *Journal of Political Economy* 98 (4): 783–802. (Cited on p. 239.)

Chari, V. V., and Patrick J. Kehoe. 1999. Optimal fiscal and monetary policy. In *Handbook of macroeconomics*, eds. John B. Taylor and Michael Woodford, Vol. 1C, 1671–1745. Amsterdam: North-Holland. Chap. 26. (Cited on p. 214.)

Chari, V. V., Lawrence J. Christiano, and Patrick J. Kehoe. 1994. Optimal fiscal policy in a business cycle model. *Journal of Political Economy* 102 (4): 617–652. (Cited on p. 213.)

Chari, V. V., Lawrence J. Christiano, and Patrick J. Kehoe. 1996. Optimality of the Friedman rule in economies with distorting taxes. *Journal of Monetary Economics* 37 (2): 203–223. (Cited on p. 213.)

Chari, V. V., Patrick J. Kehoe, and Ellen R. McGrattan. 2000. Sticky price models of the business cycle: Can the contract multiplier solve the persistence problem? *Econometrica* 68 (5): 1151–1180. (Cited on p. 160.)

Chattopadhyay, Subir, and Piero Gottardi. 1999. Stochastic OLG models, market structure, and optimality. *Journal of Economic Theory* 89 (1): 21–67. (Cited on p. 38.)

Clarida, Richard, Jordi Galí, and Mark Gertler. 1999. The science of monetary policy: A New Keynesian perspective. *Journal of Economic Literature* 37 (4): 1661–1707. (Cited on pp. 213 and 239.)

Clower, Robert W. 1967. A reconsideration of the microfoundations of monetary theory. *Western Economic Journal* 6 (1): 1–8. (Cited on p. 144.)

Cobb, Charles W., and Paul H. Douglas. 1928. A theory of production. *American Economic Review, Papers and Proceedings* 18 (1): 139–165. (Cited on p. 8.)

Cochrane, John H. 2001. *Asset pricing*. Princeton: Princeton University Press. (Cited on p. 63.)

Constantinides, George M., and Darrell Duffie. 1996. Asset pricing with heterogeneous consumers. *Journal of Political Economy* 104 (2): 219–240. (Cited on p. 86.)

Cooley, Thomas F., ed. 1995. *Frontiers of business cycle research*. Princeton: Princeton University Press. (Cited on p. 86.)

Cooper, Russell, and Andrew John. 1988. Coordinating coordination failures in Keynesian models. *Quarterly Journal of Economics* 103 (3): 441–463. (Cited on p. 160.)

Correia, Isabel, and Pedro Teles. 1999. The optimal inflation tax. *Review of Economic Dynamics* 2 (2): 325–346. (Cited on p. 213.)

Correia, Isabel, Juan Pablo Nicolini, and Pedro Teles. 2008. Optimal fiscal and monetary policy: Equivalence results. *Journal of Political Economy* 116 (1): 141–170. (Cited on p. 214.)

Correia, Isabel, Emmanuel Farhi, Juan Pablo Nicolini, and Pedro Teles. 2013. Unconventional fiscal policy at the zero bound. *American Economic Review* 103 (4): 1172–1211. (Cited on p. 214.)

Cox, John C., Jonathan E. Ingersoll, and Stephen A. Ross. 1985. A theory of the term structure of interest rates. *Econometrica* 53 (2): 385–407. (Cited on p. 63.)

Croushore, Dean. 1993. Money in the utility function: Functional equivalence to a shoppingtime model. *Journal of Macroeconomics* 15 (1): 175–182. (Cited on p. 144.)

Cvitanić, Jakša, and Fernando Zapatero. 2004. *Introduction to the economics and mathematics of financial markets*. Cambridge, Massachusetts: MIT Press. (Cited on p. 63.)

Dávila, Eduardo, and Anton Korinek. 2018. Pecuniary externalities in economies with financial frictions. *Review of Economic Studies* 85 (1): 352–395. (Cited on p. 125.)

Dávila, Julio, Jay H. Hong, Per Krusell, and José-Víctor Ríos-Rull. 2012. Constrained efficiency in the neoclassical growth model with uninsurable idiosyncratic shocks. *Econometrica* 80 (6): 2431–2467. (Cited on p. 126.)

Deaton, Angus. 1991. Saving and liquidity constraints. *Econometrica* 59 (5): 1221–1248. (Cited on p. 53.)

Deaton, Angus. 1992. *Understanding consumption*. Oxford: Oxford University Press. (Cited on pp. 24 and 53.)

Deaton, Angus, and John Muellbauer. 1980. *Economics and consumer behavior*. Cambridge, England: Cambridge University Press. (Cited on p. 259.)

Debortoli, Davide, Ricardo Nunes, and Pierre Yared. 2018. Optimal taxation and debt management without commitment, Working Paper 24522, NBER, Cambridge, Massachusetts. (Cited on p. 239.)

Debreu, Gerard. 1959. *Theory of value*. New York: John Wiley. (Cited on p. 8.)

Del Negro, Marco, and Christopher A. Sims. 2015. When does a central bank's balance sheet require fiscal support? *Journal of Monetary Economics* 73 (C): 1–19. (Cited on p. 190.)

Diamond, Peter A. 1965. National debt in a neoclassical growth model. *American Economic Review* 55 (5): 1126–1150. (Cited on pp. 38 and 189.)

Diamond, Peter A. 1975. A many-person Ramsey tax rule. *Journal of Public Economics* 4 (4): 335–342. (Cited on p. 260.)

Diamond, Peter A. 1982. Aggregate demand management in search equilibrium. *Journal of Political Economy* 90: 881–894. (Cited on p. 125.)

Diamond, Peter A., and James A. Mirrlees. 1971a. Optimal taxation and public production I: Production efficiency. *American Economic Review* 61 (1): 8–27. (Cited on p. 260.)

Diamond, Peter A., and James A. Mirrlees. 1971b. Optimal taxation and public production II: Tax rules. *American Economic Review* 61 (3): 261–278. (Cited on p. 260.)

Diamond, Peter A., and James A. Mirrlees. 1978. A model of social insurance with variable retirement. *Journal of Public Economics* 10 (3): 295–336. (Cited on p. 213.)

Dixit, Avinash K. 1989. Entry and exit decisions under uncertainty. *Journal of Political Economy* 97 (3): 620–638. (Cited on p. 125.)

Dixit, Avinash K., and Luisa Lambertini. 2003. Interactions of commitment and discretion in monetary and fiscal policies. *American Economic Review* 93 (5): 1522–1542. (Cited on p. 240.)

Dixit, Avinash K., and Robert S. Pindyck. 1994. *Investment under uncertainty*. Princeton: Princeton University Press. (Cited on p. 125.)

Dixit, Avinash K., and Joseph E. Stiglitz. 1977. Monopolistic competition and optimum product diversity. *American Economic Review* 67 (3): 297–308. (Cited on pp. 24 and 159.)

Domeij, David, and Tore Ellingsen. 2018. Rational bubbles and public debt policy: A quantitative analysis. *Journal of Monetary Economics* 96 (C): 109–123. (Cited on p. 190.)

Dornbusch, Rudiger. 1976. Expectations and exchange rate dynamics. *Journal of Political Economy* 84 (6): 1161–1176. (Cited on p. 144.)

Dornbusch, Rudiger, Stanley Fischer, and Paul A. Samuelson. 1977. Comparative advantage, trade, and payments in a Ricardian model with a continuum of goods. *American Economic Review* 67 (5): 823–839. (Cited on p. 96.)

Dotsey, Michael, Robert G. King, and Alexander L. Wolman. 1999. State-dependent pricing and the general equilibrium dynamics of money and output. *Quarterly Journal of Economics* 114 (2): 655–690. (Cited on p. 160.)

Duffie, Darrell. 2001. *Dynamic asset pricing theory*, 3. edn. Princeton: Princeton University Press. (Cited on p. 63.)

Eaton, Jonathan, and Raquel Fernandez. 1995. Sovereign debt. In *Handbook of international economics*, eds. G. M. Grossman and K. Rogoff, Vol. 3, 2031–2077. Amsterdam: North-Holland. Chap. 39. (Cited on p. 239.)

Eaton, Jonathan, and Mark Gersovitz. 1981. Debt with potential repudiation: Theoretical and empirical analysis. *Review of Economic Studies* 48 (2): 289–309. (Cited on p. 239.)

Eatwell, John, Murray Milgate, and Peter Newman, eds. 1989. *The new Palgrave: General equilibrium*. New York: Norton. (Cited on p. 9.)

Epstein, Larry G., and Stanley E. Zin. 1989. Substitution, risk aversion, and the temporal behavior of consumption and asset returns: A theoretical framework. *Econometrica* 57 (4): 937–969. (Cited on p. 260.)

Erceg, Christopher J., Dale W. Henderson, and Andrew T. Levin. 2000. Optimal monetary policy with staggered wage and price contracts. *Journal of Monetary Economics* 46 (2): 281–313. (Cited on p. 160.)

Evans, George W., and Seppo Honkapohja. 1999. Learning dynamics. In *Handbook of macroeconomics*, eds. John B. Taylor and Michael Woodford, Vol. 1A, 449–452. Amsterdam: North-Holland. Chap. 7. (Cited on p. 8.)

Evans, George W., and Seppo Honkapohja. 2001. *Learning and expectations in macroeconomics*. Princeton: Princeton University Press. (Cited on p. 8.)

Farhi, Emmanuel. 2010. Capital taxation and ownership when markets are incomplete. *Journal of Political Economy* 118 (5): 908–948. (Cited on p. 213.)

Farhi, Emmanuel, and Iván Werning. 2007. Inequality and social discounting. *Journal of Political Economy* 115 (3): 365–402. (Cited on p. 214.)

Farhi, Emmanuel, and Iván Werning. 2016a. Fiscal multipliers: Liquidity traps and currency unions. In *Handbook of macroeconomics*, eds. John B. Taylor and Harald Uhlig, Vol. 2B, 2417–2492. Amsterdam: North Holland. Chap. 31. (Cited on p. 190.)

Farhi, Emmanuel, and Iván Werning. 2016b. A theory of macroprudential policies in the presence of nominal rigidities. *Econometrica* 84 (5): 1645–1704. (Cited on p. 160.)

Feenstra, Robert C. 1986. Functional equivalence between liquidity costs and the utility of money. *Journal of Monetary Economics* 17 (2): 271–291. (Cited on p. 144.)

Fischer, Stanley. 1977. Long-term contracts, rational expectations, and the optimal money supply rule. *Journal of Political Economy* 85 (1): 191–205. (Cited on p. 160.)

Fischer, Stanley. 1980. Dynamic inconsistency, cooperation, and the benevolent dissembling government. *Journal of Economic Dynamics and Control* 2: 93–107. (Cited on p. 239.)

Fisher, Irving. 1896. Appreciation and interest. *Publications of the American Economic Association* 11 (4): 1–98. (Cited on p. 144.)

Fisher, Irving. 1930. *The theory of interest, as determined by impatience to spend income and opportunity to invest it*. New York: Macmillan. (Cited on pp. 38, 126, and 144.)

Fried, Joel. 1980. The intergenerational distribution of the gains from technical change and from international trade. *The Canadian Journal of Economics* 13 (1): 65–81. (Cited on p. 96.)

Friedman, Milton. 1957. *A theory of the consumption function*. Princeton: Princeton University Press. (Cited on pp. 24 and 53.)

Friedman, Milton. 1968. The role of monetary policy. *American Economic Review* 58 (1): 1–17. (Cited on pp. 9 and 190.)

Friedman, Milton. 1969. The optimum quantity of money. In *The optimum quantity of money and other essays*, ed. Milton Friedman, 1–50. Chicago: Aldine. Chap. 1. (Cited on p. 213.)

Fudenberg, Drew, and Eric Maskin. 1986. The folk theorem in repeated games with discounting or with incomplete information. *Econometrica* 54 (3): 533–554. (Cited on p. 240.)

Gale, David. 1973. Pure exchange equilibrium of dynamic economic models. *Journal of Economic Theory* 6 (1): 12–36. (Cited on p. 38.)

Gale, Douglas. 1990. The efficient design of public debt. In *Public debt management: Theory and history*, eds. Rudiger Dornbusch and Mario Draghi, 14–47. Cambridge, England: Cambridge University Press. Chap. 2. (Cited on p. 213.)

Galí, Jordi. 2015. *Monetary policy, inflation, and the business cycle*, 2. edn. Princeton: Princeton University Press. (Cited on pp. 160, 190, 214, and 240.)

Geanakoplos, John D., and Heraklis M. Polemarchakis. 1986. Existence, regularity, and constrained suboptimality of competitive allocations when the asset market is incomplete. In *Uncertainty, information, and communication: Essays in honor of Kenneth J. Arrow*, eds. Walter P. Heller, Ross M. Starr, and David A. Starrett, Vol. 3, 65–95. Cambridge, England: Cambridge University Press. Chap. 3. (Cited on p. 125.)

Gertler, Mark, and John Leahy. 2008. A Phillips curve with an Ss foundation. *Journal of Political Economy* 116 (3): 533–572. (Cited on p. 160.)

Gollier, Christian. 2001. *The economics of risk and time*. Cambridge, Massachusetts: MIT Press. (Cited on p. 54.)

Golosov, Mikhail, and Robert E. Lucas. 2007. Menu costs and Phillips curves. *Journal of Political Economy* 115 (2): 171–199. (Cited on p. 160.)

Golosov, Mikhail, Narayana Kocherlakota, and Aleh Tsyvinski. 2003. Optimal indirect and capital taxation. *Review of Economic Studies* 70: 569–587. (Cited on p. 213.)

Golosov, Mikhail, Aleh Tsyvinski, and Nicolas Werquin. 2016. Recursive contracts and endogenously incomplete markets. In *Handbook of macroeconomics*, eds. John B. Taylor and Harald Uhlig, Vol. 2A, 725–841. Amsterdam: North Holland. Chap. 10. (Cited on pp. 127 and 214.)

Gonzalez-Eiras, Martín, and Dirk Niepelt. 2008. The future of social security. *Journal of Monetary Economics* 55 (2): 197–218. (Cited on p. 239.)

Gonzalez-Eiras, Martín, and Dirk Niepelt. 2015. Politico-economic equivalence. *Review of Economic Dynamics* 18 (4): 843–862. (Cited on pp. 189 and 240.)

Goodfriend, Marvin, and Robert G. King. 1997. The new neoclassical synthesis and the role of monetary policy. In *NBER macroeconomics annual 1997*, eds. Ben S. Bernanke and Julio J. Rotemberg, Vol. 12, 231–283. Cambridge, Massachusetts: MIT Press. (Cited on p. 160.)

Gorman, William M. 1953. Community preference fields. *Econometrica* 21 (1): 63–80. (Cited on p. 259.)

Grandmont, Jean-Michel. 1977. Temporary general equilibrium theory. *Econometrica* 45 (3): 535–572. (Cited on p. 8.)

Grandmont, Jean-Michel. 1985. On endogenous competitive business cycles. *Econometrica* 53 (5): 995–1045. (Cited on p. 38.)

Grandmont, Jean-Michel, and Yves Younes. 1972. On the role of money and the existence of a monetary equilibrium. *Review of Economic Studies* 39 (3): 355–372. (Cited on p. 144.)

Greenwald, Bruce C., and Joseph E. Stiglitz. 1986. Externalities in economies with imperfect information and incomplete markets. *Quarterly Journal of Economics* 101 (2): 229–264. (Cited on p. 126.)

Grossman, Herschel I., and Taejoon Han. 1999. Sovereign debt and consumption smoothing. *Journal of Monetary Economics* 44 (1): 149–158. (Cited on p. 239.)

Grossman, Sanford, and Laurence Weiss. 1983. A transactions-based model of the monetary transmission mechanism. *American Economic Review* 73 (5): 871–880. (Cited on p. 190.)

Hahn, Frank H. 1965. On some problems of proving the existence of an equilibrium in a monetary economy. In *The theory of interest rates: Proceedings of a conference held by the International Economic Association*, eds. Frank H. Hahn and Frank P. R. Brechling, 126–135. London and New York: Macmillan and St. Martin's Press. Chap. 6. (Cited on p. 144.)

Hahn, Frank H. 1971. Equilibrium with transaction costs. *Econometrica* 39 (3): 417–439. (Cited on p. 8.)

Hall, Robert E. 1978. Stochastic implications of the life cycle-permanent income hypothesis: Theory and evidence. *Journal of Political Economy* 86 (6): 971–987. (Cited on p. 53.)

Hall, Robert E. 2005. Employment fluctuations with equilibrium wage stickiness. *American Economic Review* 95 (1): 50–65. (Cited on p. 125.)

Hall, Robert E., and Ricardo Reis. 2015. Maintaining central-bank financial stability under new-style central banking, Working Paper 21173, NBER, Cambridge, Massachusetts. (Cited on p. 190.)

Hansen, Gary D. 1985. Indivisible labor and the business cycle. *Journal of Monetary Economics* 16 (3): 309–327. (Cited on p. 86.)

Harms, Philipp. 2016. *International macroeconomics*. Tübingen: Mohr Siebeck. (Cited on p. 96.)

Harrod, Roy F. 1933. *International economics*. Cambridge, England: Cambridge University Press. (Cited on p. 96.)

Hart, Oliver, and John Moore. 1994. A theory of debt based on the inalienability of human capital. *Quarterly Journal of Economics* 109 (4): 841–879. (Cited on p. 126.)

Hart, Oliver, and John Moore. 1998. Default and renegotiation: A dynamic model of debt. *Quarterly Journal of Economics* 113 (1): 1–41. (Cited on p. 126.)

Hart, Oliver D. 1975. On the optimality of equilibrium when the market structure is incomplete. *Journal of Economic Theory* 11: 418–443. (Cited on p. 125.)

Hayashi, Fumio. 1982. Tobin's marginal q and average q: A neoclassical interpretation. *Econometrica* 50 (1): 213–224. (Cited on p. 125.)

Heathcote, Jonathan, Kjetil Storesletten, and Giovanni L. Violante. 2014. Consumption and labor supply with partial insurance: An analytical framework. *American Economic Review* 104 (7): 2075–2126. (Cited on p. 86.)

Heckman, James J. 1974. Life cycle consumption and labor supply: An explanation of the relationship between income and consumption over the life cycle. *American Economic Review* 64 (1): 188–194. (Cited on p. 86.)

Hicks, John Richard. 1939. *Value and capital: An inquiry into some fundamental principles of economic theory*. Oxford: Clarendon Press. (Cited on pp. 8 and 9.)

Holmström, Bengt. 1983. Equilibrium long-term labor contracts. *Quarterly Journal of Economics* 98 (Supplement): 23–54. (Cited on p. 126.)

Holmström, Bengt, and Jean Tirole. 1998. Private and public supply of liquidity. *Journal of Political Economy* 106 (1): 1–40. (Cited on p. 190.)

Homer. 800 B.C.E. *The odyssey*. (Cited on p. 24.)

Hosios, Arthur J. 1990. On the efficiency of matching and related models of search and unemployment. *Review of Economic Studies* 57 (2): 279–298. (Cited on p. 125.)

Huggett, Mark. 1993. The risk-free rate in heterogeneous-agent incomplete-insurance economies. *Journal of Economic Dynamics and Control* 17 (5–6): 953–969. (Cited on p. 53.)

Jones, Larry E., and Rodolfo Manuelli. 1990. A convex model of equilibrium growth: Theory and policy implications. *Journal of Political Economy* 98 (5): 1008–1038. (Cited on p. 86.)

Jorgensen, Dale W. 1963. Capital theory and investment behavior. *American Economic Review, Papers and Proceedings* 53 (2): 247–259. (Cited on p. 125.)

Judd, Kenneth L. 1985. Redistributive taxation in a simple perfect foresight model. *Journal of Public Economics* 28: 59–83. (Cited on p. 213.)

Kaldor, Nicholas. 1961. Capital accumulation and economic growth. In *The theory of capital*, eds. F. A. Lutz and D. C. Hague, 177–222. New York: St. Martins Press. (Cited on p. 86.)

Kaplan, Greg, Benjamin Moll, and Giovanni L. Violante. 2018. Monetary policy according to HANK. *American Economic Review* 108 (3): 697–743. (Cited on p. 160.)

Kareken, John, and Neil Wallace. 1981. On the indeterminacy of equilibrium exchange rates. *Quarterly Journal of Economics* 96 (2): 207–222. (Cited on p. 144.)

Kehoe, Timothy J., and David K. Levine. 1985. Comparative statics and perfect foresight in infinite horizon economies. *Econometrica* 53 (2): 433–453. (Cited on p. 38.)

Kehoe, Timothy J., and David K. Levine. 1993. Debt-constrained asset markets. *Review of Economic Studies* 60 (4): 865–888. (Cited on p. 126.)

Keynes, John Maynard. 1923. *A tract on monetary reform*. London: Macmillan. (Cited on p. 144.)

Keynes, John Maynard. 1936. *The general theory of employment, interest and money*. London: Macmillan. (Cited on p. 9.)

Kimball, Miles S. 1990. Precautionary saving in the small and in the large. *Econometrica* 58 (1): 53–73. (Cited on p. 53.)

King, Mervyn A. 1980. Savings and taxation. In *Public policy and the tax system*, eds. G. Hughes and G. Heal, 1–35. London: George Allen & Unwin. Chap. 1. (Cited on p. 213.)

King, Robert G., and Alexander L. Wolman. 1996. Inflation targeting in a St. Louis model of the 21st century. *Federal Reserve Bank of St. Louis Review* 78 (3): 83–107. (Cited on p. 160.)

King, Robert G., Charles I. Plosser, and Sergio T. Rebelo. 1988. Production, growth, and business cycles I: The basic neoclassical model. *Journal of Monetary Economics* 21: 195–232. (Cited on p. 86.)

King, Robert G., Charles I. Plosser, and Sergio T. Rebelo. 2002. Production, growth, and business cycles: Technical appendix. *Computational Economics* 20 (1): 87–116. (Cited on p. 86.)

Kirman, Alan P. 1992. Whom or what does the representative individual represent? *Journal of Economic Perspectives* 6 (2): 117–136. (Cited on p. 259.)

Kiyotaki, Nobuhiro, and John Moore. 1997. Credit cycles. *Journal of Political Economy* 105 (2): 211–248. (Cited on p. 125.)

Kiyotaki, Nobuhiro, and Randall Wright. 1989. On money as a medium of exchange. *Journal of Political Economy* 97 (4): 927–954. (Cited on pp. 144 and 145.)

Kiyotaki, Nobuhiro, and Randall Wright. 1993. A search-theoretic approach to monetary economics. *American Economic Review* 83 (1): 63–77. (Cited on pp. 144 and 145.)

Kocherlakota, Narayana, and Christopher Phelan. 1999. Explaining the fiscal theory of the price level. *Federal Reserve Bank of Minneapolis Quarterly Review* 23 (4): 14–23. (Cited on p. 190.)

Kocherlakota, Narayana R. 1996. Implications of efficient risk sharing without commitment. *Review of Economic Studies* 63 (4): 595–609. (Cited on p. 126.)

Kollmann, Robert. 2001. The exchange rate in a dynamic-optimizing business cycle model with nominal rigidities: A quantitative investigation. *Journal of International Economics* 55 (2): 243–262. (Cited on p. 160.)

Koopmans, Tjalling C. 1965. On the concept of optimal economic growth. In *The econometric approach to development planning*, 225–300. Amsterdam: North-Holland / Rand McNally. Chap. 4. Reissue of Pontificiae Academiae Scientiarum Scripta Varia 28. (Cited on p. 38.)

Korinek, Anton, and Alp Simsek. 2016. Liquidity trap and excessive leverage. *American Economic Review* 106 (3): 699–738. (Cited on p. 160.)

Kraay, Aart, and Jaume Ventura. 2000. Current accounts in debtor and creditor countries. *Quarterly Journal of Economics* 115 (4): 1137–1166. (Cited on p. 96.)

Kreps, David M., and Evan L. Porteus. 1978. Temporal resolution of uncertainty and dynamic choice theory. *Econometrica* 46 (1): 185–200. (Cited on p. 259.)

Kreps, David M., and Robert Wilson. 1982. Reputation and imperfect information. *Journal of Economic Theory* 27 (2): 253–279. (Cited on p. 240.)

Krugman, Paul R. 1989. Market-based debt-reduction schemes. In *Analytical issues in debt*, eds. Jacob A. Frenkel, Michael P. Dooley, and Peter Wickham, 258–278. Washington: International Monetary Fund. (Cited on p. 240.)

Krusell, Per, and José-Víctor Ríos-Rull. 1996. Vested interests in a positive theory of stagnation and growth. *Review of Economic Studies* 63 (2): 301–329. (Cited on p. 239.)

Krusell, Per, and Anthony A. Smith. 1998. Income and wealth heterogeneity in the macroeconomy. *Journal of Political Economy* 106 (5): 867–896. (Cited on p. 87.)

Krusell, Per, and Anthony A. Smith. 2003. Consumption-savings decisions with quasi-geometric discounting. *Econometrica* 71 (1): 365–375. (Cited on p. 24.)

Krusell, Per, Vincenzo Quadrini, and José-Víctor Ríos-Rull. 1997. Politico-economic equilibrium and economic growth. *Journal of Economic Dynamics and Control* 21 (1): 243–272. (Cited on p. 239.)

Kydland, Finn E., and Edward C. Prescott. 1977. Rules rather than discretion: The inconsistency of optimal plans. *Journal of Political Economy* 85 (3): 473–491. (Cited on p. 239.)

Kydland, Finn E., and Edward C. Prescott. 1982. Time to build and aggregate fluctuations. *Econometrica* 50 (6): 1345–1370. (Cited on p. 86.)

Laffont, Jean-Jacques. 1989. *The economics of uncertainty and information.* Cambridge, Massachusetts: MIT Press. (Cited on p. 54.)

Lagos, Ricardo, and Randall Wright. 2005. A unified framework for monetary theory and policy analysis. *Journal of Political Economy* 113 (3): 463–484. (Cited on p. 145.)

Laibson, David. 1997. Golden eggs and hyperbolic discounting. *Quarterly Journal of Economics* 62: 443–477. (Cited on p. 24.)

Leeper, Eric M. 1991. Equilibria under 'active' and 'passive' monetary and fiscal policies. *Journal of Monetary Economics* 27 (1): 129–147. (Cited on p. 190.)

Leland, Hayne E. 1968. Saving and uncertainty: The precautionary demand for saving. *Quarterly Journal of Economics* 82 (3): 465–473. (Cited on p. 53.)

LeRoy, Stephen F., and Jan Werner. 2014. *Principles of financial economics.* Cambridge, England: Cambridge University Press. (Cited on p. 63.)

Levhari, Jerusalem David, and T. N. Srinivasan. 1969. Optimal savings under uncertainty. *Review of Economic Studies* 36 (2): 153–163. (Cited on p. 53.)

Lewbel, Arthur. 1989. Exact aggregation and a representative consumer. *Quarterly Journal of Economics* 104 (3): 621–633. (Cited on p. 259.)

Lindbeck, Assar, and Jörgen W. Weibull. 1987. Balanced-budget redistribution as the outcome of political competition. *Public Choice* 52: 273–297. (Cited on p. 260.)

Lintner, John. 1965. The valuation of risk assets and the selection of risky investments in stock portfolios and capital budgets. *Review of Economics and Statistics* 47 (1): 13–37. (Cited on p. 63.)

Ljungqvist, Lars, and Thomas J. Sargent. 2018. *Recursive macroeconomic theory,* 4. edn. Cambridge, Massachusetts: MIT Press. (Cited on pp. 126, 214, 239, and 240.)

Long, John B., and Charles I. Plosser. 1983. Real business cycles. *Journal of Political Economy* 91 (11): 39–69. (Cited on p. 86.)

Lorenzoni, Guido. 2008. Inefficient credit booms. *Review of Economic Studies* 75 (3): 809–833. (Cited on p. 126.)

Lucas, Robert E. 1972. Expectations and the neutrality of money. *Journal of Economic Theory* 4 (2): 103–124. (Cited on pp. 8, 9, and 190.)

Lucas, Robert E. 1976. Econometric policy evaluation: A critique. *Carnegie-Rochester Conference Series on Public Policy.* (Cited on p. 9.)

Lucas, Robert E. 1978. Asset prices in an exchange economy. *Econometrica* 46 (6): 1429–1445. (Cited on p. 63.)

Lucas, Robert E. 1980. Equilibrium in a pure currency economy. In *Models of monetary economies,* eds. John H. Kareken and Neil Wallace, 131–145. Minneapolis: Federal Reserve Bank of Minneapolis. (Cited on p. 144.)

Lucas, Robert E. 1982. Interest rates and currency prices in a two-country world. *Journal of Monetary Economics* 10 (3): 335–359. (Cited on p. 144.)

Lucas, Robert E. 1987. *Models of business cycles.* New York: Basil Blackwell. (Cited on p. 87.)

Lucas, Robert E. 1990. Liquidity and interest rates. *Journal of Economic Theory* 50 (2): 237–264. (Cited on p. 190.)

Lucas, Robert E., and Edward C. Prescott. 1971. Investment under uncertainty. *Econometrica* 39 (5): 659–681. (Cited on pp. 87 and 125.)

Lucas, Robert E., and Edward C. Prescott. 1974. Equilibrium search and unemployment. *Journal of Economic Theory* 7 (2): 188–209. (Cited on p. 126.)

Lucas, Robert E., and Leonard A. Rapping. 1969. Real wages, employment, and inflation. *Journal of Political Economy* 77 (5): 721–754. (Cited on p. 86.)

Lucas, Robert E., and Nancy L. Stokey. 1983. Optimal fiscal and monetary policy in an economy without capital. *Journal of Monetary Economics* 12 (1): 55–93. (Cited on pp. 213 and 239.)

Lucas, Robert E., and Nancy L. Stokey. 1987. Money and interest rates in a cash-in-advance economy. *Econometrica* 55 (3): 491–513. (Cited on p. 144.)

Magill, Michael, and Martine Quinzii. 1996. *Theory of incomplete markets*, Vol. 1. Cambridge, Massachusetts: MIT Press. (Cited on pp. 63 and 126.)

Malinvaud, Edmond. 1953. Capital accumulation and efficient allocation of resources. *Econometrica* 21 (2): 233–268. (Cited on p. 38.)

Mankiw, N. Gregory. 1985. Small menu costs and large business cycles: A macroeconomic model of monopoly. *Quarterly Journal of Economics* 100 (2): 529–537. (Cited on p. 159.)

Mankiw, N. Gregory, and Ricardo Reis. 2002. Sticky information versus sticky prices: A proposal to replace the New Keynesian Phillips curve. *Quarterly Journal of Economics* 117 (4): 1295–1328. (Cited on pp. 160 and 190.)

Marcet, Albert, and Ramon Marimon. 1992. Communication, commitment, and growth. *Journal of Economic Theory* 58 (2): 219–249. (Cited on p. 126.)

Marcet, Albert, and Ramon Marimon. 2019. Recursive contracts. *Econometrica* (forthcoming). (Cited on p. 126.)

Martin, Alberto, and Jaume Ventura. 2012. Economic growth with bubbles. *American Economic Review* 102 (6): 3033–3058. (Cited on p. 63.)

Martin, Alberto, and Jaume Ventura. 2018. The macroeconomics of rational bubbles: A user's guide. *Annual Review of Economics* 10: 505–539. (Cited on p. 63.)

Mas-Colell, Andreu, Michael D. Whinston, and Jerry R. Green. 1995. *Microeconomic theory*. New York: Oxford University Press. (Cited on pp. 9, 243, and 260.)

McCall, J. J. 1970. Economics of information and job search. *Quarterly Journal of Economics* 84 (1): 113–126. (Cited on p. 126.)

McCallum, Bennett T., and Marvin S. Goodfriend. 1987. Demand for money: Theoretical studies. In *The new palgrave: A dictionary of economics*, eds. John Eatwell, Peter Newman, and Murray Milgate, 775–781. London: Macmillan Press. (Cited on p. 144.)

McDonald, Robert, and Donald Siegel. 1986. The value of waiting to invest. *Quarterly Journal of Economics* 101 (4): 707–727. (Cited on p. 125.)

McKenzie, Lionel. 1954. On equilibrium in Graham's model of world trade and other competitive systems. *Econometrica* 22 (2): 147–161. (Cited on p. 8.)

Merz, Monika. 1995. Search in the labor market and the real business cycle. *Journal of Monetary Economics* 36 (2): 269–300. (Cited on p. 125.)

Miao, Jianjun. 2014. *Economic dynamics in discrete time*. Cambridge, Massachusetts: MIT Press. (Cited on p. 260.)

Mirrlees, James A. 1965. Optimum accumulation under uncertainty. Unpublished. (Cited on p. 86.)

Mirrlees, James A. 1971. An exploration in the theory of optimum income taxation. *Review of Economic Studies* 38 (114): 175–208. (Cited on p. 260.)

Modigliani, Franco, and Richard Brumberg. 1954. Utility analysis and the consumption function: An interpretation of cross-section data. In *Post keynesian economics*, ed. Kenneth K. Kurihara. New Brunswick: Rutgers University Press. (Cited on pp. 24, 38, and 53.)

Modigliani, Franco, and Merton H. Miller. 1958. The cost of capital, corporation finance and the theory of investment. *American Economic Review* 48 (3): 261–297. (Cited on p. 126.)

Mortensen, Dale T. 1982. Property rights and efficiency in mating, racing, and related games. *American Economic Review* 72 (5): 968–979. (Cited on p. 125.)

Mossin, Jan. 1966. Equilibrium in a capital asset market. *Econometrica* 34 (4): 768–783. (Cited on p. 63.)

Mueller, Dennis C. 1989. *Public choice ii*. Cambridge, England: Cambridge University Press. (Cited on p. 240.)

Mulligan, Casey B., and Xavier Sala-i-Martin. 1997. The optimum quantity of money: Theory and evidence. *Journal of Money, Credit, and Banking* 29 (4): 687–715. (Cited on p. 213.)

Muth, John F. 1961. Rational expectations and the theory of price movements. *Econometrica* 29 (3): 315–335. (Cited on p. 9.)

Myers, Stewart C. 1977. Determinants of corporate borrowing. *Journal of Financial Economics* 5 (2): 147–175. (Cited on p. 240.)

Negishi, Takashi. 1960. Welfare economics and existence of an equilibrium for a competitive economy. *Metroeconomica* 12 (2–3): 92–97. (Cited on p. 38.)

Niehans, Jürg. 1994. *A history of economic theory: Classic contributions, 1720–1980*. Baltimore: Johns Hopkins University Press. (Cited on p. 9.)

Niepelt, Dirk. 2004a. The fiscal myth of the price level. *Quarterly Journal of Economics* 119 (1): 277–300. (Cited on p. 190.)

Niepelt, Dirk. 2004b. Tax smoothing versus tax shifting. *Review of Economic Dynamics* 7 (1): 27–51. (Cited on p. 213.)

Obstfeld, Maurice. 1982. Aggregate spending and the terms of trade: Is there a Laursen-Metzler effect? *Quarterly Journal of Economics* 97 (2): 251–270. (Cited on p. 96.)

Obstfeld, Maurice, and Kenneth Rogoff. 1983. Speculative hyperinflations in maximizing models: Can we rule them out? *Journal of Political Economy* 91 (4): 675–687. (Cited on p. 190.)

Obstfeld, Maurice, and Kenneth Rogoff. 1995. Exchange rate dynamics redux. *Journal of Political Economy* 103 (3): 624–660. (Cited on p. 160.)

Obstfeld, Maurice, and Kenneth Rogoff. 1996. *Foundations of international macroeconomics*. Cambridge, Massachusetts: MIT Press. (Cited on p. 96.)

Persson, Torsten, and Guido Tabellini. 2000. *Political economics*. Cambridge, Massachusetts: MIT Press. (Cited on pp. 240 and 260.)

Phelan, Christopher. 2006. Opportunity and social mobility. *Review of Economic Studies* 73 (2): 487–504. (Cited on p. 214.)

Phelan, Christopher, and Ennio Stacchetti. 2001. Sequential equilibria in a Ramsey tax model. *Econometrica* 69 (6): 1491–1518. (Cited on p. 240.)

Phelps, Edmund S. 1962. The accumulation of risky capital: A sequential utility analysis. *Econometrica* 30 (4): 729–743. (Cited on p. 53.)

Phelps, Edmund S. 1965. Second essay on the golden rule of accumulation. *American Economic Review* 55 (4): 793–814. (Cited on p. 38.)

Phelps, Edmund S., ed. 1970. *Microeconomic foundations of employment and inflation theory*. New York: Norton. (Cited on pp. 9 and 190.)

Phelps, Edmund S. 1973. Inflation in the theory of public finance. *Swedish Journal of Economics* 75: 67–82. (Cited on p. 213.)

Phelps, Edmund S., and R. A. Pollak. 1968. On second-best national saving and game-equilibrium growth. *Review of Economic Studies* 35 (2): 185–199. (Cited on p. 24.)

Pissarides, Christopher A. 1985. Short-run equilibrium dynamics of unemployment, vacancies, and real wages. *American Economic Review* 75 (4): 676–690. (Cited on p. 125.)

Pissarides, Christopher A. 1990. *Equilibrium unemployment theory*. Oxford: Basil Blackwell. (Cited on p. 125.)

Pissarides, Christopher A. 2000. *Equilibrium unemployment theory*, 2. edn. Cambridge, Massachusetts: MIT Press. (Cited on p. 125.)

Pollak, R. A. 1968. Consistent planning. *Review of Economic Studies* 35 (2): 201–208. (Cited on p. 24.)

Poole, William. 1970. Optimal choice of monetary policy instruments in a simple stochastic macro model. *Quarterly Journal of Economics* 84 (2): 197–216. (Cited on p. 190.)

Prescott, Edward C., and Rajnish Mehra. 1980. Recursive competitive equilibrium: The case of homogeneous households. *Econometrica* 48 (6): 1365–1379. (Cited on p. 87.)

Radner, Roy. 1972. Existence of equilibrium of plans, prices, and price expectations in a sequence of markets. *Econometrica* 40 (2): 289–303. (Cited on pp. 8 and 53.)

Ramsey, Frank P. 1927. A contribution to the theory of taxation. *Economic Journal* 37 (145): 47–61. (Cited on p. 260.)

Ramsey, Frank P. 1928. A mathematical theory of saving. *Economic Journal* 38 (152): 543–559. (Cited on p. 38.)

Rangel, Antonio. 1997. Social security reform: Efficiency gains or intergenerational redistribution. Unpublished, Harvard University. (Cited on p. 189.)

Rebelo, Sergio. 1991. Long-run policy analysis and long-run growth. *Journal of Political Economy* 99 (3): 500–521. (Cited on p. 86.)

Rocheteau, Guillaume, and Ed Nosal. 2017. *Money, payments, and liquidity*, 2. edn. Cambridge, Massachusetts: MIT Press. (Cited on p. 145.)

Rogerson, Richard. 1988. Indivisible labor, lotteries and equilibrium. *Journal of Monetary Economics* 21 (1): 3–16. (Cited on p. 86.)

Rogerson, William P. 1985. Repeated moral hazard. *Econometrica* 53 (1): 69–76. (Cited on p. 213.)

Rogoff, Kenneth. 1985. The optimal degree of commitment to an intermediate monetary target. *Quarterly Journal of Economics* 100: 1169–1190. (Cited on p. 239.)

Romer, Paul M. 1986. Increasing returns and long-run growth. *Journal of Political Economy* 94 (5): 1002–1037. (Cited on p. 86.)

Ross, Stephen A. 1976. The arbitrage theory of capital asset pricing. *Journal of Economic Theory* 13 (3): 341–360. (Cited on p. 63.)

Rotemberg, Julio J. 1982. Monopolistic price adjustment and aggregate output. *Review of Economic Studies* 49 (4): 517–531. (Cited on p. 160.)

Rotemberg, Julio J. 1984. A monetary equilibrium model with transactions costs. *Journal of Political Economy* 92 (1): 40–58. (Cited on p. 190.)

Rotemberg, Julio J., and Michael Woodford. 1997. An optimization-based econometric framework for the evaluation of monetary policy. In *NBER macroeconomics annual 1997*, eds. Ben S. Bernanke and Julio Rotemberg, 297–346. Cambridge, Massachusetts: MIT Press. (Cited on p. 213.)

Sachs, Jeffrey D. 1981. The current account and macroeconomic adjustment in the 1970s. In *Brookings papers on economic activity*, Vol. 12, 201–282. Washington: Brookings Institution. (Cited on p. 96.)

Salanié, Bernard. 2003. *The economics of taxation*. Cambridge, Massachusetts: MIT Press. (Cited on p. 260.)

Samuelson, Paul A. 1939. The gains from international trade. *Canadian Journal of Economics and Political Science* 5 (2): 195–205. (Cited on p. 96.)

Samuelson, Paul A. 1955. *Economics*, 3. edn. New York: McGraw-Hill. (Cited on p. 9.)

Samuelson, Paul A. 1958. An exact consumption-loan model of interest with or without the social contrivance of money. *Journal of Political Economy* 66 (6): 467–482. (Cited on pp. 38 and 144.)

Samuelson, Paul A. 1964. Theoretical notes on trade problems. *Review of Economics and Statistics* 46 (2): 145–154. (Cited on p. 96.)

Sandmo, Agnar. 1970. The effect of uncertainty on saving decisions. *Review of Economic Studies* 37 (3): 353–360. (Cited on p. 53.)

Santos, Manuel S., and Michael Woodford. 1997. Rational asset pricing bubbles. *Econometrica* 65 (1): 19–57. (Cited on p. 63.)

Sargent, Thomas J. 1971. A note on the "accelerationist" hypothesis. *Journal of Money, Credit, and Banking* 3 (3): 721–725. (Cited on p. 9.)

Sargent, Thomas J. 1987. *Dynamic macroeconomic theory*. Cambridge, Massachusetts: Harvard University Press. (Cited on p. 190.)

Sargent, Thomas J., and Neil Wallace. 1973. The stability of models of money and growth with perfect foresight. *Econometrica* 41 (6): 1043–1048. (Cited on p. 260.)

Sargent, Thomas J., and Neil Wallace. 1975. "Rational" expectations, the optimal monetary instrument, and the optimal money supply rule. *Journal of Political Economy* 83 (2): 241–254. (Cited on p. 190.)

Sargent, Thomas J., and Neil Wallace. 1981. Some unpleasant monetarist arithmetic. *Federal Reserve Bank of Minneapolis Quarterly Review* 5 (3): 1–17. (Cited on p. 190.)

Saving, Thomas R. 1971. Transactions costs and the demand for money. *American Economic Review* 61 (3): 407–420. (Cited on p. 144.)

Schlicht, Ekkehart. 2006. A variant of Uzawa's theorem. *Economics Bulletin* 5 (6): 1–5. (Cited on p. 86.)

Schmitt-Grohé, Stephanie, and Martín Uribe. 2004. Solving dynamic general equilibrium models using a second-order approximation to the policy function. *Journal of Economic Dynamics and Control* 28 (4): 755–775. (Cited on p. 87.)

Sharpe, William F. 1964. Capital asset prices: A theory of market equilibrium under conditions of risk. *Journal of Finance* 19 (3): 425–442. (Cited on p. 63.)

Shell, Karl. 1971. Notes on the economics of infinity. *Journal of Political Economy* 79 (5): 1002–1011. (Cited on pp. 38 and 144.)

Shimer, Robert. 2010. *Labor markets and business cycles.* Princeton: Princeton University Press. (Cited on p. 125.)

Shleifer, Andrei, and Robert W. Vishny. 1992. Liquidation values and debt capacity: A market equilibrium approach. *Journal of Finance* 47 (4): 1343–1366. (Cited on p. 125.)

Sidrauski, Miguel. 1967. Rational choice and patterns of growth in a monetary economy. *American Economic Review* 57 (2): 534–544. (Cited on p. 144.)

Simon, Carl P., and Lawrence Blume. 1994. *Mathematics for economists.* New York: Norton & Company. (Cited on pp. 243 and 244.)

Sims, Christopher A. 1980. Macroeconomics and reality. *Econometrica* 48 (1): 1–48. (Cited on p. 9.)

Sims, Christopher A. 1994. A simple model for study of the determination of the price level and the interaction of monetary and fiscal policy. *Economic Theory* 4 (3): 381–399. (Cited on p. 190.)

Siu, Henry E. 2004. Optimal fiscal and monetary policy with sticky prices. *Journal of Monetary Economics* 51 (3): 575–607. (Cited on p. 214.)

Stein, Jeremy C. 2012. Monetary policy as financial stability regulation. *Quarterly Journal of Economics* 127 (1): 57–97. (Cited on p. 126.)

Stiglitz, Joseph E. 1982. The inefficiency of the stock market equilibrium. *Review of Economic Studies* 49: 241–261. (Cited on p. 125.)

Stiglitz, Joseph E. 1987. Pareto efficient and optimal taxation and the new new welfare economics. In *Handbook of public economics*, eds. Alan J. Auerbach and Martin Feldstein, Vol. 2, 991–1042. Amsterdam: North-Holland. Chap. 15. (Cited on p. 260.)

Stiglitz, Joseph E., and Andrew Weiss. 1981. Credit rationing in markets with imperfect information. *American Economic Review* 71 (3): 393–410. (Cited on p. 126.)

Stigum, Bernt P. 1969. Competitive equilibria under uncertainty. *Quarterly Journal of Economics* 83 (4): 533–561. (Cited on p. 8.)

Stokey, Nancy L. 1989. Reputation and time consistency. *American Economic Review* 79 (2): 134–139. (Cited on p. 239.)

Stokey, Nancy L. 1991. Credible public policy. *Journal of Economic Dynamics and Control* 15 (4): 627–656. (Cited on p. 239.)

Stokey, Nancy L., and Robert E. Lucas. 1989. *Recursive methods in economic dynamics*. Cambridge, Massachusetts: Harvard University Press. (Cited on pp. 87, 243, 244, and 259.)

Stolper, Wolfgang F., and Paul A. Samuelson. 1941. Protection and real wages. *Review of Economic Studies* 9 (1): 58–73. (Cited on p. 96.)

Straub, Ludwig, and Iván Werning. 2014. Positive long run capital taxation: Chamley-Judd revisited, Working Paper 20441, NBER, Cambridge, Massachusetts. (Cited on p. 213.)

Strotz, Robert H. 1956. Myopia and inconsistency in dynamic utility maximization. *Review of Economic Studies* 23 (3): 165–180. (Cited on p. 24.)

Svensson, Lars E. O. 1985. Money and asset prices in a cash-in-advance economy. *Journal of Political Economy* 93 (5): 919–944. (Cited on p. 144.)

Svensson, Lars E. O., and Assaf Razin. 1983. The terms of trade and the current account: The Harberger-Laursen-Metzler effect. *Journal of Political Economy* 91 (1): 97–125. (Cited on p. 96.)

Taylor, John B. 1979. Staggered wage setting in a macro model. *American Economic Review* 69 (2): 108–113. (Cited on p. 160.)

Taylor, John B. 1993. Discretion versus policy rules in practice. *Carnegie-Rochester Conference Series on Public Policy* 39: 195–214. (Cited on p. 190.)

Taylor, John B. 1999. A historical analysis of monetary policy rules. In *Monetary policy rules*, ed. John B. Taylor, 319–348. Chicago: University of Chicago Press. Chap. 7. (Cited on p. 190.)

Thomas, Jonathan, and Tim Worrall. 1988. Self-enforcing wage contracts. *Review of Economic Studies* 55 (4): 541–553. (Cited on p. 126.)

Tirole, Jean. 1982. On the possibility of speculation under rational expectations. *Econometrica* 50 (5): 1163–1181. (Cited on p. 63.)

Tirole, Jean. 1985. Asset bubbles and overlapping generations. *Econometrica* 53 (5): 1071–1100. (Cited on p. 63.)

Tirole, Jean. 2006. *The theory of corporate finance*. Princeton: Princeton University Press. (Cited on p. 126.)

Tobin, James. 1956. The interest elasticity of the transactions demand for cash. *Review of Economics and Statistics* 38 (3): 241–247. (Cited on p. 144.)

Tobin, James. 1969. A general equilibrium approach to monetary theory. *Journal of Money, Credit, and Banking* 1 (1): 15–29. (Cited on p. 125.)

Townsend, Robert M. 1979. Optimal contracts and competitive markets with costly state verification. *Journal of Economic Theory* 21 (2): 265–293. (Cited on p. 125.)

Townsend, Robert M. 1980. Models of money with spatially separated agents. In *Models of monetary economies*, eds. John H. Kareken and Neil Wallace, 265–304. Minneapolis: Federal Reserve Bank of Minneapolis. (Cited on p. 144.)

Uribe, Martín, and Stephanie Schmitt-Grohé. 2017. *Open economy macroeconomics*. Princeton: Princeton University Press. (Cited on p. 96.)

Uzawa, Hirofumi. 1961. Neutral inventions and the stability of growth equilibrium. *Review of Economic Studies* 28 (2): 117–124. (Cited on p. 86.)

Vaughan, D. R. 1970. A non recursive algorithm solution for the discrete Ricatti equation. *IEEE Transactions on Automatic Control* AC-15: 597–599. (Cited on p. 260.)

von Neumann, John, and Oskar Morgenstern. 1944. *Theory of games and economic behavior*. Princeton: Princeton University Press. (Cited on p. 53.)

Wallace, Neil. 1980. The overlapping generations model of fiat money. In *Models of monetary economies*, eds. John H. Kareken and Neil Wallace, 49–82. Minneapolis: Federal Reserve Bank of Minneapolis. (Cited on p. 144.)

Wallace, Neil. 1981. A Modigliani-Miller theorem for open-market operations. *American Economic Review* 71 (3): 267–274. (Cited on pp. 189 and 190.)

Walras, Léon. 1874. *Éléments d'Économie politique pure, ou théorie de la richesse sociale*. Lausanne: L. Corbaz. (Cited on p. 8.)

Walsh, Carl E. 1995. Optimal contracts for central bankers. *American Economic Review* 85 (1): 150–167. (Cited on p. 239.)

Walsh, Carl E. 2017. *Monetary theory and policy*, 4. edn. Cambridge, Massachusetts: MIT Press. (Cited on pp. 126, 145, 160, 190, 214, and 240.)

Weil, Philippe. 1987. Confidence and the real value of money in an overlapping generations economy. *Quarterly Journal of Economics* 102 (1): 1–22. (Cited on p. 63.)

Weil, Philippe. 1989. The equity premium puzzle and the risk-free rate puzzle. *Journal of Monetary Economics* 24: 401–421. (Cited on p. 260.)

Werning, Iván. 2003. Standard dynamic programming for Aiyagari, Marcet, Sargent and Seppälä. Unpublished, MIT, Cambridge, Massachusetts. (Cited on p. 213.)

Werning, Iván. 2007. Optimal fiscal policy with redistribution. *Quarterly Journal of Economics* 122 (3): 925–967. (Cited on p. 213.)

Werning, Iván. 2015. Incomplete markets and aggregate demand, Working Paper 21448, NBER, Cambridge, Massachusetts. (Cited on p. 53.)

Williams, John Burr. 1938. *The theory of investment value*. Cambridge, Massachusetts: Harvard University Press. (Cited on p. 126.)

Woodford, Michael. 1990. Public debt as private liquidity. *American Economic Review* 80 (2): 382–388. (Cited on pp. 144 and 190.)

Woodford, Michael. 1995. Price level determinacy without control of a monetary aggregate. *Carnegie-Rochester Conference Series on Public Policy* 43: 1–46. (Cited on p. 190.)

Woodford, Michael. 2001. The Taylor rule and optimal monetary policy. *American Economic Review, Papers and Proceedings* 91 (2): 232–237. (Cited on p. 190.)

Woodford, Michael. 2003a. Imperfect common knowledge and the effects of monetary policy. In *Knowledge, information, and expectations in modern macroeconomics: In honor of Edmund S. Phelps*, eds. Philippe Aghion, Roman Frydman, Joseph Stiglitz, and Michael Woodford, 25–58. Princeton: Princeton University Press. Chap. 1. (Cited on p. 190.)

Woodford, Michael. 2003b. *Interest and prices*. Princeton: Princeton University Press. (Cited on pp. 160, 190, 213, 214, and 240.)

Yaari, Menahem E. 1965. Uncertain lifetime, life insurance, and the theory of the consumer. *Review of Economic Studies* 32 (2): 137–150. (Cited on p. 38.)

Yun, Tack. 1996. Nominal price rigidity, money supply endogeneity, and business cycles. *Journal of Monetary Economics* 37 (2): 345–370. (Cited on p. 160.)

Zeldes, Stephen P. 1989a. Consumption and liquidity constraints: An empirical investigation. *Journal of Political Economy* 97 (2): 305–346. (Cited on p. 53.)

Zeldes, Stephen P. 1989b. Optimal consumption with stochastic income: Deviations from certainty equivalence. *Quarterly Journal of Economics* 104 (2): 275–298. (Cited on p. 53.)

Zhu, Xiaodong. 1992. Optimal fiscal policy in a stochastic growth model. *Journal of Economic Theory* 58 (2): 250–289. (Cited on p. 213.)

Zilcha, Itzhak. 1990. Dynamic efficiency in overlapping generations models with stochastic production. *Journal of Economic Theory* 52 (2): 364–379. (Cited on p. 38.)

Author Index

Subject Index